THE

COOKIE

BIBLE

THE
COOKIE
BIBLE

ROSE LEVY BERANBAUM

Photography by Matthew Septimus

HARVEST
An Imprint of WILLIAM MORROW

To darling cousin Ada Minette, welcome
to our new generation of bakers

No part of this book may be used or reproduced in any manner whatsoever without written permission except in the case of brief quotations embodied in critical articles and reviews. For information, address HarperCollins Publishers, 195 Broadway, New York, NY 10007.

Library of Congress Cataloging-in-Publication Data is available.

ISBN 978-0-358-35399-7 (hbk)

ISBN 978-0-358-35424-6 (ebk)

Printed in Vietnam

23 SCP 10 9 8 7 6 5 4 3 2

CONTENTS

RECIPE LIST

FOREWORD

A decade ago, we were two young, enthusiastic students at The Culinary Institute of America. We loved being in school—learning, cooking, eating, making new friends. Our most favorite thing to do when we felt grown-up and adventurous and flush with cash from our on-campus jobs was to take the train down to New York City. We'd sightsee a little or just amble down the avenues, dwarfed and oddly comforted by the solid, soaring buildings around us. We'd stop to stare at the person with the floppy hat dipping strawberries in the Godiva storefront. A couple times, we rode the subway to Queens, where there were piles of shrink-wrapped goat and purple stacks of Milka and barrels of sharp feta in brine. And, of course, we ate! As much as, and sometimes more than, our budget allowed. Our day trip would often end with us quite literally holding up our stomachs with our hands as we trot-waddled back to Grand Central.

But no matter what the rest of our NYC itinerary involved, the one nonnegotiable each time was a visit to Strand Bookstore, the famously miles-long purveyor of books on every subject you'd care to read about. It was there that we happened upon a pristine copy of *The Cake Bible*, by one Rose Levy Beranbaum. We were enchanted by the tabulated lists and retro line drawings, reassured by the gushing reviews on the back, and encouraged by the exacting but approachable details in the recipes. We bought the book and spent the rest of the school year baking out of it in our dorm kitchen. We didn't know then, on that chilly evening with our coats tugged tight around us, that within the decade, we would be married to each other, living in NYC, one of us the pastry chef at a legendary New York restaurant, and—the real kicker—furiously exchanging texts with this beloved prophet of baking, Rose herself, while eating Shilpa's goat biryani and drinking Rose's blood orange sours.

To know Rose is to know the spirit of giving. She gives generously of herself—her abiding friendship, her anecdotes that will make you go *ooh* and then *aah* and then howl with laughter. Her uncanny ability to retain and recount every detail brings any story to life. She will give you her hot takes on ice cream machines and lamb sausages, bring you magazines she thinks you will like or first editions or uncorrected proofs of books you'll always cherish. But most of all, she gives you her formidable, unmatched knowledge on all things baking. Rose was one of the first authors to recognize and insist that metric weights are imperative for consistently fabulous results. She specifies whether the flour required in a recipe is bleached or not, because she knows, through exhaustive testing, just what influence this will have on the final result. She is persistent, she is unfailingly curious, and she is always, always open to learning more, all qualities we deeply respect her for. This is what makes every book of hers a smashing success; an inordinate attention to the details and science of a recipe.

We've been lucky enough to taste many cookies from this book as Rose and Woody meticulously tested them through. We went mad for her Strudel Cookies, delicate swirls of flaky dough encircling tart, amber-colored apricots and studded with nuts. Rose brought over a carefully packed box and the next day they were gone, downed with our afternoon tea on the balcony! Sturdy Pfeffernüsse, fragrant with ground pepper, cloves, and cinnamon, were all too easy to nibble on. Miro was thrilled to taste Rose's version of the caramel-bellied snickerdoodles he serves at Gramercy Tavern: For her Caramel Surprise Snickerdoodles, she's adapted them into a thin sandwich cookie that drips with dark, chewy caramel when you bite into it.

There are dozens—hundreds!—more cookies in *The Cookie Bible* that we are absolutely dying to try, from Apricot Walnut Rugelach to Woody's Luxury Brownies, from the niche little Ischler to the familiar comfort of Cranberry Chocolate Chippers. Shilpa, always a sucker for words, quickly shortlisted a few cookies she fell in love with for their names alone—Lemon Lumpies and Banana Custard Cuddle Cookies to start. You might laugh at such a child-like way of picking a recipe, but this is a Rose Levy Beranbaum production, and you just know that all the recipes are going to be great. Every verse from this bible is worth preaching about!

**WITH LOVE AND COOKIES,
MIRO AND SHILPA USKOKOVIC
APRIL 2020**

ACKNOWLEDGMENTS

Our great gratitude goes to the most amazing production team, each and every one of whom is my friend and either a professional or home baker, and it shows: Senior editor Stephanie Fletcher whose sterling judgment and commitment to excellence is the backbone of this book, senior managing editor Marina Padakis Lowry, who stewarded the book to perfection and even contributed a special family recipe, Tai Blanche, art director—the embodiment of form follows function equals beauty, production manager Kimberly Kiefer, copy editor par excellence and former pastry chef Judith Sutton, and eagle-eyed proofreaders Deri Reed and chocolatier Zach Townsend, as well as to chefs Miro and Shilpa Uskokovic for their heartfelt, eloquent, and insightful foreword.

The stunning photos that grace this book are the result of my much-esteemed colleague Erin Jeanne McDowell whose extraordinary food-styling skill, loving heart, and patience made it possible, despite the time of quarantine, for me to participate in every shot virtually, her right-hand and super-skilled assistant Kaitlin Wayne, and photographer extraordinaire Matthew Septimus, who captured the beauty and essence of every cookie.

Cookies are about sharing, and blessings to all those who contributed their special recipes, especially David Shamah, who voluntarily offered his brilliant thoughts and ideas in consultation.

Special Mentions: Dan O'Malley of American Products Group, who produces my product line, Rose's Signature Series, Thermoworks (thermometers), StretchTite (plastic wrap), Organic Valley (butter and cream), Nielsen Massey and Heilala (vanilla), India Tree (sugar), and Valrhona and Guittard (chocolate).

This book was written in full and sustaining collaboration with my longtime and much valued "partner in crème" Woody Wolston of team "RoseWood," who is now my husband.

The last words my husband Elliott spoke to me, December 2019, in his supremely generous wisdom and love were: "Never give up your work." And it is this book that was my survival through his loss and the pandemic that followed.

INTRODUCTION

Baking is the best all-encompassing lesson for children. It teaches so many important things: precision, patience, timing, sensory perception, science, art, mathematics. And of all baking, cookies are the most child-friendly and forgiving. A basic cookie is easier to make than a cake or pastry because cookie dough, due to its higher sugar content, is much more forgiving of overmixing or overhandling than a cake batter or pastry dough. Scraps of dough can be reshaped several times without changing the cookies' texture. Cookies are fun, and they make people of all ages happy.

Most cookies are a cross between cake and pastry (in fact, the word *cookie* derives from the Dutch word *koekj,* which means little cake). Some, though, such as meringues and pralines, are closer to the candy category.

When I started putting together all my favorite cookie recipes along with all the recipes I dreamed of creating, I suddenly remembered that when I was a little girl, my grandmother Sarah, who brought me up, used to call me "Cookie"! But it was years before I ever tasted a home-baked one. My mother was a dentist and orthodontist and didn't cook or bake until after her retirement.

My first cookie baking experience, in the 1960s, was a complete disaster. I made oatmeal cookies using the recipe on the back of the Quaker oatmeal box. The result was one huge inedible cookie that filled the entire pan. It was several years before I was willing to try cookie baking again. I was working at the Educational Testing Service in Princeton, NJ, and one of my co-workers gave me her favorite recipe for almond crescent cookies. It was the first home-baked cookie I had ever tasted. Over the years, as I learned more about baking and ingredients, I was inspired to tweak this simple recipe to match my idea of perfection:

Buttery, tender, flavorful, and with only five simple ingredients, it has been my longtime signature cookie (see Rose's Crescents, page 111).

In 1990, when *Rose's Christmas Cookies* was published, the National Dairy Council hired me to be their spokesperson after hearing my mantra: "I'd rather have one perfect cookie made with butter than a whole bunch made with shortening." And I still feel the same way.

Since that book, of course, cookies have graced many of my other cookbooks. But one morning, I woke up with the realization that it was time to put together all of my collection under one cover. So I revisited and updated all of my old favorites to reflect changes in ingredients and equipment, and new techniques. And being so immersed in cookie thoughts, I discovered and created many new cookies along the way. Those almond crescents, my first cookie, remain one of my favorites, but I now have a new favorite on equal par: the Chocolate Sablés (page 210).

Cookies come in so many different flavors and textures. But my favorite thing about all of them is that even after one is full to bursting, there's always room for one perfect cookie.

GOLDEN
RULES FOR
BAKING
THE BEST
COOKIES

Before You Begin

1. Read through the entire recipe to familiarize yourself with it, especially any plan-ahead notes and advance prep (referred to here as mise en place).

2. Avoid making substitutions until you have tried the recipe at least once as it is written. The variations and Baking Gems at the end of many of the recipes give you tested ideas and suggested substitutions. See the Ingredients section (page xxiv) for more on the critical importance of choosing the correct ingredients.

3. If you can, segregate equipment that could retain odors from savory ingredients, such as garlic or spices, to use only for baking. This includes cutting boards, measuring spoons and cups, wooden spoons, and silicone or rubber spatulas. (Glass does not retain odors.) The Equipment section (page xx) provides more information on the basic tools you will need.

Weighing and Measuring

4. Use care when you weigh or measure your ingredients in order to achieve optimal flavor and texture in your results. Weighing most ingredients (anything in larger quantities than teaspoons and tablespoons) with a scale makes baking easier, faster, and more reliable. It also makes it easy to measure out the right amount of dough to make cookies a consistent size. Most scales switch easily from ounces to grams and back. Grams are more precise because amounts are usually rounded off

to either 1 gram or ¼ ounce, which is equal to 7 grams.

5. Using too much flour will make your cookies dry and dense; follow the instructions on page xxiv for how to measure flour. Use "dry" measuring cups (with unbroken rims) for dry ingredients and measuring cups with spouts for liquids.

Baking

6. Make all the cookies in each batch the same size, shape, and thickness so that they will bake evenly. For cutout cookies, you can make individual batches of smaller and larger shapes as long as you divide them among different cookie sheets, because size will affect baking time. (The size of the cookies will also affect the amount of filling or topping, if any, needed for each one.)

7. Space cookies at even intervals on the cookie sheet so that they bake evenly (it is best not to leave large empty spaces).

8. Preheat the oven for a minimum of 20 to 30 minutes, or 40 minutes if baking at 375°F / 190°C or higher. Use an accurate oven thermometer to determine if your oven is properly calibrated. (Whether the cookies bake in the time range specified in the recipe will be another indicator.) Always start checking at the shortest time specified. Because cookies are relatively small, they can go from pale gold to overbrowned in a very short time. The recipe will specify the correct level for the oven rack (or racks) to ensure proper browning on both the tops and bottoms of the cookies. Cookies bake most evenly when baked only one sheet at a time.

Cooling

9. Remove the cookies from the cookie sheets as soon as they are rigid enough to transfer, and cool them on wire racks so that they remain crisp and do not continue cooking from the heat of the cookie sheets. Cool cookies completely before storing them airtight for the best possible texture.

HIGH ALTITUDE

Baking at altitudes over 3,000 feet requires adjustments to ingredients and baking temperature. Since most of my cookies contain less sugar than many recipes, there is less of a problem with spreading due to lower air pressure. First make a small batch and try baking one cookie and then, if it spreads, you can try lowering the sugar and increasing the flour slightly for the next batch. If there is baking soda in the recipe, decrease it slightly as well. It may also help to increase the baking temperature slightly, which will also shorten the baking time. To prevent them from drying out, store cookies as soon as possible after they've cooled. In her book *Pie in the Sky*, Susan Purdy gives very useful guidelines for four different altitudes, ranging from 3,000 to 10,000 feet. The USDA is a valuable online resource.

Storing Cookie Dough and Cookies

Most cookie doughs can be refrigerated for up to 3 days, or frozen for several weeks and then defrost overnight in the refrigerator. If refrigerating dough for more than 2 hours, wrap it in plastic wrap and put it in a reclosable freezer bag. However, it is easiest to shape cookie dough if it has not been refrigerated for more than 3 hours. If the chilled dough is too cold to shape, divide it into quarters and let each piece sit at room temperature for about 15 minutes, or until it is malleable and soft enough to roll but still cold. (See page xvii for more solutions for dough that cracks during rolling.)

When storing cookies, always be sure to cool them completely first. Also, store crisp cookies separately from soft ones. If you've baked more than one kind of cookie, it is best to store each variety separately to prevent transfer of flavors.

Separate layers of cookies with parchment or wax paper to keep the cookies crisp and to separate those that are sticky.

The storage times given for baked cookies are conservative estimates—because when a cookie is really good, it never stays around long enough to gauge the maximum storage time!

Many cookies will keep for weeks after baking if stored carefully. If they are stored in a cool room, some will even keep for months. There is, however, something extra special about certain cookies, especially those containing pieces of chocolate, that are freshly baked. For 4 to 6 hours after baking, the pieces of chocolate will still be slightly soft, adding an extra dimension to both texture and taste. If you like soft cookies, storing them in airtight containers in the refrigerator will keep them softer longer. Airtight containers, in addition to preserving the cookies' texture, will keep them from picking up aromas from other foods. For the best flavor and texture, let them warm to room temperature before serving.

Freezing cookies keeps them almost as fresh as the day they were baked. If you want to freeze cookies, use reclosable freezer bags, expelling as much air as possible before sealing them, or airtight containers, filling any airspace at the top with crumpled plastic wrap or wax paper. Fragile cookies can be flash-frozen in single layers on cookie sheets and then, once frozen solid, packed in airtight containers. Bar cookies can be frozen in one whole slab, before cutting, wrapped in plastic wrap and then heavy-duty aluminum foil. Individual frozen cookies taken out of their containers will thaw at room temperature in about 20 minutes.

To recrisp cookies, place them on cookie sheets and heat them in a preheated 300°F / 150°C oven for about 5 minutes. Cool them on wire racks.

Some cookies, such as biscotti, will keep for several weeks but after the first week will become very hard and need to be dunked in coffee, tea, or milk. You can soften hard cookies the same way as hardened brown sugar—moisten a paper towel, set it in a custard cup or small foil cup, and place it in the container with the cookies. Alternatively set a piece of apple in the cup. After a few days, the cookies will have softened.

Baking Gems

♥ Unless otherwise indicated, bake cookies as close to the center of the oven as possible. If they are too high, the tops will overbrown; if too low, the bottoms will overbrown. It is, therefore, ideal to bake one sheet of cookies at a time.

♥ For some recipes that take a relatively longer time to bake and a shorter time to shape, I suggest that you shape the dough for the second batch while the first batch is baking. But always be sure to keep an eye on the ones in the oven to prevent overbaking.

♥ If you prefer to bake multiple sheets of cookies at a time, make sure to allow a minimum of 2 inches between the edges of the cookie sheets and all the sides of the oven. If your oven is not large enough to hold two cookie sheets side by side, place the oven racks so that they divide the oven in thirds. Rearrange and rotate the cookie sheets from top to bottom and front to back halfway through baking for even baking. The baking time will be slightly longer if baking more than one sheet at a time.

♥ If your cookies are browning too much on the bottoms, bake them on a higher rack, or use an insulated cookie sheet or doubled sheets.

♥ Do not overbake cookies. They will continue to bake after they are removed from the oven. If you remove them too soon, they can always be returned to the oven. For softer rather than crisper cookies, underbake slightly.

♥ If cookie dough cracks during rolling, unless the dough is very dry, it works well to cover it with plastic wrap before rolling. If it still doesn't come together smoothly, spritz it with a little water and knead it together until smooth.

♥ If cookies spread too much while baking and are too flat, it can help to chill the shaped dough before baking. Flouring your hands before shaping the dough helps to make a more rounded cookie. Avoid placing cookie dough on hot or warm cookie sheets. If you find your cookies are still too flat, you can substitute a lower-protein flour (so more water is available to turn to steam and aerate the cookies) and/or decrease the sugar slightly.

♥ If cutout cookies lose their shape during baking, refrigerate the dough cutouts on the cookie sheet, lightly covered with plastic wrap, for about 30 minutes before baking.

♥ If a log of cookie dough flattens on one side during storage, insert the plastic-wrapped dough log into the cardboard tube from a roll of paper towels. If necessary, slit the tube down the length so that it can be opened up to accommodate the diameter of the log. Then secure it at either end with rubber bands and stand it on end in the freezer. If the tube is too long to fit into your freezer, cut it into sections and divide the dough log(s) accordingly.

♥ If you like softer cookies, remove them from the oven while they are still soft. Then remove them from the cookie sheet as soon as they are firm enough to lift without bending.

♥ My blog, www.realbakingwithrose.com, has an errata/corrections section for all of my books in which Woody and I post new information and changes. We welcome and will answer your questions and comments on our Ask a Question page.

The Three Basic Methods for Mixing Most Cookie Doughs

All three of these methods produce essentially the same results, but some of them are more suitable for certain types of cookies than others.

1. USING A FOOD PROCESSOR This is the fastest method. I use it in recipes where I consider it to be the best method. If you are making a small batch of dough and your food processor is large, you will need to scrape the sides of the bowl often. When using the food processor method, the butter is usually best at between 65° and 70 F° / 18° and 21°C. If the butter is too cold or too warm, you will need to scrape down the sides of the bowl more often. If the butter is on the cooler side, there is no need to chill the dough before shaping.

2. USING AN ELECTRIC MIXER Most cookie doughs come together easily in a stand mixer. My favorite thing about the mixer method compared to using a food processor is the ease of scraping the mixture out of the bowl. A few tips when using a stand mixer:

• Start the mixer on low speed and gradually increase the speed. The gradual increase in speed keeps the ingredients from jumping out of the bowl and is easier on the mixer's gears. The one exception to this practice is when beating hot syrup into stiffly beaten egg whites—starting on low for each addition would overheat and deflate the whites.

- If the butter is too firm, beat it until creamy before adding the sugar.

- Using the mixer's flat beater to mash ingredients such as butter by hand before you attach it to the mixer keeps the butter from flying out of the bowl.

- If the mixer bowl is very full, I suggest you cover the top with plastic wrap until the dry ingredients are moistened to prevent them from flying out of the bowl.

- If the volume of ingredients is small in proportion to the mixer bowl, you will need to use higher speeds.

- It is important to scrape the sides of the bowl, as indicated in the recipes, to ensure that the batter on the sides gets mixed in evenly. Always stop the mixer to scrape the sides. Also be sure to reach to the bottom of the bowl.

3. BY HAND Many cookie doughs can be mixed using a large bowl (at least 4 quart / 4 liter capacity) and a wooden spoon. Follow the same basic procedure as you would with a stand mixer, with the following modifications: Instead of beating the butter and sugar together at the start, first beat the butter until it is creamy. Then add the sugar and beat the two together for a few minutes until the mixture becomes very light in color. If there are eggs in the dough, whisk them lightly before adding them to the bowl.

DEFINITION OF MY MIXING SPEEDS

The times listed in the recipes are for a KitchenAid stand mixer. Refer to your owner's manual if using another brand. If you are using a handheld electric mixer, you will need to use a higher speed than specified and a longer beating time.

MIXING SPEEDS

Low: number 2
Medium-low: number 3
Medium: number 4
Medium-High: numbers 6 to 8
High: number 10

EQUIPMENT

OVENS Because cookies bake quickly and most evenly on the middle rack of the oven, most recipes in this book call for baking them in batches. A standard 17 by 14 inch cookie sheet was used to determine the batch size.

When having a new oven installed, make sure that it is level, or your brownies and bar cookies (and most other baked goods) will not be. Also have the installer calibrate the oven.

When to Use Convection: A convection setting circulates air in the oven for more even baking. If your oven has one, follow the manufacturer's directions. These may recommend lowering the temperature by 25°F / 15°C when using the convection setting. (If you are in the market for a new oven, and it would suit your needs, a countertop convection oven can be a fine choice, but you may need to adjust the baking temperature and time for these recipes. Note that some countertop ovens may not accommodate larger pans.)

It's fine to use convection for any cookies that are not too delicate (delicate cookies could lose their shape). For biscotti and other cookies that you want crisp, the convection setting works especially well to dry them.

Oven Temperature: Most cookies are baked at 350°F / 175°C or 375°F / 190°C. The higher temperature will set the dough faster, which helps it keep its shape, as for the Spritz Cookies (page 252). Although many factors contribute to a cookie's texture, a higher temperature usually results in a darker crust with wider range in texture, from crisper on the edges to softer in the center, as in the Oatmeal Favorites (page 9).

OVEN THERMOMETERS Not every oven is accurate. The CDN Oven Pro Accurate Thermometer and the multifunction Chefalarm (with optional oven clip) by Thermoworks are my recommendations. The most reliable test of oven temperature is baking time. If it takes more or less time than the indicated range in the recipe to bake a cookie in this book, you may need to have your oven calibrated or to adjust the oven temperature. (Creating a chart of adjustments needed can help you keep track for next time.)

INSTANT-READ THERMOMETERS The most accurate and fastest to react instant-read thermometer is the Thermapen by Thermoworks. It is useful not only for making syrups such as caramel, but also for certain cookies—for example, rugelach— to ensure that the dough is fully cooked through.

COOKIE SHEETS AND SHEET PANS Most cookies bake best on flat cookie sheets with very low or no rims to allow air to circulate over and around the cookies and make them crisp. An inverted 17¼ by 12¼ by 1 inch half sheet pan will work equally well. Use shiny heavy-gauge aluminum cookie sheets, not dark ones, so the cookies will brown evenly and not excessively. My favorites are 17 by 14 inch cookie sheets by Wearever. I also like insulated cookie sheets for cookies that are prone to overbrowning on the bottoms. Alternatively, you can create your own insulated sheets by "double-panning." For recipes that require no pan preparation, parchment is optional for ease in cleanup.

Cool cookie sheets between batches so that the dough will not start melting and thinning at the edges before the heat of the oven can set it. Alternatively, you can arrange unbaked cookies on sheets of parchment, then slip them quickly onto the hot cookie sheet and immediately place them in the oven.

WIRE COOLING RACKS Racks with the wires spaced close together offer the best support.

DIGITAL SCALE My favorite scale for the home baker is the Alimento by Escali. Choose a scale with a range that is at minimum from 1 gram up to 4 kilograms / 8.8 pounds. I list weights for very small amounts of ingredients, such as baking powder, but it's fine to use accurate measuring spoons instead. Should you prefer to weigh such small amounts, I recommend the Escali L600 "High Precision," with a range of 0.1 gram to 600 grams. I include weights for baking powder and baking soda here even though they are very small amounts, in case you want to scale up the recipe.

STAND MIXERS I find a 5 to 6 quart heavy-duty stand mixer is ideal for baking recipes. Having two bowls is useful, especially for recipes in which you need to beat egg whites separately. I find the KitchenAid 5 quart tilt-head model the most convenient for mixing cookie doughs and batters. If you want to make double or triple batches of a recipe, I recommend the Cuisinart 7 quart mixer.

HANDHELD MIXERS Handheld electric mixers are useful for small quantities of ingredients, such as whipped cream. Powerful models, like the Breville brand, can also be used in place of a stand mixer. If your mixer is less powerful, use a higher speed than indicated in the recipe for a stand mixer.

FOOD PROCESSORS A processor with a 7 to 12 cup / 1.6 to 3 liter capacity will work for almost all of the recipes in this book. It is also very useful to have a small-capacity food processor.

SPICE MILLS AND ROTARY NUT GRINDERS If you need to grind nuts into an even and fine consistency and do not have a food processor, a spice mill or Mouli or Zyliss hand grater, fitted with the finest drum, works well.

ROLLING PINS AND DOUGH MATS I created Rose's Signature Series nonstick rolling pins, produced by the American Products Group, to require the least amount of added flour to prevent sticking when rolling out dough. I also designed a 9 inch version, which works wonderfully for smaller pieces of dough and individual cookies. The dough mats are also truly nonstick. My silicone dough-thickness rails, called Fast Tracks, come in three heights; simply set them around the edges of the cookie dough before rolling to ensure even thickness.

A Note About the Dough Mat: To keep the mat from sliding, lightly wet the clean countertop. Start at the edge of the counter and slide the dough mat forward to create suction that will hold it securely in place.

SILICONE SPATULAS You'll need these for high-heat stirring as well as for scraping bowls. I also created, for the American Products Group, a "reduction spatula" with raised markings to help you measure liquids as you reduce them on the cooktop or in the microwave. If the spatula is left in the microwavable container, it makes stirring to prevent liquid bursts unnecessary. Its rigid texture makes it ideal for scraping out narrow containers.

FINE- AND MEDIUM-MESH STRAINERS For sifting powdered sugar and straining mixtures.

COOKIE CUTTERS Plain or scalloped, and decorative shapes for holiday cookies.

DISPOSABLE PASTRY BAGS AND TIPS Disposable plastic pastry bags are available in cake decorating supply stores and online. Small tubes, referred to as decorating tips, are used for small decorations. Larger tubes, referred to as pastry tubes, are used to pipe some cookies. I give suggested diameters for the tubes but not size numbers, because the numbers vary by manufacturer.

I also like to use heavy-duty quart- and gallon-size reclosable freezer bags for beginners and children, because the bags are readily available and disposable and because the tops can be sealed shut so the filling can't work its way out should your grip be too relaxed.

If using a large pastry tube, simply cut off a small semicircular piece of plastic from one corner of the bag and insert the tube through the opening. If using a small decorating tip that could work its way back into the bag, insert the nozzle portion of a coupler first, then add the tip and secure it with the coupler. Before filling the bag, seal off the tube opening by twisting the bag directly above the tube and pushing it into the

tube to keep the filling from leaking out. Invert the edges of the bag over a wire bag holder or large glass, fill the bag with the mixture, and close it securely.

If using a pastry bag without a decorating tip or tube, fold up the tip and use a paper clamp to close it until you have filled the bag and are ready to pipe the mixture.

SMALL STRAIGHT AND OFFSET METAL SPATULAS For leveling measuring spoons, unmolding cookies baked in muffin pans, and applying toppings to cookies.

METAL CAKE TESTERS AND WOODEN SKEWERS For testing doneness.

PASTRY BRUSH Preferably silicone.

WOODEN SPOON For very stiff mixtures, because it is firmer than a silicone spatula.

PLASTIC AND METAL BENCH SCRAPERS For scraping bowls and lifting and cutting doughs.

ASSORTED WHISKS Small and medium whisks are useful for mixing small amounts of liquid ingredients and for mixing together dry ingredients.

MICROPLANE GRATER For grating citrus zest.

MEASURING SPOONS The most accurate spoons I've found are the POURfect brand. When measuring flour, dip the measuring spoon into the flour and then level it off. Be sure to wipe off any flour that sticks to the bottom of the spoon.

A DEMITASSE SPOON A tiny spoon comes in very handy for filling small openings in cookies.

DRY CUP MEASURES If you're not using a scale, use these for dry ingredients. They have unbroken rims, so they can be leveled off. When measuring flour, lightly spoon it into the cup and level off. (The volume measures listed in these recipes are as close as possible to correlate with the weights; sometimes they are rounded off slightly.) Again, I prefer Pourfect brand, which I find to be the most accurate.

GLASS CUP MEASURES If measuring liquids instead of weighing them, use a liquid measuring cup and read it at eye level. Water measures should be read below the meniscus (the curved upper surface of the water). I prefer the Anchor Hocking brand for greatest accuracy. Metric markings are usually in 25 ml increments and correlate as closely as possible with fluid ounces. If using the metric system, it's fine to eyeball and go slightly under or over the mark as needed.

PARCHMENT PAPER Preferably flat sheets, for lining pans.

COOKIE SCOOPS Weighing is the best method to get uniformly sized cookies that will all bake at the same time, and using a cookie scoop is a speedy way to dispense cookie dough before weighing it. The cookie scoops I use most often are 1¼ inches (2 teaspoons), 1½ inches (3½ teaspoons), 1¾ inches (5¾ teaspoons), and 2 inches (8 teaspoons). When shopping online, it is useful to know the approximate volume, because most sites don't list diameters. By the nature of their design, cookie scoops are not as precise as measuring spoons, because they don't release 100 percent of the dough.

PLASTIC WRAP Stretch-Tite is my favorite plastic wrap because it clings tightly to the bowl or whatever you are wrapping. Plastic wraps are not entirely impermeable and, therefore, they are suitable for freezing baked goods only if used in a couple of layers. Freeze-Tite is one and a half times thicker than most other brands, but I still advise using more than one layer when freezing. Freeze-Tite is also wider (15 inches) than most others, which makes it great for rolling out cookie dough.

INGREDIENTS

Flour and sugar are the two most important ingredients for a cookie dough; the types used and how they are measured will have a great effect on the quality of the baked cookies. But understanding the essential details about all the ingredients is invaluable for giving you the ultimate cookie control.

In my recipes, weight is listed first, as the primary method of measuring, because it is the most accurate, fastest, and easiest. Volume is given in measuring spoons, cups, and milliliters. In some instances but not all, volume is rounded off, so you may find a slightly different weight for the same volume when the quantity may need to be more precise. If using volume rather than weight for measuring liquids, you will need to use the nearest marking on the measuring cup.

WATER All the recipes in this book were tested with tap water; however, if the water in your region is not suitable, use spring water. (Mineral water that is high in minerals will affect the outcome of baked goods.) To measure water, set the measuring cup on a level surface and read the volume at eye level from the bottom of the meniscus (the curved upper surface of the water).

FLOURS With the exception of flourless cookies, including meringues, flour is the most important ingredient in cookie baking. The type of flour used, particularly its protein content and whether it is bleached or unbleached, is critical to the texture and appearance of the baked cookies. It is important to use a national brand such as Gold Medal or King Arthur, because protein content varies widely in regional brands.

Flour contributes a major part of a cookie's structure. I use bleached all-purpose flour in most of these recipes because it has just the right protein content to create the ideal texture. Unbleached all-purpose flour and bread flour contain higher amounts of protein and produce cookies that are browner, flatter, and chewier, because the higher level of protein absorbs more liquid-forming gluten, leaving less available liquid in the dough to turn to steam and aerate the cookies. Bleached all-purpose and cake flours contain less protein, so because less water is tied up by the flour, it turns to steam and makes the cookies puffier. Less gluten forms as well, which makes the cookies more tender. And the cookies brown less, because it is the protein that is largely responsible for browning.

Wondra flour is not a necessity, but it is ideal for dusting cookie dough when rolling because it is precooked and its granularity means less flour will be absorbed into the dough. Buckwheat flour is also a good choice for rolling dough. It is very fine, so it helps the dough roll beautifully, and it gives a lovely crisp texture to the outsides of the cookies. It also adds a slightly deeper flavor.

To Measure Flour by Volume: Lightly spoon it into the cup and level it off. Avoid shaking or tapping the cup as you add the flour, as that will cause the flour to settle, increasing the amount of flour and resulting in cookies that are heavy, dry, and crumbly.

SUGAR The sugar in many of my basic cookie doughs is a little less than half the weight of the flour—or more if the cookie contains spices. Sugar lowers the setting point of the dough during baking, so a cookie dough with a higher amount of sugar can spread more before setting, resulting in a thinner, crisper cookie.

I often prefer superfine sugar for my cookie recipes. The finer the granulation of the sugar, the less the cracking in the surface of the dough during baking. The fine granulation also results in a finer crumb and lighter texture in the baked cookies because the smaller crystals provide more surface area to trap air. In the mixing or creaming process, the sharp or angular surfaces of the sugar crystals catch air. If the surface of the grains of sugar were smooth, as in powdered sugar, the grains would clump together and not allow air in between them. The more crystals there are, the more air will be incorporated. The finer sugar dissolves more easily and makes lighter, more delicate meringues. Using powdered sugar, or part powdered sugar, however, does result in delightfully fragile cookies in some recipes. Granulated sugar, which is coarser, can be processed in a food processor to simulate superfine. The two most common brands of superfine sugar are C & H and Domino; C & H is slightly finer.

Brown Sugar and Muscovado Sugar: Brown sugar is sugar that contains molasses that was added back to the refined sugar after processing. Muscovado sugar still contains some molasses that was not extracted during processing. My preference is India Tree light or dark Muscovado for its delicious complexity of flavor. In terms of molasses content, light Muscovado is close to a combination of light and dark brown sugar. For recipes where more molasses would overwhelm the other flavors, I list light brown sugar as a substitute for Muscovado. In those recipes where more molasses would enhance the flavor, I give dark brown sugar as a substitute.

Brown sugar will harden on storage. I store it in a tightly sealed canning jar, and if I need to soften it, I moisten a paper towel, set it in a small foil cup, and place it in the jar with the sugar. If the sugar is very dry and hard, it can take as long as 24 hours to soften it.

BUTTER Use a high-quality AA or A unsalted butter with standard fat content unless high-fat butter is called for in the recipe or you are making clarified butter. Clarifying butter is the process of heating butter to remove the water it contains and separating the pure butter oil (the fat) from the milk solids. These milk solids can also be browned, turning anywhere from pale golden to deep brown, depending on the desired flavor; the browned milk solids have a rich, nutty flavor and will also impart some of their flavor to the butter oil. For some cookies, I use both the clarified butter and the milk solids to give extra flavor; for other cookies, I use only the clarified butter. If the butter is cooked until the milk solids are deeply browned, I refer to it as browned butter whether or not the solids have been left in. When butter is clarified and the solids removed, it will be only 75 percent the volume or weight of its original amount. If the milk solids are removed, clarified butter can be stored in the refrigerator for many months or in the freezer for at least a year. (Clarified butter with the milk solids removed is ideal for sautéing, because it is the milk solids that can cause burning.)

Grade AA or A butter contains about 81 percent fat and 15.5 percent water. The rest of it is milk solids. Lower grades usually contain more water, which will have a detrimental effect on the texture of a cookie dough, and they will not work well at all in mousseline buttercream (see page 361), will make a less tender piecrust (page 130), and will result in puffier cookies.

I recommend using unsalted butter because it allows you to control the amount of salt added to the cookies (which in many recipes is only a pinch) and because it usually has a fresher flavor. I recommend a top-quality butter such as Organic Valley's cultured, Hotel Bar, or Land O'Lakes. The flavor of cultured butter is especially delicious. It is best to weigh butter, because a 113 gram / 4 ounce stick of butter, when unwrapped, sometimes weighs only 109 grams / 3.86 ounces.

Butter freezes well for many months, with no perceptible difference in flavor or performance. However, because butter absorbs other aromas or odors readily, be sure to wrap it well in plastic wrap and place it in a resealable freezer bag.

CREAM CHEESE Full-fat Philadelphia brand cream cheese is the best choice for both flavor and texture.

HEAVY CREAM Heavy cream, also referred to as heavy whipping cream, contains 56.6 percent water and 36 to 40 percent butter fat (36 percent is the norm). Cream labeled "whipping cream" has only 30 percent fat. The higher the butterfat and the colder the cream, the easier it is to whip and the more stable the whipped cream. To determine the fat content, on the side of the container 40 percent cream will be listed as 6 grams total fat per serving. Organic Valley and Stonyfield are two brands that contain 40 percent butterfat. Heavy cream will not whip if it has been frozen, but thawed frozen heavy cream can be used for making ganache.

EGGS I use USDA-graded large eggs, which requires that 12 eggs in the shell weigh a minimum of 24 ounces / 680 grams and a maximum of 30 ounces / 850 grams. However, this does not mean that each egg is the same weight. Also, the ratio of white to yolk in an egg can vary to such a degree that a recipe calling for 6 yolks may actually need as many as 9. It is therefore advisable to weigh or measure yolks and whites. (The weights given for eggs on the recipe charts are without the shells.)

Eggs in the shell can be brought to room temperature by setting them in a bowl of hot tap water for 5 minutes.

Cracking and Separating Eggs: Eggshells break most cleanly when tapped firmly on a flat surface, not on the edge of a bowl. To separate egg yolks from egg whites, clean hands work better than any separating device. If you will be beating the whites, use an extra small bowl for the whites, separating the whites one at a time and then adding each white to a larger bowl, because even a drop of yolk will prevent egg whites from whipping to stiff peaks. However, if just a drop of yolk gets into the white as you are separating the egg, the broken shell works like a magnet to remove it; this also works for any tiny bits of shell.

Beating Egg Whites: Make sure the bowl, whisk beater, and egg whites are entirely free of oil or fat. Use a metal bowl; glass is slippery and the whites won't whip as well. Avoid plastic bowls, which can retain residual oils. As added insurance, if you haven't used a dishwasher, wet a paper towel, add a little white vinegar to it, and wipe the inside of the bowl, then rinse it thoroughly and dry with a clean paper towel.

Start whipping the egg whites on medium-low speed, then gradually raise the speed to medium-high and whip until soft peaks form when the beater is raised. Sugar, if used, should be added gradually in most cases, with the mixer on, to maintain maximum air bubbles. Continue whipping until stiff peaks form when the beater is raised slowly.

Cream of Tartar: Also known as potassium acid tartrate, this acidic by-product of the wine industry, if added in the correct amount, stabilizes egg whites so that it becomes impossible to dry them out by overbeating. Cream of tartar has an indefinite shelf life if not exposed to moisture or humidity. Use 1 teaspoon cream of tartar per 240 grams / 1 cup egg whites (⅛ teaspoon cream of tartar per 1 egg white / 30 grams / 2 tablespoons); *double if using eggs that are pasteurized in the shell*. If using an electric mixer, it is fine to add the cream of tartar right at the beginning of beating, but if using a hand whisk, add it after the egg whites have started foaming.

Storing Eggs: For maximum freshness, store eggs in the carton or in a covered container, bottom (larger) sides up. Egg whites keep in an airtight container in the refrigerator for up to 10 days. Unbroken yolks, sprayed with nonstick cooking spray or covered with water to prevent drying, will keep in an airtight container in the refrigerator for up to 3 days.

Egg whites freeze perfectly and keep for at least 1 year. Store them in small containers to be used as needed, as they should not be refrozen after thawing. It is also possible to freeze yolks. Stir ½ teaspoon of sugar per yolk into the container of yolks to keep them from becoming sticky after they thaw. (Mark the amount of sugar on the container so that you remember to subtract this amount of sugar from any recipe in which you use them.)

Egg Safety for Raw or Partially Cooked Eggs: Food safety experts warn that the risk of salmonella from raw or partially cooked eggs is highest for young children, the elderly, pregnant women, and those whose immune systems are impaired.

To prevent salmonella in preparations calling for uncooked or lightly cooked eggs, the American Egg Board recommends using pasteurized eggs in the shell, such as Safest Choice (available in some markets; "pasteurized" will be marked on the carton) or pasteurized egg whites. Pasteurized egg whites contain minute quantities of triethyl citrate to improve whipping (cream of tartar can still be added for stability). They keep refrigerated for up to 4 months and more than a year in the freezer.

Pasteurization makes eggs safe for buttercreams and prevents contamination of the work area. When beating egg whites without additives or from eggs pasteurized in the shell, double the amount cream of tartar specified in the recipe (¼ teaspoon / 30 grams per 2 tablespoons / 30 ml per egg white). Longer beating (a total of about

10 minutes) will be required, but the result will be an exceptionally stable meringue.

SALT Fine sea salt contains no additives and is easy to measure accurately and consistently. Transfer the salt to a container to make it easier to measure.

BAKING POWDER Baking powder is a mixture of a dry acid or acid salts and baking soda, with starch or flour added to help stabilize the mixture. "Double-acting" means the baking powder will react (liberate carbon dioxide) on contact with moisture during the mixing stage and then again when exposed to heat during baking. Choose an all-phosphate product containing calcium acid phosphate. I recommend Rumford baking powder, found in most supermarkets or health food stores. It lacks the bitter aftertaste from the aluminum in SAS (sodium aluminum sulfate) baking powders.

Baking powder should be stored in an airtight container to avoid humidity, which will activate it. Baking powder will lose much of its power after about a year. Date the top or bottom of the can after you buy it. To test if it is still active, sprinkle a little of it over hot water. If it fizzes actively, you can still use it.

The weight of a volume measure of baking powder varies widely depending on storage and humidity. I find that the average weight of a teaspoon is 4.5 grams. For consistency when measuring, stir the baking powder lightly with a small spatula or spoon before measuring it.

BAKING SODA Also known as sodium bicarbonate, baking soda has an indefinite shelf life if not exposed to moisture or humidity. After opening it, transfer it to a canning jar or another container with a tight-fitting lid. It usually clumps on storage, so when measuring it, first use a spoon to mash any large lumps. Then dip the measuring spoon into it and slice through it with the edge of a small spatula about three times before sweeping off the excess with the flat part of the blade. Baking soda will cause a cookie dough to brown faster, especially if the dough has been stored for several hours before baking.

CORN SYRUP I prefer light corn syrup to dark for its neutral flavor. A small amount added to sugar when caramelizing is an excellent way to prevent crystallization. Corn syrup is also useful in cookies where a moist chewy consistency is desired.

GOLDEN SYRUP This by-product of sugar refining has a delicious butterscotch flavor. It can be used interchangeably with light corn syrup. If it crystallizes on storage, set the jar in a pan of simmering water and stir the syrup often until the crystals have dissolved.

A Note About Measuring Syrups: Syrups are sticky, so when measuring by volume rather than weighing, it helps either to spray the cup or measuring spoon with nonstick cooking spray or rinse it with water before adding the syrup. Syrups are susceptible to fermentation if contaminated, which results in a sour taste, so avoid returning any unused portion to the bottle.

VANILLA EXTRACT Pure vanilla extract imparts a lovely flavor to baked goods and also serves as a flavor enhancer. High-quality brands are available in some supermarkets, many specialty food stores, and online. My favorite brands are Nielsen-Massey, Heilala, and The Vanilla Company. (Weights are not listed for vanilla in my recipes because weight varies according to the brand.)

CHOCOLATE Dark chocolate is a combination of cocoa solids and cocoa butter, referred to collectively as cacao. The rest is sugar. The higher the percentage of cacao, the lower the percentage of sugar. Almost all the chocolate recipes in this book were developed using chocolate with 60 to 62 percent cacao. A different percentage will affect both the flavor and the texture of the recipe. When purchasing white chocolate, be sure to choose a brand that contains only cocoa butter.

COCOA Unsweetened cocoa powder is pulverized pure chocolate liquor that has had three quarters of its cocoa butter removed. I prefer the flavor of Dutch-processed, aka alkalized, cocoa. These terms refer to a process in which the cocoa powder is treated with a mild alkali to mellow its flavor by neutralizing its acidity, which also makes it easier to dissolve.

NUTS Always taste nuts before using them, because the oils they contain can become rancid; it is not usually possible to detect this from smell alone (unless they are very rancid). Store nuts in an airtight container in a cool place or the freezer. If frozen, they will keep for over a year. Be sure to bring the nuts to room temperature if processing them. Lightly toasting nuts will bring out their flavor and, in the case of walnuts, helps to loosen their bitter skins.

CITRUS ZEST The zest is the colored portion of citrus peel or rind. When grating zest, avoid the pith, or white portion beneath it, as it is bitter. Citrus fruits should be zested before squeezing

(unless the peels are frozen), which is why zest is sometimes listed in the ingredients charts slightly out of order from where it is added to the recipe. Scrub the fruit using liquid detergent and hot water and rinse it well before zesting it, or it will add a bitter taste to the recipe. If a recipe calls for finely grated zest, after grating it with a Microplane grater, use a chef's knife to chop it finely; or process the grated zest in a food processor or spice mill with some of the sugar in the recipe.

NONSTICK COOKING SPRAY This useful product, which contains oil and lecithin, is ideal for keeping baked cookies from sticking to a wire cooling rack. PAM brand is odor-free.

BAKING SPRAY WITH FLOUR This spray, a combination of oil, flour, and lecithin, is used on cookie sheets and baking pans to ensure clean release. It is faster, neater, and more effective than greasing and flouring the pans. Baker's Joy brand is odor-free and releases the best.

Approximate Yield of Juice and Zest from One Orange or Lemon

	ZEST	JUICE
1 orange	2 to 3 tablespoons / 12 to 18 grams	¼ to ½ cup / 59 to 118 ml
1 lemon	1¼ to 2 teaspoons / 2 to 4 grams	3 to 4 tablespoons / 45 to 59 ml

CHAPTER 1

ROLLED

BY HAND

MY DREAM CHOCOLATE CHIP COOKIES

Makes: Twenty-two 2¾ inch round cookies

My dream chocolate chip cookie has crisp edges and is moist and chewy inside. Here's how I accomplish that: I brown the butter to remove the water, which promotes crispness and also adds flavor. Then I add golden or corn syrup to make the inside of the cookies moist and chewy. Golden syrup adds a delicious butterscotch note. Unbleached all-purpose flour gives the cookies a slightly chewier texture than bleached flour. I like to add walnuts, but the cookies are still delicious without nuts. And to achieve moist, chewy interiors, I remove them from the oven when the centers are still soft—and eat them while still warm from the oven. I also love the thinner, crisper variation that follows.

Oven Temperature: 350°F / 175°C	**Baking Time:** 5 minutes for the walnuts; 8 to 10 minutes for the cookies (for each of two batches)

Special Equipment: Two 17 by 14 inch cookie sheets, lined with parchment

DOUGH *Makes: 690 grams*

unsalted butter	113 grams	8 tablespoons (1 stick)
1 large egg	50 grams	3 tablespoons plus ½ teaspoon (47.5 ml)
pure vanilla extract	·	1 teaspoon (5 ml)
walnut halves	75 grams	¾ cup
all-purpose flour, preferably unbleached	161 grams	1⅓ cups (lightly spooned into the cup and leveled off)
baking soda	2.7 grams	½ teaspoon
fine sea salt	·	¼ teaspoon
light brown sugar, preferably Muscovado	81 grams	¼ cup plus 2 tablespoons (firmly packed)
granulated sugar	25 grams	2 tablespoons
golden syrup (or corn syrup)	42 grams	2 tablespoons (30 ml)
dark chocolate chips, 52% to 63% cacao (see Baking Gems)	170 grams (6 ounces)	1 cup

PREHEAT THE OVEN

Twenty minutes or longer before baking, set an oven rack at the middle level. Set the oven at 350°F / 175°C.

MISE EN PLACE

Thirty minutes to 1 hour ahead, cut the butter into tablespoon-size pieces. Set on the counter to soften.

Thirty minutes ahead, into the bowl of a stand mixer, weigh or measure the egg. Whisk in the vanilla extract. Cover tightly with plastic wrap.

Brown the Butter: Have ready by the cooktop a 1 cup / 237 ml glass measure with a spout.

In a small heavy saucepan, melt the butter over very low heat, stirring often with a light-colored silicone spatula. Raise the heat to low and boil, stirring constantly, until the milk solids on the spatula have become little brown specks. An instant-read thermometer should read 285° to 290F° / 140° to 143°C. Immediately pour the

Continues

butter into the glass measure, scraping in the browned solids as well. You should have about 94 grams / ½ cup minus 1 tablespoon / 104 ml. Allow the browned butter to cool to 80°F / 27°C.

Toast and Chop the Walnuts: Spread the walnuts evenly on a baking sheet and bake for 5 minutes. Turn the walnuts onto a clean dish towel and roll and rub them around to loosen the skins. Discard any loose skins and let the nuts cool completely, then chop into coarse pieces.

In a small bowl, whisk together the flour, baking soda, and salt.

MAKE THE DOUGH

1. Into the bowl of the stand mixer fitted with the flat beater, add the browned butter with the solids, the sugars, and golden syrup and mix on low speed for 1 minute.

2. Add the flour mixture. Starting on the lowest speed, beat just until the flour is moistened. Continue beating on low speed for 30 seconds, or until well mixed. Add the chocolate chips and walnuts and continue beating just until evenly incorporated.

3. Divide the dough in half (about 345 grams each). Wrap each piece in plastic wrap. If the dough is very sticky, refrigerate for about 30 minutes.

SHAPE THE DOUGH

4. Divide one piece of dough into 11 walnut-size pieces (31 grams each). Roll each piece of dough in the palms of your hands to form a 1½ inch ball.

5. Place the balls 2 inches apart on a cookie sheet. Flatten the cookies to about 2 inches wide by ½ inch high.

BAKE THE COOKIES

6. Bake for 4 minutes. Rotate the cookie sheet halfway around. Continue baking for 4 to 6 minutes, or until the cookies are just beginning to brown on the tops. When gently pressed with a fingertip, they should still feel soft in the middle.

COOL THE COOKIES

7. Set the cookie sheet on a wire rack and let the cookies cool for 1 minute, or until firm enough to lift from the sheet. Use a thin pancake turner to transfer the cookies to another wire rack. Cool completely.

8. Repeat with the second batch.

STORE Airtight: room temperature, 2 weeks; refrigerated, 1 month; frozen, 3 months.

Baking Gems

♥ Use your favorite chocolate chips here. My favorites are: Valrhona dark chocolate chips (52% or 60%), and Guittard dark chocolate chips (63%).

♥ Use an AA butter, as a lower quality would result in a lesser amount of browned butter.

♥ It's also fine to use butter that is softened, not browned, but it will result in a less flavorful and puffier cookie.

♥ For a cookie that is crisp all the way through, bake at 325°F / 160°C for 12 to 14 minutes, until set but still soft. The cookie will become firm and crisp as it cools.

♥ You can freeze the shaped cookie dough to bake at a later time: Freeze it on the cookie sheet until firm, then transfer to a freezer bag. The baking time will be about 2 minutes longer when baked from frozen. For the ideal texture, preheat the oven to 325°F / 160°C and then raise the temperature to 350°F / 175°C once the cookies are in the oven.

VARIATIONS

Many variations work with this cookie base; for example, use a mix of chocolate chips, such as white, milk, and dark chocolate, or use butterscotch chips instead of chocolate. You can use pecans or your favorite nut instead of walnuts, or no nuts at all. You could also add an equal volume of dried fruit, such as cranberries or raisins.

Thin, Crisp, and Chewy Chocolate Chip Cookies

- Replace the egg with 30 grams / 2 tablespoons / 30 ml milk. This will cause the dough to spread more, so you should use a little less dough for each cookie (the yield will then be greater).

- Replace the chocolate chips with mini chocolate chips and chop the nuts medium-fine.

- Divide each batch of dough into 14 pieces (25 grams / about 2 tablespoons). Roll each piece of dough in the palms of your hands to form a 1⅜ inch ball.

- Place the balls 2 inches apart on the cookie sheet. Flatten them to about 2 inches wide and ⅜ inch high. (If planning to freeze or refrigerate the shaped dough, flatten them to 2¼ inches.)

- Bake for 8 to 10 minutes, or until the cookies are just beginning to brown but the entire tops are still soft. Allow the cookies to cool for 3 minutes before transferring them to a wire rack.

Chocolate Chocolate Chip Cookies

Marvelously fudgy on the inside and deeply chocolaty throughout. It's especially pleasing to eat these still warm, to experience the little pools of melted chocolate chips contrasting with the fudginess.

- Omit the walnuts and add 19 grams / ¼ cup unsweetened alkalized cocoa powder (sifted into the cup and leveled off) to the flour mixture.

- Add 30 grams / 2 tablespoons / 30 ml brewed espresso or strong coffee, cooled to room temperature, to the egg along with the vanilla.

- Flour your hands lightly when shaping this slightly sticky dough.

- Bake the cookies for 8 minutes, or just until the edges are set and slightly firmer but the tops are still soft.

CRANBERRY CHOCOLATE CHIPPERS

Makes: Thirty-two 2½ inch round cookies

This recipe, which features a winning combination of dark chocolate chips, tart cranberries, orange zest, and walnuts, is from my dear cousin Marion. An older version was one of the most popular recipes in my 1990 book *Rose's Christmas Cookies*. That recipe featured fresh cranberries, giving the cookies a slightly cakier texture, but I also like the chewy quality of dried cranberries, which means I can make the cookies all year round. The food processor is a great advantage for this recipe because it makes it easy to chop the cranberries and walnuts. It also keeps the batter from turning pink if you use fresh cranberries.

Oven Temperature: 350°F / 175°C	
Baking Time: 5 minutes for the walnuts; 14 to 16 minutes (for each of two batches)	
Special Equipment: Two 17 by 14 inch cookie sheets, no preparation needed or lined with parchment	

DOUGH *Makes: 860 grams*

Ingredient	Weight	Volume
unsalted butter	113 grams	8 tablespoons (1 stick)
1 large egg	50 grams	3 tablespoons plus ½ teaspoon (47.5 ml)
pure vanilla extract	·	1 teaspoon (5 ml)
orange zest, finely grated	12 grams	2 tablespoons (loosely packed)
walnut halves	50 grams	½ cup
bleached all-purpose flour	161 grams	1⅓ cups (lightly spooned into the cup and leveled off)
baking soda	2.7 grams	½ teaspoon
fine sea salt	·	¼ teaspoon
light brown sugar, preferably Muscovado	81 grams	¼ cup plus 2 tablespoons (firmly packed)
granulated sugar	75 grams	¼ cup plus 2 tablespoons
dried cranberries (or fresh cranberries, see Baking Gems)	150 grams	1 cup plus 2 tablespoons (lightly packed) (1½ cups)
dark chocolate chips, 52% to 63% cacao (see Baking Gems, page 4)	170 grams (6 ounces)	1 cup

PREHEAT THE OVEN

Twenty minutes or longer before baking, set an oven rack at the middle level. Set the oven at 350°F / 175°C.

MISE EN PLACE

Thirty minutes to 1 hour ahead, cut the butter into tablespoon-size pieces. Set on the counter to soften.

Thirty minutes ahead, into a 1 cup / 237 ml glass measure with a spout, weigh or measure the egg. Whisk in the vanilla extract. Cover tightly with plastic wrap and set on the counter.

With dish washing liquid, wash, rinse, and dry the orange before zesting it.

Toast the Walnuts: Spread the walnuts evenly on a baking sheet and bake for 5 minutes. Turn the walnuts onto a clean dish towel and roll and rub them around to loosen the skins. Discard any loose skins and cool completely.

In a small bowl, whisk together the flour, baking soda, and salt.

Continues

MAKE THE DOUGH
Food Processor Method

1. In a food processor, process the sugars and orange zest until the zest is very fine.

2. With the motor running, add the butter one piece at a time, processing until smooth and creamy. Scrape down the sides of the bowl as needed.

3. Add the egg mixture and process just until incorporated, scraping down the sides of the bowl.

4. Add the cranberries and pulse until coarsely chopped, scraping down the sides of the bowl a few times.

5. Add the flour mixture and walnuts and pulse just until the flour is incorporated and the nuts are coarsely chopped.

6. Scrape the dough into a bowl and, with a silicone spatula or large spoon, stir in the chocolate chips.

Stand Mixer Method

1. Coarsely chop the cranberries and walnuts and set them in a small bowl.

2. In the bowl of a stand mixer fitted with the flat beater, beat the butter, sugars, and grated orange zest on medium speed for 2 to 3 minutes, or until lighter in color and fluffy.

3. Gradually add the egg mixture, beating until incorporated. Scrape down the sides of the bowl.

4. On low speed, gradually beat in the flour mixture just until incorporated, scraping down the sides of the bowl as needed.

5. Add the cranberries, nuts, and chocolate chips and beat only until incorporated.

Both Methods

7. Divide the dough in half (about 430 grams each). Wrap each piece in plastic wrap and flatten into a 5 inch disc. Refrigerate for about 30 minutes, until firm enough to shape.

ROLL THE DOUGH INTO BALLS
8. Divide one piece of the dough into 16 walnut-size pieces (about 27 grams each). Roll each piece of dough in the palms of your hands to form a 1 inch ball.

9. Place the balls about 1½ inches apart on a cookie sheet, in 4 rows of 4 cookies.

BAKE THE COOKIES
10. Bake for 10 minutes. Rotate the cookie sheet halfway around. Continue baking for 4 to 6 minutes, or until the cookies are lightly browned but still soft.

COOL THE COOKIES
11. Set the cookie sheet on a wire rack and let the cookies cool for 3 to 5 minutes, until firm enough to lift from the sheet. Use a thin pancake turner to transfer the cookies to another wire rack. Cool completely.

12. Repeat with the second batch.

STORE Airtight: room temperature, 2 weeks; refrigerated, 1 month; frozen, 3 months.

Baking Gems

♥ The sugar is higher in this recipe to balance the tartness of the cranberries. Note, though, that dried cranberries contain added sugar; this amount of dried cranberries contains 6 grams / ½ tablespoon extra sugar. If desired, you can reduce the sugar in the recipe to 69 grams / ¼ cup plus 1½ tablespoons.

♥ Do not use frozen cranberries, as the juices from thawing would bleed into the dough and cause the bottoms of the cookies to burn during baking.

♥ If using fresh cranberries, the dough will be moister, so it is best to drop rounded tablespoons or rounded 1½ inch cookie scoops of dough onto the cookie sheets instead of shaping the balls by hand.

OATMEAL FAVORITES

Makes: Eighteen 3 inch round cookies

There is a reason these cookies are "favorites." They satisfy on every level: crispy, crunchy, chewy, and flavorful. They store well but will become slightly softer in the middle. (Not a bad thing!)

Oven Temperature: 325°F / 160°C for the walnuts; 375°F / 190°C for the cookies

Baking Time: 7 minutes for the walnuts; 8 to 12 minutes for the cookies (for each of two batches)

Special Equipment: Two 17 by 14 inch cookie sheets, no preparation needed or lined with parchment

DOUGH *Makes: 755 grams*

unsalted butter	113 grams	8 tablespoons (1 stick)
1 large egg	50 grams	3 tablespoons plus ½ teaspoon (47.5 ml)
pure vanilla extract	·	1 teaspoon (5 ml)
walnut halves	50 grams	½ cup
bleached all-purpose flour	151 grams	1¼ cups (lightly spooned into the cup and leveled off)
baking powder, preferably an aluminum-free variety	2.2 grams	½ teaspoon
baking soda	2.7 grams	½ teaspoon
fine sea salt	3 grams	½ teaspoon
raisins	108 grams	¾ cup
old-fashioned rolled oats	52 grams	1¼ cups
dark chocolate chips, 52% to 63% cacao	85 grams (3 ounces)	½ cup
light Muscovado (or dark brown sugar)	108 grams	½ cup (firmly packed)

PREHEAT THE OVEN

Twenty minutes or longer before baking, set an oven rack at the middle level. Set the oven at 325°F / 160°C.

MISE EN PLACE

Thirty minutes to 1 hour ahead, cut the butter into tablespoon-size pieces. Set on the counter to soften.

Thirty minutes ahead, into a 1 cup / 237 ml glass measure with a spout, weigh or measure the egg. Whisk in the vanilla extract. Cover tightly with plastic wrap and set on the counter.

Toast and Chop the Walnuts: Spread the walnuts evenly on a baking sheet and bake for 7 minutes. Turn the walnuts onto a clean dish towel and roll and rub them around to loosen the skins. Discard any loose skins and cool completely, then chop into coarse pieces.

In a small bowl, whisk together the flour, baking powder, baking soda, and salt.

In a medium bowl, toss together the walnuts, raisins, oats, and chocolate chips.

MAKE THE DOUGH

1. In the bowl of a stand mixer fitted with the flat beater, beat the sugar and butter on medium

Continues

speed until smooth and creamy, about 1 minute. Scrape down the sides of the bowl.

2. Add the egg mixture and beat for 30 seconds, or until incorporated. Scrape down the sides of the bowl.

3. Add the flour mixture and beat on low speed just until all the flour disappears.

4. Add the nut mixture and beat on low speed just until incorporated.

5. Scrape the dough onto a sheet of plastic wrap, *wrap*, and refrigerate it for a minimum of 30 minutes, up to 24 hours.

PREHEAT THE OVEN

Thirty minutes or longer before baking, set an oven rack at the middle level. Set the oven at 375°F / 190°C.

ROLL THE DOUGH INTO BALLS

6. Divide the dough in half (about 375 grams each). Rewrap one of the pieces in the plastic wrap and refrigerate it while you shape the other piece.

7. Divide the dough into 9 pieces (2 level tablespoons / 41 grams). Roll each piece between the palms of your hands to form a 1¾ inch ball.

8. Place the balls 2 inches apart on a cookie sheet. Press them down to about 2½ inches wide.

BAKE THE COOKIES

9. Bake the cookies for 6 minutes. Rotate the cookie sheet halfway around. Continue baking for 2 to 6 minutes, or until the cookies are lightly browned but still feel soft when gently pressed with a fingertip.

COOL THE COOKIES

10. Set the cookie sheet on a wire rack and let the cookies cool for 1 minute. Use a thin pancake turner to transfer the cookies to another wire rack. They will firm up as they cool and are most delicious when eaten slightly warm.

11. Repeat with the second batch.

STORE Airtight: room temperature, 2 weeks; refrigerated, 1 month; frozen, 3 months.

Baking Gem

♥ It is best for the dough to rest for a minimum of 30 minutes before shaping to allow the oats to absorb some of the moisture and soften and to allow the rest of the moisture to be evenly absorbed. Otherwise, the oats will be harder and the excess moisture in the dough will cause it to spread more.

VARIATION

The nuts can be replaced with mini chocolate chips or chopped chocolate.

JUMBLES

Makes: Thirty-six 2¼ inch round cookies

Leave it to my longtime friend chef David Shamah to create a cookie that is the perfect marriage of a chocolate chip cookie and a Chunky candy bar. The cookie is chock-full of nuts, chocolate chips, and the tangy sweetness of raisins, with just enough dough to hold it all together. I even enjoy it as a breakfast cookie!

Oven Temperature: 325°F / 160°C for the nuts; 375°F / 190°C for the cookies	**Baking Time:** 5 minutes for the nuts; 14 to 16 minutes for the cookies (for each of two batches)
Special Equipment: Two 17 by 14 inch cookie sheets, no preparation needed or lined with parchment; A 1¾ inch cookie scoop or a tablespoon	

DOUGH *Makes: 1,170 grams*

unblanched whole almonds	240 grams	2 cups
pecan halves	75 grams	¾ cup
unsalted butter	113 grams	8 tablespoons (1 stick)
1 large egg	50 grams	3 tablespoons plus ½ teaspoon (47.5 ml)
pure vanilla extract	·	1 teaspoon (5 ml)
bleached all-purpose flour	161 grams	1⅓ cups (lightly spooned into the cup and leveled off)
baking soda	5.5 grams	1 teaspoon
fine sea salt	·	¼ teaspoon
dark chocolate chips, 52% to 63% cacao (see Baking Gems)	170 grams (6 ounces)	1 cup
raisins (see Baking Gems)	216 grams	1½ cups
granulated sugar	100 grams	½ cup
light brown sugar, preferably Muscovado	54 grams	¼ cup (firmly packed)

PREHEAT THE OVEN

Twenty minutes or longer before baking, set an oven rack at the middle level. Set the oven at 325°F / 175°C.

MISE EN PLACE

Toast and Chop the Nuts: Divide the almonds and pecans on a baking sheet and bake for 5 minutes. Cool completely, then use a sharp knife to chop the nuts very coarsely. I like to cut the almonds in halves and the pecans into thirds.

Raise the oven temperature to 375°F / 190°C.

Thirty minutes to 1 hour ahead, cut the butter into tablespoon-size pieces. Set on the counter to soften.

Thirty minutes ahead, into a 1 cup / 237 ml glass measure with a spout, weigh or measure the egg. Whisk in the vanilla extract. Cover tightly with plastic wrap and set on the counter.

In a small bowl, whisk together the flour, baking soda, and salt.

In a medium bowl, stir together the nuts, chocolate chips, and raisins.

Continues

MAKE THE DOUGH

1. In the bowl of a stand mixer fitted with the flat beater, beat the butter and sugars on medium speed for 2 to 3 minutes, until lighter in color and fluffy.

2. Gradually add the egg mixture, beating until incorporated. Scrape down the sides of the bowl.

3. On low speed, gradually beat in the flour mixture just until incorporated, scraping down the sides of the bowl as needed.

4. Add the nut mixture and beat until it is incorporated and the dough holds together.

5. Divide the dough in half (about 585 grams each). Wrap each piece in plastic wrap and flatten into a 6 inch disc. Refrigerate for about 30 minutes, or until firm enough to shape.

SHAPE THE DOUGH

6. Scoop out 18 pieces of dough (a rounded scoop / 32 to 33 grams). Roll each piece of dough firmly between the palms of your hands to form a 1⅝ inch ball.

7. Place the balls 1½ inches apart on a cookie sheet. Press them down to 2 inches wide.

BAKE THE COOKIES

8. Bake for 10 minutes. Rotate the cookie sheet halfway around. Continue baking for 4 to 6 minutes, or until the cookies are golden brown but still soft.

COOL THE COOKIES

9. Set the cookie sheet on a wire rack and let the cookies cool for 3 to 5 minutes, until firm enough to lift from the sheet. Use a thin pancake turner to transfer the cookies to another wire rack. Cool completely.

10. Repeat with the second batch.

STORE Airtight: room temperature, 2 weeks; refrigerated, 1 month; frozen, 3 months.

Baking Gems

♥ A larger amount of baking soda than usual is needed for this recipe because the dough carries so many nuts, chocolate, and raisins that it needs to puff up around them to hold everything together.

♥ If dropped straight from the scoop rather than rolled by hand, the baked cookies will have a rougher, more jumbled effect, but some will split or separate.

♥ Use your favorite chocolate chips. Mine are Valrhona dark chocolate chips (52% or 60%) and Guittard dark chocolate chips (63%).

♥ If the raisins are dried out, put them in a small bowl, sprinkle with hot water, and allow them to sit, covered, for a minimum of 30 minutes to soften.

FREEDOM TREASURE COOKIES

Have you ever wondered what wonderful things you could do with all the leftover additions to cookies, aside from munching on them as snacks? What follows is a base recipe for rolled or dropped cookies with which you can build and create your own favorite cookie using a mixture of those treasures. Here are guidelines for baking temperature and range of additions that will give you the freedom to make your own dream cookie.

ABOUT THE BASIC INGREDIENTS: ALL-PURPOSE FLOUR, SUGAR, BUTTER, EGG, BAKING SODA, FINE SEA SALT, AND VANILLA EXTRACT

Unbleached all-purpose flour, brown sugar, and baking soda will result in browner cookies than those made with bleached all-purpose flour, granulated sugar, and baking powder. Unbleached all-purpose flour will also produce slightly flatter, less tender cookies than bleached all-purpose flour because the higher protein not only browns faster, it also ties up some of the liquid, which prevents the cookie from puffing as much. The egg helps to bind the dough together and assists a little in aeration and puffiness. The salt should be an accent, not rise above the other flavors.

BASIC PROPORTIONS OF INGREDIENTS: 161 grams / 1⅓ cups flour: about 100 to 156 grams / ½ to ¾ cup sugar, depending on the amount of brown sugar (which is slightly heavier due to its molasses) used and the sweetness of the added ingredients. If you are adding tart ingredients such as cranberries, or if you have more of a sweet tooth, use the higher amount of sugar; if you are adding sweet ingredients such as coconut or raisins, use the lower amount. Adding a higher amount of sugar will result in a flatter, crisper cookie.

BAKING TEMPERATURE

Baking at 375°F / 190°C will brown the cookies faster, keeping the centers softer and moister. Baking at 350°F / 175°C will take a little longer and the cookies' texture will be more uniform, thinner, and crisper.

Continues

TREASURE ADDITIONS

These additions all vary in weight, so this is a rare instance when I find volume more useful. The cookie dough can hold anywhere from 3 cups to as much as 5¼ cups of add-ins. Cookies made with the highest amount have the bare minimum of dough to keep all the additions together and have more of a candy than a cookie profile.

SUGGESTED ADD-INS

Note: If mixing the dough in a food processor, there is no need to coarsely chop any of the ingredients.

CHOCOLATE CHUNKS OR CHIPS: dark, white, or milk chocolate; butterscotch or peanut butter chips

NUTS: such as almonds, walnuts, pistachios, cashews, hazelnuts, or macadamia, coarsely chopped

Note: If adding nuts that are not already toasted, to bring out the flavor, you can toast them for 5 to 7 minutes in a preheated 325°F / 160°C oven. Allow them to cool completely. Walnut skins are slightly bitter, but it's fine to leave them on. Alternatively, while the walnuts are still hot, roll them in a clean dish towel to remove any skins that come off easily. When chopping or breaking them into coarse pieces, some of the skins will separate and should be discarded.

COCONUT: shredded sweetened or unsweetened

ROLLED OATS: old-fashioned or instant. Old-fashioned oats are slightly thicker and the cookies will be chewier. Oats absorb moisture, so the dough will be less smooth and will produce a drier, crisper cookie. Recommended maximum amount: 1¼ cups / 90 grams. Be sure to allow the dough to rest for a minimum of 30 minutes to allow the oats to absorb the moisture evenly, or the cookies will be harder and the extra moisture in the dough itself will cause the cookies to spread more during baking.

DRIED FRUIT, COARSELY CHOPPED IF NEEDED: including cherries, cranberries, candied ginger, raisins, currants

GRATED CITRUS ZEST: 12 grams / 2 tablespoons loosely packed is usually the ideal amount to be present without overpowering the other ingredients.

SIZE

For 2½ inch cookies, use about 1½ table-spoons dough for 1 inch balls (walnut-size)

For 3 inch cookies, use 2 tablespoons dough for 1¾ inch balls (ping pong ball–size)

THE BASIC FREEDOM TREASURE COOKIE RECIPE

Makes: 36 to 64 round cookies, depending on size (see above)

Oven Temperature: 350°F / 175°C for flatter, crisper cookies; 375°F / 190°C for browner cookies with softer centers

Baking Time: 8 to 16 minutes (for each of two batches)

Special Equipment: Two 17 by 14 inch cookie sheets, no preparation needed or lined with parchment; A 1¾ inch cookie scoop or a tablespoon

DOUGH *Makes: 430 grams (before Treasure Additions)*

unsalted butter	113 grams	8 tablespoons (1 stick)
1 large egg	50 grams	3 tablespoons plus ½ teaspoon (47.5 ml)
pure vanilla extract	·	1 teaspoon (5 ml)
all-purpose flour, preferably bleached	161 grams	1⅓ cups (lightly spooned into the cup and leveled off)
baking soda	2.7 grams	½ teaspoon
fine sea salt	3 grams	½ teaspoon
light Muscovado (or dark brown sugar)	56 grams	¼ cup (firmly packed)
granulated sugar	50 grams	¼ cup
Treasure Additions	·	3 to 5¼ cups

PREHEAT THE OVEN

Twenty minutes or longer before baking, set an oven rack at the middle level. Set the oven at 350°F / 175°C. (If baking at 375°F / 190°C—see Oven Temperature, above—preheat for 30 minutes or longer.)

MISE EN PLACE

Thirty minutes to 1 hour ahead, cut the butter into tablespoon-size pieces. Set on the counter to soften.

Thirty minutes ahead, into a 1 cup / 237 ml glass measure with a spout, weigh or measure the egg. Whisk in the vanilla extract. Cover tightly with plastic wrap and set on the counter.

In a small bowl, whisk together the flour, baking soda, and salt.

MAKE THE DOUGH
Food Processor Method

1. In a food processor, process the sugars until as fine as possible.

2. With the motor running, add the butter one piece at a time and process until smooth and creamy, scraping down the sides of the bowl as needed.

3. Add the egg mixture and process just until incorporated, scraping down the sides of the bowl.

4. Add the flour mixture and Treasure Additions except for chocolate or other chunks or chips and

Continues

pulse just until the flour is incorporated and the added ingredients are coarsely chopped.

5. If using chocolate or other chunks or chips, scrape the dough into a bowl and stir them in with a silicone spatula or large spoon.

Stand Mixer Method

1. In the bowl of a stand mixer fitted with the flat beater, beat the butter and sugars on medium speed for 2 to 3 minutes, or until lighter in color and fluffy.

2. Gradually add the egg mixture, beating until incorporated. Scrape down the sides of the bowl.

3. On low speed, gradually beat in the flour mixture just until incorporated, scraping down the sides of the bowl as needed.

4. Add the Treasure Additions and beat only until incorporated.

Both Methods

6. Divide the dough in half. Wrap each piece in plastic wrap and flatten into a disc. Refrigerate for about 30 minutes (a minimum of 30 minutes if adding rolled oats), or until firm enough to shape.

ROLL THE DOUGH INTO BALLS

7. Divide one piece of the dough into 1½ level tablespoon pieces to form 1 inch balls for 2½ inch cookies or 2 level tablespoons to form 1¾ inch balls for 3 inch cookies. (Alternatively, use a 1¾ to 2 inch cookie scoop or a tablespoon to drop the cookies onto the cookie sheet. If adding more than 4 cups of Treasures, it is best to roll the cookies in the palms of your hands to help press the additions into the dough.)

8. Place the balls 1½ to 2 inches apart on a cookie sheet.

BAKE THE COOKIES

9. Bake for 6 minutes. Rotate the cookie sheet halfway around. Continue baking for 2 to 10 minutes, or until the cookies are lightly browned but still soft.

COOL THE COOKIES

10. Set the cookie sheet on a wire rack and let the cookies cool for 3 to 5 minutes, until firm enough to lift from the sheet. Use a thin pancake turner to transfer the cookies to another wire rack. Cool completely.

11. Repeat with the second batch.

STORE Airtight: room temperature, 2 weeks; refrigerated, 1 month; frozen, 3 months.

LEMON POPPY SEED COOKIES

Makes: Eighteen 2 inch round cookies

Lemon and poppy seeds are a classic well-loved combination. These extraordinary cookies are buttery, crunchy, and filled with flavorful crackly poppy seeds, with a firm yet dissolving texture.

Oven Temperature:
350°F / 175°C

Baking Time: 18 to 20 minutes

Special Equipment: One 17 by 14 inch cookie sheet, no preparation needed or lined with parchment

DOUGH *Makes: 342 grams*

unsalted butter	113 grams	8 tablespoons (1 stick)
1 (to 2) large egg yolk (see page xxvi)	19 grams	1 tablespoon plus ½ teaspoon (17.5 ml)
pure vanilla extract	·	½ teaspoon (2.5 ml)
lemon zest, finely grated (from 1 to 2 lemons)	6 grams	1 tablespoon (loosely packed)
bleached all-purpose flour	113 grams	1 cup (lightly spooned into the cup and leveled off) minus 1 tablespoon
poppy seeds	27 grams	3 tablespoons
fine sea salt	·	⅛ teaspoon
sugar	75 grams	¼ cup plus 2 tablespoons

MISE EN PLACE

Thirty minutes to 1 hour ahead, cut the butter into tablespoon-size pieces. Set on the counter to soften.

Thirty minutes ahead, into a 1 cup / 237 ml glass measure with a spout, weigh or measure the egg yolk. Whisk in the vanilla extract. Cover tightly with plastic wrap and set on the counter.

With dishwashing liquid, wash, rinse, and dry the lemons before zesting them.

In a small bowl, whisk together the flour, poppy seeds, and salt.

MAKE THE DOUGH

Food Processor Method

1. In a food processor, process the sugar and lemon zest until the zest is very fine.

2. With the motor on, add the butter one piece at a time and process until smooth and very creamy. Scrape down the sides of the bowl.

3. Add the egg yolk mixture and pulse just until incorporated. Scrape down the sides of the bowl.

4. Add the flour mixture and pulse just until blended. Scrape down the sides of the bowl.

Stand Mixer Method

1. Chop the lemon zest very fine.

2. In the bowl of a stand mixer fitted with the flat beater, beat the butter, sugar, and lemon zest on medium speed for 2 to 3 minutes, until lighter in color and fluffy.

3. On low speed, add the egg yolk mixture, beating just until incorporated. Scrape down the sides of the bowl.

Continues

4. Gradually beat in the flour mixture just until smoothly incorporated, scraping down the sides of the bowl as needed.

Both Methods

5. Scrape the dough into a bowl. Cover and refrigerate for a minimum of 1 hour, up to overnight.

PREHEAT THE OVEN

Twenty minutes or longer before baking, set an oven rack at the middle level. Set the oven at 350°F / 175°C.

ALMOND COATING

sliced blanched almonds	42 grams	½ cup

6. Finely grind the almonds in a food processor, or grind in a spice mill in batches; or use a rotary nut grinder. Set in a small bowl.

ROLL THE DOUGH INTO BALLS AND COAT THEM

7. Scoop out 18 pieces of dough (1 gently rounded tablespoon / 19 grams each). One at a time, roll each piece in the palms of your hands to form a 1⅛ inch ball and then, while the dough is still soft, set the ball in the bowl with the ground almonds and twirl it around to coat it with nuts. Place the balls a minimum of 2 inches apart on the cookie sheet.

BAKE THE COOKIES

8. Bake for 10 minutes. Rotate the cookie sheet halfway around. Continue baking for 8 to 10 minutes, or until the cookies are golden and beginning to brown around the edges.

COOL THE COOKIES

9. Set the cookie sheet on a wire rack and use a thin pancake turner to transfer the cookies to another wire rack. Cool completely.

STORE Airtight: room temperature, 2 weeks; frozen, 3 months.

Baking Gems

♥ Poppy seeds are high in oil, so to prevent rancidity, store them in the freezer.

♥ If not using the nut coating, flour your hands lightly when rolling the dough into balls; this will help them keep a rounder shape when baked.

LEMON LUMPIES

Makes: Thirty-two 2 inch by 1 inch high round cookies

My dear friend Annie Baker sells wonderful "cookie dough cookies"—crunchy on the outside and chewy and doughy on the inside—at Napa farmers' markets and online at anniethebaker.com. When I stopped in the Bay Area while promoting my book *Rose's Heavenly Cakes,* she gifted me with a bag of her famous cookies for the road. Of course, her recipe is top secret, as her vast array of cookie dough cookies are her claim to fame. Here is my version. The candied lemon peel adds a sparkly counterpoint to the sweetness of the white chocolate. You can use this recipe as a base for any number of variations (see page 25).

Oven Temperature: 400°F / 200°C

Baking Time: 10 to 11 minutes (for each of two batches)

Special Equipment: Two 17 by 14 inch cookie sheets, lined with parchment

---

DOUGH *Makes: about 1,180 grams*

unsalted butter	200 grams	14 tablespoons (1¾ sticks)
candied lemon peel, preferably homemade (page 398); see Baking Gems	74 grams	½ cup (chopped)
high-quality white chocolate	113 grams (4 ounces)	·
all-purpose flour, preferably unbleached	400 grams	3¼ cups (lightly spooned into the cup and leveled off) plus 1 tablespoon
baking soda	·	⅛ teaspoon
fine sea salt	6 grams	1 teaspoon
light brown sugar, preferably Muscovado	217 grams	1 cup (firmly packed)
golden syrup (or corn syrup)	126 grams (120 grams)	¼ cup plus 2 tablespoons (89 ml)
pure vanilla extract	·	1 teaspoon (5 ml)
milk	121 grams	½ cup (118 ml)
granulated sugar, for coating	40 grams	3 tablespoons

MISE EN PLACE

Brown the Butter: Have ready by the cooktop a 1 cup / 237 ml glass measure with a spout.

In a small heavy saucepan, melt the butter over very low heat, stirring often with a light-colored silicone spatula. Raise the heat to low and boil, stirring constantly, until the milk solids on the spatula become little brown specks. An instant-read thermometer should read 285° to 290°F / 140° to 143°C. Immediately pour the butter into the glass measure, scraping in the browned solids as well. You should have about 140 grams / ¾ cup / 177 ml. Allow the browned butter to cool to 80°F / 27°C.

Chop the candied lemon peel into ¼ inch pieces. You should have ½ cup.

Chop the white chocolate into ¼ inch pieces. You should have ⅔ cup.

In a medium bowl, whisk together the flour, baking soda, and salt.

Continues

MAKE THE DOUGH

1. In the bowl of a stand mixer fitted with the flat beater, mix the browned butter, brown sugar, golden syrup, and vanilla extract on low speed for 1 minute, or until blended.

2. Gradually beat in the milk. The batter will look curdled.

3. Add the flour mixture. Beat on the lowest speed just until the flour is moistened. Then beat on low speed for 30 seconds.

4. Add the white chocolate and candied lemon peel and beat just until evenly incorporated.

ROLL THE DOUGH INTO BALLS

5. In a small custard cup, place the granulated sugar for coating.

6. Divide the dough into 32 walnut-size pieces (37 grams each). If the dough is too soft to roll easily, refrigerate it briefly until it is firmer. One at a time, roll each piece of dough in the palms of your hands to form a 1½ inch ball, then roll the ball in the sugar, while it is still soft enough to coat evenly.

7. Set the balls on a small sheet pan. Cover with plastic wrap and freeze for a minimum of 1 hour, up to 3 months. (If planning to store these for longer than 1 hour, it is best to transfer the frozen balls to an airtight container or freezer bag.)

PREHEAT THE OVEN

Thirty minutes or longer before baking, set an oven rack at the middle level. Set the oven at 400°F / 200°C.

8. Place half of the balls 1½ inches apart on a prepared cookie sheet.

BAKE THE COOKIES

9. Bake for 5 minutes. Rotate the cookie sheet halfway around. Continue baking for 5 to 6 minutes, or until the cookies are just beginning to brown on the top; when gently pressed with thumb and index finger on the sides, they should yield to pressure. An instant-read thermometer inserted into a cookie should read 145° to 165°F / 63° to 74°C.

COOL THE COOKIES

10. Set the cookie sheet on a wire rack and use a thin pancake turner to transfer the cookies to another wire rack. Cool completely.

11. Repeat with the second batch.

STORE Airtight: room temperature, 3 days; refrigerated, 5 days; frozen, 3 months.

Baking Gems

♥ If using store-bought candied lemon peel, it is a good idea to boost the flavor by adding 12 grams / 2 tablespoons loosely packed freshly grated lemon zest to the dough.

♥ Use an AA or A butter, as a lower quality will result in a lesser amount of browned butter.

VARIATIONS

You can replace the candied lemon peel with other ingredients of your choice, such as candied ginger, in equal volume. Candied orange peel with milk or dark chocolate is another fantastic combination. You could also replace both the lemon peel and the white chocolate with the same volume of another ingredient, such as peanut butter chips. Chopped nuts are also a good substitution for the white chocolate, with or without the candied citrus peel.

PEANUT BUTTER AND JELLY BUTTONS

Makes: Thirty 1¼ inch round cookies

The combination of crisp, sandy peanut butter cookies and tart sticky cherry jam could not be better (other than with the addition of a chocolate topping; see the Variation). Or you could skip the cherry jam altogether and opt for the milk chocolate filling variation instead.

Oven Temperature: 375°F / 190°C	Baking Time: 10 to 12 minutes (for each of two batches)	Special Equipment: Two 17 by 14 inch cookie sheets, no preparation needed or lined with parchment; Optional: A disposable pastry bag fitted with a ¼ inch star decorating tip if making the Milk Chocolate Filling

DOUGH *Makes: 360 grams*

unsalted butter	57 grams	4 tablespoons (½ stick)
½ large egg, lightly beaten before measuring	25 grams	1½ tablespoons (22.5 ml)
pure vanilla extract	·	¼ teaspoon (1.25 ml)
bleached all-purpose flour	71 grams	½ cup (lightly spooned into the cup and leveled off) plus 4 teaspoons
baking soda	2.7 grams	½ teaspoon
fine sea salt	·	1/16 teaspoon (a pinch)
light brown sugar, preferably Muscovado (or dark brown sugar)	54 grams	¼ cup (firmly packed)
sugar, preferably superfine	25 grams	2 tablespoons
smooth peanut butter, preferably Jif	133 grams	½ cup

MISE EN PLACE

Thirty minutes to 1 hour ahead, cut the butter into tablespoon-size pieces. Set on the counter to soften.

Thirty minutes ahead, into a 1 cup / 237 ml glass measure with a spout, weigh or measure the egg. Whisk in the vanilla extract. Cover tightly with plastic wrap and set on the counter.

In a medium bowl, whisk together the flour, baking soda, and salt.

MAKE THE DOUGH

1. In the bowl of a stand mixer fitted with the flat beater, beat the sugars on medium speed until well mixed.

2. Add the butter and peanut butter and beat for 2 to 3 minutes, until very smooth and creamy.

3. Gradually add the egg mixture, beating until incorporated. Scrape down the sides of the bowl.

4. On low speed, gradually beat in the flour mixture just until incorporated, scraping down the sides of the bowl as needed.

5. Scrape the dough into a medium bowl, cover, and refrigerate for a minimum of 1 hour, up to overnight, to keep it from cracking when shaped.

PREHEAT THE OVEN

Twenty minutes or longer before baking, set an oven rack at the middle level. Set the oven at 375°F / 190°C.

SHAPE THE DOUGH

6. Divide the dough in half (about 180 grams each). Wrap one of the pieces in plastic wrap and set it aside while you shape the other piece.

7. Measure out 15 pieces of dough (2 level teaspoons / 12 grams each).

8. One at a time, roll each piece between the palms of your hands to form a 1 inch ball. As soon as you shape the cookie, while the dough is still soft, set it on a cookie sheet, spacing the cookies 1½ inches apart, and use your index finger or the handle of a wooden spoon to make a depression in the middle of the dough, going down almost to the cookie sheet.

BAKE THE COOKIES

9. Bake for 6 minutes. Rotate the cookie sheet halfway around. Continue baking for 4 to 6 minutes, until the cookies are lightly browned and set.

COOL THE COOKIES

10. Set the cookie sheet on a wire rack and let the cookies cool for 3 to 5 minutes, until firm enough to lift from the sheet. Use a thin pancake turner to transfer the cookies to another wire rack. If the depressions have become more shallow, while the cookies are still hot, use the handle of a wooden spoon, lightly coated with nonstick cooking spray, to deepen them again. Cool completely.

11. Repeat with the second batch.

SOUR CHERRY PRESERVES FILLING AND TOPPING

sour cherry preserves	255 grams	about ¾ cup

1. In a 2 cup / 473 ml microwavable measure with a spout (or in a small saucepan over low heat stirring constantly) heat the preserves just until boiling. Strain the jelly into a small saucepan.

2. Place the cherries remaining in the strainer into the depressions of the cookies, piecing together any crushed pieces.

3. Bring the jelly to a boil over medium heat and boil for about 5 minutes, stirring constantly with a metal spoon, until when a little of the jelly is dropped from the spoon, the last drops come together to form one large sticky drop that hangs from the spoon. The jelly will be reduced to about 6 tablespoons / 90 ml.

4. Let the jelly cool until it stops bubbling (about 1 minute). Spoon a heaping ¼ to ½ teaspoon over the cherry in each cookie depression.

STORE Filled, Airtight: room temperature, 1 month. Unfilled, Airtight: room temperature, several months.
If you are not adding the chocolate topping, the cherry topping will stay pleasantly sticky, so the cookies will need to be stored in a single layer.

Baking Gem

♥ Superfine sugar will result in fewer cracks on the cookies' surface. You can also use just half the peanut butter, which will prevent cracking and result in flatter, crisper cookies.

Continues

Chocolate-Covered Cherry Cookies

Coarsely chop 43 grams / 1.5 ounces dark chocolate and finely chop 28 grams / 1 ounce milk chocolate. Melt the dark chocolate (see melting instructions below). Remove it from the heat and stir in the milk chocolate until completely melted. Pipe the chocolate, or use a small spoon, to coat the cherry centers with the chocolate. Place the cookies in the refrigerator for 5 minutes, or until the chocolate is set and no longer shiny.

Peanut Butter and Chocolate Buttons

Use this in place of the sour cherry preserves.

MILK CHOCOLATE FILLING

milk chocolate	85 grams (3 ounces)	·
dark chocolate, 60% to 62% cacao	85 grams (3 ounces)	·
unsalted butter, softened	43 grams	3 tablespoons

Chop the milk chocolate into fine pieces.

Chop the dark chocolate into coarse pieces. In a medium microwavable bowl, heat the dark chocolate, stirring every 15 seconds with a silicone spatula, until completely melted. Or heat it in the top of a double boiler set over hot, not simmering, water—do not let the bottom of the container touch the water—stirring often, until completely melted.

Remove the dark chocolate from the heat, add the milk chocolate, and stir until completely cool to the touch.

Whisk in the softened butter just until incorporated. The mixture will thicken instantly.

Scrape the chocolate mixture into the prepared pastry bag and fill the cookies. Alternatively, use a small spoon or metal spatula.

Traditional Peanut Butter Cookies

These are classic peanut butter cookies, without any filling. The recipe uses less peanut butter than the "buttons" to keep the dough from cracking along the edges when pressed flat. Adding ground peanuts ensures a full peanut flavor, and the result is an appealingly soft, chewy cookie with crisp edges.

For twenty-two 3 inch round cookies, double all the ingredients except for the peanut butter. Along with the peanut butter in step 2, add 80 grams / $\frac{2}{3}$ cup lightly salted dry-roasted peanuts, ground in a food processor, spice mill, or rotary nut grinder.

Divide the dough in half (340 grams each), wrap one half in plastic, and keep refrigerated while you shape the other half. When shaping the dough in Step 7, measure out 11 pieces of dough (2 level tablespoons / 31 grams each). Roll each piece of dough in the lightly floured palms of your hands to form a 1½ inch ball. Set the cookies 2 inches apart on a parchment-lined cookie sheet. Use the tines of a fork, dipped in cold water to prevent sticking, to flatten the cookies to 2 inches wide, first in one direction and then perpendicular to it, to create the traditional crosshatched effect.

Bake in a preheated 350°F / 175°C oven for 6 minutes. Rotate the cookie sheet halfway around. Continue baking for 6 to 8 minutes, or until the cookies are golden but still slightly soft when pressed lightly with your finger.

Set the cookie sheet on a wire rack and let the cookies cool for 3 to 5 minutes, until firm enough to lift from the cookie sheet. Use a thin pancake turner to transfer the cookies to another wire rack. Cool completely.

Repeat with the second batch.

TAHINI CRISPS

Makes: Twenty 2¼ inch round cookies

These cookies are crisp and amazingly light and tender, with an appealingly addictive sesame flavor.

Oven Temperature: 375°F / 190°C	**Baking Time:** 12 to 15 minutes (for each of two batches)	**Special Equipment:** Two 17 by 14 inch cookie sheets, no preparation needed or lined with parchment; A 1 tablespoon measure

DOUGH *Makes: 360 grams*

unsalted butter	57 grams	4 tablespoons (½ stick)
tahini, preferably Soom (see Baking Gems)	143 grams	½ cup plus 1 tablespoon
½ large egg, lightly beaten before measuring	25 grams	1½ tablespoons (22.5 ml)
pure vanilla extract	·	¼ teaspoon (1.25 ml)
bleached all-purpose flour	71 grams	½ cup (lightly spooned into the cup and leveled off) plus 1½ tablespoons
baking soda	2.7 grams	½ teaspoon
fine sea salt	·	¹⁄₁₆ teaspoon (a pinch)
light brown sugar, preferably Muscovado	54 grams	¼ cup (firmly packed)
granulated sugar	25 grams	2 tablespoons
hulled sesame seeds, for coating	42 grams	¼ cup

MISE EN PLACE

Thirty minutes to 1 hour ahead, cut the butter into tablespoon-size pieces. Set on the counter to soften.

About 30 minutes ahead, stir the tahini until the oil that has separated is completely incorporated.

Then weigh or measure the tahini into a small bowl and set on the counter to come to room temperature (65° to 75°F / 18° to 24°C).

Thirty minutes ahead, into a 1 cup / 237 ml glass measure with a spout, weigh or measure the egg. Whisk in the vanilla extract. Cover tightly with plastic wrap and set on the counter.

In a small bowl, whisk together the flour, baking soda, and salt.

MAKE THE DOUGH

Food Processor Method

1. In a food processor, process the sugars for several minutes, until very fine.

2. With the motor running, add the butter one piece at a time and process until smooth and creamy. Scrape down the sides of the bowl as needed.

3. Add the tahini and process until smooth and creamy.

4. Add the egg mixture and process until incorporated, scraping down the sides of the bowl as needed.

5. Add the flour mixture and pulse just until incorporated. Scrape the dough into a bowl.

Stand Mixer Method

1. Grind the sugars in a spice mill until very fine.

Continues

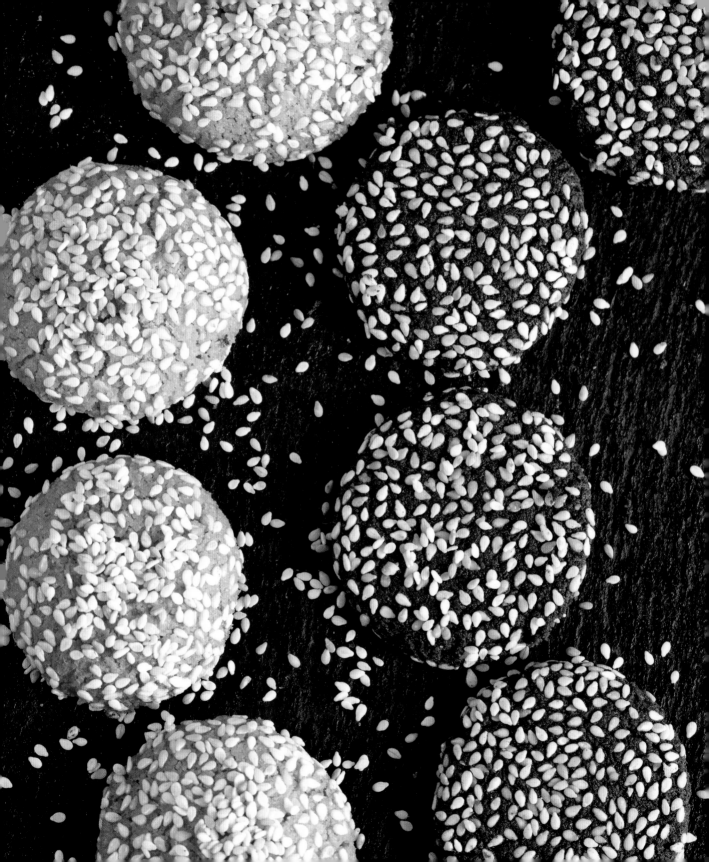

2. In the bowl of a stand mixer fitted with the flat beater, beat the butter and sugar on medium speed for 2 to 3 minutes, until lighter in color and fluffy.

3. Add the tahini and process until smooth and creamy.

4. Gradually add the egg mixture, beating until incorporated. Scrape down the sides of the bowl.

5. Add the flour mixture and beat on low speed just until incorporated, scraping down the sides of the bowl as needed.

Both Methods

6. Cover and refrigerate for a minimum of 1 hour, up to overnight, to firm for shaping.

PREHEAT THE OVEN

Thirty minutes or longer before baking, set an oven rack at the middle level. Set the oven at 375°F / 190°C.

ROLL THE DOUGH INTO BALLS

7. Into a small custard up, place the sesame seeds.

8. Measure out 10 pieces of dough (1 level tablespoon / 18 grams each). One at a time, roll each piece of dough between the palms of your hands to form a 1 inch ball, then roll each ball in the sesame seeds while it is still soft enough to coat.

9. Place the balls 1½ inches apart on a cookie sheet.

BAKE THE COOKIES

10. Bake for 6 minutes. Rotate the cookie sheet halfway around. Continue baking for 6 to 9 minutes, or until the cookies are lightly browned and the centers, when lightly pressed, have barely any give.

COOL THE COOKIES

11. Set the cookie sheet on a wire rack and let the cookies cool for 1 minute, or until firm enough to lift from the cookie sheet. Use a thin pancake turner to transfer the cookies to another wire rack. Cool completely.

12. Repeat with the second batch.

STORE Airtight: room temperature, 1 week; frozen, 3 months.

Baking Gems

♥ Soom tahini is made with 100 percent roasted beige sesame seeds. If you use another brand, it may be thicker, so you may need to flatten the cookies before baking. I suggest baking a test cookie and then, if necessary, for the rest of the batch, flatten the dough balls to 1½ inches, as for the Black Tuxedo Tahini Cookies variation.

♥ Kevala organic black tahini, produced in the United States, is made with 100 percent lightly roasted unhulled black sesame seeds. The Roland brand from Israel is made with 100 percent lightly roasted hulled black sesame seeds. Both are excellent alternatives.

♥ You can make the dough a day ahead and refrigerate it overnight. Unlike some other doughs using baking soda, longer storage before baking will not cause these cookies to darken.

VARIATION

Black Tuxedo Tahini Cookies

These cookies resemble chocolate nonpareils. Use black tahini. The flavor is the same with either type, but I love the black variety for its dramatic appearance and contrast with the sesame seeds. The only difference is that when it is made with black tahini, the dough does not spread, so be sure to flatten the dough balls to 1½ inches after setting them on the cookie sheet.

MEXICAN WEDDING CAKES

Makes: Twenty-four 2 inch round cookies

I like to call these tender, explosive little cookies powder puffs. I think of them as explosive because if you don't eat them in one bite, you risk having powdered sugar fly off the cookie and onto you! The classic Mexican version uses pecans, but for the most intense flavor, try walnuts.

Oven Temperature: 350°F / 175°C

Baking Time: 5 minutes for the pecans; 15 to 20 minutes for the cookies (for each of two batches)

Special Equipment: Two 17 by 14 inch cookie sheets, no preparation needed or lined with parchment

DOUGH *Makes: 320 grams*

unsalted butter	113 grams	8 tablespoons (1 stick)
pecan halves (or walnut halves—see Baking Gem)	37 grams	¼ cup plus 2 tablespoons
powdered sugar	57 grams	½ cup (lightly spooned into the cup and leveled off)
fine sea salt	·	1/16 teaspoon (a pinch)
pure vanilla extract	·	¼ teaspoon (1.25 ml)
bleached all-purpose flour	125 grams	1 cup (lightly spooned into the cup and leveled off) plus ½ tablespoon
powdered sugar, for coating	57 grams	½ cup (lightly spooned into the cup and leveled off)

PREHEAT THE OVEN

Twenty minutes or longer before baking, set an oven rack at the middle level. Set the oven at 350°F / 175°C.

MISE EN PLACE

Thirty minutes to 1 hour ahead, cut the butter into tablespoon-size pieces. Set on the counter to soften.

Toast the Pecans: Spread the pecans evenly on a baking sheet and bake for about 5 minutes, just until they start to smell fragrant but are not beginning to brown. Stir once or twice to ensure even toasting and avoid browning. Set the baking sheet on a wire rack and cool completely.

MAKE THE DOUGH

Food Processor Method

1. In a food processor, process the pecans with the 57 grams / ½ cup powdered sugar and the salt until powder fine.

2. With the motor running, add the butter one piece at a time and process until smooth and creamy. Scrape down the sides of the bowl as needed.

3. Pulse in the vanilla extract.

4. Pulse in the flour just until the dough starts to hold together in clumps. Scrape down the sides of the bowl as needed.

Stand Mixer Method

1. Finely grind the pecans in a spice mill with a little of the flour, or use a rotary nut grinder.

2. In a small bowl, whisk together the ground pecans, the (remaining) flour, and salt.

3. In the bowl of a stand mixer fitted with the flat beater, beat the butter and sugar on medium

Continues

speed for 2 to 3 minutes, until lighter in color and fluffy. Beat in the vanilla extract. Scrape down the sides of the bowl.

4. On low speed, gradually add the flour mixture, beating just until incorporated. Scrape down the sides of the bowl as needed.

Both Methods

5. Scrape the dough onto a large sheet of plastic wrap and use the plastic and your knuckles to knead it just until it comes together smoothly.

6. Divide the dough in half (about 160 grams each). Wrap each piece in plastic wrap and set them on a baking sheet. Refrigerate for a minimum of 1 hour, up to 3 hours.

ROLL THE DOUGH INTO BALLS

7. Remove one piece of dough from the refrigerator. Measure out 12 pieces of dough (1 scant tablespoon / 13 grams each). Roll each piece of dough between the palms of your hands to form a 1¼ inch ball (flour your hands if necessary).

8. Set the balls a minimum of 1½ inches apart on a cookie sheet.

BAKE THE COOKIES

9. Bake for 8 minutes. Rotate the cookie sheet halfway around. Continue baking for 7 to 12 minutes, or until the cookies are lightly browned.

10. Shape the second batch while the first batch is baking.

COOL THE COOKIES

11. Set the cookie sheet on a wire rack for 2 to 3 minutes.

12. Bake the second batch.

COAT THE COOKIES WITH POWDERED SUGAR

13. Lay a sheet of parchment on the counter and place a wire rack on top. Spoon the powdered sugar into a small bowl. One at a time, use a thin pancake turner to transfer each cookie from the sheet to the bowl and roll it in the powdered sugar while still hot, then set the cookie on the rack.

14. Spoon the remaining powdered sugar into a sifter or fine-mesh strainer and sift over the cookies to coat them. Let them cool completely.

15. Lift away the rack and reserve any remaining sugar to coat the cookies when storing.

STORE THE COOKIES

16. Layer the cookies in a parchment-lined container, coating them with any reserved powdered sugar and placing parchment between each layer to keep moisture from softening the sugar and making it sticky. Then leave the container uncovered for 8 hours before covering it tightly, to maintain the powdery sugar coating.

STORE Airtight: room temperature, 1 month; frozen, 6 months (recoat with powdered sugar before serving).

Baking Gem

🖤 If using walnuts, for deeper flavor, do not remove the skins after toasting.

KOURAMBIETHES

Makes: Eighteen 2½ inch round cookies

There are many cookies in the family of explosively light, crunchy with nuts, powdery with a sugar coating, and with a lingering taste of butter; the Mexican Wedding Cakes on page 33 are one such cookie. But Greek kourambiethes are the star of the family. My dear friend David Shamah suggested using clarified butter in these cookies, as many Mideastern cookies that are made with clarified butter have an exceptional melt-in-the-mouth quality. He mentioned that the esteemed cookbook author Paula Wolfert beats the chilled clarified butter, which lightens the texture of the cookies. The result is so exquisitely fragile compared to cookies made with other methods that this is the only way I now make them.

Oven Temperature: 350°F / 175°C

Baking Time: 5 minutes for the almonds; 15 to 20 minutes for the cookies (for each of two batches)

Special Equipment: Two 17 by 14 inch cookie sheets, no preparation needed or lined with parchment

DOUGH *Makes: 570 grams*

unsalted butter	227 grams	16 tablespoons (2 sticks)
1 (to 2) large egg yolk (see page xxvi)	19 grams	1 tablespoon plus ½ teaspoon (17.5 ml)
pure vanilla extract	·	½ teaspoon (2.5 ml)
brandy, or orange juice, freshly squeezed and strained	21 grams	1½ tablespoons (22.5 ml)
slivered almonds	60 grams	½ cup
bleached all-purpose flour (see Baking Gems)	242 grams	2 cups (lightly spooned into the cup and leveled off)
baking powder, preferably an aluminum-free variety	9 grams	2 teaspoons
powdered sugar	57 grams	½ cup (lightly spooned into the cup and leveled off)
powdered sugar, for coating	57 grams	½ cup (lightly spooned into the cup and leveled off)

MISE EN PLACE

Thirty minutes ahead, cut the butter into tablespoon-size pieces. Set on the counter to soften.

Clarify the Butter: Have ready by the cooktop a fine-mesh or cheesecloth-lined strainer suspended over a medium bowl, preferably silicone (see Baking Gems).

In a small heavy saucepan, melt the butter over very low heat, stirring often with a light-colored silicone spatula. Raise the heat to low and boil, stirring constantly, until the milk solids on the spatula barely begin to color (the bubbling will diminish). Immediately pour the butter through the strainer into the bowl. You should have about 170 grams / ¾ cup plus 2 tablespoons / 207 ml.

Chill the clarified butter until solid, about 2 hours. Refrigerate or freeze the milk solids for future use (see page xxvi) or discard them.

PREHEAT THE OVEN

Twenty minutes or longer before baking, set an oven rack at the middle level. Set the oven at 350°F / 175°C.

Thirty minutes ahead, into a 1 cup / 237 ml glass measure with a spout, weigh or measure the egg yolk. Whisk in the vanilla extract and brandy. Cover tightly with plastic wrap and set on the counter.

Toast the Almonds: Spread the almonds evenly on a baking sheet and bake for about 5 minutes, or until pale gold. Stir once or twice to ensure even toasting and avoid overbrowning. Set the baking sheet on a wire rack and cool completely, then chop medium-fine.

In a medium bowl, whisk together the flour and baking powder.

MAKE THE DOUGH

1. Unmold the chilled butter onto a cutting board. (If not using a silicone bowl, dip the bowl into a bowl of very hot water for a few seconds, or until the butter can be unmolded.) Cut the butter into ½ inch cubes. Set them in the bowl of a stand mixer fitted with the flat beater.

2. Add the 57 grams / ½ cup powdered sugar and beat on low speed until the sugar is mixed into the butter. Raise the speed to medium and beat for 10 minutes. The mixture will lighten in color and be very creamy. Scrape down the sides of the bowl.

3. Add the egg yolk mixture and beat for 1 minute.

4. Add the almonds and beat on low speed for a few seconds, just to combine thoroughly.

5. Add the flour mixture and beat just until incorporated, about 20 seconds. The dough will be soft and slightly tacky.

6. Cover the bowl with plastic wrap and refrigerate for 20 to 30 minutes to firm slightly.

ROLL THE DOUGH INTO BALLS

7. Transfer half (about 285 grams) of the dough from the mixer bowl to a small bowl. Cover the mixer bowl and return it to the refrigerator.

8. Pinch off 9 walnut-size pieces of dough (31 grams each). Roll each piece of dough gently between the palms of your hands to form a 1½ inch ball. Do not be concerned if there are small cracks around the edges (see Baking Gems). (If you have any leftover dough, add it to the second batch.)

9. Place the balls a minimum of 1½ inches apart on a cookie sheet. Flatten them to 2 inches wide by ½ inch high.

BAKE THE COOKIES

10. Bake for 8 minutes. Rotate the cookie sheet halfway around. Continue baking for 7 to 12 minutes, or just until the cookies begin to brown very lightly.

11. While the first batch is baking, shape the second batch of cookies.

COOL THE COOKIES

12. Set the cookie sheet on a wire rack. Lay a sheet of parchment on the counter and place another wire rack on top. Use a pancake turner to transfer the cookies to the second wire rack.

13. Bake and cool the second batch.

COAT THE COOKIES WITH POWDERED SUGAR

14. Spoon the powdered sugar for coating into a sifter or fine-mesh strainer and coat the cookies. After giving the cookies a first coat, coat them again so that they are heavily coated with the sugar. Let them cool completely.

Continues

15. Lift away the rack and sift any remaining powdered sugar onto the parchment. Set the cookies on top to coat the bottoms with sugar.

STORE THE COOKIES

16. Layer the cookies in a parchment-lined container, coating them with powdered sugar and placing parchment between each layer to keep moisture from softening the sugar and making it sticky. Then leave the container uncovered for 8 hours before covering it tightly, to maintain the powdery sugar coating.

STORE Airtight: room temperature, 1 month.

Baking Gems

♥ I find the texture of the baked cookie to be perfect using the full amount of flour, but if you prefer an even lighter cookie, reduce the flour to 212 grams / 1¾ cups; this will make 17 cookies. The dough will be softer and will not crack around the edges.

♥ The baking powder will not cause the dough to puff. Its function here is to add tenderness.

♥ A silicone container is ideal for the clarified butter, as its flexibility makes unmolding so easy.

CLOUD NINES

Makes: Twenty-two 1¾ inch round cookies

These buttery, cinnamon-dusted yeast-raised cookies are exceptionally crispy and crumbly-tender.

Oven Temperature: 350°F / 175°C	**Baking Time:** 20 to 25 minutes (for each of two batches)	**Special Equipment:** Two 17 by 14 inch cookie sheets, preferably insulated, lined with parchment or nonstick; A third cookie sheet to serve as a double pan if not using insulated cookie sheets

DOUGH *Makes: 317 grams*

unsalted butter	113 grams	8 tablespoons (1 stick)
1 large egg	50 grams	3 tablespoons plus ½ teaspoon (47.5 ml)
water	45 grams	3 tablespoons (45 ml)
pure vanilla extract	·	½ teaspoon (2.5 ml)
bleached all-purpose flour	121 grams	1 cup (lightly spooned into the cup and leveled off)
sugar	37 grams	3 tablespoons
instant yeast	1.5 grams	½ teaspoon
fine sea salt	·	⅛ teaspoon

MISE EN PLACE

Thirty minutes ahead or longer, cut the butter into ½ inch cubes. Wrap and refrigerate.

Thirty minutes ahead or longer, into a 1 cup / 237 ml glass measure with a spout, weigh or measure the egg. Whisk in the water and vanilla extract. Cover tightly with plastic wrap and refrigerate.

MAKE THE DOUGH

Food Processor Method

1. In a food processor, process the flour, sugar, and yeast for a few seconds, until evenly mixed. Pulse in the salt (see Baking Gems).

2. Add the butter and pulse until the mixture reaches the consistency of coarse meal and no large pieces of butter remain.

3. Add the egg mixture and pulse until incorporated and the dough is in large clumps.

4. Scrape the mixture into a small bowl and, using your fingers, press it just until it holds together.

Stand Mixer Method

1. In the bowl of a stand mixer fitted with the flat beater, beat together the flour, sugar, and yeast on low speed until evenly mixed. Mix in the salt (see Baking Gems).

2. Add the butter and beat on medium-low speed until the mixture reaches the consistency of coarse meal.

3. On low speed, beat in the egg mixture until well blended.

Continues

Both Methods

5. Cover the bowl tightly and refrigerate for a minimum of 1 hour, up to overnight (see Baking Gems).

PREHEAT THE OVEN

Twenty minutes or longer before baking, set an oven rack at the middle level. Set the oven at 350°F / 175°C.

CINNAMON SUGAR TOPPING

sugar	50 grams	¼ cup
ground cinnamon	·	½ teaspoon

6. In a small bowl, whisk together the sugar and cinnamon.

ROLL THE DOUGH INTO BALLS

7. Divide the dough in half (about 158 grams each). Wrap one piece in plastic wrap and refrigerate it.

8. Measure out 11 pieces of dough (1 level tablespoon / about 14 grams each). The dough will be soft and a little sticky. One at a time, roll each piece of dough in the sugar mixture, roll in the palms of your hands to form a 1¼ inch ball, and then roll it again in the sugar mixture.

9. Place the balls a minimum of 2 inches apart on a cookie sheet. Set the cookie sheet on top of another cookie sheet; this will keep the sugar-coated bottoms of the cookies from overbrowning.

BAKE THE COOKIES

10. Bake for 10 minutes. Rotate the cookie sheets halfway around. Continue baking for 10 to 15 minutes, or until the cookies are golden brown and baked through. An instant-read thermometer inserted in a cookie should read 212°F / 100°C; or you can cut one cookie in half to test. Only a very small part in the center should be slightly moist. the cookies will continue to dry while cooling.

COOL THE COOKIES

11. Set the cookie sheet on a wire rack and let the cookies cool completely. Use a thin pancake turner to transfer the cookies to a storage container.

12. Repeat with the second batch.

STORE Airtight: room temperature, 1 week.

Baking Gems

♥ Do not coat the cookie sheets with nonstick cooking spray or butter, as this would cause the dough to spread too much and the thin edges would overbrown.

♥ The salt is added after the yeast is mixed in to avoid inhibiting the yeast activity.

♥ If you refrigerate the dough overnight, the cookies will brown a little less, because the yeast will have eaten some of the sugar. Otherwise the taste and texture are the same.

FILBERTINES

Makes: Twenty-two 1½ inch round cookies

I discovered a version of this cookie in the files of *Ladies' Home Journal* in the 1970s, when I was working on their annual Christmas cookie issue. I enjoy both the taste and texture of filberts, aka hazelnuts. The very subtle but bright note of cardamom increases a day after the cookies are baked. The cookies are very firm until you bite into them, at which point they reveal their tenderness. That firmness makes them ideal for shipping.

Oven Temperature: 350°F / 175°C	Baking Time: 13 to 16 minutes	Special Equipment: One 17 by 14 inch cookie sheet, nonstick or lined with parchment

DOUGH *Makes: 260 grams*

unsalted butter	57 grams	4 tablespoons (½ stick)
½ large egg, lightly beaten before measuring	25 grams	1½ tablespoons (22.5 ml)
pure vanilla extract	·	¼ teaspoon (1.25 ml)
bleached all-purpose flour	96 grams	¾ cup (lightly spooned into the cup and leveled off) plus ½ tablespoon
baking soda	·	¼ teaspoon
ground cardamom	·	¼ teaspoon
fine sea salt	·	1/16 teaspoon (a pinch)
unblanched hazelnuts	71 grams	½ cup, *divided*
sugar	50 grams	½ cup

PREHEAT THE OVEN

Twenty minutes or longer before baking, set an oven rack at the middle level. Set the oven at 350°F / 175°C.

MISE EN PLACE

Thirty minutes to 1 hour ahead, cut the butter into tablespoon-size pieces. Set on the counter to soften.

Into a 1 cup / 237 ml glass measure with a spout, weigh or measure the egg. Whisk in the vanilla extract. Cover tightly with plastic wrap and set on the counter.

In a small bowl, whisk together the flour, baking soda, cardamom, and salt.

MAKE THE DOUGH

Food Processor Method

1. In a food processor fitted with the grater or shredder disc, grate the hazelnuts.

2. Switch to the metal blade and process the nuts until very fine.

3. Spoon half the nuts (36 grams / ⅓ cup) into a small wide bowl and set aside for coating the dough balls.

4. Add the sugar to the remaining nuts in the food processor and process until the nuts are powder fine.

5. With the motor on, add the butter one piece at a time and process until smooth and very creamy. Scrape down the sides of the bowl.

6. With the motor on, add the egg mixture and process until incorporated. Scrape the sides and bottom of the bowl.

7. Add the flour mixture and pulse until blended and the dough is just beginning to clump together.

Stand Mixer Method

1. Grind the hazelnuts in a spice mill, or use a rotary nut grinder. Add half the nuts (36 grams / ⅓ cup) to the bowl with the flour mixture and whisk them in. Transfer the remaining nuts to a small wide bowl and set aside for coating the dough balls.

2. In the bowl of a stand mixer fitted with the flat beater, beat the butter and sugar on medium speed for 2 to 3 minutes, until lighter in color and fluffy.

3. On low speed, add the egg mixture and beat just until incorporated. Scrape down the sides of the bowl.

4. Gradually beat in the flour mixture just until smoothly incorporated, scraping down the sides of the bowl as needed.

Both Methods

8. Scrape the dough onto a large piece of plastic wrap and use the wrap to press it together.

9. Refrigerate the dough for about 30 minutes, until it is firm enough to roll into balls.

ROLL THE DOUGH INTO BALLS

10. Measure out the dough into 22 pieces (2 level teaspoons / 11 grams each). One at a time, shape each piece of dough in the palms of your hands,

first pressing it to flatten and smooth it and then forming a 1 inch ball, then drop it into the grated hazelnuts and roll it around until it is completely coated with nuts.

11. Place the cookies a minimum of 1½ inches apart on the cookie sheet.

BAKE THE COOKIES

12. Bake for 7 minutes. Rotate the cookie sheet halfway around. Continue baking for 6 to 9 minutes, or until the cookies are just beginning to brown very lightly. They should be firm to the touch.

COOL THE COOKIES

13. Set the cookie sheet on a wire rack and use a thin pancake turner to lift each cookie onto another wire rack. Cool completely.

STORE Airtight: room temperature, 1 month; frozen, 3 months.

Baking Gem

♥ For this cookie, I do not remove the skins of the nuts, because they add a more robust flavor. I do not toast the nuts, because then the nut coating would get too brown during baking.

ALMOND COFFEE CRISPS

Makes: Thirty-six 2½ inch round cookies

This crisp, exquisitely fragile, coffee-imbued cookie is based on a recipe given to me many years ago by a friend of the late Charlie Trotter. It remains one of my favorites, and I even purchased a special brush just for this cookie to create the most gossamer possible dusting of espresso powder.

Oven Temperature: 350°F / 175°C	Baking Time: 5 minutes for the almonds; 10 to 15 minutes for the cookies (for each of three batches)	Special Equipment: Two 17 by 14 inch cookie sheets, no preparation needed or lined with parchment; Optional: a makeup brush designed for applying blush (but used only for these cookies or any time you may want the lightest dusting of espresso, powdered sugar, or even cocoa!)

DOUGH *Makes: 378 grams*

unsalted butter	113 grams	8 tablespoons (1 stick)
sliced blanched or unblanched almonds	50 grams	½ cup
unbleached all-purpose flour	80 grams	⅔ cup (lightly spooned into the cup and leveled off)
instant espresso powder	2.4 grams	2 teaspoons
baking powder, preferably an aluminum-free variety	6.8 grams	1½ teaspoons
fine sea salt	·	⅛ teaspoon
sugar	133 grams	⅔ cup
pure vanilla extract	·	½ tablespoon (7.5 ml)
instant espresso powder, for sprinkling	1.2 grams	1 teaspoon

PREHEAT THE OVEN
Twenty minutes or longer before baking, set an oven rack at the middle level. Set the oven at 350°F / 175°C.

MISE EN PLACE
Thirty minutes to 1 hour ahead, cut the butter into tablespoon-size pieces. Set on the counter to soften.

Toast the Almonds: Spread the almonds evenly on a baking sheet and bake for about 5 minutes, until pale gold. Stir once or twice to ensure even toasting and avoid overbrowning. Set the baking sheet on a wire rack and cool completely.

MAKE THE DOUGH
Food Processor Method

1. In a food processor, combine the almonds, flour, the 2 teaspoons instant espresso powder, the baking powder, and salt and process until the almonds are powder fine, about 2 minutes. Empty the mixture onto a piece of parchment or into a bowl.

2. Process the sugar in the food processor until very fine. With the motor running, add the butter 1 tablespoon at a time and process for a few seconds, until smooth, scraping down the sides of the bowl as needed.

3. Add the vanilla extract and pulse just to incorporate. Scrape down the sides of the bowl.

4. Add the flour mixture and pulse just until combined.

Stand Mixer Method

1. Grind the sugar in a spice mill until very fine. (Alternatively, use superfine sugar.)

2. Finely grind the nuts in batches in a spice mill with a little of the sugar, or use a rotary nut grinder.

3. In a medium bowl, whisk together the almonds, flour, the 2 teaspoons instant espresso powder, the baking powder, and salt.

4. In the bowl of a stand mixer fitted with the flat beater, beat the butter and (remaining) sugar on medium speed for 2 to 3 minutes, until lighter in color and fluffy.

5. On low speed, gradually beat in the flour mixture just until incorporated, scraping down the sides of the bowl as needed.

6. Add the vanilla extract and beat just until incorporated.

Both Methods

7. Scrape the mixture onto a large sheet of plastic wrap and use the plastic wrap to knead the dough together until it is completely even and there are no visible streaks of butter.

8. Divide the dough into thirds (about 126 grams each). Wrap two of the pieces in plastic wrap and refrigerate them while you roll the first piece.

SHAPE THE DOUGH

9. Measure out 12 pieces of dough (1 rounded teaspoon / 10 g each). Roll each piece of dough between the palms of your hands to form a 1 inch ball. Working with one ball at a time, roll it again to soften (so it will have smooth edges) and press it down to 1¾ inches on a cookie sheet. Repeat with the remaining balls, leaving 2 inches of space in between each flattened cookie.

BAKE THE COOKIES

10. Bake the cookies for 5 minutes. Rotate the cookie sheet halfway around. Continue baking for 5 to 10 minutes: The cookies should just begin to brown and should still feel slightly soft when pressed very gently with a fingertip but not keep the impression.

COOL THE COOKIES

11. Set the cookie sheet on a wire rack. Lay a sheet of parchment on the counter and place another wire rack on top. Use a pancake turner to transfer the cookies to the second wire rack.

12. Place the remaining 1 teaspoon instant espresso powder in a small bowl and use your thumb and index finger to sprinkle it over the surface of the cookies. Alternatively, use the makeup brush, dipping it into the espresso powder and then lightly tapping it over the cookies.

13. While the first batch of cookies is baking, roll the dough balls for the second batch. Repeat baking, cooling, and applying the espresso powder with that batch and then the third batch.

STORE Airtight: room temperature, 3 weeks; frozen, 3 months.

Baking Gem

♥ Any visible streaks of butter left in the dough will melt and form holes during baking. If there are visible pieces of butter, continue kneading the dough, or use the heel of your hand to press the pieces in a forward motion to smear them into the dough.

PUMPKIN PECAN COOKIES

Makes: Eighteen 3 inch round cookies

These cookies, which have the slightly earthy flavor of pumpkin, are lightly spiced like pumpkin pie and studded with chopped pecans. Because pumpkin contains a high percentage of water, I cook it with the sugar to remove as much of the moisture as possible, which produces a delightfully crunchy top crust with soft interior. The optional turbinado sugar gives the cookie a slight sparkle.

| Oven Temperature: 350°F / 175°C | Baking Time: 12 to 15 minutes (for each of two batches) | Special Equipment: Two 17 by 14 inch cookie sheets, nonstick or lined with parchment |

DOUGH *Makes: 470 grams*

unsalted butter	57 grams	4 tablespoons (½ stick)
canned pumpkin	182 grams	¾ cup
light brown sugar, preferably Muscovado	54 grams	¼ cup (firmly packed)
granulated sugar	50 grams	¼ cup
bleached all-purpose flour	71 grams	½ cup (lightly spooned into the cup and leveled off) plus 4 teaspoons
baking soda	2.7 grams	½ teaspoon
fine sea salt	.	¼ teaspoon
ground ginger	1.8 grams	1 teaspoon
ground cinnamon	.	¾ teaspoon
pecans	100 grams	1 cup
1 medium egg yolk	16 grams	1 tablespoon (15 ml)
pure vanilla extract	.	¼ teaspoon (1.25 ml)

MISE EN PLACE

Thirty minutes to 1 hour ahead, cut the butter into 4 pieces. Set it on the counter to soften.

Prepare the Pumpkin: In a small heavy saucepan, stir together the pumpkin, brown sugar, and granulated sugar. Bring the mixture to a sputtering simmer over medium heat, stirring constantly. Reduce the heat to low and cook, stirring constantly, for 10 minutes, or until the mixture is very thick and shiny. It will hold together like a paste. You will have about 241 grams / ¾ cup plus 2 tablespoons.

Spread the pumpkin mixture thinly on a silicone baking mat or piece of aluminum foil. Allow it to cool, uncovered, to room temperature.

In a small bowl, whisk together the flour, baking soda, salt, ginger, and cinnamon.

Chop the pecans into medium-small pieces, less than ¼ inch.

MAKE THE DOUGH

1. In the bowl of a stand mixer fitted with the flat beater, beat the butter for 1 to 2 minutes on medium speed, until smooth and creamy.

2. Add the pumpkin mixture, egg yolk, and vanilla extract and beat on low speed for 1 to 2 minutes, until incorporated.

3. Add the flour mixture and beat on low speed just until incorporated, scraping down the sides of the bowl as needed.

4. Add the chopped pecans and beat for a few seconds, just until incorporated.

5. Divide the dough evenly between two small bowls (about 235 grams each). Cover and refrigerate for at least 1 hour, up to 6 hours.

PREHEAT THE OVEN

Twenty minutes or longer before baking, set an oven rack at the middle level. Set the oven at 350°F / 175°C.

SUGAR COATING AND TOPPING

granulated sugar (see Baking Gems)	38 grams	3 tablespoons
turbinado sugar (optional)	17 grams	4 teaspoons

SHAPE THE DOUGH

6. Measure the granulated sugar into a small bowl. If desired, measure the turbinado sugar into another small bowl; the turbinado sugar will give the cookies extra sparkle.

7. The dough will be sticky and is easiest to work with when cold, so keep the second bowl of dough refrigerated while you work with the first batch. Using a tablespoon and a small metal spatula or teaspoon, one at a time, measure out 9 pieces of dough (1 rounded tablespoon / 25 grams). Drop each piece into the sugar. Toss it to coat and then roll it between the palms of your hands into a roughly 1 inch ball. Drop the ball back into the sugar and roll it around to coat a second time. Then flatten it in your palm, patting it into a disc about 2 inches in diameter. If necessary, dip it in the sugar again.

8. Place the dough discs evenly spaced on a cookie sheet. Set a small piece of plastic wrap on top of a disc and smooth the dough, using a circular motion, into a 2¾ inch disc that is about ¼ inch thick. Carefully peel off the plastic wrap. Repeat with the remaining discs.

9. Sprinkle the turbinado sugar on top of the discs if using.

BAKE THE COOKIES

10. Bake for 5 minutes. Rotate the cookie sheet halfway around. Continue baking for 7 to 10 minutes, or until the cookies are deep golden brown and the centers are only a little soft when pressed lightly with your finger. Or, if you prefer totally crispy cookies, continue baking for another 2 minutes, or until the centers are firm.

COOL THE COOKIES

11. Set the cookie sheet on a wire rack and use a thin pancake turner to transfer the cookies to another wire rack. Cool completely.

12. Repeat with the second batch.

STORE Airtight, layered between sheets of parchment: room temperature, 1 week; refrigerated, 2 weeks; frozen, 3 months.

Baking Gems

♥ If the dough is made more than 6 hours ahead, the baked cookies will be much darker because of the baking soda.

♥ The granulated sugar is used for rolling the dough to sweeten it, to keep it from sticking to your fingers, and to give the crust a crunchy texture.

♥ The cookies are the most crisp on the day of baking, but they can be recrisped by setting them on a rack set on a cookie sheet in a preheated 350°F / 175°C oven for about 10 minutes.

GINGERSNAPS

Makes: Thirty-two 3 inch round cookies

The best gingersnaps I ever tasted were in the home of Kate Coldrick, a friend and excellent home baker in Devon, England. Golden syrup and golden baker's sugar, both common in the UK, contributed to their robust and complex flavor. Because the flour in the U.S. is different from what is available in the UK, I have adapted the recipe by adding an extra egg white plus leavening and salt equal to that of British self-raising flour. The result is wonderfully crisp and chewy. If you live in the UK, see Baking Gems for the original recipe ingredients.

Oven Temperature: 350°F / 175°C

Baking Time: 10 to 12 minutes (for each of three batches)

Special Equipment: Two 17 by 14 inch cookie sheets, nonstick or lined with parchment

DOUGH *Makes: 850 grams*

unsalted butter	113 grams	8 tablespoons (1 stick)
golden syrup (or corn syrup)	113 grams (109 grams)	⅓ cup (79 ml)
1 large egg	50 grams	3 tablespoons plus ½ teaspoon (47.5 ml)
1 large egg white	30 grams	2 tablespoons (30 ml)
bleached all-purpose flour (see Baking Gems)	348 grams	2¾ cups (lightly spooned into the cup and leveled off) plus 1½ tablespoons
golden baker's sugar (see Baking Gems)	200 grams	1 cup
baking powder, preferably an aluminum-free variety	18 grams	4 teaspoons
baking soda	11 grams	2 teaspoons
fine sea salt	3 grams	½ teaspoon
ground ginger	5.4 grams	1 tablespoon

PREHEAT THE OVEN

Twenty minutes or longer before baking, set an oven rack at the middle level. Set the oven at 350°F / 175°C.

MISE EN PLACE

Thirty minutes ahead, cut the butter into tablespoon-size pieces. Place them in a medium heavy saucepan. Add the golden syrup to the saucepan.

Thirty minutes ahead, into a 1 cup / 237 ml glass measure with a spout, weigh or measure the egg and egg white. Whisk lightly. Cover tightly with plastic wrap and set on the counter.

MAKE THE DOUGH

1. Set the saucepan over low heat and, stirring constantly with a silicone spatula, heat the butter and golden syrup until the butter is almost fully melted. Remove the pan from the heat and stir until the butter is fully melted. Let the mixture cool for about 10 minutes, until cool to the touch.

2. In the bowl of a stand mixer fitted with the flat beater, beat together the flour, sugar, baking powder, baking soda, salt, and ginger on low speed for 30 seconds, or until well blended.

3. Add the butter mixture and beat for 1 minute, or until evenly combined. The mixture will be crumbly.

4. Add the egg mixture and mix for about 30 seconds, until well mixed. Scrape down the sides of the bowl.

5. Divide the dough in thirds (about 283 grams each). Wrap each piece in plastic wrap and refrigerate for a minimum of 30 minutes, up to 24 hours.

ROLL THE DOUGH INTO BALLS

6. If the dough has been chilled for more than 30 minutes, remove each batch about 10 minutes before rolling to make it malleable. Pinch off 10 heaping tablespoons of dough (26 grams each) from one batch of dough. Roll each piece in the palms of your hands to form a 1¼ inch ball. (Add any leftover dough to the third batch of dough.)

7. Place the balls a minimum of 2 inches apart on a cookie sheet.

BAKE THE COOKIES

8. Bake for 5 minutes. Rotate the cookie sheet halfway around. Continue baking for 5 to 7 minutes, until cracks appear on the surface and it is golden brown. The cookies should still feel slightly soft when pressed lightly with a fingertip. (An instant-read thermometer inserted in the center of a cookie should read from 200° to 212°F / 93° to 100°C.)

COOL THE COOKIES

9. Set the cookie sheet on a wire rack and let the cookies cool for 5 minutes, or until firm enough to lift from the sheet. Use a thin pancake turner to transfer the cookies to another wire rack. They will firm up as they cool, resulting in a crispy surface and soft, chewy interior. (Baking longer will result in a darker-looking cookie that is crisper throughout.)

10. Repeat with the remaining batches (add any leftover dough from the second batch to the third batch, which will make 12 cookies).

STORE Airtight: room temperature, 1 week; refrigerated, 2 weeks; frozen, 3 months.

Baking Gems

♥ Golden baker's sugar contains a small amount of residual molasses, giving it a unique flavor. You can substitute a combination of 150 grams / ¾ cup granulated sugar and 54 grams / ¼ cup lightly packed light brown sugar. (If you use superfine sugar, the surface of the cookies will not have cracks.)

♥ For UK bakers, use 340 grams self-raising flour, eliminate the baking powder and salt, and use only one whole egg. If the dough is too crumbly, mix in more egg.

♥ Heating the butter until it is just melted and then cooling the butter mixture until cool to the touch will give the cookies the nicest shape. If the mixture is warmer, the cookies will spread more and puff less.

♥ Baking the cookies in batches and keeping the remaining dough cold to minimize activation of the baking soda ensures that the cookies will be uniform in size and shape. The time it takes to roll 10 dough balls is about the same as it takes to bake each batch.

DOUBLE GINGER MOLASSES COOKIES

Makes: Thirty-five 2½ inch round cookies

I love ginger and molasses so much that I decided to turn my favorite molasses sugar cookie into a ginger cookie, with double the ground ginger and an ample amount of crystallized ginger. The crystallized ginger gives the cookies extra chew and, of course, amplifies the flavor.

Oven Temperature: 375°F / 190°C	**Baking Time:** 8 to 10 minutes (for each of three batches)

Special Equipment: Two 17 by 14 inch cookie sheets, no preparation needed or lined with parchment

DOUGH *Makes: 630 grams*

unsalted butter	150 grams	10½ tablespoons (1 stick plus 2½ tablespoons)
1 large egg	50 grams	3 tablespoons plus ½ teaspoon (47.5 ml)
crystallized ginger	75 grams	⅓ cup
bleached all-purpose flour	204 grams	1¾ cups (lightly spooned into the cup and leveled off) minus 1 tablespoon
baking soda	8.2 grams	1½ teaspoons
fine sea salt	·	⅜ teaspoon
ground ginger	1.8 grams	1 teaspoon
ground cinnamon	·	¾ teaspoon
ground cloves	·	⅜ teaspoon
superfine sugar	128 grams	½ cup plus 2 tablespoons
light molasses, preferably Grandma's brand	60 grams	3 tablespoons (45 ml)
superfine sugar (see Baking Gems), for rolling the dough balls	25 grams	2 tablespoons

MISE EN PLACE

Brown the Butter: Have ready by the cooktop a 1 cup / 237 ml glass measure with a spout.

In a medium heavy saucepan, melt the butter over very low heat, stirring often with a light-colored silicone spatula. Raise the heat to low and boil, stirring constantly, until the milk solids on the spatula become a deep brown. Immediately pour the butter into the glass measure, scraping in the browned solids as well. You should have about 112 grams / ½ cup plus 1 tablespoon / 133 ml. Allow the browned butter to cool to 80°F / 27°C (see Baking Gems).

About 30 minutes ahead, into a 1 cup / 237 ml glass measure with a spout, weigh or measure the egg. Cover tightly with plastic wrap and set on the counter.

Cut the crystallized ginger into ¼ inch pieces.

In a medium bowl, whisk together the flour, baking soda, salt, ginger, cinnamon, and cloves.

Continues

MAKE THE DOUGH

1. In the bowl of a stand mixer fitted with the flat beater, mix the browned butter, sugar, molasses, and egg on low speed for 1 minute.

2. Add the flour mixture and crystallized ginger and beat on the lowest speed to moisten the flour. Raise the speed to low and beat for 30 seconds.

3. Scrape the dough onto a piece of plastic wrap and divide it in half (about 315 grams each). Wrap each piece in plastic wrap and refrigerate for 1 hour, or until firm enough to handle (see Baking Gems).

PREHEAT THE OVEN

Thirty minutes or longer before baking, set an oven rack at the middle level. Set the oven at 375°F / 190°C.

ROLL THE DOUGH INTO BALLS

4. In a small bowl or large custard cup, place the sugar for rolling the dough balls.

5. Remove one piece of dough from the refrigerator. Measure out 12 pieces of dough (1 level tablespoon / 18 grams each). Roll each piece in the palms of your hands to form a 1¼ inch ball. (Add any remaining dough to the second batch.)

6. Roll each ball around in the bowl of sugar to coat it well, then place it on a cookie sheet, spacing the balls a minimum of 1½ inches apart.

BAKE THE COOKIES

7. Bake for 4 minutes. Rotate the cookie sheet halfway around. Continue baking for 4 to 6 minutes: Cracks will appear on the surface toward the very end of baking, but the inside will look slightly underbaked. When they are ready, the cookies will have flattened, and when gently pressed with a fingertip, they should still feel soft except at the edges. (Baking longer will give a darker and crisper cookie.)

COOL THE COOKIES

8. Set the cookie sheet on a wire rack and let the cookies cool for 3 minutes, or until firm enough to lift from the cookie sheet. Use a thin pancake turner to transfer the cookies to another wire rack. They will firm up as they cool, resulting in a crispy surface and soft chewy interior.

9. Repeat with the remaining two batches.

STORE Airtight: room temperature, 1 week; refrigerated, 2 weeks; frozen, 3 months.

Baking Gems

♥ It is essential to clarify the butter to remove the liquid. Simply melting the butter will result in a thinner cookie that doesn't bake through. Use an AA butter, as a lower quality will result in a lesser amount of browned butter.

♥ If the browned butter is warmer than 80°F / 27°C, the cookies will not expand to 2¾ inches and will not form cracks. They will also require another 2 minutes or so of baking.

♥ Superfine sugar will give the finest, most even crunch to the surface of the cookies, but if desired, turbinado sugar, which will offer more sparkle, can be used instead.

♥ Keeping the second half of the dough cool in the refrigerator until ready to shape will prevent the baking soda from activating, which would otherwise darken the cookies. It also results in a smoother surface when baked and ensures that the cookies will be uniform in size and shape.

♥ The dough freezes nicely; however, if it is not baked on the same day as it is mixed, the baked cookies will be slightly larger, flatter, and darker in color because of the baking soda.

HAZELNUT PRALINE COOKIES

Makes: Thirty 2 inch round cookies

Making your own hazelnut praline powder is easy and makes the crispest, nuttiest, chewiest hazelnut cookies ever. Any extra praline powder is delightful sprinkled over ice cream, particularly coffee, chocolate, or vanilla.

Oven Temperature:	Baking Time: About	Special Equipment: *For the hazelnut*	*For the hazelnut cookies:*
350°F / 175°C for the hazelnuts; 375°F / 190°C for the cookies	15 minutes for the hazelnuts; 12 to 14 minutes for the cookies (for each of two batches)	*powder:* One 17¼ by 12¼ inch half sheet pan, no preparation needed or lined with a silicone baking mat; If not using a mat, a second half sheet pan lined with aluminum foil and lightly coated with nonstick cooking spray	Two 17 by 14 inch cookie sheets, no preparation needed or lined with parchment

HAZELNUT PRALINE POWDER

Makes: 265 grams / 2⅓ cups

water	710 grams	3 cups (710 ml)
baking soda	66 grams	¼ cup
hazelnuts	213 grams	1½ cups
sugar	67 grams	⅓ cup
water	79 grams	⅓ cup (79 ml)

PREHEAT THE OVEN

Twenty minutes or longer before baking, set an oven rack at the middle level. Set the oven at 350°F / 175°C.

REMOVE THE HAZELNUT SKINS

Have ready a colander placed in the sink and a large bowl filled half full with cold water.

1. In a 3 quart or larger saucepan, bring the 710 grams / 3 cups (710 ml) water to a boil. Remove from the heat and stir in the baking soda. The water will bubble vigorously.

2. Add the hazelnuts and return the pan to the heat. Boil the nuts for 3 minutes. The water will turn a deep maroon from the color of the skins. Test a nut by running it under cold water: The skin should slip off easily. If necessary, boil the nuts for a couple of minutes longer.

3. Pour the nuts into the colander and rinse them under cold running water. Place several nuts in a bowl of cold water. Slide off the skins and place the nuts on a clean dish towel. Repeat with the remaining nuts in batches; as necessary, empty the bowl and refill with cold water. Roll and rub the nuts around in the towel to dry them.

TOAST THE HAZELNUTS

4. Set the hazelnuts on the half sheet pan and bake for about 15 minutes, until the oils rise to the surface and the nuts become slightly shiny and deep golden brown. Shake the pan once or twice to ensure even toasting.

5. Set the sheet pan on a wire rack. Or, if not using a silicone mat, transfer the nuts to the second half sheet pan and set it on the rack.

Continues

MAKE THE PRALINE POWDER

6. In a small saucepan, preferably nonstick (coat the sides lightly with nonstick cooking spray if the pan is not nonstick), with a silicone spatula, stir together the sugar and the 79 grams / ⅓ cup / 79 ml water and heat, stirring constantly, over medium heat until the sugar has dissolved and the syrup is bubbling.

7. Continue boiling, without stirring, until the syrup caramelizes to deep amber. (An instant-read thermometer should read about 370°F / 188°C, or a few degrees lower, because its temperature will continue to rise.)

8. Immediately remove the pan from the heat and pour the caramel over the hazelnuts. Let it harden completely, about 15 to 30 minutes.

9. Remove the praline from the sheet and break it into several pieces.

10. In a food processor, pulse the praline until it is powder fine.

DOUGH *Makes: 318 grams*

unsalted butter	57 grams	4 tablespoons (½ stick)
½ large egg, lightly beaten before measuring	25 grams	1½ tablespoons (22.5 ml)
pure vanilla extract	·	¼ teaspoon (1.25 ml)
bleached all-purpose flour	80 grams	⅔ cup (lightly spooned into the cup and leveled off)
baking soda	2.7 grams	½ teaspoon
fine sea salt	·	¹⁄₁₆ teaspoon (a pinch)
superfine sugar (see Baking Gem)	37 grams	3 tablespoons
hazelnut praline powder	113 grams	1 cup
canola or safflower oil	4 grams	1 teaspoon (5 ml)

MISE EN PLACE

For the Food Processor Method: Thirty minutes ahead or longer, cut the butter into ½ inch cubes. Wrap and refrigerate.

For the Stand Mixer Method: Thirty minutes to 1 hour ahead, cut the butter into tablespoon-size pieces. Set on the counter to soften.

Thirty minutes ahead, into a 1 cup / 237 ml glass measure with a spout, weigh or measure the egg. Whisk in the vanilla extract. Cover tightly with plastic wrap and set on the counter.

In a small bowl, whisk together the flour, baking soda, and salt.

MAKE THE DOUGH

Food Processor Method

1. In a food processor, place the sugar. With the motor running, add butter cubes one at a time.

2. Add the praline powder and oil and process until the mixture is smooth and creamy, about 20 seconds.

3. With the motor running, add the egg mixture and process until incorporated. Scrape down the sides of the bowl.

4. Add the flour mixture and pulse just until incorporated.

Stand Mixer Method

1. In the bowl of a stand mixer fitted with the flat beater, beat together the sugar, butter, praline powder, and oil on medium speed for several minutes, or until very smooth and creamy.

2. Add the egg mixture and beat until incorporated, scraping down the sides of the bowl.

3. On low speed, gradually beat in the flour mixture just until incorporated.

Both Methods

5. Scrape the dough onto a piece of plastic wrap and divide it in half (about 159 grams each). Wrap each piece and refrigerate for a minimum of 1 hour, up to 6 hours, before shaping.

PREHEAT THE OVEN

Thirty minutes or longer before baking, set an oven rack at the middle level. Set the oven at 375°F / 190°C.

SHAPE THE DOUGH

6. Remove one piece of dough from the refrigerator. Measure out 15 pieces (1 rounded teaspoon / 10 grams each) of dough. Roll each piece between the palms of your hands to form a 1 inch ball.

7. Place the balls a minimum of 1½ inches apart on a cookie sheet. Press them down to 1½ inches wide by ½ inch high.

BAKE THE COOKIES

8. Bake for 7 minutes. Rotate the cookie sheet halfway around. Continue baking for 5 to 7 minutes, or until the cookies are lightly browned and set. When pressed gently with a fingertip the top of a cookie will yield slightly to the pressure.

COOL THE COOKIES

9. Set the cookie sheet on a wire rack and let the cookies cool for 1 minute, or until firm enough to lift from the sheet. Use a thin pancake turner to transfer the cookies to another wire rack. Cool completely.

10. Repeat with the second batch.

STORE Airtight: room temperature, 3 weeks; frozen, 6 months.

Baking Gems

♥ The extra hazelnut praline powder can be stored in an airtight container, refrigerated, for 2 months, or frozen for 6 months.

♥ Granulated sugar can be used for the dough instead of superfine if processed in a food processor for larger amounts or a spice mill for several minutes, or until very fine.

SCOTTISH SHORTBREAD COOKIES

Makes: 8 wedges

If there were only one cookie in the world, it would have to be this one, since it has so few ingredients, is so easy to mix, and is so versatile. Buttery and tender, with a perfectly balanced touch of sweetness, it is delightful in all shapes from round to wedges. It also makes the ideal base for lemon curd bar cookies; see Lemon Butter Squares, page 316. Mixing the dough in a food processor or by hand results in a more delicate texture than using a stand mixer.

Oven Temperature: 300°F / 150°C	Baking Time: 50 to 60 minutes	Special Equipment: One 9½ inch by 1 inch fluted tart pan with a removable bottom, set on a cookie sheet and, if not nonstick, coated lightly with baking spray with flour

DOUGH *Makes: 355 grams*

unsalted butter	142 grams	10 tablespoons (1¼ sticks)
granulated sugar	25 grams	2 tablespoons
powdered sugar	14 grams	2 tablespoons plus 2 teaspoons
bleached all-purpose flour	181 grams	1½ cups (lightly spooned into the cup and leveled off)
fine sea salt	·	a small pinch

MISE EN PLACE

For the Food Processor Method: Thirty minutes ahead or longer, cut the butter into ½ inch cubes. Wrap and refrigerate.

For the Hand Method: Thirty minutes to 1 hour ahead, cut the butter into tablespoon-size pieces. Set on the counter to soften.

MAKE THE DOUGH

Food Processor Method

1. In a food processor, process the sugars for 1 minute, or until the granulated sugar is very fine.

2. Add the butter and pulse until all the sugar coats the butter.

3. Add the flour and salt and pulse until the butter pieces are the size of tiny peas. The dough will be crumbly but will hold together when pinched.

4. Scrape the mixture into a plastic bag and, using your knuckles and the heels of your hands, press it together.

Hand Method

For the finest texture, use superfine sugar in place of the granulated sugar.

1. In a large bowl, whisk together the sugars and salt.

2. With a wooden spoon, mix in the butter until light and creamy.

3. Add the flour and use your fingers to mix it in until incorporated.

Continues

Both Methods

5. Transfer the dough to a large sheet of plastic wrap and use the wrap to knead it lightly just until it holds together.

SHAPE THE COOKIES

6. Roll the dough between sheets of plastic wrap into an 8 or 9 inch disc. Remove the bottom sheet and use the top sheet to press the dough into the tart pan. (Alternatively, using the bottom sheet of plastic wrap, lift the dough disc into an 8 or 9 inch round cake pan and use the top sheet to press it into the pan. Then lift it out of the pan and set it, without the plastic wrap, on a cookie sheet.)

7. Use the tines of a fork to press ¾ inch lines, radiating to resemble sun rays, all around the perimeter of the dough. Prick the rest of the dough all over with the fork or a wooden skewer to help it bake evenly. With the tip of a sharp knife, score the dough into 8 wedges, going almost to the bottom.

8. Cover the dough with plastic wrap and refrigerate for 30 minutes to set the design.

PREHEAT THE OVEN

While the dough is chilling, set an oven rack at the middle level. Set the oven at 300°F / 150°C.

BAKE THE COOKIES

9. Bake for 30 minutes. Rotate the cookie sheet halfway around and continue baking for 20 to 30 minutes, or until the shortbread is pale golden.

COOL AND CUT THE COOKIES

10. Set the pan on a wire rack, and while the shortbread is still hot, cut along the score lines again. Cool completely in the pan.

11. If using a tart pan, unmold the shortbread. Use a thin-bladed sharp knife to cut the wedges all the way through.

STORE Airtight: room temperature or frozen, 3 months.

Baking Gem

♥ To unmold the shortbread from a tart pan, set the pan on top of a canister that is smaller than the bottom opening of the tart pan's rim. Press down on both sides of the tart ring; it should slip away easily. Then carefully slide a long metal spatula between the bottom of the pan and the shortbread and slide it onto a cutting board. If it sticks, heat the bottom of the pan briefly by setting it on a hot surface, such as an inverted cake pan that has been filled with hot water, emptied, and dried.

VARIATION

Shape as rounds, following the instructions for Muscovado Shortbread Cookies on page 59. This will make twenty-four 1½ inch round cookies.

MUSCOVADO SHORTBREAD COOKIES

Makes: Twenty-seven 2 inch round cookies

Light brown sugar adds a uniquely complex flavor to classic shortbread, but to keep the molasses in the sugar from overriding the buttery flavor, I've added a little extra butter, which also makes its texture more smooth. A food processor results in the best texture, because it distributes the brown sugar more evenly.

Oven Temperature:
275°F / 135°C

Baking Time: 55 to 65 minutes

Special Equipment: Two 17 by 14 inch cookie sheets, no preparation needed or lined with parchment

---

DOUGH *Makes: 385 grams*

unsalted butter	156 grams	11 tablespoons (1 stick plus 3 tablespoons)
light brown sugar, preferably Muscovado	54 grams	¼ cup (firmly packed)
bleached all-purpose flour	181 grams	1½ cups (lightly spooned into the cup and leveled off)
fine sea salt	·	a small pinch

PREHEAT THE OVEN

Twenty minutes or longer before baking, set oven racks in the upper and lower thirds of the oven. Set the oven at 275°F / 135°C.

MISE EN PLACE

For the Food Processor Method: Thirty minutes ahead or longer, cut the butter into ½ inch cubes. Wrap and refrigerate.

For the Hand Method: Thirty minutes to 1 hour ahead, cut the butter into tablespoon-size pieces and set on the counter to soften.

MAKE THE DOUGH

Food Processor Method

1. In a food processor, process the brown sugar for a few minutes, until it is free of all lumps.

2. Add the butter and pulse until all the sugar coats the butter.

3. Add the flour and salt and pulse until the butter pieces are the size of tiny peas. The dough will be crumbly but will hold together when pinched with your fingers.

4. Scrape the mixture into a plastic bag and, using your knuckles and the heels of your hands, press it together.

Hand Method

1. In a large bowl, whisk together the sugar and salt.

2. With a wooden spoon, mix in the butter until light and creamy.

3. Add the flour and use your fingers to mix it in until incorporated.

Both Methods

5. Transfer the dough to a large sheet of plastic wrap and use the wrap to knead it lightly just until it holds together.

Continues

SHAPE THE COOKIES

6. Measure out 27 pieces of dough (1 scant tablespoon / about 14 grams each). One at a time, flatten each piece between the palms of your hands and then roll it into a 1 inch ball. (This will keep the dough from cracking when pressed flat.) Place the ball on a cookie sheet and flatten it gently with your fingers or the bottom of a flat glass tumbler, lightly moistened with water, into a 1½ inch disc. Continue with the remaining dough, spacing the cookies a minimum of 1 inch apart on both cookie sheets.

7. Use the tines of a fork to make press ⅜ inch lines around the edges of each cookie and to prick holes in the center.

8. For the best shape and design, cover the cookies with plastic wrap and refrigerate for 30 minutes.

BAKE THE COOKIES

9. Bake for 30 minutes. Rotate the cookie sheets halfway around and from top to bottom. Continue baking for 25 to 35 minutes, or until the shortbread is deep golden.

COOL THE COOKIES

10. Set the cookie sheets on wire racks and use a thin pancake turner to transfer the cookies to another wire rack. Cool completely.

STORE Airtight: room temperature or frozen, 3 months.

VARIATION

Shape as wedges, following the instructions for Scottish Shortbread Cookies on page 56.

PEANUT BUTTER AND CHOCOLATE CHIP SHORTBREAD

Makes: Thirty-five 2 inch round cookies

These marvelous cookies, created by my dear friend and food writer Marissa Rothkopf Bates, have the classic melt-in-the-mouth texture of shortbread but are deliciously peanut-buttery and chocolatey.

Oven Temperature: 325°F / 160°C

Baking Time: 12 to 15 minutes (for each of two batches)

Special Equipment: Two 17 by 14 inch cookie sheets, lined with parchment

DOUGH *Makes: 572 grams*

unsalted butter	113 grams	8 tablespoons (1 stick)
smooth peanut butter, preferably Jif	88 grams	⅓ cup
bleached all-purpose flour	174 grams	1½ cups (lightly spooned into the cup and leveled off) minus 1 tablespoon
powdered sugar	35 grams	¼ cup (lightly spooned into the cup and leveled off) plus 1 tablespoon
fine sea salt	·	¼ teaspoon
pure vanilla extract	·	½ teaspoon (2.5 ml)
mini semisweet chocolate chips, 46% to 50% cacao	170 grams (6 ounces)	1 cup

PREHEAT THE OVEN

Twenty minutes or longer before baking, set an oven rack at the middle level. Set the oven at 325°F / 160°C.

MISE EN PLACE

Thirty minutes to 1 hour ahead, cut the butter into tablespoon-size pieces. Set on the counter to soften.

Thirty minutes to 1 hour ahead, in a small bowl, place the peanut butter.

In a small bowl, whisk together the flour, sugar, and salt.

MAKE THE DOUGH

1. In the bowl of a stand mixer fitted with the flat beater, mix the butter and peanut butter together on medium speed for 2 to 3 minutes, or until very smoothly combined.

2. Add the vanilla extract and mix for a few seconds, until incorporated.

3. Add the flour mixture and beat on low speed just until the dry ingredients are moistened and the dough is beginning to hold together.

4. Add the chocolate chips and continue beating for just a few seconds, until evenly incorporated. If the dough seems very soft, cover and refrigerate it for a few minutes.

Continues

SHAPE THE COOKIES

5. Measure out 18 pieces of dough (1 level tablespoon / about 16 grams each). One at a time, flatten each piece between the palms of your hands and then roll it into a 1¼ inch ball. (This keeps the dough from cracking when pressed flat.) Flatten the ball slightly in the palm of your hand and then place it on a cookie sheet.

6. Top the cookie with a small piece of plastic wrap. Use your index finger, in a circular motion, to press it gently into a 1¾ inch disc. If necessary, press against the sides with your finger to make it smooth. Continue with the remaining pieces, spacing the cookies a minimum of ½ inch apart on the cookie sheet.

7. Cover the remaining dough with plastic wrap.

BAKE THE COOKIES

8. Bake for 6 minutes. Rotate the cookie sheet halfway around. Continue baking for 6 to 9 minutes, or just until the cookies begin to take on the faintest bit of color.

COOL THE COOKIES

9. Set the cookie sheet on a wire rack and use a thin pancake turner to transfer the cookies to another wire rack. Cool completely.

10. Repeat with the second batch.

STORE Airtight: room temperature, 1 month; frozen, 3 months.

CARAMEL SURPRISE SNICKERDOODLES

Makes: Thirty 3 inch round sandwich cookies

When my pastry chef friend Miro Uskokovic served these at Gramercy Tavern, I was charmed by the unexpected flow of extraordinary bourbon caramel inside the cookies. But I found re-creating them at home very challenging. Finally, after countless tries, with the caramel escaping through cracks in the dough and losing its consistency within, I tried one more thing—rolling his dough very thin so that the cookies baked up crisp, and sandwiching them with a thin layer of chewy caramel. It's a labor of love to shape the dough and make the caramel, but oh so worth it.

Oven Temperature: 350°F / 175°C	**Baking Time:** 12 to 15 minutes (for each of four batches)

Plan Ahead: For ease in shaping the cookies, it is best to make the dough at least 1 day, up to 3 days ahead.

Special Equipment: Two 17 by 14 inch cookie sheets, lined with parchment

DOUGH *Makes: 990 grams*

unsalted butter	227 grams	16 tablespoons (2 sticks)
2 large eggs	100 grams	⅓ cup plus 1 tablespoon (94 ml)
pure vanilla extract	·	1 teaspoon (5 ml)
unbleached all-purpose flour	371 grams	3 cups (lightly spooned into the cup and leveled off) plus 1 tablespoon
baking powder, preferably an aluminum-free variety	8 grams	1¾ teaspoons
fine sea salt	3 grams	½ teaspoon
ground cinnamon	4 grams	1½ teaspoons
sugar, preferably superfine	267 grams	1⅓ cups

MISE EN PLACE

Thirty minutes to 1 hour ahead, cut the butter into tablespoon-size pieces. Set on the counter to soften.

Thirty minutes ahead, into a 1 cup / 237 ml glass measure with a spout, weigh or measure the eggs. Whisk in the vanilla extract. Cover tightly with plastic wrap and set on the counter.

MAKE THE DOUGH

1. In a medium bowl, whisk together the flour, baking powder, salt, and cinnamon.

2. In the bowl of a stand mixer fitted with the flat beater, beat the butter and sugar on medium speed for 2 to 3 minutes, until lighter in color and fluffy.

3. Gradually add the egg mixture, beating until incorporated. Scrape down the sides of the bowl.

Continues

4. On low speed, gradually beat in the flour mixture just until incorporated, scraping down the sides of the bowl as needed.

5. Refrigerate the dough in the bowl, tightly covered, until firm, preferably 1 day ahead. Or scrape the dough onto a sheet of plastic wrap, wrap tightly, and refrigerate for up to 3 days.

PREHEAT THE OVEN

Twenty minutes or longer before baking, set an oven rack at the middle level. Set the oven at 350°F / 175°C.

CINNAMON SUGAR TOPPING

sugar	125 grams	½ cup plus 2 tablespoons
ground cinnamon	6 grams	2½ teaspoons

6. In a wide shallow bowl, whisk together the sugar and cinnamon.

SHAPE THE DOUGH

7. Divide the dough into fourths (about 247 grams each). Wrap each one in plastic wrap.

8. Work with one fourth of dough at a time. Measure out 15 pieces (about 1 tablespoon / 16 grams each). Knead each piece to soften and smooth the dough and then roll it between the palms of your hands to form a 1¼ inch ball. Cover the dough and the balls as you work to keep them moist and soft, which makes it easier to press into the sugar.

9. Flatten each dough ball and press it into the cinnamon sugar, flipping it over and pressing several times to coat well with sugar, until it is about 2 inches in diameter. Then lift it out and press it between your thumbs and index fingers, avoiding the edges, to enlarge it to 2½ inches. Then press it again into the cinnamon sugar, on both sides. Set it on a parchment-lined cookie sheet, spacing the cookies 1 inch apart.

BAKE THE COOKIES

10. Bake for 6 minutes. Rotate the cookie sheet halfway around. Continue baking for 6 to 9 minutes, or until the cookies are lightly browned and set.

COOL THE COOKIES

11. Set the cookie sheet on a wire rack and use a thin pancake turner to transfer the cookies to another wire rack. Cool completely.

12. Repeat shaping, baking, and cooling with the remaining batches.

BOURBON CARAMEL

Makes: about 600 grams / 2 cups / 473 ml

unsalted butter	57 grams	4 tablespoons (½ stick)
heavy cream	174 grams	¾ cup (177 ml)
sugar	400 grams	2 cups
bourbon	120 grams	½ cup (118 ml)
corn syrup	82 grams	¼ cup (59 ml)
cream of tartar	·	¾ teaspoon
pure vanilla extract	16 grams	4 teaspoons (20 ml)

MISE EN PLACE

Thirty minutes to 1 hour ahead, cut the butter into tablespoon-size pieces. Set on the counter to soften.

Have ready a 4 cup / 1 liter canning jar or heatproof container, lightly coated with nonstick cooking spray.

MAKE THE CARAMEL

1. Into a 1 cup / 237 ml microwavable measure with a spout (or in a small saucepan over medium heat) weigh or measure the cream. Heat until hot, then cover.

2. In a medium heavy saucepan, preferably nonstick (coat the sides lightly with nonstick

Continues

cooking spray if the pan is not nonstick), with a silicone spatula, stir together the sugar, bourbon, corn syrup, and cream of tartar until all the sugar is moistened. Heat, stirring constantly, over medium heat until the sugar has dissolved and the syrup is bubbling.

3. Continue boiling, without stirring, until the syrup caramelizes to deep amber. (An instant-read thermometer should read about 370°F / 188°C, or a few degrees lower, because its temperature will continue to rise.) Just as soon as it reaches the correct temperature, pour in the hot cream. The mixture will bubble up furiously.

4. Use a clean silicone spatula to stir the mixture gently, scraping up the thicker part that has settled on the bottom.

5. Remove the caramel from the heat and gently stir in the butter until incorporated. The mixture will be a little streaky, but it will become uniform once cooled and stirred. When the bubbling slows down, return the pan to the heat and bring the caramel to 250°F / 121°C.

6. Immediately pour and scrape the caramel into the prepared glass jar, then let it cool for 3 minutes. Gently stir in the vanilla extract and let it cool until no longer hot—about 120°F / 49°C—stirring gently once or twice. This can take as long as an hour.

If you are not using the caramel immediately, cover with plastic wrap and set it in a warm place. If it starts to become too firm, reheat it with 3-second bursts in the microwave or set it in a pot of very hot water.

The caramel can be stored at room temperature for up to 2 days or refrigerated for up to 6 months (reheat as stated above before using).

SANDWICH THE COOKIES

13. Use a small spoon to spread about 2 teaspoons / 16 grams of the caramel onto the bottom side of a cookie. It is best to make one sandwich at a time so that the caramel stays fluid; if necessary, reheat the caramel as described above.

14. Set second cookie, bottom side down, on top of the caramel to create a sandwich. Press gently so that the caramel comes just to the edges. Repeat with the remaining cookies.

STORE Unfilled, airtight: room temperature, 1 week; frozen, 2 months.
Filled, airtight: room temperature, 2 days; frozen, 2 months.

Baking Gem

♥ The caramel does not crystallize on stirring because of the acidity of the cream of tartar and because the corn syrup is an invert sugar. But if you need to rewarm it to make it fluid, do not overheat it or bring it to a boil; thickening the caramel further would make it harder to chew.

CRANBERRY SCONETTES

Makes: Twenty-eight 2¼ inch round cookies

These are my favorite scones—shaped into cookies! I've doubled the lemon zest in the original recipe, which complements the dried cranberries; chopped the cranberries for better distribution in the smaller cookies; and used a lower-protein flour for a more tender result.

Oven Temperature: 375°F / 190°C	**Baking Time:** 20 to 25 minutes (for each of two batches)

Special Equipment: Two 17 by 14 inch cookie sheets, preferably insulated, lined with parchment; A third cookie sheet to serve as a double pan if not using insulated cookie sheets

DOUGH *Makes: 856 grams*

unsalted butter	142 grams	10 tablespoons (1¼ sticks)
heavy cream	232 grams	1 cup (237 ml)
lemon zest, finely grated (2 medium lemons)	12 grams	2 tablespoons (loosely packed)
dried cranberries	100 grams	¾ cup (lightly packed)
all-purpose flour, preferably bleached	300 grams	2½ cups (lightly spooned into the cup and leveled off)
sugar	50 grams	¼ cup
baking powder, preferably an aluminum-free variety	13.5 grams	1 tablespoon
fine sea salt	·	⅜ teaspoon
honey	28 grams	1 tablespoon plus 1 teaspoon (20 ml)

PREHEAT THE OVEN

Thirty minutes or longer before baking, set an oven rack in the middle of the oven. Set the oven at 375°F / 190°C.

MISE EN PLACE

Thirty minutes ahead or longer, cut the butter into ½ to ¾ inch cubes. Wrap and refrigerate.

Into a medium bowl, weigh or measure the heavy cream. Refrigerate for a minimum of 15 minutes. (Chill the mixer's beaters alongside the bowl.)

Whip the cream just until soft peaks form when the beater is lifted. Place in the refrigerator.

With dishwashing liquid, wash, rinse, and dry the lemons, then zest them.

Using a chef's knife, chop the cranberries together with the lemon zest until the cranberries are in coarse pieces.

MAKE THE DOUGH

1. In a large bowl, whisk together the flour, sugar, baking powder, and salt. Add the butter and, with a fork, toss to coat with the flour. Press the butter cubes between your fingers to form very thin flakes.

2. Stir in the cranberry mixture. Make a well in the center. Place the whipped cream into the well, add the honey, and, with a silicone spatula, stir the flour mixture into the cream mixture until all of it is moistened.

Continues

3. Lightly knead the dough in the bowl just until it holds together.

4. Divide the dough in half (about 428 grams each). Work with one batch at a time, keeping the second one covered, and refrigerate if the dough softens.

SHAPE THE SCONETTES

5. Measure out 14 pieces of dough (1 rounded tablespoon / 30 grams each) from the first batch of dough. Roll each piece of dough in the palms of your hands to form a 1½ inch ball. Place the balls about 2 inches apart on a prepared cookie sheet. Flatten into 2 inch discs.

6. Cover the sconettes with plastic wrap and refrigerate for a minimum of 20 minutes, up to 24 hours.

7. Repeat the shaping with the second batch; refrigerate.

BAKE THE SCONETTES

8. Bake the first batch for 10 minutes. Rotate the cookie sheet halfway around. Continue baking for 10 to 15 minutes, or until the sconettes are golden brown. (An instant-read thermometer inserted in the center should read 212° to 215°F / 100° to 102°C.)

COOL THE SCONETTES

9. Set the cookie sheet on a wire rack and use a pancake turner to transfer the sconettes to another wire rack. Cool completely.

10. Repeat baking and cooling with the second batch.

STORE Airtight: room temperature, 2 days; frozen, 3 months.

CHOCOLATE CRACKLE COOKIES

Makes: Sixteen 2 inch round cookies

These bittersweet flourless cookies come from my sister-in-law Alice, who is a terrific cook and baker. They have fudgy brownie-like interiors and exceptionally attractive exteriors—crisp on the outside but moist inside. They are the most crisp before storing but will regain their texture if allowed to sit uncovered for about an hour before serving. For a stronger nut flavor, substitute ground hazelnuts or walnuts in equal weight or measure for the almonds.

Oven Temperature: 350°F / 175°C | **Baking Time:** 10 to 12 minutes | **Special Equipment:** One 17 by 14 inch cookie sheet, lined with parchment

DOUGH *Makes: 264 grams*

1 large egg	50 grams	3 tablespoons plus ½ teaspoon (47.5 ml)
pure vanilla extract	.	½ teaspoon (2.5 ml)
sliced blanched almonds (or almond flour)	56 grams	½ cup plus 1 tablespoon sliced almonds (or ½ cup plus 3 tablespoons almond flour)
dark chocolate, 60% to 62% cacao	113 grams (4 ounces)	.
unsalted butter	14 grams	1 tablespoon
instant espresso powder	2.4 grams	2 teaspoons
fine sea salt	.	⅛ teaspoon
sugar	31 grams	2½ tablespoons

MISE EN PLACE

Thirty minutes ahead, into a 1 cup / 237 ml glass measure with a spout, weigh or measure the egg. Whisk in the vanilla extract. Cover tightly with plastic wrap and set on the counter.

MAKE THE DOUGH

1. If using sliced almonds, in a small food processor or a spice mill, or using a rotary nut grinder, grind the almonds as fine as possible.

2. Chop the chocolate into coarse pieces. In the top of a double boiler set over hot, not simmering, water—do not let the bottom of the container touch the water—heat the chocolate and butter, stirring often with a silicone spatula, until completely melted.

3. Remove the top of the double boiler from the heat and stir in the almonds or almond flour, espresso powder, and salt.

4. In a medium bowl, with a handheld mixer, beat the egg mixture with the sugar on medium-high speed for 2 to 3 minutes, until paler in color and thicker.

5. With a silicone spatula, fold in the chocolate mixture. Scrape about half the mixture into a second bowl. Cover both bowls tightly and refrigerate for a minimum of 2 hours, up to 2 days.

PREHEAT THE OVEN

Twenty minutes or longer before baking, set an oven rack at the middle level. Set the oven at 350°F / 175°C.

ROLL THE DOUGH INTO BALLS

6. Keep one bowl of dough refrigerated while you work with the dough in the other bowl. Line a small pan or flat plate with plastic wrap. Scoop out 8 pieces of dough (1 level tablespoon / 15 to 16 grams each), setting the dough mounds on the pan as you go.

7. Roll each mound of dough in the palms of your hands to form a 1¼ inch ball. They will be quite sticky. Set the balls back on the pan. If the dough starts getting too soft to work with, return it briefly to the refrigerator.

SUGAR COATINGS

granulated sugar	25 grams	2 tablespoons
powdered sugar	29 grams	¼ cup (lightly spooned into the cup and leveled off)

8. Spoon the granulated sugar into a small bowl. Sift the powdered sugar into another small bowl.

9. One at a time, coat the dough balls: First swirl a ball in the granulated sugar to coat evenly, then lift it out with your fingers, set it in the powdered sugar, and swirl it around to coat thickly.

10. Place the balls 2 inches apart on the cookie sheet.

11. Repeat with the second bowl of dough, placing the balls on the same sheet.

BAKE THE COOKIES

12. Bake for 5 minutes. Rotate the cookie sheet halfway around. Continue baking for 5 to 7 minutes.

Cracks will appear on the surface of the cookies, but the insides will look slightly underbaked. The edges of the cookies will appear dry and will be firm when pressed lightly.

COOL THE COOKIES

13. Set the cookie sheet on a wire rack and let the cookies cool for 3 to 5 minutes, until firm enough to lift cleanly from the sheet. Use a thin pancake turner to transfer the cookies to another wire rack. Cool completely.

STORE Airtight: room temperature, 1 week.

Baking Gems

♥ Rolling the dough balls in granulated sugar before rolling them in powdered sugar makes them easier to handle and results in a more even and attractive design on the baked cookies. Coating the balls with sugar draws out moisture from the surface before the interior sets in the oven, which causes the cookies to form cracks on the top as they continue to expand.

♥ Grinding almonds yourself rather than using almond flour, which is finer, will make the cookies' texture crunchier.

♥ Overbaking will result in a flatter shape and drier texture.

DOUBLE CHOCOLATE ORIOLOS

Makes: Thirty-four 2¼ inch round cookies

These intensely chocolate cookies have been in my repertoire for many years; I dedicated them to designer Richard Oriolo, who was the art director for many of my cookbooks, because he loved the cookies so much. They are buttery but still light in texture. The plain cookies make a fabulous addition to Bourbon Balls (page 260), but they are terrific on their own, with or without the chocolate walnut buttercream.

Oven Temperature: 325°F / 160°C	**Baking Time:** 7 minutes for the walnuts; 20 to 25 minutes for the cookies (for each of three batches)	**Special Equipment:** Two 17 by 14 inch cookie sheets, no preparation needed or lined with parchment

DOUGH *Makes: 429 grams*

walnut halves	125 grams	1¼ cups, *divided*
unsalted butter	142 grams	10 tablespoons (1¼ sticks)
granulated sugar	67 grams	⅓ cup
powdered sugar	38 grams	⅓ cup (lightly spooned into the cup and leveled off)
unsweetened alkalized cocoa powder	24 grams	¼ cup plus 1 tablespoon (sifted before measuring)
bleached all-purpose flour	110 grams	¾ cup (lightly spooned into the cup and leveled off) plus 2 tablespoons
granulated sugar, for pressing down the dough balls	100 grams	½ cup

PREHEAT THE OVEN

Twenty minutes or longer before baking, set an oven rack at the middle level. Set the oven at 325°F / 160°C.

MISE EN PLACE

Toast and Chop the Walnuts: Spread the walnuts evenly on a baking sheet and bake for 7 minutes. Turn the walnuts onto a clean dish town and roll and rub them around to loosen the skins. Discard any loose skins, and cool completely.

Chop the walnuts medium-coarse. Reserve 75 grams / ¾ cup in a small bowl for sprinkling on the cookies.

Thirty minutes ahead or longer, **for the food processor method,** cut the butter into ½ inch cubes. Wrap and refrigerate. **For the stand mixer method,** cut the butter into tablespoon-size pieces and set on the counter to soften.

MAKE THE DOUGH

Food Processor Method

1. In a food processor, process the 50 grams / ½ cup walnuts, the sugars, and cocoa until the walnuts are finely ground.

2. Add the butter and pulse until the nut mixture is absorbed by the butter.

Continues

3. Add the flour and pulse it in until there are a lot of little moist crumbly pieces and no dry flour particles remain.

Stand Mixer Method

1. Finely grind the walnuts in a spice mill with a little of the granulated sugar, or use a rotary nut grinder.

2. Into the bowl of a stand mixer fitted with the flat beater, sift the cocoa. Add the ground nuts and the (remaining) sugars and beat on low speed for about 30 seconds, until evenly mixed.

3. Add the butter and beat on medium speed for 2 to 3 minutes, until the mixture is lighter in color and fluffy.

4. On low speed, gradually beat in the flour just until incorporated, scraping down the sides of the bowl as needed.

Both Methods

5. Empty the dough into a plastic bag and press it from the outside of the bag just until it holds together.

6. Remove the dough from the plastic bag and place it on a very large sheet of plastic wrap. Using the plastic wrap, knead the dough only a few times, just until it becomes one smooth piece.

7. Divide the dough into thirds (about 143 grams each). Wrap two of the pieces in plastic wrap and refrigerate them while you roll the first piece.

SHAPE THE DOUGH

8. In a small bowl or large custard cup, place the sugar for pressing down the dough balls.

9. Measure out 12 pieces of dough (1 scant tablespoon / about 12 grams each). Roll each piece of dough between the palms of your hands to form a 1 inch ball. Place the balls a minimum of 2 inches apart on a cookie sheet.

10. Spray the bottom of a flat glass tumbler with nonstick cooking spray. Press it into the sugar and then use it to flatten a dough ball to a disc about 1½ inches in diameter. Recoat the tumbler with sugar before flattening each of the remaining dough balls.

BAKE THE COOKIES

11. Bake for 10 minutes. Rotate the cookie sheet halfway around. Continue baking for 10 to 15 minutes, or until the cookies are firm enough to lift from the sheet but still soft when pressed lightly on top.

12. While each batch of cookies is baking, shape the dough for the next batch, then bake once the previous batch is done.

COOL THE COOKIES

13. Set the cookie sheet on a wire rack and let the cookies cool for 2 minutes, or until firm enough to lift from the cookie sheet. Use a thin pancake turner to transfer the cookies to another wire rack. Cool completely.

CHOCOLATE BUTTERCREAM WITH WALNUTS

Makes: 135 grams / ½ cup

unsalted butter	42 grams	3 tablespoons
dark chocolate, 60% to 62% cacao	85 grams (3 ounces)	.
corn syrup	.	½ teaspoon (2.5 ml)
pure vanilla extract	.	½ teaspoon (2.5 ml)
chopped walnuts reserved from above, for topping	75 grams	⅔ cup

MAKE THE BUTTERCREAM

1. Thirty minutes ahead, cut the butter into ½ inch pieces. Set on the counter to soften slightly.

2. Chop the chocolate into coarse pieces. In a small microwavable bowl, heat the chocolate, stirring every 15 seconds with a silicone spatula, until almost completely melted (or heat the chocolate in the top of a double boiler set over hot, not simmering, water—do not let the bottom of the container touch the water—stirring often, until almost completely melted).

Remove the chocolate from the heat source and stir until fully melted.

3. Add the butter to the melted chocolate 1 tablespoon at a time, stirring until blended. If the butter is not warm enough and does not incorporate, scrape the mixture into the top of a double boiler set over hot, not simmering, water (do not microwave) and stir briefly just until incorporated; remove it from the heat. Stir in the corn syrup and vanilla extract.

4. Let the buttercream stand at room temperature for about 1 hour, or until thick enough to spread.

COMPOSE THE COOKIES

14. Use a small metal spatula to spread the buttercream over the cookies. Sprinkle the reserved walnuts on top.

15. Let the topping set overnight at room temperature, or refrigerate for 30 minutes, before storing the cookies.

STORE Without buttercream, airtight: room temperature, 3 weeks; frozen, 6 months. With buttercream, airtight: room temperature, 1 day; frozen, 6 months.

CHAPTER 2

DROPPED
OR PIPED

MOM'S COCONUT SNOWBALL KISSES

Makes: Twenty-four 1¾ inch round cookies

My mother's last word to me was over the phone. It was just one word, and she sang it to me. It was *love*. For me, this recipe is love. It is very special, because coconut macaroons are the only cookie my mother ever made. It is such an easy recipe to make that it's worth using freshly grated coconut for the best flavor. But the cookies are still lovely when made with packaged coconut. They are ideal for Passover, as well as for anyone who does not eat flour or eggs.

Oven Temperature: 400°F / 200°C for the fresh coconut; 350°F / 175°C for the cookies	**Baking Time:** 20 minutes for the fresh coconut; 15 to 20 minutes for the cookies (for each of two batches)

Special Equipment: Two 17 by 14 inch cookie sheets, lined with parchment or silicone baking mats; An ice pick or nail and hammer; A food processor fitted with the shredding disc or a handheld shredder; A 1½ inch cookie scoop or a tablespoon

DOUGH *Makes: 570 grams*

fresh coconut, shredded (see Mise en Place and Baking Gems)	276 grams	3½ cups
cornstarch	15 grams	2 tablespoons
lemon juice, freshly squeezed and strained	5 grams	1 teaspoon (5 ml)
pure vanilla extract	·	1 teaspoon (5 ml)
fine sea salt	·	1⁄16 teaspoon (a pinch)
sweetened condensed milk	276 grams	¾ cup plus 2 tablespoons (207 ml), *divided*

PREHEAT THE OVEN

Thirty minutes or longer before baking, set an oven rack at the middle level. Set the oven at 400°F / 200°C.

MISE EN PLACE

Bake and Shred the Coconut: With an ice pick or nail and a hammer, pierce the 3 eyes at one end of the coconut. Drain the liquid and reserve it, if desired, for another use. Bake the coconut until the shell cracks, about 20 minutes. Remove from the oven. Lower the oven temperature to 350°F / 175°C.

Wrap the coconut in a towel to contain the shell and use the hammer to crack open the shell. Separate the coconut meat from the shell with the help of a peeler or butter knife and then, with a small knife, peel away and discard the dark outer skin.

In a food processor fitted with the fine shredding disc, shred the coconut meat. Weigh or measure out the amount of coconut you need and place in a medium bowl.

MAKE THE DOUGH

1. Add the cornstarch, lemon juice, vanilla extract, salt, and 250 grams / ¾ cup / 177 ml of the condensed milk to the coconut.

Continues

2. With a large spoon, mix all the ingredients together until well blended. The mixture should be moist and hold together. If necessary, add some or all of the remaining 26 grams / 2 tablespoons / 30 ml of the condensed milk.

SHAPE THE COOKIES

3. Use a cookie scoop to measure out 12 mounds, or use a scant tablespoon and your fingers to form 1½ inch high mounds (about 23 grams each) and arrange in 3 rows of 4 each on a cookie sheet.

BAKE THE COOKIES

4. Bake for 10 minutes. Rotate the cookie sheet halfway around. Continue baking for 5 to 10 minutes, or until most of the cookies' surfaces are light golden.

COOL THE COOKIES

5. Set the cookie sheet on a wire rack and use a thin pancake turner to transfer the cookies to another wire rack. Cool completely.

6. Repeat with the second batch.

STORE Airtight: room temperature, 1 day; refrigerated, 2 months; frozen, 3 months.

Baking Gems

♥ Shredding the coconut in the food processor rather than using the round grating holes of a grater will give the roundest shape to the cookies.

♥ Freshly grated coconut is far superior for these cookies, but it can be replaced with an equal weight or volume of packaged shredded coconut (sweetened or unsweetened). If using the sweetened variety, which is moister than fresh, you may need to start with slightly less condensed milk.

CHOCOLATE PHANTOMS

Makes: Thirty 1½ inch round cookies

These little cookies first appeared in 1985 in my friend Lora Brody's charming memoir *Growing Up on the Chocolate Diet*. She called them phantoms because they are so delicious they disappear quickly. The cookies are super-chocolatey and moist, with almost half their weight in macadamia nuts, which contribute their unique, slightly waxy crunch. The chocolate and nuts are held together by just one egg and a tiny bit of flour.

Oven Temperature:	Baking Time:	Special Equipment:
350°F / 175°C	9 to 10 minutes (for each of two batches)	Two 17 by 14 inch cookie sheets, nonstick or lined with parchment

DOUGH *Makes: 455 grams*

1 large egg	50 grams	3 tablespoons plus ½ teaspoon (47.5 ml)
pure vanilla extract	·	½ teaspoon (2.5 ml)
dark chocolate, 60% to 62% cacao	113 grams (4 ounces)	·
unsalted butter	14 grams	1 tablespoon
bleached all-purpose flour	14 grams	1½ tablespoons
baking powder, preferably an aluminum-free variety	·	⅛ teaspoon
sugar	50 grams	¼ cup
semisweet chocolate chips, 46% to 50% cacao	113 grams (4 ounces)	⅔ cup
unsalted whole macadamia nuts (see Baking Gems)	100 grams	¾ cup

PREHEAT THE OVEN

Twenty minutes or longer before baking, set an oven rack at the middle level. Set the oven at 350°F / 175°C.

MISE EN PLACE

Thirty minutes ahead, into a 1 cup / 237 ml glass measure with a spout, weigh or measure the egg. Whisk in the vanilla extract. Cover tightly with plastic wrap and set on the counter.

Melt the Chocolate and Butter: In the top of a double boiler set over hot, not simmering, water—do not let the bottom of the container touch the water—heat the chocolate and butter, stirring often, until completely melted. Set aside in a warm place.

MAKE THE DOUGH

1. In a small bowl, whisk together the flour and baking powder.

2. In the bowl of a stand mixer fitted with the flat beater, beat the egg mixture and sugar on medium speed for about 1 minute, until well blended.

Continues

3. On low speed, beat in the melted chocolate mixture until combined.

4. Add the flour mixture and beat just until incorporated.

5. Remove the bowl from the stand. Use a silicone spatula to scrape down the sides of the bowl and then mix in the chocolate chips, along with the macadamia nuts.

SHAPE THE COOKIES

6. Scoop rounded teaspoons of the dough (15 grams each) in 3 rows of 5 mounds each onto each cookie sheet. They should be about 1 inch wide. If the dough starts to get too stiff, set the bowl in a larger bowl or pan of hot tap water.

BAKE THE COOKIES

7. Bake the first cookie sheet for 6 minutes. Rotate the cookie sheet halfway around. Continue baking for 3 to 4 minutes, until the tops of the cookies are dry and set. The insides should still be very soft.

COOL THE COOKIES

8. Set the cookie sheet on a wire rack and let the cookies cool until just warm or at room temperature. Use a thin pancake turner to transfer the cookies to another wire rack. Cool completely.

9. Repeat with the second batch.

STORE Airtight: room temperature, 2 days.

Baking Gems

♥ If you can find only salted macadamia nuts, set them in a strainer and rinse them under hot tap water. Then recrisp them in the preheated oven for 5 to 10 minutes.

♥ The cookies release most easily from the cookie sheet or parchment while still warm.

BENNE WAFERS

Makes: Eighteen 2½ inch round wafers

These sesame cookies are a treasured South Carolina tradition. They are incredibly crisp and crunchy because the dough contains more sesame seeds than flour by weight.

Oven Temperature: 350°F / 175°C	**Baking Time:** 5 minutes for the sesame seeds; 8 to 10 minutes for the cookies (for each of two batches)	**Special Equipment:** Two 17 by 14 inch cookie sheets, lined with parchment (see Baking Gem)

DOUGH *Makes: 286 grams*

unsalted butter	57 grams	4 tablespoons (½ stick)
½ large egg, lightly beaten before measuring	25 grams	1½ tablespoons (22.5 ml)
pure vanilla extract	·	¼ teaspoon (1.25 ml)
hulled sesame seeds	71 grams	½ cup
bleached all-purpose flour	60 grams	½ cup (lightly spooned into the cup and leveled off)
baking soda	·	⅛ teaspoon
fine sea salt	·	1⁄16 teaspoon (a pinch)
light brown sugar, preferably Muscovado	54 grams	¼ cup (firmly packed)
granulated sugar	25 grams	2 tablespoons

PREHEAT THE OVEN

Thirty minutes or longer before baking, set an oven rack at the middle level. Set the oven at 350°F / 175°C.

MISE EN PLACE

Thirty minutes to 1 hour ahead, cut the butter into tablespoon-size pieces. Set on the counter to soften.

Thirty minutes ahead, into a 1 cup / 237 ml glass measure with a spout, weigh or measure the egg. Whisk in the vanilla extract. Cover tightly with plastic wrap and set on the counter.

Toast the Sesame Seeds: Spread the sesame seeds evenly on a baking sheet and bake for about 5 minutes, or until pale gold. Shake the pan gently one or two times to ensure even toasting and avoid overbrowning. Set the baking sheet on a wire rack and cool completely.

In a small bowl, whisk together the flour, baking soda, and salt.

MAKE THE DOUGH

1. In the bowl of a stand mixer fitted with the flat beater, beat the butter and sugars on medium speed for about 2 minutes, until smooth and creamy. Gradually add the egg mixture, beating until incorporated.

2. Add the flour mixture and mix on low speed just until no flour particles are visible.

3. Add the sesame seeds and mix just until incorporated.

SPOON THE DOUGH
4. Use a tablespoon measure to drop 9 mounds of dough (about 15 grams each) 1½ inches apart onto a cookie sheet.

BAKE THE COOKIES
5. Bake for 5 minutes. Rotate the cookie sheet halfway around. Continue baking for 3 to 5 minutes, or until the cookies are golden brown.

COOL THE COOKIES
6. Set the cookie sheet on a wire rack and let the cookies cool for 1 minute, or until firm enough to lift from the sheet. Use a thin pancake turner to transfer the cookies to another wire rack. Cool completely.

7. Repeat with the second batch.

STORE Airtight: room temperature, 1 week; frozen, 3 months.

Baking Gem
♥ If you don't use parchment, the wafers will spread to 3 inches.

FLORENTINES

Makes: Thirty 3½ inch round cookies

I love the combination of orange, chocolate, and caramel. Using your own candied orange peel makes this crisp, lacy, slightly caramelized cookie a special delight! The thin, even coating of chocolate on the underside of each cookie offers the ideal balance of chocolate to the orange and caramel flavors of the cookie. I love how the chocolate coating rises up through the openings in the cookies and forms tiny pools.

Oven Temperature: 350°F / 175°C

Baking Time: 10 to 12 minutes (for each of four batches)

Special Equipment: Two 17 by 14 inch cookie sheets, lined with parchment or silicone baking mats

BATTER *Makes: 540 grams*

unsalted butter	57 grams	4 tablespoons (½ stick)
candied orange peel (page 398)	37 grams	¼ cup (chopped)
sliced blanched almonds	200 grams	2 cups
all-purpose flour, bleached or unbleached	22 grams	2½ tablespoons
fine sea salt	·	¼ teaspoon
heavy cream	116 grams	½ cup (118 ml)
sugar	100 grams	½ cup
golden syrup (or corn syrup)	42 grams	2 tablespoons (30 ml)
pure vanilla extract	·	1 teaspoon (5 ml)

PREHEAT THE OVEN

Twenty minutes or longer before baking, set an oven rack at the middle level. Set the oven at 350°F / 175°C.

MISE EN PLACE

Thirty minutes to 1 hour ahead, cut the butter into tablespoon-size pieces. Set on the counter to soften.

Use a chef's knife to chop the candied orange peel into fine pieces. You will have about ¼ cup.

MAKE THE BATTER

1. In a food processor, process the almonds into fine but not powder-fine pieces. (Alternatively, grind in a spice mill in batches, or use a rotary nut grinder.)

2. Empty the almonds into a medium bowl. Add the flour and salt and stir to incorporate evenly.

3. In a small saucepan, preferably nonstick, combine the butter, heavy cream, sugar, and golden syrup. Bring the mixture to a full boil over medium heat, stirring constantly with a silicone spatula. Boil for 1 minute to make sure the sugar is fully dissolved. Remove the pan from the heat and add the vanilla extract and candied orange peel.

4. Pour the butter mixture into the flour mixture and stir until evenly combined. Allow to cool and thicken for 10 to 15 minutes, stirring once or twice.

Continues

SPOON THE BATTER

5. Spoon the batter into mounds (about 1 level tablespoon / 18 grams each) 3½ inches apart on the prepared cookie sheets, 8 to a sheet. Use a small offset spatula or the back of a spoon, dipped in water, to flatten the mounds into 2½ inch rounds.

BAKE THE COOKIES

6. Bake the first cookie sheet for 5 minutes. Rotate the sheet halfway around. Continue baking for 5 to 7 minutes, watching carefully, just until the cookies are evenly deep golden.

COOL THE COOKIES

7. Set the cookie sheet on a wire rack and allow the cookies to cool for 5 minutes, or until firm enough to lift from the cookie sheet. Use a thin pancake turner to transfer the cookies onto another wire rack. Cool completely.

8. Repeat with the remaining three batches.

DARK CHOCOLATE COATING

dark chocolate, 61% to 70% cacao	227 grams (8 ounces)	.

MAKE THE CHOCOLATE COATING

9. In a small microwavable bowl, heat the chocolate, stirring every 15 seconds with a silicone spatula, until almost completely melted (or heat it in the top of a double boiler set over hot, not simmering, water—do not let the bottom of the container touch the water—stirring often, until almost completely melted). Remove the chocolate from the heat source and stir until fully melted (see Baking Gems).

COAT THE COOKIE BOTTOMS

10. Lift each cookie in one hand and use a small offset spatula to spread a thin, even coating of chocolate onto the smooth underside. Set the cookies on a tray, chocolate side up, and let stand until the chocolate dulls and sets.

STORE Airtight, layered between sheets of parchment: room temperature, 1 week; refrigerated, 10 days.

Baking Gems

♥ Golden syrup gives a slightly butterscotch flavor to the cookie.

♥ If you only have one or two cookie sheets, keep the batter covered with plastic wrap to prevent evaporation. For this delicate cookie, it is especially important to bake only one sheet at a time to ensure that the cookies are evenly baked.

♥ I prefer parchment to silicone baking mats for these cookies because with parchment, the lacy holes that develop in the cookies go all the way to the bottom. The silicone mats cause the cookies to bake a little faster and seal the holes so that they don't go all the way through the cookies.

♥ You can make 2 inch cookies and sandwich the chocolate between them.

♥ The cookies stay most crisp when refrigerated.

♥ You need to quick-temper the chocolate by removing it from the heat before it is fully melted and then stirring until it is completely melted and the temperature is no higher than 94°F / 34°C. This will keep the chocolate from "blooming" (forming gray streaks) and will give it a sharp snap when you bite into it.

♥ Keep the chocolate warm and in temper as you work by placing the container on a heating pad wrapped with foil and set to the lowest temperature, or by setting it over a bowl of warm water (no warmer than 120°F / 49°C). Stir often to equalize and maintain the temperature.

CASHEW COMFORTS

Makes: Thirty-six 1¾ inch round cookies

These slightly airy, firm, and crunchy mounds of mellow cashew nuts, sour cream, and buttery dough are perfect cookies for shipping because they hold up well and have a long shelf life. They are so pleasing and comforting in the face of life's vicissitudes that the name came to me one day as I enjoyed one.

Oven Temperature: 375°F / 190°C	**Baking Time:** 10 to 13 minutes (for each of two batches)

Special Equipment: Two 17 by 14 inch cookie sheets, nonstick or lightly coated with nonstick cooking spray or lined with parchment

DOUGH *Makes: 474 grams*

unsalted butter	57 grams	4 tablespoons (½ stick)
½ large egg, lightly beaten before measuring	25 grams	1½ tablespoons (22.5 ml)
pure vanilla extract	·	½ teaspoon (2.5 ml)
unsalted roasted cashews (see Baking Gem)	93 grams	⅔ cup
bleached all-purpose flour	145 grams	1 cup (lightly spooned into the cup and leveled off) plus 2½ tablespoons
baking powder, preferably an aluminum-free variety	·	⅜ teaspoon
baking soda	·	⅜ teaspoon
fine sea salt	·	⅛ teaspoon
light brown sugar, preferably Muscovado	95 grams	½ cup (firmly packed) minus 1 tablespoon
full-fat sour cream	60 grams	¼ cup

PREHEAT THE OVEN

Twenty minutes or longer before baking, set an oven rack at the middle level. Set the oven at 375°F / 190°C.

MISE EN PLACE

Thirty minutes to 1 hour ahead, cut the butter into tablespoon-size pieces. Set on the counter to soften.

Thirty minutes ahead, into a 1 cup / 237 ml glass measure with a spout, weigh or measure the egg. Whisk in the vanilla extract. Cover tightly with plastic wrap and set on the counter.

With a long sharp knife, coarsely chop the nuts.

In a medium bowl, whisk together the flour, baking powder, baking soda, and salt. Mix in the nuts.

MAKE THE DOUGH

1. In the bowl of a stand mixer fitted with the flat beater, beat the butter and sugar on medium speed for 2 to 3 minutes, until lighter in color and fluffy.

2. Gradually add the egg mixture, beating until incorporated. Scrape down the sides of the bowl.

Continues

3. Add the sour cream and beat until incorporated.

4. On low speed, gradually beat in the flour mixture just until incorporated, scraping down the sides of the bowl as needed.

SPOON THE DOUGH

5. Use two teaspoons to drop eighteen 1 inch mounds of dough (13 grams each) 1½ inches apart onto a cookie sheet.

BAKE THE COOKIES

6. Bake for 6 minutes. Rotate the cookie sheet halfway around. Continue baking for 4 to 7 minutes, until the cookies are golden brown and firm, with only a very slight give when pressed lightly in the centers.

COOL THE COOKIES

7. Set the cookie sheet on a wire rack and let the cookies cool for 3 to 5 minutes, until firm enough to lift from the sheet. Use a thin pancake turner to transfer the cookies to another wire rack. Cool completely.

8. Repeat with the second batch.

STORE Airtight: room temperature, 1 month; frozen, 3 months.

Baking Gem

♥ If the cashew nuts are salted, rinse them in a colander or sieve under hot tap water, then crisp them for 10 minutes in the preheated 350°F / 175°C oven. Cool completely before chopping them.

CLINTON STREET BROOKIES

Makes: Twenty-four 2½ to 2¾ inch round cookies

This is the felicitous offspring of a cookie that is married to a brownie. They sport crackly brownie-like tops with delightfully chewy and slightly cakey interiors and sweet, deep chocolate flavor. They are at their very melty best when still warm, but they are still soft and chewy at room temperature. I adapted this recipe from the *Clinton Street Baking Company Cookbook* with permission from its creator, pastry chef Ernie Rich.

Oven Temperature: 350°F / 175°C	**Baking Time:** 10 to 12 minutes (for each of two batches)	**Special Equipment:** Two 17 by 14 inch cookie sheets, nonstick or lined with nonstick liners or parchment; Optional: a 1½ inch / 1 tablespoon cookie scoop

DOUGH *Makes: 564 grams*

dark chocolate, 60% to 62% cacao	227 grams (8 ounces)	*divided* (see Baking Gem for an alternative choice)
canola or safflower oil	13 grams	1 tablespoon (15 ml)
unsalted butter	5 grams	1 teaspoon
2 large eggs	100 grams	⅓ cup plus 1 tablespoon (94 ml)
pure vanilla extract	·	¼ teaspoon (1.25 ml)
bleached all-purpose flour	65 grams	½ cup (lightly spooned into the cup and leveled off) plus ½ tablespoon
baking powder, preferably an aluminum-free variety	·	¼ teaspoon
fine sea salt	·	¼ teaspoon
light Muscovado (or dark brown sugar)	163 grams	¾ cup (firmly packed)

PREHEAT THE OVEN

Twenty minutes or longer before baking, set an oven rack at the middle level. Set the oven at 350°F / 175°C.

MISE EN PLACE

Melt the Chocolate: Thirty minutes to 1 hour ahead, chop the chocolate into coarse pieces. In the top of a double boiler set over hot, not simmering, water—do not let the bottom of the container touch the water—stir together half of the chocolate (113 grams / 4 ounces), the oil, and butter. Heat the mixture, stirring often, until the chocolate is fully melted. Remove from the heat and let cool to room temperature.

Thirty minutes ahead, into a medium bowl, weigh or measure the eggs. Whisk in the vanilla extract. Cover tightly with plastic wrap and set on the counter.

MAKE THE DOUGH

1. In a small bowl, whisk together the flour, baking powder, and salt.

2. Add the brown sugar to the eggs and whisk until combined. Use the whisk to fold the melted chocolate mixture into the egg mixture.

3. With a silicone spatula or wooden spoon, mix the flour mixture into the chocolate mixture until evenly combined. Fold in the remaining chopped chocolate.

CHILL THE DOUGH
4. Scrape the mixture onto a shallow pan, such as a quarter sheet pan or pie plate lined with plastic wrap that has been lightly coated with nonstick cooking spray. The dough will be very soft. Cover it with another coated sheet of plastic wrap, coated side down, and set it in the freezer for about 15 minutes, or until it is firm enough to scoop.

SCOOP THE DOUGH
5. Using a cookie scoop, drop 12 scoops of dough (23 grams each), about 1½ inches in diameter, about 2 inches apart onto a prepared cookie sheet. You can use a small metal spatula to help release the sticky dough from the scoop. (Alternatively, use 2 teaspoons to drop and mound the dough.) If your kitchen is hot and the dough becomes very soft, return it to the freezer to firm for about 15 minutes as necessary.

BAKE THE COOKIES
6. Bake for 5 minutes. Rotate the cookie sheet halfway around. Continue baking for 5 to 7 minutes, or until the tops of the cookies are dry and cracked. When pressed lightly on top, they should give slightly; they should feel firm around the edges but still a little soft all over the tops.

7. While the first batch of cookies is baking, shape the dough for the second batch.

COOL THE COOKIES
8. Set the cookie sheet on a wire rack and let the cookies cool for 3 minutes, or until firm enough to lift from the sheet. Use a thin pancake turner to transfer the cookies to another wire rack. Cool completely.

9. Bake and cool the second batch.

STORE Airtight: room temperature, 4 days; refrigerated, 1 week; frozen, 2 months.

Baking Gem

♥ I prefer to use an 85% cacao chocolate for the chopped chocolate that gets folded into the dough, to temper the sweetness of the cookie. But the sweeter lower-percentage chocolate is needed to form the attractive cracks in the surface.

LANGUES DE CHATS (CATS' TONGUES)

Makes: about Twenty-four 2½ inch by 1½ to 1¾ inch piped cookies (12 sandwiches) or Eighty 3 inch by 2 inch stenciled butterfly cookies (40 sandwiches)

There are two styles of this delicate cookie: piped free-form, which are ½ inch thick, and smoother, paper-thin stenciled cookies, which are a mere ¹⁄₁₆ inch thick. The first time I made the recipe was when I was studying with Roland Mesnier, the former White House pastry chef, at L'Academie de Cuisine. The only oven available was a commercial convection oven, which was too powerful for these delicate cookies—they literally flew off the parchment! The cookies are lovely as is, but because their flavor is so subtle, they marry well with just about any filling, making them perfect for sandwiches.

Oven Temperature:
400°F / 200°C for piped;
350°F / 175°C for stenciled

Baking Time: 10 to 12 minutes for piped cookies (for each of two batches); 6 to 8 minutes for butterflies (number of batches depends on the type of stencil)

Special Equipment: Two 17 by 14 inch cookie sheets lined with silicone baking mats and/or parchment templates—see Mise en Place (if using silicone baking mats, slide the parchment templates under the baking mats); A large disposable pastry bag fitted with a ½ inch round pastry tube for piped cookies, or a stencil (preferably a butterfly)

BATTER

Makes: 420 grams using the extra flour for piped cookies, 390 grams for stenciled cookies

unsalted butter	100 grams	7 tablespoons (¾ stick plus 1 tablespoon)
3 large egg whites	90 grams	¼ cup plus 2 tablespoons (89 ml)
pure vanilla extract	.	1 teaspoon (5 ml)
powdered sugar	100 grams	¾ cup (lightly spooned into the cup and leveled off) plus 2½ tablespoons
unbleached all-purpose flour	130 grams for piped cookies OR 100 grams for stenciled cookies	1 cup (lightly spooned into the cup and leveled off) plus 1 tablespoon OR ¾ cup (lightly spooned into the cup and leveled off) plus 1 tablespoon

PREHEAT THE OVEN

Thirty minutes or longer before baking, set an oven rack at the middle level. Set the oven at 400°F / 200°F for piped cookies, 350°F / 175°C for stenciled cookies.

MISE EN PLACE

Thirty minutes to 1 hour ahead, cut the butter into tablespoon-size pieces. Set on the counter to soften.

Thirty minutes ahead, into a 1 cup / 237 ml glass measure with a spout, weigh or measure the egg whites. Whisk in the vanilla extract. Cover tightly with plastic wrap and set on the counter.

For piped cookies, make 2 parchment templates: Starting 2 inches from one long edge, draw 2 pairs of guidelines the length of the parchment, (in rows), with the guidelines 2½ inches apart and each pair spaced 2 inches apart. Then, starting 2 inches from one short edge, draw 7 vertical lines, spaced 2 inches apart, to serve as piping guides for each row. You will be able to pipe 7 vertical cookies on each row. If not using silicone mats, invert the parchment so that the pencil or ink marks are facing against the cookie sheet and not the cookies.

MAKE THE BATTER

1. In the bowl of a stand mixer fitted with the flat beater, beat the butter and sugar on medium speed for 2 to 3 minutes, until lighter in color and very creamy.

2. Gradually add the egg white mixture, beating until incorporated. The butter will be in little clumps.

3. Gradually add the flour, beating on low speed just until incorporated. Scrape down the sides of the bowl.

PIPE OR STENCIL THE BATTER

4. **If piping the thicker batter,** have ready a small metal spatula and a bowl of water for cutting off each piece. Scrape the batter into the prepared pastry bag and pipe 2½ inch long by ¾ inch wide fingers, using the piping lines on the template as a guide, 2 inches apart, on a prepared cookie sheet, starting at the top guideline. Stop piping about ½ inch from the bottom guideline and cut off the batter, using the moistened spatula. Each piece will be about 15 grams. If necessary, you can perfect the shape using the moistened spatula.

If using the stencil for the thinner batter, use pieces of tape to hold the stencil in place on the parchment (no tape is needed if using a silicone baking mat). Use a small offset spatula to spread the batter over each of the cutouts. Then remove the tape, hold down the parchment, and carefully lift off the stencil, starting from the bottom. Scrape any excess batter on the stencil back into the bowl.

Continues

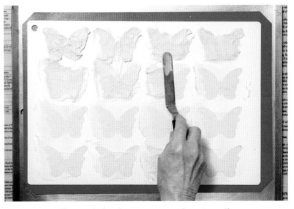
Spread the batter over the stencil.

Carefully lift off the stencil.

BAKE THE COOKIES

5. **Bake piped cookies** for 6 minutes. Rotate the cookie sheet halfway around. Continue baking for 4 to 6 minutes, or until the cookies are browned around the edges and firm to the touch.

Bake stenciled cookies for 3 minutes. Rotate the cookie sheet halfway around. Continue baking for 3 to 5 minutes, or until the cookies are browned around the edges and firm to the touch.

COOL THE COOKIES

6. Set the cookie sheet on a wire rack and let the cookies cool completely. Use a thin pancake turner to transfer the cookies to an airtight storage container.

7. Repeat with the remaining batch(es).

STORE Airtight: room temperature, 3 weeks; frozen, 2 months.

Baking Gems

♥ Stencils are available at JB Prince, jbprince.com.

♥ Silicone baking mats are my first choice for the thin butterfly cookies because they will hold the stencil firmly in place and will not lift up when you remove the stencil. And, unlike parchment, they will not wrinkle, so the cookies bake perfectly flat, with no rippling.

♥ Traditionally, langues de chats are piped pencil-thin, using a ¼ inch round decorating tip. I prefer a wider cookie that resembles Pepperidge Farm Milanos (see Variation).

♥ The batter for piped cookies needs more flour to be stiff enough to yield an even shape on baking.

VARIATION
"Milano" Sandwich Cookies

Arrange the cookies in matched pairs, flat sides up.

You will need 57 grams / 2 ounces of dark chocolate, coarsely chopped, to sandwich the cookies with a hairline thin layer of melted chocolate.

In a small microwavable bowl, heat the chocolate, stirring every 15 seconds with a silicone spatula, until almost completely melted (or heat the chocolate in the top of a double boiler set over hot, not simmering, water—do not let the bottom of the container touch the water—stirring often, until almost completely melted).

Remove the chocolate from the heat source and stir until fully melted (see Baking Gems).

Using an offset spatula, apply a very thin layer of melted chocolate to the bottom of a cookie, coming as close as possible to the edges. (Work with one cookie at a time so that the chocolate stays melted.) Gently set the second cookie of the pair, flat side down, on top.

Baking Gems

♥ You need to quick-temper the chocolate by removing it from the heat before it is fully melted and then stirring until it is melted and the temperature is no higher than 94°F / 34°C. This will keep the chocolate from "blooming" (forming gray streaks) and will give it a sharp snap when you bite into it.

♥ Keep the chocolate warm and in temper as you work by placing the container on a heating pad wrapped with foil and set to the lowest temperature, or by setting it over a bowl of warm water (no warmer than 120°F / 49°C). Stir often to equalize and maintain the temperature.

FRENCH TUILES

Makes: Fifty 3½ inch curved cookies

I learned to make tuiles during a visit to Maurice Bernachon's bakery in Lyon, France, when I was translating his cookbook *La Passion du Chocolat* into English. *Tuiles* means tiles in English, and the cookies are said to resemble Spanish roof tiles.

I loved Bernachon's formula, which used an equal weight of almonds and sugar, a convention French bakers call *tant pour tant*. It has been over thirty years since my translation was published, and I have only recently worked out how to make the batter in a food processor, which makes it very easy to prepare. The only challenge with these cookies is keeping them warm and flexible so that they can curve without cracking. The Bernachons used baguette pans as the molds, but a rolling pin works well if set on a towel to prevent it from rolling.

Oven Temperature: 350°F / 175°C	Baking Time: 10 to 12 minutes (for each of five batches)	Plan Ahead: It is preferable to let the tuile batter sit for 2 hours before baking.	Special Equipment: Two 17 by 14 inch cookie sheets, lined with silicone baking mats or lightly coated with melted butter or nonstick cooking spray; A rolling pin, lightly coated with nonstick cooking spray; Optional: A 1¼ inch cookie scoop or a disposable pastry bag fitted with a ¾ inch round pastry tube

BATTER *Makes: 800 grams*

5 large egg whites	150 grams	½ cup plus 2 tablespoons (148 ml)
pure vanilla extract	·	1 teaspoon (5 ml)
unsalted butter	65 grams	2½ tablespoons
sugar	250 grams	1¼ cups
blanched sliced almonds	250 grams	2½ cups
all-purpose flour, preferably bleached	100 grams	¾ cup (lightly spooned into the cup and leveled off) plus 1 tablespoon
fine sea salt	·	1/16 teaspoon (a pinch)

MISE EN PLACE

Thirty minutes to 1 hour ahead, into a 2 cup / 473 ml glass measure with a spout, weigh or measure the egg whites. Whisk in the vanilla extract. Cover tightly with plastic wrap and set on the counter.

Melt the butter and allow it to cool until no longer hot but still liquid.

MAKE THE BATTER
Food Processor Method

1. Process the sugar in a food processor for about 1 minute, or until very fine. Add the almonds, flour, and salt and process until the almonds are coarsely chopped.

Continues

2. Add about half the egg whites and pulse just until incorporated. Scrape down the sides of the bowl and pulse in the remaining egg whites. Scrape down the sides of the bowl.

3. Add the melted butter and pulse until incorporated.

Stand Mixer Method

1. In a spice mill, grind the sugar in batches until very fine. (Alternatively, use superfine sugar.)

2. Chop the almonds into medium-coarse pieces.

3. In a medium bowl, whisk together the almonds, flour, and salt.

4. In the bowl of a stand mixer fitted with the flat beater, beat the egg white mixture and sugar on medium speed for 2 to 3 minutes, until lighter in color and fluffy.

5. Add the almond mixture and beat on low speed just until incorporated, scraping down the sides of the bowl as needed.

6. Gradually beat in the melted butter just until incorporated.

Both Methods

7. Scrape the batter into a medium bowl. Cover it tightly and allow to sit at cool room temperature for 2 hours.

PREHEAT THE OVEN

Twenty minutes or longer before baking, set an oven rack at the middle level. Set the oven at 350°F / 175°C.

SHAPE THE COOKIES

8. Use the cookie scoop (slightly rounded scoops), a spoon, or the prepared pastry bag to dispense ten 1½ inch wide mounds of batter (16 grams each) at least 2½ inches apart onto a prepared cookie sheet. Use the back of a fork dipped in water to spread the mounds into 3 inch discs.

BAKE THE COOKIES

9. Bake for 5 minutes. Rotate the cookie sheet halfway around. Continue baking for 5 to 7 minutes, or until the cookies are golden and browned around the edges.

SHAPE AND COOL THE COOKIES

10. Working quickly, using a thin pancake turner, remove the cookies from the sheet one at a time and place them, top side up, over the rolling pin, removing each one as it firms. Cool completely (they will cool very quickly).

11. Repeat with the remaining 4 batches.

STORE Airtight low humidity: room temperature, 3 days.

Baking Gems

🤍 If some of the cookies are browning faster than others, remove them first and return the cookie sheet to the oven for a few seconds more to finish baking the remaining cookies.

🤍 If you are using a curved baguette pan as a mold, set the cookies top side down in it.

🤍 In order to be flexible to shape, the center of the tuiles are still a bit soft and are susceptible to humidity, and therefore could lose their shape if refrigerated or frozen.

LES BIARRITZ

Makes: Thirty 2½ inch round cookies

These cookies, flavorful with hazelnuts, are crisp yet slightly chewy when freshly baked. A dark chocolate coating is traditional, but the golden cookies are delicious even without it. They are as elegant as the famous beach resort on France's Atlantic Coast for which they are named. When I was working at the legendary patisserie Bernachon years ago (as I describe on page 99), these were my favorites.

Oven Temperature: 350°F / 175°C

Baking Time: About 10 minutes for the hazelnuts; 8 to 12 minutes for the cookies (for each of two batches)

Special Equipment: Two 17 by 14 inch cookie sheets, nonstick or very lightly coated with nonstick cooking spray; A large disposable pastry bag fitted with a 5⁄16 inch plain round decorating tube, or a teaspoon; Optional: A triangular cake decorating comb

BATTER *Makes: 290 grams*

unsalted butter	37 grams	2 tablespoons plus 2 teaspoons
1 extra-large egg white	37 grams	2½ tablespoons (37 ml)
cream of tartar	·	⅛ teaspoon
water	237 grams	1 cup (237 ml)
baking soda	16.5 grams	1 tablespoon
hazelnuts	62 grams	½ cup minus 1 tablespoon
all-purpose flour, preferably bleached	50 grams	⅓ cup (lightly spooned into the cup and leveled off) plus 1 tablespoon
superfine sugar	62 grams	¼ cup plus 1 tablespoon, *divided*
fine sea salt	·	1⁄16 teaspoon (a pinch)
milk	60 grams	¼ cup (59 ml)
pure vanilla extract	·	½ teaspoon (2.5 ml)

PREHEAT THE OVEN

Twenty minutes or longer before baking, set an oven rack at the middle level. Set the oven at 350°F / 175°C.

MISE EN PLACE

Thirty minutes to 1 hour ahead, cut the butter into 3 pieces. Set on the counter to soften.

Thirty minutes to 1 hour ahead, into a small mixing bowl, weigh or measure the egg white. Add the cream of tartar, cover tightly with plastic wrap, and set on the counter.

Have ready a colander placed in the sink and a large bowl filled half full with cold water.

REMOVE THE HAZELNUT SKINS

1. In a medium saucepan, bring the water to a boil. Remove from the heat and stir in the baking soda. The water will bubble vigorously.

2. Add the hazelnuts and return the pan to the heat. Boil for 3 minutes. The water will turn a deep maroon from the color of the skins. Test a nut by

Continues

running it under cold water. The skin should slip off easily. If necessary, boil the nuts for a couple of minutes longer.

3. Pour the nuts into the colander and rinse them under cold running water. Place the nuts in the bowl of cold water. Use both hands to slide off the skins under water. As each nut is peeled, set it on a clean towel to dry. Then roll and rub the nuts around in the towel to dry them.

TOAST THE HAZELNUTS
4. Spread the hazelnuts evenly on a rimmed baking sheet and bake for about 10 minutes, until their oils rise to the surface and they become slightly shiny and turn a deep golden brown. Shake the pan two or three times to ensure even toasting. Set the baking sheet on a wire rack and cool completely.

MAKE THE BATTER
5. In a food processor, process the hazelnuts with the flour, 12 grams / 1 tablespoon of the sugar, and the salt until finely chopped.

6. Add the milk and vanilla and pulse just to combine. Scrape down the sides of the bowl.

7. Add the butter and pulse several times to combine well. Scrape the mixture into a large bowl.

8. With a handheld mixer, beat the egg white mixture on medium-low speed until foamy. Raise the speed to medium-high and beat until soft peaks form when the beater is raised slowly. Raise the speed to high and gradually beat in the remaining 50 grams / ¼ cup sugar, then continue beating until very stiff but gently curved peaks form when the beater is raised slowly.

9. Stir about 2 tablespoons of the meringue into the nut mixture to lighten it. Using a large silicone spatula, scrape in the rest of the meringue and gently but thoroughly fold it in until evenly combined.

PIPE THE COOKIES
10. Scoop the batter into the prepared pastry bag and pipe fifteen 1¼ inch wide rounds (about 8 grams each) of the batter onto one of the prepared cookie sheets, leaving about 2 inches between them (pipe 3 rows of 5 each). (Alternatively, use a teaspoon to dispense the batter.) Tap the cookie sheet on the counter several times to spread and flatten the batter into 2 inch discs. If necessary, use a small offset metal spatula to widen them.

BAKE THE COOKIES
11. Bake the cookies for 5 minutes. Rotate the cookie sheet halfway around. Continue baking for 3 to 7 minutes, or until the cookies begin to brown around the edges and are set but feel just slightly soft to the touch when pressed in the centers.

12. While the cookies are baking, pipe the rest of the batter onto the second cookie sheet; set it in the oven after the first batch comes out.

COOL THE BIARRITZ
13. Allow the Biarritz to cool on the cookie sheet for about 5 minutes before transferring them to wire racks to finish cooling. Carefully slip a small offset spatula under the edges of each cookie, and it will lift off the sheet easily. Transfer them onto a wire rack to cool completely.

DARK CHOCOLATE COATING

dark chocolate, 60% to 62% cacao	213 grams (7.5 ounces)

MAKE THE CHOCOLATE COATING
14. In a small microwavable bowl, heat the chocolate, stirring every 15 seconds with a silicone spatula, until almost completely melted (or heat the chocolate in the top of a double boiler set over hot, not simmering, water—do not let the bottom of the container touch the water—stirring often, until almost completely melted).

Continues

Remove the chocolate from the heat source and stir until fully melted (see Baking Gems).

GLAZE THE BIARRITZ

15. Using an offset spatula, apply a thick, smooth layer of melted chocolate onto the flat bottom of each Biarritz. If you like, just before the chocolate sets and starts to dull, use the decorating comb to make an attractive wavy design. (Alternatively, you can sandwich the cookies with the melted chocolate; you will end up with half the number of cookies.)

STORE Airtight, layered between sheets of parchment: room temperature, 1 month; frozen, 3 months.

Baking Gems

♥ The Biarritz have the best shape when baked on nonstick cookie sheets, which give them a very slightly rounded edge.

♥ The hazelnuts will have the best flavor if they are toasted until deep golden brown.

♥ I do not advise making a larger batch of this batter, because the meringue will start to lose air and the cookies will have a denser texture.

♥ The unglazed Biarritz freeze well; the chocolate glaze will have the best appearance if applied after they are thawed.

♥ You need to quick-temper the chocolate by removing it from the heat before it is fully melted and then stirring until it is completely melted and the temperature is no higher than 94°F / 34°C. This will keep the chocolate from "blooming" (forming gray streaks) and will give it a sharp snap when you bite into it.

♥ Keep the chocolate warm and in temper as you work by placing the container on a heating pad wrapped with foil and set to the lowest temperature, or by setting it over a bowl of warm water (no warmer than 120°F / 49°C). Stir often to equalize and maintain the temperature.

CHURRO NUGGETS

Makes: Twenty-eight 1 to 1¼ inch round churros

Churros are a favorite deep-fried treat usually shaped as slender crunchy cylinders, rolled in cinnamon sugar, and served warm. Woody developed these little nuggets that are easier to make. The craggy round shapes, with their thin outer shells and incredibly light and melt-in-the-mouth interiors also lend themselves to a filling of creamy, flavorful cajeta (see the Variations, page 107).

Frying Temperature: 350°F / 175°C

Frying Time: 6 to 7 minutes (for each of two batches)

Special Equipment: A slotted skimmer or slotted spoon

BATTER *Makes: 320 grams / 1¼ cups*

unsalted butter	57 grams	4 tablespoons (½ stick)
2 large eggs	100 grams	⅓ cup plus 1 tablespoon (94 ml)
unbleached all-purpose flour	106 grams	¾ cup (lightly spooned into the cup and leveled off) plus 2 tablespoons, *divided*
ground cinnamon	·	¼ teaspoon
fine sea salt	·	⅛ teaspoon
cold water	118 grams	½ cup (118 ml)
frying oil, preferably canola	645 grams	3 cups (711 ml)

MISE EN PLACE

Thirty minutes ahead, cut the butter into tablespoon-size pieces. Set on the counter to soften.

Thirty minutes ahead, into a 1 cup / 237 ml glass measure with a spout, weigh or measure the eggs. Whisk lightly, cover tightly with plastic wrap, and set on the counter.

MAKE THE BATTER

1. In a small bowl, whisk together 76 grams / ½ cup plus 2 tablespoons of the flour, the cinnamon, and salt.

2. Place the remaining 30 grams / ¼ cup flour in a large custard cup or shallow bowl for coating the nuggets.

3. In a medium saucepan, combine the water and butter. Bring to a rolling boil over medium heat, stirring constantly with a silicone spatula, and boil until the butter has melted.

4. Remove the pan from the heat and add the flour mixture all at once, stirring constantly until it is moistened. Then use the silicone spatula to fold and mash in the flour mixture until it is completely incorporated.

5. Return the pan to the cooktop and stir the mixture constantly until the dough is shiny and uniform in consistency (similar to cream puff pastry dough).

6. Remove the pan from the heat and transfer the dough to a medium bowl. Spread the dough onto the sides and bottom of the bowl to speed cooling and set aside to cool for 20 to 30 minutes, or just until warm to the touch.

7. With a handheld mixer on medium speed, add the eggs to the dough in two parts, beating until the mixture becomes smooth and thick, similar to the consistency of peanut butter.

8. Cover tightly with plastic wrap and set the bowl in the refrigerator. Let the dough cool to 65° to

Continues

70°F / 18° to 21°C, stirring occasionally; it should be stiff but sticky.

The dough can be refrigerated for up to 2 days before shaping and frying.

HEAT THE OIL

Ten minutes or longer before frying, in a medium heavy saucepan, heat the oil over medium-high heat to 350°F / 175°C.

Set the slotted skimmer and a couple of paper towels on a cookie sheet near the cooktop.

SHAPE AND FRY THE CHURRO NUGGETS

Flour your fingers with some of the reserved flour.

9. Work with one piece of dough at a time: Use a tablespoon to scoop out a piece of dough (about ½ tablespoon / 10 to 11 grams) and, with your fingers, roll the dough into a ¾ inch ball.

10. Roll the dough ball in the reserved flour to coat it lightly, then set it on a plate.

11. Continue scooping, rolling, and flouring until you have 14 dough balls.

12. Carefully drop the dough balls into the hot oil. Fry for 2 minutes. (You will need to adjust the heat to keep the oil at around the correct temperature.)

13. Continue frying for another 4 to 5 minutes, using the slotted skimmer to submerge the dough balls gently and turn them over so they fry as evenly as possible on all sides, until they are golden brown.

14. With the slotted skimmer, lift out the churro nuggets, draining the oil back into the pot, and transfer them to the paper towels.

COOL THE CHURRO NUGGETS

15. Let the churro nuggets cool for a few minutes. Then, with the paper towels, roll and pat them to remove as much excess oil as possible. If necessary, transfer to another set of paper towels.

16. Repeat with the second batch.

17. Cool the churros just until warm to the touch.

CINNAMON SUGAR COATING

sugar	50 grams	¼ cup
ground cinnamon	·	½ teaspoon

18. In a small shallow bowl, whisk together the sugar and cinnamon.

19. Roll the nuggets in the cinnamon sugar to coat lightly. Sugar only as many as you plan to serve, because on storage, the sugar would make them soggy.

Churros taste best when freshly made and still warm.

STORE Airtight: room temperature, 2 days (without the cinnamon sugar).

Baking Gem

♥ Stored unsugared churro nuggets can be reheated on a cookie sheet in a preheated 400°F / 200°C oven for a few minutes. Set them on paper towels and then roll them in the cinnamon sugar.

VARIATIONS

Cajeta-Filled Churro Nuggets

With the tip of a small knife, make a shallow ¼ inch hole in each nugget. Use a small pastry bag, fitted with a ¼ inch round decorating tip to pipe about ½ teaspoon of Cajeta (see page 395) into each nugget.

Piped Churro Nuggets

You can also use a pastry bag fitted with a ½ inch round or star pastry tube to pipe the churro nuggets. Carefully pipe the mixture directly into the hot oil, using scissors to cut off ½ inch lengths as you go. You will not need the extra 30 grams / ¼ cup of flour for dusting the churros with this method, so the churros will be a little lighter in texture.

CHAPTER 3

SHAPED
BY HAND

ROSE'S CRESCENTS

Makes: Thirty 2½ inch by 1 inch cookies

I first made this totally exquisite cookie almost sixty years ago—it was my first cookie success. The high proportion of ground almonds to flour (1 part almonds to 3 parts flour) makes this buttery cookie perfectly tender and delicate without falling apart. It remains one of my top favorites; in fact, if I had just one cookie to crave, this would be it.

Oven Temperature: 325°F / 160°C

Baking Time: 14 to 16 minutes (for each of two batches)

Special Equipment: Two 17 by 14 inch cookie sheets, no preparation needed or lined with parchment

DOUGH *Makes: 280 grams*

unsalted butter	113 grams	8 tablespoons (1 stick)
blanched sliced almonds	28 grams	¼ cup plus ½ tablespoon
sugar, preferably superfine	33 grams	2 tablespoons plus 2 teaspoons
bleached all-purpose flour	118 grams	1 cup (lightly spooned into the cup and leveled off) minus 1 teaspoon
fine sea salt	·	⅛ teaspoon

MISE EN PLACE

Thirty minutes to 1 hour ahead, cut the butter into tablespoon-size pieces. Set on the counter to soften.

MAKE THE DOUGH

Food Processor Method

1. In a food processor, process the almonds and sugar until the almonds are ground very fine.

2. With the motor running, add the butter one piece at a time. Scrape down the sides of the bowl.

3. Add the flour, sprinkle the salt on top, and pulse in just until incorporated.

Stand Mixer Method

1. Grind the almonds in a spice mill with a little of the sugar, or use a rotary nut grinder.

2. In the bowl of a stand mixer fitted with the flat beater, beat the butter, almonds, and (remaining) sugar on medium speed for 2 to 3 minutes, until lighter in color and fluffy.

3. Add the flour, sprinkle the salt evenly on top, and beat on low speed just until incorporated. Scrape down the sides of the bowl.

Both Methods

4. Scrape the soft, sticky dough onto a sheet of plastic wrap. Press it into a thick disc. Wrap and refrigerate for 1 to 2 hours, or until the dough is firm.

PREHEAT THE OVEN

Twenty minutes or longer before baking, set an oven rack at the middle level. Set the oven at 325°F / 160°C.

Continues

CINNAMON SUGAR TOPPING

superfine sugar	50 grams	¼ cup
ground cinnamon	·	¼ teaspoon

5. In a small wide bowl whisk together the sugar and cinnamon.

SHAPE THE DOUGH

6. Divide the dough into quarters (about 70 grams each). Rewrap three of the pieces and refrigerate them while you shape the first piece.

7. Allow the first piece of dough to sit at room temperature for about 10 minutes, or until softened slightly. Then knead it between floured hands until malleable.

8. Pinch off ½ tablespoons of dough (about 9 grams each) and roll each piece into a 1 inch ball.

9. Spoon a little flour into a custard cup. Gently roll each ball in the flour to coat it lightly, then roll it on a lightly floured dough mat or counter into a cylinder about 2½ inches long, tapering the ends. Gently curve each cylinder into a crescent shape, and place the crescents a minimum of 1 inch apart on a cookie sheet. Cover lightly with plastic wrap.

10. Repeat with the second piece of dough to fill the cookie sheet.

BAKE THE COOKIES

11. Bake for 8 minutes. Rotate the cookie sheet halfway around. Continue baking for 6 to 8 minutes, or until the cookies are firm to the touch but not beginning to brown.

COOL AND COAT THE COOKIES

12. Set the cookie sheet on a wire rack and let the cookies cool for 5 minutes, until just warm.

13. Use a thin pancake turner to lift each cookie and gently dip it on both sides in the cinnamon sugar topping, then transfer to another wire rack. Cool completely.

14. Repeat with the second batch, using the remaining pieces of dough.

STORE Airtight: room temperature, 3 weeks; refrigerated, 1 month; frozen, 3 months.

Baking Gem

♥ Superfine sugar makes a finer texture and coating for this delicate cookie. If you don't have it, you can process granulated sugar for a few minutes in a food processor until it is as fine as sand.

MELTING MOMENTS

Makes: Twenty-four 2½ inch crescent cookies

There is a reason these are called "melting." Of all the cookies I know, they are the most dissolving in the mouth. They have the most delicate crumb when made with cassava starch but are almost as lovely in texture when made with cornstarch. They are actually very similar in makeup to Alfajores (page 177), but with almost three times the butter and no egg.

Oven Temperature: 375°F / 190°C | **Baking Time:** 10 to 15 minutes (for each of two batches) | **Special Equipment:** Two 17 by 14 inch cookie sheets, lined with parchment

DOUGH *Makes: 248 grams*

unsalted butter	113 grams	8 tablespoons (1 stick)
cassava starch (ground tapioca) or cornstarch	60 grams	½ cup (sifted, then lightly spooned into the cup and leveled off)
all-purpose flour, preferably bleached	57 grams	½ cup (lightly spooned into the cup and leveled off) minus 1 teaspoon
fine sea salt	·	1/16 teaspoon (a pinch)
powdered sugar	29 grams	¼ cup (lightly spooned into the cup and leveled off)
pure vanilla extract	·	½ teaspoon (2.5 ml)
powdered sugar, for dusting	57 grams	½ cup (lightly spooned into the cup and leveled off)

MISE EN PLACE

Thirty minutes to 1 hour ahead, cut the butter into tablespoon-size pieces. Set on the counter to soften.

In a medium bowl, whisk together the cassava, flour, and salt.

MAKE THE DOUGH

Food Processor Method

1. In a food processor, process the sugar for about a minute, until smooth and lump free.

2. With the motor running, add the butter one piece at a time, processing until smooth and creamy. Scrape down the sides of the bowl as needed.

3. Pulse in the vanilla extract.

4. Add the cassava mixture and pulse a few times to begin to incorporate it. Scrape down the sides of the bowl and process for about 5 seconds more, just until the dough is in crumbly pieces. (If processed longer, the dough will be harder to scrape out of the bowl.)

Stand Mixer Method

1. In the bowl of a stand mixer fitted with the flat beater, beat the butter and sugar on medium speed for 2 to 3 minutes, until lighter in color and fluffy.

2. On low speed, gradually beat in the cassava mixture just until incorporated, scraping down the sides of the bowl as needed.

3. Beat in the vanilla extract.

Continues

Both Methods

5. Scrape the dough onto a piece of plastic wrap. Use the plastic wrap to shape it into a flat disc. Wrap the dough and refrigerate it for 1 to 2 hours.

PREHEAT THE OVEN

Thirty minutes or longer before baking, set an oven rack at the middle level. Set the oven at 375°F / 190°C.

6. Divide the dough into quarters (about 62 grams each). Work with one piece at a time, keeping the rest of the dough covered in a cool spot or the refrigerator.

SHAPE THE DOUGH

7. Knead the piece of dough lightly to make it malleable. Gently roll the dough with floured hands on a floured dough mat or countertop into a ½ inch thick rope. Add more flour as needed to prevent sticking.

8. Cut the rope into 2½ inch long pieces and place them a minimum of 1½ inches apart on a prepared cookie sheet. Curve them slightly into crescent shapes. Knead any leftover dough into the next portion.

9. Shape the rest of the dough, setting 12 cookies on each sheet. Cover one sheet with plastic wrap and refrigerate it while you bake the first batch.

BAKE THE COOKIES

10. Bake for 7 minutes. Rotate the pan halfway around. Continue baking for 3 to 8 minutes, or just until the bottom edges of the cookies begin to brown.

COOL THE COOKIES

11. Set the cookie sheet on a wire rack and let the cookies cool for about 3 minutes, until firm enough to lift from the sheet. Lay a sheet of

parchment on the counter and place another wire rack on top. Use a thin pancake turner to transfer the cookies to the wire rack.

12. Bake the second batch of cookies. While they are baking, dust the first batch with powdered sugar (see below).

DUST THE COOKIES WITH POWDERED SUGAR

13. Spoon half of the powdered sugar for dusting into a fine-mesh strainer and coat the baked cookies. After giving them a first coat, repeat, dusting them with a second coat so that they are more evenly coated with the sugar.

14. Cool the second batch as directed and dust with the remaining powdered sugar. Allow the cookies to cool completely.

15. Lift away the rack (with the cookies) and sift any remaining sugar onto the parchment. Set the cookies on top of the parchment to coat the bottoms with the sugar.

STORE THE COOKIES

16. Layer the cookies in a container between sheets of parchment, dusting each layer with powdered sugar. To keep moisture from softening the sugar and making it sticky, leave the container uncovered for 8 hours before covering it tightly. This will maintain the powdery sugar coating.

For the best appearance, dust the cookies again lightly before serving.

STORE Airtight: room temperature, 1 month.

VARIATIONS

The traditional shape for Melting Moments is a ball. One inch balls need to bake for 10 to 12 minutes, or until firm and golden and just beginning to brown at the bottom.

Continues

Chocolate-Dipped Melting Moments

MELT THE CHOCOLATE

Coarsely chop about 85 grams / 3 ounces of dark chocolate.

In a small microwavable bowl, heat the chocolate, stirring every 15 seconds with a silicone spatula, until almost completely melted (or heat the chocolate in the top of a double boiler set over hot, not simmering, water—do not let the bottom of the container touch the water—stirring often, until almost completely melted).

Remove the chocolate from the heat source and stir until fully melted (see Baking Gems).

Lay sheets of aluminum foil or parchment on the counter. Lightly brush away the powdered sugar from one end of a crescent and dip that end into the chocolate. (When dipping the cookies, tilt the container so that all of the chocolate collects in one corner.) Gently tap the chocolate-dipped end against the back of the silicone spatula to remove excess chocolate. Set the cookie on the foil and push it forward a tiny bit to cover any chocolate spread. Repeat with the remaining cookies. When the chocolate sets, it will dull and harden.

The chocolate dipped melting moments will have their best appearance within 3 weeks after dipping.

Baking Gems

♥ You need to quick-temper the chocolate by removing it from the heat before it is fully melted and then stirring until it is completely melted and the temperature is no higher than 94°F / 34°C. This will keep the chocolate from "blooming" (forming gray streaks) and will give it a sharp snap when you bite into it.

♥ Keep the chocolate warm and in temper as you work by placing the container on a heating pad wrapped with foil and set to the lowest temperature, or by setting it over a bowl of warm water (no warmer than 120°F / 49°C). Stir often to equalize and maintain the temperature.

MRS. SWALLOWS'S PERFECT LEMON COOKIES

Makes: Twelve 3 inch round sandwich cookies

These extraordinary cookies have a sweet meringue-like crunch, but the sweetness of the sugar is tempered by the lemon in the dough and a gilding of tart lemon curd filling. The recipe was given to me by an old friend from my childhood, Colin Streeter, whose family hailed from England. It was handed down from Colin's grandmother's cook, Mrs. Grace Swallows, and enhanced by Colin's clever addition of lemon juice, lemon oil, and a whisper of cardamom and by sandwiching the cookies with lemon curd.

Oven Temperature:
350°F / 175°C

Baking Time: 12 to 15 minutes
(for each of two batches)

Special Equipment: Two 17 by 14 inch cookie sheets, lined with parchment; Two cardboard tubes from rolls of paper towels (1⅝ inch inside diameter); A sharp heavy knife with a 1½ to 2 inch wide blade

DOUGH *Makes: 520 grams*

unsalted butter	113 grams	8 tablespoons (1 stick)	lemon zest, finely grated (1 large lemon)	4 grams	2 teaspoons (loosely packed)
1 large egg	50 grams	3 tablespoons plus ½ teaspoon (47.5 ml)	lemon juice, freshly squeezed and strained	16 grams	1 tablespoon (15 ml)
pure vanilla extract	·	⅛ teaspoon (0.6 ml)	lemon oil, preferably Boyajian (or lemon extract)	·	4 drops (¼ teaspoon / 1.25 ml)
unbleached all-purpose flour	140 grams	1 cup (lightly spooned into the cup and leveled off) plus 2 tablespoons	granulated sugar	200 grams	1 cup
cornstarch	9 grams	1 tablespoon	½ recipe Lemon Curd (page 403)	177 grams	⅔ cup
baking powder, preferably an aluminum-free variety	4.5 grams	1 teaspoon	powdered sugar, for dusting	9 grams	1½ tablespoons
ground cardamom	·	¼ teaspoon			

Continues

MISE EN PLACE

Thirty minutes to 1 hour ahead, cut the butter into tablespoon-size pieces. Set on the counter to soften.

Into a 1 cup / 237 ml glass measure with a spout, weigh or measure the egg. Whisk in the vanilla extract. Cover tightly with plastic wrap and set on the counter.

In a medium bowl, whisk together the flour, cornstarch, baking powder, and cardamom.

With dishwashing liquid, wash, rinse, and dry the lemon, then zest it.

Into a small bowl, weigh or measure the lemon juice. Stir in the zest and lemon oil. Cover with plastic wrap and set on the counter.

Cut the cardboard tubes into four 4 inch lengths (discard the excess).

MAKE THE DOUGH

1. In the bowl of a stand mixer fitted with the flat beater, beat the butter and granulated sugar on medium speed for 2 to 3 minutes, until lighter in color and fluffy.

2. Add the lemon juice mixture and, starting on low speed and increasing to medium, beat for a few seconds, until incorporated.

3. On low speed, gradually add the egg mixture, beating until incorporated. Scrape down the sides of the bowl.

4. Gradually beat in the flour mixture just until incorporated, scraping down the sides of the bowl as needed. The dough will be very soft and sticky.

5. Scrape the dough onto a sheet of plastic wrap. Lay a second piece of plastic wrap on top and flatten the dough into a rectangle about 8 by 6 inches. Slip it onto a baking sheet and refrigerate it to firm for at least 30 minutes. (An instant-read thermometer inserted in the chilled dough should read about 60°F / 15°C.)

SHAPE THE DOUGH INTO LOGS

6. Divide the dough into quarters (about 130 grams each). Wrap each piece in plastic wrap. Work with one piece at a time, keeping the rest refrigerated.

7. Use the plastic wrap to shape the dough, adding a little flour as necessary to keep it from sticking: Roll the dough into a log just under 1⅝ inches in diameter and about 3½ inches long. Lightly tamp each end on the countertop to flatten it.

8. Wrap the dough log in the plastic wrap and slide it into one of the cardboard tubes. Stand the tube on end on the countertop. With your fingers, press the dough log down until it reaches the bottom and fits snugly into the tube. Wrap the tube with plastic wrap to keep the dough from slipping out and stand it on end in the freezer. Repeat with the other three pieces of dough. (Alternatively, if not using cardboard tubes, roll the dough into logs about 1⅝ inches in diameter. Wrap and freeze them for 30 minutes; remove them from the freezer, and quickly roll them again to minimize flattening. Then stand the logs on end in the freezer again.)

9. Freeze the dough logs for a minimum of 1 hour so that they are firm enough to cut.

The dough logs can be frozen for up to 3 months.

PREHEAT THE OVEN

Twenty minutes or longer before baking, set an oven rack at the middle level. Set the oven at 350°F / 175°C.

CUT THE COOKIES

10. Remove one of the frozen dough logs from the freezer and let it soften slightly if necessary. Cut into 6 slices (each ½ inch thick). While you are cutting the dough, the log will start to flatten; simply roll it lightly to maintain the round shape. Set the dough rounds on a prepared

Continues

cookie sheet as you cut them, spacing them 2 inches apart. Smooth any rough edges with your fingertips. Repeat with a second dough log.

BAKE THE COOKIES

11. Bake for 7 minutes. Rotate the cookie sheet halfway around. Continue baking for 5 to 8 minutes, or until the cookies are beginning to brown around the edges and feel just a little soft when pressed lightly with a fingertip.

COOL THE COOKIES

12. Set the cookie sheet on a wire rack and let the cookies cool completely on the cookie sheet; this will allow them to be removed cleanly. Use a thin pancake turner to transfer the cookies to another cookie sheet if you are ready to fill them, or transfer to a storage container.

13. Repeat with the second batch.

SANDWICH THE COOKIES

Fill the cookies as close to serving as possible to prevent softening, and dust with the powdered sugar shortly before serving to keep the sugar from being absorbed into the cookies.

14. Use an offset spatula to spread a thin layer of lemon curd onto the bottom sides of half the cookies. Set the remaining cookies on top, bottom side down, to create sandwiches. Press gently so that the lemon curd oozes a little beyond the edges.

DUST WITH THE POWDERED SUGAR

15. Set a piece of parchment on the countertop. Place the cookies on top. Spoon the powdered sugar into a fine-mesh strainer. Dust each cookie lightly with powdered sugar.

STORE Filled, airtight: room temperature, 3 hours; frozen, 3 months.
Unfilled, airtight: room temperature, 1 month; frozen, 3 months.

SOFT SESAME CYLINDERS

Makes: Twenty 2¼ inch round cookies (2½ inch if shaped free-form)

Pastry chef and dear friend Miro Uskokovic created this deeply satisfying, dense-with-sesame cookie. For shaping, he likes using pastry rings to make it easier to pack the cookies, which is also my preference, because the cookies then bake evenly and look so unusual and appealing. But you can also shape them free-form, which gives them a lovely slightly rounded shape.

Oven Temperature:	Baking Time: 12 to 15	Special Equipment: Two 17 by 14 inch cookie sheets, no
350°F / 175°C	minutes (for each of two batches)	preparation needed or lined with parchment; Optional: Ten or more 2⅜ inch pastry rings (⅝ inch high), see Baking Gems

DOUGH *Makes: 600 grams*

unsalted butter	142 grams	10 tablespoons (1¼ sticks)
tahini	110 grams	¼ cup plus 2½ tablespoons (stirred before measuring)
½ large egg, lightly beaten before measuring	25 grams	1½ tablespoons (22.5 ml)
hulled sesame seeds, for coating	50 grams	⅓ cup plus 1 teaspoon
unbleached all-purpose flour, preferably King Arthur	181 grams	1½ cups (lightly spooned into the cup and leveled off)
bread flour, preferably King Arthur	38 grams	¼ cup (lightly spooned into the cup and leveled off) plus 2 teaspoons
baking soda	·	¼ teaspoon
fine sea salt	·	¼ teaspoon
sugar	106 grams	½ cup plus ½ tablespoon

MISE EN PLACE

One hour ahead, cut the butter into tablespoon-size pieces. Set on the counter to soften.

One hour ahead, stir the tahini until any oil that has separated is integrated. Into a small bowl, weigh or measure the tahini. Cover tightly and set on the counter.

Thirty minutes ahead, into a 1 cup / 237 ml glass measure with a spout, weigh or measure the egg. Whisk lightly, cover tightly with plastic wrap, and set on the counter.

Into a small bowl, weigh or measure the sesame seeds and set on the counter.

MAKE THE DOUGH

1. In a medium bowl, whisk together the all-purpose and bread flours, baking soda, and salt.

2. In the bowl of a stand mixer fitted with the flat beater, beat the butter and sugar on medium speed for 1 to 2 minutes, until well mixed.

3. Add the tahini and beat until smoothly incorporated.

Continues

4. Gradually add the egg, beating until incorporated.

5. Add the flour mixture and beat on low speed just until the dough comes together. Scrape down the sides of the bowl and beat for a few seconds more.

6. Scrape the dough into a bowl. Cover and refrigerate for 30 minutes, or just until firm enough to shape. If the dough becomes too stiff, the cookies may develop cracks around the edges when baking.

PREHEAT THE OVEN

Twenty minutes or longer before baking, set an oven rack at the middle level. Set the oven at 350°F / 175°C.

SHAPE AND COAT THE DOUGH

7. Measure out 10 pieces of dough (2 level tablespoons / 30 grams each). One at a time, roll each piece of dough in the palms of your hands to form a 1½ inch ball. Set the ball in the bowl of sesame seeds and flatten it to about 2 inches in diameter. Turn it over and press it into the sesame seeds so both sides are coated lightly.

8. If using pastry rings, set them on a cookie sheet and press each sesame-coated piece of dough evenly into a ring. You can use your fingers or a cookie press to make them level. (Alternatively, set the dough rounds a minimum of 1½ inches apart on the cookie sheet.)

BAKE THE COOKIES

9. Bake for 8 minutes. Rotate the cookie sheet halfway around. Continue baking for 4 to 7 minutes, or until the cookies are lightly browned.

COOL THE COOKIES

10. Set the cookie sheet on a wire rack and, if using rings, let the cookies cool for about 10 minutes, or until the rings are cool enough to lift off. Or, if baking the cookies free-form, let them cool for 2 to 3 minutes, until firm enough to lift from the cookie sheet. Use a thin pancake turner to transfer the cookies to another wire rack. Cool completely.

11. Repeat with the second batch.

STORE Airtight: room temperature, 1 week.

Baking Gems

♥ You can substitute Japanese white sesame paste for the tahini, but I do not recommend Chinese sesame paste, because it is darker and more intense.

♥ For extra texture and flavor, Miro sometimes stirs about 30 grams (5 percent of the weight of the dough) crumbled halvah into the dough after mixing.

♥ Disposable pastry rings can be made easily from heavy-duty aluminum foil, or reusable rings can be cut from aluminum flashing (available at most hardware and home improvement stores); see page 297.

DATE CRESCENTS

Makes: Twenty-four 2½ inch long crescents

Chef David Shamah used to make this recipe with his Syrian grandmother. The dough is unlike any other I have experienced. Incredibly delicate, tender, and buttery, with a pleasingly slightly gritty texture from the semolina flour, it rolls like a dream and marries well with both sweet and savory fillings.

Oven Temperature: 350°F / 175°C

Baking Time: 14 to 15 minutes

Special Equipment: One 17 by 14 inch cookie sheet, no preparation needed or lined with parchment

SYRIAN PASTRY DOUGH

Makes: 300 grams

unsalted butter	113 grams	8 tablespoons (1 stick)
bleached all-purpose flour	70 grams	½ cup (lightly spooned into the cup and leveled off) plus 1 tablespoon
durum semolina flour	70 grams	½ cup (lightly spooned into the cup and leveled off) minus ½ tablespoon
fine sea salt	·	¼ teaspoon
warm water	55 grams	¼ cup minus 1 teaspoon (55 ml)

PREHEAT THE OVEN

Twenty minutes or longer before baking, set an oven rack at the middle level. Set the oven at 350°F / 175°C.

MISE EN PLACE

Thirty minutes to 1 hour ahead, cut the butter into tablespoon-size pieces. Set on the counter to soften.

MAKE THE DOUGH

1. In a medium bowl, whisk together the all-purpose flour, semolina flour, and salt until well mixed.

2. Add the butter and, with a fork, toss to coat it with the flour. Press the butter pieces between your fingers to form 1 inch wide flakes.

3. Sprinkle the warm water evenly on top of the mixture, stirring with a silicone spatula until it is moistened enough to hold together and form a rough dough with pieces of butter still visible throughout.

4. Scrape the dough onto a piece of plastic wrap. Dust it all over with a little flour, wrap it with the plastic wrap, and set it aside while you make the filling.

DATE FILLING AND SUGAR DUSTING

Makes: 152 grams / ½ cup filling

date spread (see Baking Gems)	152 grams	½ cup
ground cinnamon	·	¼ teaspoon
orange flower water (optional)	·	to taste (see Baking Gems)
walnuts (optional)	14 grams	about 2 tablespoons, chopped medium-fine
powdered sugar, for dusting	6 grams	1 tablespoon

Continues

MAKE THE DATE FILLING

1. Into a small bowl, weigh or measure the date spread.

2. Stir in the cinnamon and, if using, orange flower water to taste.

3. If using walnuts, stir them into the date mixture.

FILL AND SHAPE THE DOUGH

5. Pinch off 24 pieces of dough (about 12 grams each). Roll each piece of dough between the palms of your hands into a 1 inch ball.

6. Working with one piece at a time, on a lightly floured dough mat or counter, roll the dough into a 3 inch disc, flipping it over a few times in the flour to keep it from sticking.

7. Measure a level teaspoon (about 6 grams) of date mixture onto the upper third of the dough, near the edge. Pat the mixture into a rectangle about 1 by 2 inches.

8. Starting at the top, roll the filling up in the dough. Gently pinch the edges to seal them, then curve the ends into a crescent shape.

9. Set the crescents, seam side down, 1 inch apart on the cookie sheet.

BAKE THE CRESCENTS

10. Bake for 8 minutes. Rotate the cookie sheet halfway around. Continue baking for 6 to 7 minutes, until the ends of the crescents just start to brown. (An instant-read thermometer inserted into the pastry—not the filling—should read 212°F / 100°C.)

COOL THE CRESCENTS AND DUST WITH SUGAR

11. Set the cookie sheet on a wire rack and use a thin pancake turner to transfer the cookies to another wire rack. Cool completely.

12. Spoon the powdered sugar into a fine-mesh strainer and dust the cookies very lightly with the sugar before serving.

STORE Airtight: room temperature, 1 day; refrigerated, 5 days; frozen, 2 months.

Baking Gems

♥ Search out a fine-quality date spread, such as Lior.

♥ Orange flower water varies in flavor and intensity by brand, so it is best to start with ½ teaspoon / 2.5 ml and add more to taste.

DATE-NIGHT COOKIES

Makes: Twenty-eight 2¼ by 2¾ inch oval cookies

This treasured family recipe, originally called Date Nut Roll Cookies, was given to me by my friend Sally Longo. The cookie dough is rolled around a delicious date nut citrus filling. The cookies are crisp on the outside when first baked, but the sticky dates render them moist and chewy after storing (see Baking Gems).

Oven Temperature: 375°F / 190°C	**Baking Time:** 12 to 16 minutes (for each of two batches)

Plan Ahead: The dough has to be chilled for a minimum of 2 hours (or frozen briefly) before filling. The filled dough log needs to be frozen for a minimum of 3 hours before cutting and baking.

Special Equipment: Two 17 by 14 inch cookie sheets, nonstick or lightly coated with nonstick cooking spray

DOUGH *Makes: 275 grams*

unsalted butter	57 grams	4 tablespoons (½ stick)
½ large egg, lightly beaten before measuring	25 grams	1½ tablespoons (22.5 ml)
pure vanilla extract	·	½ tablespoon (7.5 ml)
bleached all-purpose flour	121 grams	1 cup (lightly spooned into the cup and leveled off)
light brown sugar, preferably Muscovado	54 grams	¼ cup (firmly packed)
baking powder, preferably an aluminum-free variety	·	¼ teaspoon
baking soda	·	¼ teaspoon
fine sea salt	·	1/16 teaspoon (a pinch)
milk	8 grams	½ tablespoon (7.5 ml)

MISE EN PLACE

One hour ahead or longer, cut the butter into tablespoon-size pieces. Set on the counter to soften.

Thirty minutes ahead, into a 1 cup / 237 ml glass measure with a spout, weigh or measure the egg. Whisk in the vanilla extract. Cover tightly with plastic wrap and set on the counter.

MAKE THE DOUGH

1. In the bowl of a stand mixer fitted with the flat beater, combine the butter, egg mixture, flour, brown sugar, baking powder, baking soda, salt, and milk. Starting on low speed and gradually increasing it to medium, beat until smooth and evenly blended.

2. Scrape the dough onto a large piece of plastic wrap. Knead it lightly just until it comes together smoothly, then flatten it to form a rectangle. Cover with another large piece of plastic wrap. Roll the dough into a 12 by 9 inch rectangle (about 1/16 inch thick). If the dough softens, slip it onto a cookie sheet and refrigerate it until firm enough to roll. Press along the edges of the plastic wrap to seal in the dough.

Continues

3. Slide a cookie sheet or cutting board under the dough and refrigerate for a minimum of 2 hours, up to overnight. (Alternatively, set it in the freezer until firm, then refrigerate it until ready to spread with the filling.)

DATE NUT FILLING

walnut or pecan halves	50 grams	½ cup
pitted dates, preferably medjool (about 20)	142 grams	1 cup plus 2 tablespoons
sugar	50 grams	¼ cup
orange zest, finely grated (see Baking Gems)	2 grams	1 teaspoon (loosely packed)
orange juice, freshly squeezed	60 grams	¼ cup (59 ml)

MAKE THE DATE NUT FILLING

1. Chop the nuts medium-fine.

2. Cut the dates into halves or thirds and place them in a food processor. Add the sugar and process the dates until finely chopped. (Alternatively, chop the dates using a sharp knife that has been lightly coated with nonstick cooking spray.)

3. Transfer the dates and sugar to a small saucepan and add the orange zest and orange juice. Bring to a boil over medium heat, stirring occasionally with a silicone spatula. Reduce the heat to a simmer and cook for about 3 minutes, until most of the liquid has been absorbed.

4. Remove from the heat, stir in the chopped nuts, and let cool completely. The filling should have a jam-like consistency. If necessary, add a little more orange juice to loosen it to a spreadable consistency.

MAKE THE DOUGH LOG

4. Slip the dough from the cookie sheet onto a counter so that one of the shorter sides faces you. Peel off the top sheet of plastic wrap and set it loosely back onto the dough. Using the bottom sheet of plastic wrap, flip the dough over and peel off the bottom sheet of plastic wrap.

5. Use a small offset spatula to spread the filling evenly over the dough, going almost all the way to the edges.

6. Starting at one of the shorter sides, using the plastic wrap to assist in lifting the dough, tightly roll up the dough. The dough log will be about 9½ inches long by 2 inches in diameter.

7. Divide the dough log into 2 equal lengths. Wrap each piece tightly with plastic wrap. Freeze for a minimum of 3 hours, up to 3 months; to maintain the round shape, set the dough logs on end in the freezer.

PREHEAT THE OVEN

Thirty minutes or longer before baking, set an oven rack at the middle level. Set the oven at 375°F / 190°C.

CUT THE DOUGH LOGS INTO COOKIES

8. Remove one of the frozen dough logs from the freezer and place it on a cutting board. Use a sharp knife to cut the roll in half. This dough softens very quickly, so wrap one of the halves in plastic wrap and return it to the freezer.

9. Mark the other half of the log into 1 inch long sections. Use the marks as guides to slice the log into seven ⅓ inch thick discs. While cutting the dough, the log will start to flatten. This creates an attractive oval shape, but if you prefer a round shape, simply roll it lightly after each cut.

10. Set the dough slices 1½ inches apart on a cookie sheet. Smooth any rough edges with a small metal spatula. Repeat with the other half of the dough log.

BAKE THE COOKIES

11. Bake for 7 minutes. Rotate the cookie sheet halfway around. Continue baking for 5 to 9 minutes, or until the cookies are lightly browned and puffed.

COOL THE COOKIES

12. Set the cookie sheet on a wire rack and use a thin pancake turner to transfer the cookies to another wire rack. Cool completely.

13. Repeat with the second batch.

STORE Airtight: room temperature, 1 month; frozen, 3 months.

Baking Gems

♥ Wash the orange with dishwashing liquid, rinse, and dry before zesting it.

♥ The cookies will be crispy after cooling. After being stored airtight for several hours, though, they will become soft from the moisture in the filling. If you prefer crisper cookies, do not seal them airtight. That will, however, shorten their shelf life.

CREAM CHEESE–BUTTER DOUGH FOR RUGELACH

This is not only my favorite piecrust dough, it also makes the best dough for rugelach (even if you use frozen dough scraps); use it to make the Apricot Walnut Rugelach on page 132. The scraps are also great for making Rosebuds (page 236). For maximum flakiness, keep the dough cool, and if it softens while working with it, refrigerate briefly. I like to use a reclosable freezer bag instead of my bare hands to knead the dough because it keeps the dough cooler and makes it easier to transfer in and out of the freezer, but using your hands is fine, especially if you wear latex gloves to keep the dough from sticking (see Baking Gems).

DOUGH *Makes: 312 grams*

unsalted butter, cold	85 grams	6 tablespoons (¾ stick)
pastry flour (or bleached all-purpose flour, see Baking Gems)	145 grams	1¼ cups (or 1 cup plus 2½ tablespoons) (lightly spooned into the cup and leveled off)
fine sea salt	·	¼ teaspoon
baking powder, preferably an aluminum-free variety	·	⅛ teaspoon
full-fat cream cheese, cold	64 grams	¼ cup
heavy cream	22 grams	1½ tablespoons (22.5 ml)
cider vinegar	·	½ tablespoon (7.5 ml)

MISE EN PLACE

For the Food Processor Method: Cut the butter into ½ inch cubes. Wrap in plastic wrap and freeze it for at least 30 minutes, until frozen solid.

For the Hand Method: Cut the butter into ½ inch cubes. Wrap in plastic wrap and refrigerate for at least 30 minutes. Place a medium bowl in the freezer.

For both methods: In a gallon-size reclosable freezer bag, combine the flour, salt, and baking powder. Freeze for at least 30 minutes.

MAKE THE DOUGH

Food Processor Method

1. Empty the flour mixture into the food processor (set the bag aside).

2. Cut the cream cheese into 3 or 4 pieces and add it to the flour. Process for about 20 seconds, or until the mixture resembles coarse meal.

3. Add the frozen butter cubes and pulse until none of the butter pieces is larger than the size of a pea. (Toss with a fork so you can see this better.)

4. Remove the cover and drizzle the cream and vinegar evenly over the flour mixture. Pulse until most of the butter pieces are the size of small peas. The mixture will be in particles and will not hold together unless pinched.

5. Spoon the mixture into the freezer bag.

Hand Method

1. Empty the flour mixture into the chilled bowl (set the bag aside). Whisk to combine.

2. Add the cream cheese and rub the mixture between your fingers to blend the cream cheese into the flour until it resembles coarse meal.

3. Spoon the mixture, together with the cold butter, back into the freezer bag. Express any air from the bag and close it.

4. With a rolling pin, flatten the butter into thin flakes. Place the bag in the freezer for at least 10 minutes, until the butter is very firm. Transfer the mixture back to the chilled bowl, scraping the sides of the bag. Set the bag aside. (Alternatively, instead of using the bag, you can use your fingers to flatten the butter into flakes.)

5. Sprinkle the mixture with the cream and vinegar, tossing lightly with a silicone spatula. Spoon the mixture back into the plastic bag.

Both Methods

6. With the bag open, hold either side of the bag at the opening and alternate using the heel of your hand and your knuckles to knead and press the mixture from the outside of the bag until most of it holds together in one piece.

7. Cut open the bag and empty the dough onto a large sheet of plastic wrap. Use the plastic wrap to continue kneading the dough just until it feels slightly stretchy when pulled.

8. Divide the dough in half (about 156 grams each). Use your hands and the plastic wrap to shape each piece of dough into a rough disc. Use a rolling pin to flatten each one into a 5 inch disc. With your hands, press in the edges, which tend to crack, to make them smooth. There should be thin flakes of butter throughout the dough. If there are any large pieces, smear them into the dough using the heel of your hand.

9. Wrap each disc in plastic wrap and refrigerate for a minimum of 45 minutes before using.

STORE Airtight: refrigerated, 2 days; frozen, 3 months.

Baking Gems

🤍 If using all-purpose flour, add 13 grams / 1 tablespoon sugar to the flour mixture to ensure equal tenderness. The cookies will brown a little more, and faster, if using unbleached all-purpose flour.

🤍 In place of the freezer bag and plastic wrap, latex gloves also work well to press together the dough directly on a lightly floured countertop, and also to shape the dough into a disc.

🤍 This recipe makes enough for a single-crust 9 inch pie or tart. Flatten the entire dough into a 6 to 7 inch disc before chilling. I always save dough scraps when making this pie dough and freeze them. When I have enough scraps to add up to about 156 grams, I make a half recipe of rugelach.

APRICOT WALNUT RUGELACH

Makes: Twenty-four 3 by 1½ by ¾ inch high cookies

Rugelach rules as one of the top cookies of all time. For my version, I use my favorite cream cheese–butter dough, which is tender, flaky, and flavorful. I love everything about this cookie, especially the sweet tang of the apricot preserves and golden raisin filling, and the crunch of walnuts against the buttery crust.

Oven Temperature:	Baking Time:	Special Equipment: Two 17 by 14 inch cookie sheets, lined with
350°F / 175°C	15 to 20 minutes (for each of two batches)	parchment or lightly coated with nonstick cooking spray; Two wire racks, one coated with nonstick cooking spray

COOKIE DOUGH

Cream Cheese–Butter Dough (page 130)	312 grams	1 recipe

FILLING

granulated sugar	37 grams	3 tablespoons
light brown sugar, preferably Muscovado	27 grams	2 tablespoons (firmly packed)
ground cinnamon	·	¼ teaspoon
golden raisins	54 grams	¼ cup plus 2 tablespoons
walnut halves	50 grams	½ cup
apricot preserves	104 grams	⅓ cup

MISE EN PLACE

In a medium bowl, using your fingers, mix together the sugars and cinnamon, pinching and flattening any lumps of brown sugar. Divide the mixture equally between two small bowls.

Cut the raisins in half or coarsely chop them. Divide them equally between two small bowls. (If they are not soft before cutting, soak them in 118 grams / ½ cup / 118 ml boiling water for about 30 minutes and drain well.)

Coarsely chop the walnuts and add half of them to each of the bowls of raisins.

Divide the apricot preserves between two more small bowls,. Mash them with a fork, or snip them with small scissors, to break up any large pieces.

ROLL THE DOUGH AND CUT THE TRIANGLES

1. Remove one piece of dough from the refrigerator and allow it to sit on the counter for 5 to 10 minutes, or until it is malleable enough to roll.

2. Using a floured rolling pin, on a floured dough mat or lightly floured surface, roll out the dough into a 10 to 11 inch circle; it will be less than ⅛ inch (³⁄₃₂ inch) thick (see Baking Gems). Rotate the dough often and add flour as necessary to ensure that it doesn't stick. If the dough becomes too soft or sticky at any time, briefly refrigerate it until it is firm enough to roll.

3. Use a pizza wheel or sharp knife to cut the dough into 12 triangles. (Cut the dough first into quarters and then cut each quarter into thirds; see Baking Gems.) Use a pair of small scissors or

Continues

a small sharp knife to make a ¼ inch notch in the middle of each triangle's outer edge.

4. Use a small offset spatula or the back of a tablespoon to spread the dough evenly with half the preserves, avoiding a 1 inch circle in the center of the dough (the preserves will push forward when rolling the dough triangles) and going only up to ¼ inch from the edges.

5. Sprinkle half the sugar mixture evenly over the preserves and scatter half the walnuts and raisins on top. Press them in gently.

6. If necessary, slip a thin knife blade or spatula under each piece of dough to loosen it from the surface. Starting at the wide ends, roll up the triangles, then bend the ends around to form a slight crescent shape, turning the ends toward the point.

CINNAMON SUGAR COATING

milk	15 grams	1 tablespoon (15 ml)
sugar	25 grams	2 tablespoons
ground cinnamon	·	1 teaspoon

7. Into a small bowl, pour the milk.

8. In a medium bowl, stir together the sugar and cinnamon.

COAT THE RUGELACH

9. Lift each rugelach with your fingers and, with a pastry feather or brush, coat it all over with milk. Then hold it over the bowl with the sugar mixture and sprinkle it all over, letting the excess sugar fall back into the bowl.

10. Place the rugelach, points underneath, about 1½ inches apart on a prepared cookie sheet, making sure that the ends are still curved.

11. Cover the rugelach with plastic wrap and refrigerate for a minimum of 30 minutes, up to overnight.

12. Repeat with the second batch.

PREHEAT THE OVEN

Twenty minutes or longer before baking, set an oven rack at the middle level. Set the oven at 350°F / 175°C.

BAKE THE RUGELACH

13. Bake the first batch for 10 minutes. Rotate the cookie sheet halfway around. Continue baking for 5 to 10 minutes, or until the rugelach are lightly browned.

COOL THE RUGELACH

14. Set the cookie sheet on the uncoated wire rack and let the rugelach cool for 2 minutes to firm slightly. During baking, a little of the preserves always melts out onto the parchment or pan, so you need to remove the rugelach before the preserves harden completely. Use a thin pancake turner to transfer the rugelach to the coated wire rack. Cool completely.

15. Repeat with the second batch.

STORE Airtight: room temperature, 5 days; frozen (baked or unbaked), 3 months (if baking from frozen, add about 5 minutes to the baking time).

Baking Gems

♥ Search out fine-quality apricot preserves, such as Darbo from Austria.

♥ I prefer rolling the dough under ⅛ inch for these cookies (as well as for most pies so I designed silicone Fast Tracks that are ³⁄₃₂ inch thick. Set them on two opposite sides of the dough when rolling to ensure the precise thickness throughout the dough.

♥ To cut the dough into 12 triangles, a 30-60-90-degree drafting / arts triangle is very helpful. After cutting the dough into quarters, use the triangle to cut each quarter into 3 equal wedges.

AUNT LIL'S MERINGUE RUGELACH

Makes: Twenty-four 3 by 1¼ by 1 inch high cookies

I have known and admired Bonnie Stern for close to half a century, since I first visited her at her cooking school in Toronto. When I saw her unusual recipe for her Aunt Lil's rugelach in the *Jewish Ledger,* I was intrigued. The pastry dough is crisp on the outside, slightly softer on the inside, and wonderfully tender. The small amount of yeast relaxes the dough, making rolling it a breeze, but the puff comes from the meringue filling. And the small amount of sugar in the dough makes it brown beautifully.

| **Oven Temperature:** 350°F / 175°C | **Baking Time:** 15 to 20 minutes (for each of two batches) | **Plan Ahead:** The dough needs to be made a minimum of 8 hours ahead. | **Special Equipment:** Two 17 by 14 inch cookie sheets, no preparation needed or lined with parchment; Two wire racks, one coated with nonstick cooking spray |

DOUGH *Makes: 280 grams*

unsalted butter	113 grams	8 tablespoons (1 stick)
1 (to 2) large egg, separated: 1 yolk (reserve 1 white for the meringue)	19 grams	1 tablespoon plus ½ teaspoon (17.5 ml)
water	30 grams	2 tablespoons (30 ml)
all-purpose flour, preferably unbleached	121 grams	1 cup (lightly spooned into the cup and leveled off)
sugar	4 grams	1 teaspoon
instant yeast	4 grams	1¼ teaspoons
fine sea salt	·	⅛ teaspoon

MISE EN PLACE

Thirty minutes ahead or longer, cut the butter into ½ inch cubes. Wrap and refrigerate.

Thirty minutes ahead, separate the egg: Into a small bowl, weigh or measure 1 egg white to equal 30 grams / 2 tablespoons / 30 ml for the meringue filling (see page 136). Cover tightly with plastic wrap and refrigerate until 30 minutes before making the meringue filling.

Into a 1 cup / 237 ml glass measure with a spout, weigh or measure the egg yolk. Whisk the water into the egg yolk. Cover tightly with plastic wrap and set on the counter.

MAKE THE DOUGH

1. In a medium bowl, whisk together the flour, sugar, and yeast. Then whisk in the salt.

2. Add the butter and use your fingertips to mix it in until the butter pieces are the size of small pebbles.

3. Use a silicone spatula or wooden spoon to stir the egg yolk mixture into the flour mixture until evenly mixed and the dough holds together. The dough will be soft and there should still be visible bits of butter.

4. Divide the dough in half (about 140 grams each). Shape each piece into a ball and then flatten it into

Continues

a 4 inch disc. Wrap each one in plastic wrap and refrigerate for a minimum of 8 hours, up to 2 days.

NUT MERINGUE FILLING

walnut halves	20 grams	3 tablespoons
ground cinnamon	·	½ teaspoon
1 large egg white (reserved from above)	30 grams	2 tablespoons (30 ml)
cream of tartar	·	⅛ teaspoon
sugar, preferably superfine	50 grams	¼ cup

PREHEAT THE OVEN

Twenty minutes or longer before baking, set an oven rack at the middle level. Set the oven at 350°F / 175°C.

TOAST AND CHOP THE WALNUTS

1. Spread the walnuts on a small baking sheet and bake for 5 minutes. Turn the walnuts onto a small cutting mat or board and discard any skins that have separated. Finely chop the nuts.

2. Set the walnuts in a small bowl and whisk in the cinnamon.

MAKE THE MERINGUE FOR THE FILLING

3. Add the cream of tartar to the egg white and, using a handheld electric mixer, beat on medium speed until foamy. Gradually raise the speed to medium-high and beat until soft peaks form when the beater is raised slowly.

4. Raise the speed to high and gradually beat in the sugar. Continue beating until the meringue is shiny and stiff but floppy peaks form when the beater is raised slowly.

ROLL THE DOUGH AND CUT THE TRIANGLES

5. Remove one piece of dough from the refrigerator and allow it to sit on the counter for about 5 to 10 minutes, or until it is malleable enough to roll.

6. Using a floured rolling pin, on a floured dough mat or lightly floured surface, roll out the dough into a 12 inch circle; it will be less than ⅛ inch (³⁄₃₂ inch) thick. Rotate it often and add flour as necessary to ensure that it doesn't stick. If the dough becomes too soft or sticky at any time, briefly refrigerate it until it is firm enough to roll.

7. Use a pizza wheel or sharp knife to cut the dough into 12 triangles. (Cut the dough first into quarters and then cut each quarter in thirds; see Baking Gems.) Use a pair of small scissors or a small sharp knife to make a ¼ inch cut in the middle of each triangle's outer edge.

8. Spoon a rounded ½ teaspoon of meringue onto the wide end of each wedge, just under the ¼ inch cut.

9. Sprinkle half the walnut mixture on top of the meringue.

10. Starting at the wide ends, roll up the triangles gently, without pressing, to keep the meringue from squeezing out the ends.

11. Place the rugelach, points underneath, about 1½ inches apart on a cookie sheet.

12. Repeat with the second batch of dough and remaining filling.

BAKE THE RUGELACH

13. Bake the first batch for 10 minutes. Rotate the cookie sheet halfway around. Continue baking for 5 to 10 minutes, or until the rugelach are lightly browned.

COOL THE COOKIES

14. Set the cookie sheet on the uncoated wire rack and let the rugelach cool for 1 minute to firm slightly.

POWDERED SUGAR TOPPING

powdered sugar	21 grams	3½ tablespoons

15. Use a thin pancake turner to transfer the rugelach to the coated wire rack. Set the rack on a sheet of parchment to catch any falling sugar. Spoon the powdered sugar into a fine-mesh strainer and dust it lightly onto the rugelach. Cool completely.

16. Repeat with the second batch.

17. To store, layer the rugelach in an airtight container, separating the layers with parchment or plastic wrap.

STORE Airtight: room temperature, 5 days; frozen, 3 months.

Baking Gems

♥ It's fine to mix the dough in a stand mixer, but be careful not to overmix it.

♥ To cut the dough into 12 triangles, a 30-60-90-degree drafting / arts triangle is very helpful. After cutting the dough into quarters, use the triangle to cut each quarter into 3 equal wedges.

STRUDEL COOKIES

Makes: Two 10 by 2½ inch strudels (20 cookies total)

This unusual sour cream–based dough is very low in flour, so it is exceptionally tender and flaky. It is easy to mix but requires more flour than usual when rolling to keep it from sticking. The original recipe is an heirloom created by Dorothy Thompson, whose daughter owned the charming Mercersburg Inn in Pennsylvania. Because the dough gets rolled with the filling, I prefer to treat the strudel like biscotti and bake the slices for a short time to ensure that all the dough gets fully cooked, which also adds crispness. I first dip the slices in sugar to balance the deliciously tart filling of apricots, currants, and nuts.

Oven Temperature: 350°F / 175°C	**Baking Time:** 50 to 60 minutes, plus 10 minutes for the strudel slices
Plan Ahead: These are best made a minimum of 6 hours in advance.	**Special Equipment:** Two 17 by 14 inch cookie sheets, one lined with parchment, the other nonstick or lined with foil

DOUGH *Makes: 354 grams*

unsalted butter	113 grams	8 tablespoons (1 stick)
bleached all-purpose flour	128 grams	1 cup (lightly spooned into the cup and leveled off) plus 2 teaspoons
fine sea salt	·	⅛ plus ¹⁄₁₆ teaspoon
full-fat sour cream	121 grams	½ cup

MISE EN PLACE

Thirty minutes to 1 hour ahead, cut the butter into tablespoon-size pieces. Set on the counter to soften.

MAKE THE DOUGH

1. In a medium bowl, whisk together the flour and salt. Add the butter and sour cream and stir and mash with a wooden spoon until the mixture starts to come away from the sides of the bowl and you can form it into a ball.

2. Scrape the dough onto a floured sheet of plastic wrap and use the wrap to knead the dough lightly until it holds together. Dust it with flour.

CHILL THE DOUGH

3. Divide the dough in half (about 177 grams each). Scrape each portion onto a sheet of plastic wrap. Press and form each piece into a 4 inch square, ½ inch thick. Refrigerate for a minimum of 2 hours, up to overnight.

APRICOT NUT FILLING

pecans or walnuts	57 grams	½ cup
dried currants	56 grams	¼ cup plus 2 tablespoons
ground cinnamon	·	⅛ teaspoon
apricot preserves (or lekvar; see page 404)	200 grams	½ cup plus 2 tablespoons

4. Chop the nuts into coarse pieces. In a medium bowl, use a fork to stir together the nuts, currants, and cinnamon until well mixed.

ROLL THE COOKIE STRUDEL

5. Roll out half the dough at a time: Using a floured rolling pin, on a floured pastry cloth (or between sheets of plastic wrap, flouring both sides of

Continues

the dough), roll the dough into an 11 by 9 inch rectangle. While rolling, flip over the dough two or three times and flour it as necessary to be sure it does not stick.

6. Spread half the apricot preserves (100 grams / ¼ cup plus 1 tablespoon) evenly over the dough, leaving a margin of about ½ inch all around. Sprinkle half the filling mixture evenly over the preserves.

7. Using the pastry cloth (or plastic wrap), lift the dough along one long side and gently roll it up, brushing off the excess flour as you go. Flip the roll over onto the parchment-lined cookie sheet, seam side down. Tuck ½ inch of the ends under the dough. The strudel will be 10 by 2 inches.

8. Repeat with the remaining dough and filling. Place the second strudel next to the first one, a minimum of 1 inch apart.

9. With a small sharp knife, cut 3 or 4 small horizontal steam vents into the top of each strudel.

10. Bake at once, or cover the strudels with plastic wrap and refrigerate for up to 24 hours before baking.

PREHEAT THE OVEN
Twenty minutes or longer before baking, set an oven rack at the upper level. Set the oven at 350°F / 175°C.

CINNAMON SUGAR TOPPING

sugar	6 grams	½ tablespoon
ground cinnamon	·	¼ teaspoon
milk	15 grams	1 tablespoon (15 ml)

11. In a small bowl, stir together the sugar and cinnamon.

BAKE AND TOP THE STRUDEL
12. Bake for 30 minutes. Remove the pan from the oven and use a pastry brush to coat each roll with the milk. Then sprinkle the rolls evenly with the cinnamon sugar topping. Rotate the cookie sheet halfway around and continue baking for 20 to 30 minutes, or until lightly browned.

COOL THE STRUDEL
13. Set the cookie sheet on a wire rack. Cool completely.

CUT AND COAT THE STRUDEL

sugar, preferably superfine	50 grams	¼ cup

14. Slip a large pancake turner underneath the strudels and slide them onto a cutting board.

15. Using a serrated knife, slice each strudel on an angle into 10 cookies, about ½ inch wide.

16. Set the sugar on a quarter sheet pan or small plate. Dip each slice into the sugar, coating both sides, and set them on the nonstick or foil-lined cookie sheet, cut side down. They can be very close together, without touching.

BAKE THE SLICES
17. Return the cookies to the oven and bake for 10 minutes, rotating the cookie sheet halfway around after the first 5 minutes.

COOL THE SLICES
18. Set the cookie sheet on a wire rack and allow the cookies to cool completely on the sheet. Then use your fingers or a thin spatula to transfer them to a serving plate or storage container.

STORE Airtight: room temperature, 5 days; refrigerated, 8 days; frozen, 3 months.

Baking Gem
♥ If the currants are dry, spritz them with a little water, cover tightly, and allow them to sit for about 30 minutes.

THREE-NUT OVALS

Makes: Thirty-six 2 by 1¼ inch cookies

This is the nuttiest cookie I know: It boasts equal weights of nuts, butter, and flour. The high proportion of nuts and butter makes it not only flavorful, but also extraordinarily tender. Amazingly, the cookies are firm enough that you can lift one with your fingers and take a bite without it breaking apart, but then it literally dissolves in your mouth, leaving a deliciously nutty flavor with a lingering trail of hazelnut. These are also delightful crumbled on top of ice cream.

Oven Temperature: 350°F / 175°C	**Baking Time:** 5 to 7 minutes for the nuts; 13 to 16 minutes for the cookies (for each of two batches)	**Special Equipment:** Two 17 by 14 inch cookie sheets, no preparation needed or lined with parchment

DOUGH *Makes: 360 grams*

unsalted butter	113 grams	8 tablespoons (1 stick)
sliced unblanched almonds	45 grams	½ cup minus 1 tablespoon
pecan halves	33 grams	⅓ cup
whole hazelnuts	35 grams	¼ cup
bleached all-purpose flour	113 grams	1 cup (lightly spooned into the cup and leveled off) minus 1 tablespoon
fine sea salt	·	⅛ teaspoon
light brown sugar, preferably Muscovado	27 grams	2 tablespoons (firmly packed)
water	7.5 grams	½ tablespoon (7.5 ml)
pure vanilla extract	·	½ teaspoon (2.5 ml)
superfine sugar, for topping (see Baking Gem)	100 grams	½ cup

PREHEAT THE OVEN

Twenty minutes or longer before baking, set an oven rack at the middle level. Set the oven at 350°F / 175°C.

MISE EN PLACE

Thirty minutes to 1 hour ahead, cut the butter into tablespoon-size pieces. Set on the counter to soften.

Toast the Nuts: Arrange the nuts evenly, in three separate groups, on a half sheet pan and bake for 5 to 7 minutes, or just until the almonds are pale golden. Stir each group of nuts partway through to ensure even browning. Set the sheet pan on a wire rack. Spoon the hazelnuts onto a clean dish towel, wrap them in the towel, and let them sit for a few minutes. Use the towel to rub off as much of the skins as possible. Discard any loose skins and cool all the nuts completely.

In a small bowl, whisk together the flour and salt.

Continues

MAKE THE DOUGH

Food Processor Method

1. In a food processor, process the nuts and brown sugar until the nuts are very fine.

2. With the motor on, add the butter one piece at a time and process until smooth and very creamy. Scrape down the sides of the bowl as needed.

3. Add the water and vanilla extract and pulse just until incorporated. Scrape down the sides of the bowl.

4. Add the flour mixture and pulse just until blended. Scrape down the sides of the bowl.

Stand Mixer Method

1. Grind the nuts in batches in a spice mill with a little of the brown sugar, or use a rotary nut grinder. Whisk the nuts into the flour mixture.

2. In the bowl of a stand mixer fitted with the flat beater, beat the butter and (remaining) brown sugar on medium speed for 2 to 3 minutes, until lighter in color and fluffy.

3. On low speed, add the water and vanilla extract and beat just until incorporated. Scrape down the sides of the bowl.

4. Gradually beat in the flour mixture just until incorporated, scraping down the sides of the bowl as needed.

Both Methods

5. Scrape the dough into a bowl. It will be very soft but firm enough to shape.

SHAPE THE DOUGH

6. Scoop out 36 pieces of dough (2 teaspoons / 10 grams each). Dust your palms with a little flour when rolling the pieces of dough. Roll each piece in the palms of your hands to form a 1¾ inch

long by ¾ inch oblong, resembling a date. Place the cookies on the cookie sheets a minimum of 1½ inches apart, 18 to a sheet.

BAKE THE COOKIES

7. Bake the first sheet of cookies for 7 minutes. Rotate the cookie sheet halfway around. Continue baking for 6 to 9 minutes, or until the cookies are just beginning to brown very lightly. They will be firm to the touch with only a little give at the top.

COOL AND COAT THE COOKIES

8. Set the cookie sheet on a wire rack and let the cookies cool for 3 to 5 minutes, until firm enough to lift from the sheet.

9. Meanwhile, in a small shallow bowl, place the superfine sugar.

10. One at a time, use a thin pancake turner to lift each cookie and very gently dip it on both sides in the sugar topping. The cookies will be very fragile but will firm on cooling. Then transfer each cookie onto another wire rack. Cool completely. If desired, for a slightly thicker coating, dip a second time in the sugar.

11. Repeat with the second batch.

STORE Airtight: room temperature, 3 weeks; frozen, 3 months.

Baking Gem

♥ Superfine sugar makes a finer coating for this delicate cookie. If you don't have it, you can process granulated sugar for a few minutes in a food processor, until it is as fine as sand.

PISTACHIO PAVÉS

Makes: Forty-eight 3 by 1½ inch crescent cookies

For these super-buttery crescent cookies, paved with studs of pistachios, it is worth searching out the most flavorful bright green variety of the nut, which is typically imported from places such as Sicily, Iran, Turkey, and Greece. What is most special about these cookies is that about one third of the pistachios gets mixed into the dough and the rest is used to coat the outside, giving the cookies a toasty quality.

Oven Temperature: 350°F / 175°C	**Baking Time:** 12 to 15 minutes (for each of two batches)	**Special Equipment:** Two 17 by 14 inch cookie sheets, no preparation needed or lined with parchment

DOUGH *Makes: 775 grams (without the nut coating)*

unsalted butter	227 grams	16 tablespoons (2 sticks)
1 large egg	50 grams	1 tablespoon plus ½ teaspoon (47.5 ml)
pure vanilla extract	·	2 teaspoons (10 ml)
shelled unsalted pistachio nuts	112 grams	¾ cup
sugar	150 grams	¾ cup
bleached all-purpose flour	248 grams	2 cups (lightly spooned into the cup and leveled off) plus 2 teaspoons
fine sea salt	·	¹⁄₁₆ teaspoon (a pinch)
shelled unsalted pistachio nuts, for coating	200 grams	1⅓ cups

MISE EN PLACE

Thirty minutes to 1 hour ahead, cut the butter into tablespoon-size pieces. Set on the counter to soften.

Thirty minutes ahead, into a 1 cup / 237 ml glass measure with a spout, weigh or measure the egg.

Whisk in the vanilla extract. Cover tightly with plastic wrap and set on the counter.

MAKE THE DOUGH

Food Processor Method

1. In a food processor, process the 112 grams / ¾ cup pistachios and the sugar until the nuts are powder-fine.

2. With the motor on, add the butter one piece at a time and process until smooth and creamy. Scrape down the sides of the bowl as needed.

3. Add the egg mixture and pulse until incorporated.

4. Add the flour and salt and pulse just until blended. Scrape the dough into a bowl.

Stand Mixer Method

1. In a spice mill, grind the 112 grams / ¾ cup pistachios with 50 grams / ¼ cup of the sugar, in batches, until the nuts are powder-fine. (Alternatively, use a rotary nut grinder for the nuts.)

2. In the bowl of a stand mixer fitted with the flat beater, beat the butter and the remaining 100 grams / ½ cup sugar on medium speed for 2 to 3 minutes, until lighter in color and fluffy.

Continues

3. Add the grated nut mixture and then gradually beat in the egg mixture until incorporated.

4. On low speed, gradually add the flour, beating just until incorporated, and then beat in the salt.

Both Methods

5. Cover the bowl tightly with plastic wrap and refrigerate for about 1 hour, or until the dough is firm enough to shape. It will still be quite soft.

PREHEAT THE OVEN

Thirty minutes or longer before baking, set an oven rack at the middle level. Set the oven at 350°F / 175°C.

6. Chop the remaining 200 grams / 1⅓ cups pistachios medium-fine. Discard any of the skin that comes off the nuts. Spread the nuts on a sheet pan or the counter.

SHAPE THE DOUGH

7. Remove one quarter of the dough (about 194 grams) from the bowl, leaving the rest in the refrigerator while you work. Scoop out level tablespoons of dough (16 grams each). One at a time, roll each piece in the palms of your hands to form a little log. When the log starts to soften and get sticky, transfer it to the nut-lined surface and roll the dough back and forth over the nuts until it is 3 inches long. The stickier the dough, the more nuts it will pick up. If the log becomes too soft to roll, transfer it briefly to the refrigerator to firm.

8. Curve each dough log into a crescent and set it on a cookie sheet, spacing the cookies no closer than 1 inch apart. Remove and shape another

quarter of the dough. Cover the shaped dough lightly with plastic wrap and refrigerate for a minimum of 5 minutes, up to overnight, before baking. (If refrigerating overnight, shape all the dough at once; if not, shape the second batch while the first batch is baking.)

BAKE THE COOKIES

9. Bake for 6 minutes. Rotate the cookie sheet halfway around. Continue baking for 6 to 9 minutes, or until the cookies just begin to brown lightly. They should still feel a little soft to the touch.

COOL THE COOKIES

10. Set the cookie sheet on a wire rack and let the cookies cool for 3 to 5 minutes, until firm enough to lift from the sheet. Use a thin pancake turner to transfer the cookies to another wire rack. Cool completely.

11. Repeat with the second batch, using the third and fourth pieces of dough.

STORE Airtight: room temperature or refrigerated, 1 month; frozen, 3 months.

Baking Gems

♥ If using a stand mixer, superfine sugar will give the smoothest texture.

♥ This cookie dough has a high butter content, so refrigerating the cookies before baking will give them the best shape.

PECAN TASSIES

Makes: Sixty-four 1⅝ inch mini tartlets

This recipe makes a large quantity of mini tartlets, perfect for a party. I enjoy pecan tassies in this small size because they offer one or two bites with a pleasing balance of soft buttery crust to sticky pecan filling. But if you're reluctant to craft sixty-four little tartlets, it's fine to divide the recipe in half or make the double-size tassies using mini muffin tins (see the Variation).

Oven Temperature: 350°F / 175°C	Baking Time: 18 to 20 minutes (for each of two batches)	Special Equipment: Sixty-four mini tartlet or brioche pans, 1 inch at the bottom, 1¾ inches at the top (1 tablespoon capacity), uncoated (if you do not have enough molds, bake in batches), set on two 17¼ by 12¼ half sheet pans; A long thin sewing needle for unmolding; A disposable pastry bag if making the optional chocolate drizzle glaze

DOUGH *Makes: 512 grams*

unsalted butter	170 grams	12 tablespoons (1½ sticks)
full-fat cream cheese	128 grams	½ cup
bleached all-purpose flour	218 grams	1¾ cups (lightly spooned into the cup and leveled off) plus 2 teaspoons
fine sea salt	·	1/16 teaspoon (a pinch)

PREHEAT THE OVEN
Twenty minutes or longer before baking, set an oven rack at the middle level. Set the oven at 350°F / 175°C.

MISE EN PLACE
For the Food Processor Method: Thirty minutes ahead or longer, cut the butter and cream cheese into 1 inch cubes. Wrap and refrigerate.

For the Mixer Method: Thirty minutes ahead, cut the butter and cream cheese into tablespoon-size pieces. Set on the counter to soften.

MAKE THE DOUGH
Food Processor Method
1. In a food processor, process the flour and salt for a few seconds.

2. Add the butter and cream cheese and pulse until the mixture is the consistency of fine meal and will hold together when pinched.

Stand Mixer Method
1. In the bowl of a stand mixer fitted with the flat beater, beat together the butter and cream cheese on low speed until blended.

2. Add the flour and salt and beat just until incorporated.

Both Methods
3. Scrape the mixture into a gallon-size reclosable freezer bag and press the dough together from the outside of the bag. Scrape the dough onto a piece of plastic wrap and use the plastic wrap to shape it into a smooth ball.

LINE THE TARTLET (OR BRIOCHE) PANS
4. Measure rounded teaspoons of dough (8 grams each) and roll them between the palms of your

hands into balls; you should have 64 balls. If the dough softens and becomes sticky as you work, refrigerate it briefly. Set the balls of dough in the mini tart pans.

5. Press the dough into the pans, using the knuckle of your index finger. Dip your knuckle in flour if the dough sticks. Then use your fingertip or the handle of a small wooden spoon to tap the dough evenly into each pan. Be sure the dough covers the entire pan in order to keep the filling from sticking to it.

6. Set the pans ½ inch apart on the sheet pans. Cover with plastic wrap and refrigerate while you make the filling.

PECAN FILLING

1 large egg	50 grams	3 tablespoons plus ½ teaspoon (47.5 ml)
pure vanilla extract	·	1 teaspoon (5 ml)
pecan halves	113 grams	1 cup plus 2 tablespoons
unsalted butter	28 grams	2 tablespoons
golden syrup (or corn syrup)	170 grams (164 grams)	½ cup (118 ml)
light brown sugar, preferably Muscovado	80 grams	⅓ cup (firmly packed)
fine sea salt	·	¹⁄₁₆ teaspoon (a pinch)

MISE EN PLACE

Thirty minutes ahead, into a 1 cup / 237 ml glass measure with a spout, weigh or measure the egg. Whisk in the vanilla extract. Cover tightly and set on the counter.

Coarsely chop the pecans.

Shortly before you make the filling, in a 1 cup / 237 ml glass measure with a spout, melt the butter in the microwave; or melt it in a small saucepan over medium-low heat.

MAKE THE FILLING

7. In a medium bowl, stir together the egg mixture, golden syrup, brown sugar, melted butter, and salt. Stir in the pecans.

8. Use a demitasse spoon or teaspoon measure to fill each tart shell no more than two-thirds full with the pecan filling. Stir the mixture from time to time to keep it uniform in consistency.

BAKE THE TASSIES

9. Set the first pan of tassies in the oven and bake for 10 minutes. Rotate the pan halfway around. Continue baking for 8 to 10 minutes, or just until the filling is set but still soft in the center.

COOL THE TASSIES

10. Set the sheet pan on a wire rack and allow the tassies to cool for a few minutes, just until the pans are cool enough to lift. It is easiest to unmold the tassies while still warm, before the sticky filling hardens. If necessary, slip the needle between the edge of the pastry and the pan to loosen it. Set the tassies on a serving plate or storage container. If using the optional glaze, set them on a cookie sheet.

11. Repeat with the second batch.

*If desired, garnish with the chocolate drizzle glaze.

OPTIONAL: DARK CHOCOLATE DRIZZLE GLAZE

dark chocolate, 60% to 62% cacao	57 grams (2 ounces)

MAKE THE DRIZZLE GLAZE

1. Chop the chocolate into coarse pieces. In a small microwavable bowl, heat the chocolate, stirring every 15 seconds with a silicone spatula, until almost completely melted (or heat the chocolate in the top of a double boiler set over

Continues

hot, not simmering, water—do not let the bottom of the container touch the water—stirring often, until almost completely melted).

Remove the chocolate from the heat source and stir until fully melted.

2. Spoon the chocolate into the disposable pastry bag. Close it securely and cut a very small curved opening into the tip.

GLAZE THE PECAN TASSIES

3. Allow the chocolate to cool until slightly thickened, then drizzle it over the tops of the tassies.

STORE Airtight: room temperature, 2 weeks.

VARIATION

The recipe can be baked in three mini muffin pans to make 32 tassies. Increase the baking time to 25 to 30 minutes.

CHOCOLATE TRUFFLE COOKIES

Makes: Fourteen 3 inch round cookies

Several years ago, I created a chocolate lava cake for my book *Rose's Heavenly Cakes* with a ganache truffle for the center to ensure that it would have a flow even if overbaked. But it was my kindred spirit, chocolatier Zach Townsend, who recently crafted these stellar chocolate cookies using the same concept. The cookies have a chewy, brownie-like texture, with a pleasing crunch from the undissolved sugar and the tiny bits of chocolate—but oh, the centers! They are chocolate at its finest moment: lusciously, enticingly creamy.

Oven Temperature: 350°F / 175°C	Baking Time: 14 to 15 minutes for each of two batches	Special Equipment: Six or twelve 3 to 3¼ by ¾ inch high or higher pastry rings (measured from the inside)—see Baking Gems on page 297; Two 17 by 14 inch cookie sheets, lined with silicone baking mats or parchment

CHOCOLATE GANACHE TRUFFLE CENTERS

(can be made several weeks ahead and frozen)

Makes: 172 grams

unsalted butter	14 grams	1 tablespoon
heavy cream	78 grams	⅓ cup (79 ml)
dark chocolate, 61% to 66% cacao	88 grams (3 ounces)	.

MISE EN PLACE

Thirty minutes or longer ahead, set the butter on the counter to soften.

Into a 1 cup / 237 ml microwavable measure with a spout, or a small saucepan, weigh or measure the cream.

MAKE THE GANACHE

1. Chop the chocolate into coarse pieces. In a food processor, pulse the chocolate until finely chopped. (Alternatively, use a chef's knife to chop it.) Empty it into a medium bowl.

2. In the microwave (or in the saucepan over medium heat, stirring often), scald the cream (heat it to the boiling point; small bubbles will form around the periphery).

3. Pour the hot cream on top of the chocolate. Cover with plastic wrap and let sit for 1 minute.

4. With a silicone spatula, start stirring vigorously in the center of the bowl until the mixture turns dark and smooth. Then continue stirring in larger concentric circles until the cream is incorporated and the mixture is completely smooth. Add the butter and stir until fully melted and incorporated. The mixture should be glossy and smooth.

5. Let the ganache stand for a few minutes, or until cooled, then cover the bowl with plastic wrap and refrigerate until firm, 30 minutes or longer.

SHAPE THE GANACHE

6. At least 1 hour before making the cookies, remove the ganache from the refrigerator. Have ready a small plate or tray lined with plastic wrap.

Continues

7. Using a spoon, scrape up 12 to 14 medium balls (12 grams each) from the ganache for the truffle centers. It works well to set each ball of chocolate onto a piece of plastic wrap as you scoop it and then use the plastic wrap to help shape the ball. The centers do not need to be perfectly round.

8. Place the ganache balls on the plate, cover with plastic wrap, and place in the freezer until the balls are completely frozen, 30 minutes to 1 hour.

DOUGH *Makes: 710 grams*

unsalted butter	126 grams	9 tablespoons (1 stick plus 1 tablespoon)
1 large egg	50 grams	3 tablespoons plus ½ teaspoon (47.5 ml)
turbinado sugar, preferably Sugar in the Raw	155 grams	¾ cup plus 1 teaspoon
instant espresso powder	·	¼ teaspoon
pure vanilla extract	·	½ teaspoon (2.5 ml)
bleached all-purpose flour	202 grams	1⅔ cups (lightly spooned into the cup and leveled off)
unsweetened alkalized cocoa powder	19 grams	¼ cup (sifted before measuring)
baking soda	2.7 grams	½ teaspoon
fine sea salt	·	⅛ teaspoon
dark mini chocolate chips or finely chopped chocolate, 52% to 62% cacao	150 grams (5.3 ounces)	·

MISE EN PLACE
Thirty minutes or longer ahead, cut the butter into tablespoon-size pieces. Set on the counter to soften.

Into a 1 cup / 237 ml glass measure with a spout, weigh or measure the egg. Beat it lightly, then cover tightly with plastic wrap and set on the counter.

Into the bowl of a stand mixer, weigh or measure the sugar.

MAKE THE DOUGH
1. In a 2 cup / 473 ml or larger microwavable measure with a spout (or in a small saucepan over medium-low heat, stirring often) melt the butter. Allow the butter to cool slightly so that it is not hot when added to the sugar, or it could dissolve some of it.

2. In a custard cup, dissolve the coffee granules in the vanilla. Add to the melted butter and stir to combine.

3. Scrape the melted butter mixture into the sugar in the stand mixer bowl. Whisk by hand until smooth (the sugar will not dissolve).

4. Whisk in the egg until thoroughly combined.

5. In a medium bowl, whisk together the flour, cocoa, baking soda, and salt. Then sift into another bowl.

6. Set the mixer bowl on the stand and attach the flat beater.

7. Add the flour mixture to the mixture in the bowl in three parts, mixing on low speed and incorporating each addition before adding the next. Scrape down the sides of the bowl as needed and mix just until a smooth dough is formed.

8. Add the chocolate chips and beat just until evenly incorporated.

SHAPE THE DOUGH LOG AND CUT THE COOKIES
9. Scrape the dough onto a large piece of plastic wrap and shape it into a 14 inch long log, 1¾ inches in diameter, with flat or slightly rounded ends. Wrap the log in the plastic wrap and refrigerate until firm, a minimum of 1 hour, up to 24 hours.

10. Using a sharp knife, cut off 1 inch from each end of the dough log to form a 12 inch long log. (Wrap and refrigerate the cut-off pieces to make 2 more cookies.) Slice the dough into twelve 1 inch thick cookies.

SHAPE THE COOKIES

11. If necessary, let the cookies sit at room temperature for about 10 minutes to soften slightly. Lightly dust a dough mat or the counter with flour. Using a rolling pin (preferably a small one), roll the cookies into discs measuring about 3¼ inches in diameter. They do not have to be perfectly round.

12. Remove the frozen ganache balls from the freezer (for one batch at a time). Place a frozen ganache ball in the center of each cookie and wrap the dough around the ganache ball to encase it completely. Pinch the dough together at the top and press all around the cookie in places where it may have cracked to ensure that the ganache ball is well sealed inside.

13. Using the palm of your hand, press down gently on the cookie to flatten it to about 2¼ inches in diameter. Place the cookies on a tray, cover with plastic wrap, and set in the freezer or refrigerator while the oven preheats.

*You can also wrap the unbaked cookies individually with plastic wrap and freeze for up to 1 month.

PREHEAT THE OVEN

Thirty minutes or longer before baking, set an oven rack at just below the middle level. Set the oven at 350°F / 175°C.

BAKE THE COOKIES

14. Working with one batch at a time, place six of the pastry rings evenly spaced on a prepared cookie sheet. Set a chilled or frozen cookie in the center of each ring.

15. Bake for 14 to 15 minutes, or until the edges of the cookies are firm when pressed gently with your fingertip but the centers still feel soft. (The centers will dip slightly on removal from the oven.)

COOL THE COOKIES

16. Set the cookie sheet on a wire rack and let the cookies cool for 10 minutes. Slowly lift off the rings from the cookies; if necessary, gently press down on one edge of each cookie to release it. With a thin pancake turner, carefully transfer the fragile cookies to another wire rack.

17. Allow the cookies to cool for at least 5 minutes before eating. A warm cookie will be more liquid in the center, but for the best flavor, allow them to cool completely. They keep moist and chewy if stored airtight.

18. Repeat with the second batch (and the extra 2 cookies).

STORE Airtight: room temperature, 5 days; refrigerated, 1 week; frozen, 2 months.

Baking Gems

♥ Disposable pastry rings can be made easily from heavy-duty aluminum foil (see the Baking Gems on page 297), or reusable rings can be cut from aluminum flashing (available at most hardware and home improvement stores).

♥ For the best consistency, the ganache balls should remain frozen until baking. Freezing the shaped cookies is also ideal. I like to freeze a few individually wrapped unbaked cookies, giving me the advantage of an impulse bake!

FUDGY CHOCOLATE ICE CREAM SANDWICH COOKIES

Makes: Twenty-four 2¾ inch round sandwiches

This deeply chocolate cookie stays fudgy even when frozen. The secret is the heavy cream and corn syrup in the dough, added to bittersweet chocolate in the same proportion as in ganache. My favorite ice creams for filling the cookie sandwiches are cherry vanilla, salted caramel, and chocolate.

Oven Temperature: 350°F / 175°C

Baking Time: 8 to 10 minutes (for each of four batches)

Plan Ahead: The dough must be frozen for 3 hours before baking; it can be frozen for 3 months. The optional chocolate dipping sauce should be made at least 2 hours ahead, but it can be made well in advance and reheated.

Special Equipment: Two 17 by 14 inch cookie sheets, nonstick or lined with parchment; Two cardboard tubes from rolls of paper towels (1⅝ inch inside diameter); A sharp heavy knife with a 1½ to 2 inch wide blade; A 2 inch ice cream scoop or a ¼ cup measure

DOUGH *Makes: 600 grams*

unsalted butter	142 grams	10 tablespoons (1¼ sticks)
1 large egg	50 grams	3 tablespoons plus ½ teaspoon (47.5 ml)
heavy cream	43 grams	3 tablespoons (45 ml)
corn syrup	14 grams	2 teaspoons (10 ml)
pure vanilla extract		1 teaspoon (5 ml)
dark chocolate, 60% to 62% cacao	42 grams (1.5 ounces)	.
bleached all-purpose flour	144 grams	1 cup (lightly spooned into the cup and leveled off) plus 2½ tablespoons
unsweetened alkalized cocoa powder	37 grams	½ cup (sifted before measuring)
baking soda	2.7 grams	½ teaspoon
fine sea salt	·	⅛ teaspoon
superfine sugar	150 grams	¾ cup

MISE EN PLACE

Thirty minutes to 1 hour ahead, cut the butter into tablespoon-size pieces. Set on the counter to soften.

Thirty minutes to 1 hour ahead, into a 1 cup / 237 ml glass measure with a spout, weigh or measure the egg. Whisk in the cream, corn syrup, and vanilla extract. Cover tightly with plastic wrap and set on the counter.

Melt the Chocolate: Twenty to 30 minutes before baking, chop the chocolate into coarse pieces. In a small microwavable bowl, heat the chocolate, stirring every 15 seconds with a silicone spatula, until almost completely melted (or heat the chocolate in the top of a double boiler set over hot, not simmering, water—do not let the bottom of the container touch the water—stirring often, until almost completely melted).

Continues

Remove the chocolate from the heat source and stir until fully melted. Let it cool for about 10 minutes, or until it is no longer warm to the touch but is still fluid.

In a small bowl, whisk together the flour, cocoa, baking soda, and salt. Sift this mixture onto a sheet of parchment.

Cut the cardboard tubes into halves.

MAKE THE DOUGH

1. In the bowl of a stand mixer fitted with the flat beater, beat the sugar and butter on medium speed until well mixed, about 1 minute. Scrape down the sides of the bowl.

2. Gradually add the egg mixture, beating until incorporated. Scrape down the sides of the bowl.

3. Scrape in the melted chocolate and beat until thoroughly incorporated, about 1 minute. Scrape down the sides of the bowl.

4. Detach the flat beater and add the flour mixture to the bowl. Use the flat beater to stir in the flour until moistened. Then reattach the beater and beat on low speed until the flour mixture is incorporated. The dough will be like a thick, fluffy butter-cake batter.

5. Scrape the dough onto a piece of plastic wrap. Lay a second piece of plastic wrap on top and flatten the dough into a rectangle about 6 by 5 inches. Slip it onto a cookie sheet and refrigerate for at least 1½ hours, until the dough is firm enough to shape. (An instant-read thermometer inserted into the dough should read about 60°F / 15°C.)

SHAPE THE DOUGH INTO LOGS

6. Divide the dough into quarters (about 150 grams each). Wrap each piece in plastic wrap. Work with one piece at a time and keep the rest refrigerated.

7. Use the plastic wrap to shape and roll the piece of dough into a log just under 1⅝ inches

in diameter and about 5½ inches long. Lightly tamp each end on the countertop to flatten it.

8. Wrap the dough log in the plastic wrap and slide it into one of the cardboard tubes. Stand the tube on end on the countertop. With your fingers, press the dough log down until it reaches the bottom and fits snugly into the tube. Wrap the tube with plastic wrap to keep the dough from slipping out and stand it on end in the freezer. Repeat with the other three pieces of dough. (Alternatively, if you don't have cardboard tubes, roll the dough logs to about 1⅝ inches in diameter. Wrap the logs and freeze for 30 minutes; remove them from the freezer and quickly roll them again to minimize flattening. Then stand them on end in the freezer again.)

9. Freeze the dough logs for at least 3 hours (an instant-read thermometer should read below 32°F / 0°C) to firm them for even cutting.

The dough can be frozen for up to 3 months.

PREHEAT THE OVEN

Twenty minutes or longer before baking, set an oven rack at the middle level. Set the oven at 350°F / 175°C.

CUT THE DOUGH INTO COOKIES

If the dough has become too firm on longer freezing, allow it to soften slightly at room temperature.

It is best to bake these one sheet at a time to ensure that the cookies can be removed from the cookie sheet as soon after baking as possible so that they stay soft.

10. Remove one of the frozen dough logs from the freezer and cut it into twelve ⅜ inch thick slices. Place them 2 inches apart on a cookie sheet and smooth any rough edges with your fingertips. Bake at once.

BAKE THE COOKIES

11. Bake for 4 minutes. Rotate the cookie sheet halfway around. Continue baking for 4 to 6 minutes, or just until the cookies are set but are still soft to the touch.

COOL THE COOKIES

12. Set the cookie sheet on a wire rack and let the cookies cool for about 1 minute, until firm enough to lift from the sheet. Use a thin pancake turner to transfer the cookies to another wire rack. (Do not leave them on the cookie sheet, or they will continue to bake and become brittle.) They will bend slightly when set on the wire rack to cool.

13. As soon as the cookies are cool, sandwich them with the ice cream, or store them airtight.

14. While each batch of cookies is baking, cut the dough log for the next batch.

The cookies can be stored in an airtight container for 1 week at room temperature; 2 weeks refrigerated; 1 month frozen.

ICE CREAM FILLING

ice cream of your choice, softened (see Baking Gem)	.	about 1½ quarts

Assemble only half of the ice cream sandwiches at a time to prevent the ice cream from melting.

Set two cookie sheets in the freezer to chill.

SANDWICH THE COOKIES WITH ICE CREAM

15. Set 12 of the cookies bottom side up on one of the chilled cookie sheets. Set a scoop of ice cream, about ¼ cup, on top of each cookie. Place a second cookie bottom side down on top.

16. When the ice cream is soft enough to press down easily, evenly press the top of each cookie

until the ice cream comes almost to the edges. The ice cream should be about ½ inch thick.

17. Cover the sandwiches with plastic wrap and set them in the freezer until firm. Then wrap each sandwich separately in plastic wrap and store in an airtight container in the freezer.

18. Repeat with the remaining cookies.

STORE Airtight: frozen, 3 days.

Baking Gem

🍦 Refrigerate the ice cream for 20 minutes before sandwiching the cookies to soften it slightly.

OPTIONAL: CUSTOM ROSE BLEND GANACHE DIPPING SAUCE

Makes: 564 grams / 2 cups plus 2 tablespoons / 503 ml

white chocolate containing cocoa butter, preferably Valrhona	232 grams (8.2 ounces)	.
dark chocolate, 60% to 62% cacao	116 grams (4.1 ounces)	.
heavy cream	232 grams	1 cup (237 ml)

MAKE THE GANACHE DIPPING SAUCE

Have ready a fine-mesh strainer suspended over a medium glass bowl.

1. Chop the white and dark chocolates into coarse pieces. In a food processor, process the chocolates until very fine.

2. In a 1 cup / 237 ml microwavable measure with a spout (or in a small saucepan, stirring often) scald the cream (heat it to the boiling point; small bubbles will form around the periphery).

Continues

3. With the motor running, pour the cream through the feed tube in a steady stream. Process for a few seconds, until the ganache is smooth.

4. Press the ganache through the strainer into the bowl, and scrape any ganache clinging to the underside into the bowl. Let it sit for about 2 hours, or until it puddles thickly and then disappears when dropped from the tip of a spatula. Cover it after the first hour to prevent evaporation.

5. If needed, reheat the glaze in the top of a double boiler set over hot, not simmering, water (or heat very carefully in the microwave with 3-second bursts, stirring gently to ensure that it doesn't overheat or incorporate air.) The best consistency is at 72° to 75°F / 22° to 24°C.

6. Serve as a dipping sauce or spoon some on top of each sandwich cookie.

The sauce can be stored for 2 weeks refrigerated; 3 months frozen.

LION'S PAWS

Makes: Twenty-four 2½ by 1⅞ inch cookies

I created these whimsical cookies many years ago as part of an article about a "safari supper" for the now-defunct *Co-ed Magazine*. The main course was a mixture of spiced dry cereals I called Habitat. Celery stalks filled with cream cheese and topped with sesame seeds became "Ants Climbing a Tree." But it was these cookies that were the theme winners.

In order for the cookies to hold their cunning shape, the dough needs to be quite sturdy; it is low in sugar and relatively low in butter to prevent spreading. In this version, which I've improved from the original, I have increased the butter for more flavor and used unbleached all-purpose flour for more structure. Chocolate chips, hidden in the dough, form the knuckles and are a nice surprise treat. The cookies do require a lot of shaping, but it's part of the fun.

Oven Temperature:
325°F / 160°C for the almonds;
350°F / 175°C for the cookies

Baking Time: 4 to 6 minutes for the almonds; 14 to 18 minutes for the cookies (for each of two batches)

Special Equipment: Two 17 by 14 inch cookie sheets, no preparation needed or lined with parchment

DOUGH *Makes: 414 grams*

unsalted butter	100 grams	7 tablespoons (¾ stick plus 1 tablespoon)
1 large egg	50 grams	3 tablespoons plus ½ teaspoon (47.5 ml)
pure vanilla extract	·	1 teaspoon (5 ml)
slivered blanched almonds	60 grams	½ cup
unbleached all-purpose flour	212 grams	1¾ cups (lightly spooned into the cup and leveled off)
baking powder, preferably an aluminum-free variety	2.2 grams	½ teaspoon
fine sea salt	3 grams	½ teaspoon
sugar	50 grams	¼ cup
semisweet chocolate chips, 46% to 50%, such as Nestlé's Toll House	85 grams (3 ounces)	½ cup

PREHEAT THE OVEN

Twenty minutes or longer before baking, set an oven rack at the middle level. Set the oven at 325°F / 160°C.

MISE EN PLACE

Thirty minutes to 1 hour ahead, cut the butter into tablespoon-size pieces. Set on the counter to soften.

Thirty minutes ahead, into a 1 cup / 237 ml glass measure with a spout, weigh or measure the egg. Whisk in the vanilla extract. Cover tightly with plastic wrap and set on the counter.

Toast the Almonds: Spread the almonds evenly on a baking sheet and bake for 4 to 6 minutes, until lightly browned. Transfer the almonds to a small bowl. Cool completely.

In a medium bowl, whisk together the flour, baking powder, and salt.

Continues

MAKE THE DOUGH

1. In the bowl of a stand mixer fitted with the flat beater, beat the butter and sugar on medium speed for 2 to 3 minutes, until light and fluffy.

2. Gradually beat in the egg mixture until incorporated.

3. On low speed, gradually add the flour mixture, beating just until the flour is completely incorporated.

4. Scrape the dough onto a large piece of plastic wrap. Flatten it slightly and wrap tightly. Refrigerate for a minimum of 30 minutes, up to 24 hours. (The dough can be shaped directly from the refrigerator.)

PREHEAT THE OVEN

Twenty minutes or longer before baking, set an oven rack at the middle level. Set the oven at 350°F / 175°C.

CINNAMON SUGAR TOPPING

1 large egg white	30 grams	2 tablespoons (30 ml)
sugar	50 grams	¼ cup
ground cinnamon	·	⅛ teaspoon

MAKE THE CINNAMON SUGAR TOPPING

5. Into a small bowl, weigh or measure the egg white. Whisk the egg white to break it up and make it fluid. Cover tightly with plastic wrap.

6. In a small bowl, whisk together the sugar and cinnamon.

SHAPE THE DOUGH

It is best to shape one cookie at a time to keep the dough malleable and prevent drying. Keep the rest of the dough covered with plastic wrap. If the dough softens or becomes sticky, return it to the refrigerator for a few minutes to firm.

You will need a slightly rounded measuring teaspoon / 6 grams of dough to shape a ⅞ inch ball for the bottom of each cookie and 2 scant teaspoons / 10 grams of dough to shape a 1 inch ball for the top of each cookie.

7. Pinch off a piece of dough for the bottom cookie (see above). Knead it in the palm of your hand to make it smooth, then roll it into a ball. Flatten it slightly and set it between two small sheets of plastic wrap (this will help prevent cracks from forming). Use a small rolling pin and the side of your thumb to flatten and shape the dough into a rounded 2 inch long triangle, 1¾ inches at its widest point, to resemble a paw.

8. Set 3 chocolate chips, pointed ends down, near the edge of the wide end of the triangle to form the paw's knuckles. Set another 3 chocolate chips wide end down on top of the first set of chips.

9. Shape the dough for the top of the cookie the same way as for the bottom, but make a triangle 2½ inches long and 2½ inches at the widest point. Try to keep the wider end, which will cover the chocolate chips, thicker than the narrower end.

10. Starting at the wider end of the triangle, drape the top piece of dough evenly over the bottom piece of dough so that the edges align. Gently press the edges of the dough together. Don't be concerned if the dough covering the chocolate chips cracks a little. During baking, it will puff up and cover them completely.

11. Press down on the area between the chocolate chips and the point of the triangle. If desired, use a fork to create "fur" lines.

12. Use a small brush to coat the bottom of each almond sliver with a little of the egg white before pressing an almond sliver firmly between each set of chocolate chips and on either side to resemble claws.

Continues

13. Set the finished cookie on a sheet of parchment or dough mat for coating with the cinnamon sugar. Repeat with the remaining dough.

COAT THE COOKIES

14. Brush the tops of the cookies with the remaining egg white. Use a fine-mesh strainer to dust them with the cinnamon sugar.

15. Use a small offset spatula to lift the cookies and arrange them on the cookie sheet, alternating the direction of the pointed and rounded ends, a minimum of ½ inch apart.

BAKE THE COOKIES

16. Bake for 7 minutes. Rotate the cookie sheet halfway around. Continue baking for 7 to 11 minutes, or until the cookies start to brown very lightly. If you lift one of the cookies, the bottom should be golden brown.

17. Repeat to shape and bake the second batch.

COOL THE COOKIES

18. Set the cookie sheet on a wire rack and use a thin pancake turner to transfer the cookies to another wire rack. Cool completely.

STORE Airtight: room temperature, 1 week; frozen, 2 months.

Baking Gem

♥ A small flexible ruler is great for smoothing any rough edges of dough; curve the ruler and press it against the dough.

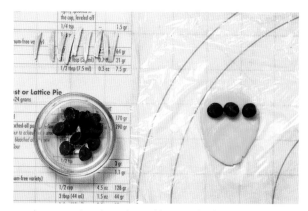
Arrange the chocolate chips on the bottom piece of dough.

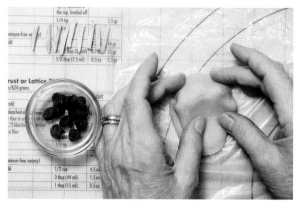
Drape the top piece of dough over the chocolate chips.

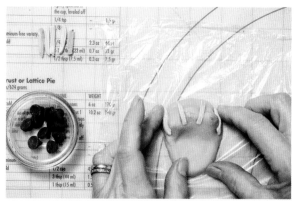
Add the almond "claws."

PEPPARKAKORS

Makes: Sixty to sixty-eight 2 inch round cookies

Woody's T'ai Chi Sifu (master), Paul Abdella, gave Woody his treasured family recipe for this unusual, flavorful, wafer-thin Norwegian cookie. The black pepper gives the cookie a subtle underlying sensation of heat on the palate, bringing the spicy flavors into harmony. These are absolutely addictive and have become a top favorite of ours. They are perfect as they are, but they also make a delicious and unusual hors d'oeuvre when spread with a soft goat cheese.

Oven Temperature: 350°F / 175°C	**Baking Time:** 8 to 11 minutes (for each of three batches)	**Plan Ahead:** Freeze the dough for at least 8 hours before baking the cookies.	**Special Equipment:** Two 17 by 14 inch cookie sheets, lightly coated with nonstick cooking spray and then wiped to leave just a thin coating; Optional: a cardboard tube from a paper towel roll (1⅝ inches inside diameter), cut into thirds; A sharp heavy knife with a 1½ to 2 inch wide blade

DOUGH *Makes: 460 grams*

unsalted butter	113 grams	8 tablespoons (1 stick)
bleached all-purpose flour	167 grams	1⅓ cups (lightly spooned into the cup and leveled off) plus 2 teaspoons
baking soda	2.7 grams	½ teaspoon
fine sea salt	1.5 grams	¼ teaspoon
ground ginger	2.7 grams	½ tablespoon
ground cloves	2.5 grams	1 teaspoon
ground cinnamon	2.2 grams	1 teaspoon
black pepper	2 grams	¾ teaspoon
sugar	100 grams	½ cup
light molasses, preferably Grandma's brand	80 grams	¼ cup (59 ml)
pearl or demerara sugar, for topping	50 grams	¼ cup

MISE EN PLACE

Thirty minutes to 1 hour ahead, cut the butter into tablespoon-size pieces. Set on the counter to soften.

MAKE THE DOUGH

1. In a medium bowl, whisk together the flour, baking soda, salt, ginger, cloves, cinnamon, and black pepper.

2. In the bowl of a stand mixer fitted with the flat beater, beat the butter and sugar on medium speed for 1 to 2 minutes, until light and creamy. Scrape down the sides of the bowl.

3. Scrape in the molasses and beat until incorporated. Scrape down the sides of the bowl.

4. Detach the beater and use it to stir in the dry ingredients until moistened. Reattach the beater and beat on the lowest speed until the dry ingredients are evenly incorporated, about 15 seconds. The dough will resemble a thick, fluffy buttercream.

Continues

5. Scrape the dough onto a large sheet of plastic wrap. Use it to knead the dough a few times until it becomes one smooth piece. Wrap the dough loosely with the plastic wrap and flatten it into a 5 by 4 inch rectangle.

6. Refrigerate the dough for at least 1 hour, until firm enough to shape. (An instant-read thermometer inserted into the center should read below 63°F / 17°C.)

SHAPE THE DOUGH INTO LOGS

7. Divide the dough into thirds (about 153 grams each). Wrap each piece in plastic wrap. Work with one piece at a time and keep the rest refrigerated.

8. Begin by rolling the dough between the palms of your hands, then use plastic wrap to shape the dough into a log just under 1⅝ inches in diameter and about 4 inches long. Lightly tamp each end on the countertop to flatten it.

9. Wrap the dough log in plastic wrap and slide it into one of the cardboard tubes, if using. Stand the tube on end on the countertop. With your fingers, press the dough log down until it reaches the bottom and fits snugly into the tube. Wrap the tube with plastic wrap to keep the dough from slipping out and stand it on end in the freezer. (Alternatively, if not using the cardboard tube, roll the dough logs to 1⅝ inches in diameter. Wrap and freeze the dough logs for 1 hour, remove them from the freezer, and quickly roll them again to minimize flattening. Then stand them on end in the freezer.)

10. Repeat with the other two pieces of dough.

11. Freeze the dough logs for at least 8 hours to firm them for even cutting. The dough cuts most easily when frozen solid.

The dough can be frozen for up to 3 months.

PREHEAT THE OVEN

Twenty minutes or longer before baking, set an oven rack at the middle level. Set the oven at 350°F / 175°C.

CUT THE DOUGH INTO COOKIES

12. In a small bowl, place the pearl sugar.

13. Remove one of the frozen dough logs from the freezer and let it sit for 10 minutes on the counter. Cut it into twenty to twenty-three ⅛ inch thick slices. While you are cutting the dough, the log will start to flatten. Simply roll it lightly to maintain the round shape.

14. Place the dough rounds ½ inch apart on a prepared cookie sheet. Smooth any rough edges with a small metal spatula. Sprinkle each cookie with some of the pearl sugar and bake at once.

BAKE THE COOKIES

15. Bake for 4 minutes. Rotate the cookie sheet halfway around. Continue baking for 4 to 7 minutes, or until the cookies are set to the touch. Pressing on a cookie should only leave a slight impression.

16. While each batch of cookies is baking, remove the next dough log to soften slightly and then slice it for the next batch.

COOL THE COOKIES

17. Set the cookie sheet on a wire rack and let the cookies cool for about 1 minute, or just until they can be lifted with a thin pancake turner without distorting their shapes. (Do not leave them on the cookie sheet, as they will continue to bake and become too brittle.)

18. Continue with the remaining two batches.

STORE Airtight: room temperature, 2 weeks; refrigerated, 1 month; frozen, 4 months.

VARIATION

Hot Nick Pepparkakors

This variation comes from fellow T'ai Chi student and chef Nick Cronin. Replace ¼ teaspoon of the black pepper with ⅛ teaspoon cayenne pepper. This not only increases the fire, it also intensifies the peppery flavor.

CANDIED PINEAPPLE BISCOTTI

Makes: Twenty-four 4½ by 1¼ inch cookies

My cousin Marion always makes these exceptional cookies as part of her glorious Thanksgiving feast. What I find most compelling about these biscotti is that they are very crisp but at the same time chewy and a little moist, thanks to the candied pineapple.

Oven Temperature: 325°F / 160°C

Baking Time: 20 to 25 minutes for the loaves, then 20 to 25 minutes for the slices

Special Equipment: One 17 by 14 inch cookie sheet, lined with aluminum foil

DOUGH *Makes: 980 grams*

unblanched whole almonds or walnuts	200 grams	2 cups
2 large eggs	100 grams	⅓ cup plus 1 tablespoon (94 ml)
pure vanilla extract	·	½ teaspoon (2.5 ml)
pure almond extract	·	½ teaspoon (2.5 ml)
cointreau or other orange liqueur such as triple sec	15 grams	1 tablespoon (15 ml)
unbleached all-purpose flour	236 grams	2 cups (lightly spooned into the cup and leveled off) minus 2 teaspoons
baking powder, preferably an aluminum-free variety	4.5 grams	1 teaspoon
sugar	200 grams	1 cup
candied pineapple	227 grams	1 cup

PREHEAT THE OVEN

Twenty minutes or longer before baking, set an oven rack at the middle level. Set the oven at 325°F / 160°C.

MISE EN PLACE

Chop the nuts into coarse pieces.

Into a 1 cup / 237 ml glass measure with a spout, weigh or measure the eggs. Whisk in the vanilla and almond extracts and Cointreau. Cover tightly with plastic wrap and set on the counter.

MAKE THE DOUGH

1. In a food processor, process the flour, baking powder, and sugar until evenly mixed.

2. Add the egg mixture and pulse to combine; the flour mixture will be moistened and in small particles.

3. Add the candied pineapple and pulse until it is chopped into pieces under ½ inch. Add the nuts and pulse just to mix them in.

SHAPE THE DOUGH

4. With a large spoon, scrape the dough into 2 rough strips (490 grams each) on the cookie sheet. Use your hands to shape the slightly sticky dough into rectangular loaves 8 inches long by 3 inches wide by 1¼ inches high.

BAKE THE BISCOTTI LOAVES

5. Bake for 15 minutes. Rotate the cookie sheet halfway around. Continue baking for 5 to 10 minutes, or until the loaves are light golden brown. When pressed with a fingertip, they will have a very slight give, but they will firm up on cooling.

COOL THE BISCOTTI LOAVES

6. Set the cookie sheet on a wire rack and let the loaves cool for 10 minutes.

CUT THE BISCOTTI

7. Slip a large pancake turner underneath each baked loaf and slide onto a cutting mat or board. Set a new piece of aluminum foil on the cookie sheet.

8. Using a serrated knife, slice each loaf on an angle into 12 cookies, about ¾ inch wide. Return them, cut side down, to the cookie sheet. They can be very close together, without touching.

BAKE THE BISCOTTI

9. Bake the biscotti for 15 minutes. Remove the end pieces. Flip over the remaining slices and rotate the pan halfway around. Continue baking for 5 to 10 minutes, until the biscotti are crisp and golden.

COOL THE BISCOTTI

10. Set the cookie sheet on a wire rack and use a thin pancake turner to transfer the biscotti to another wire rack. Cool completely.

STORE Airtight: room temperature, 3 weeks; frozen, 3 months.

Baking Gem

🤍 The biscotti need to be removed from the foil while still hot to prevent the candied pineapple from sticking.

MANDELBROT

Makes: Thirty 3½ by 1⅜ inch cookies

Mandelbrot means almond bread in German. It is a traditional Jewish cookie that is related to the Italian biscotti. This recipe was given to me by my long-time friend Arnie Civins. It came from his mother, Edie Kaplan Civins.

Edie's recipe used oil, rather than butter, to make the cookies pareve—that is, they can be eaten after a meal of meat and still be true to Jewish kashrut dietary laws. The high amount of oil and the nuts make the cookies less brittle than most biscotti. I've added orange zest for its beautiful color and flavor.

Oven Temperature: 350°F / 175°C; 325°F / 160°C for the second bake	**Baking Time:** 30 to 40 minutes for the cylinders, then 16 to 20 minutes for the slices	**Special Equipment:** Two 17 by 14 inch cookie sheets, nonstick or lined with parchment

DOUGH *Makes: 800 grams*

2 large eggs	100 grams	⅓ cup plus 1 tablespoon (94 ml)
pure vanilla extract	·	1½ teaspoons (7.5 ml)
pure almond extract	·	½ teaspoon (2.5 ml)
canola or safflower oil	143 grams	⅔ cup (158 ml)
unbleached all-purpose flour	282 grams	2⅓ cups (lightly spooned into the cup and leveled off), *divided*
baking powder, preferably an aluminum-free variety	3.4 grams	¾ teaspoon
fine sea salt	·	¼ teaspoon
sugar	133 grams	⅔ cup
orange zest, finely grated (see Baking Gems)	12 grams	2 tablespoons (loosely packed)
sliced unblanched almonds	142 grams	1½ scant cups
unblanched whole almonds (optional)	32 grams	¼ cup

PREHEAT THE OVEN

Twenty minutes or longer before baking, set two oven racks in the upper and lower thirds of the oven. Set the oven at 350°F / 175°C.

MISE EN PLACE

Thirty minutes ahead, into a 1 cup / 237 ml glass measure with a spout, weigh or measure the eggs. Whisk in the vanilla and almond extracts. Cover tightly with plastic wrap and set on the counter.

Into a 1 cup / 237 ml glass measure with a spout, weigh or measure the oil.

Into a medium bowl, weigh or measure the flour. Remove 30 grams / ¼ cup to a custard cup for dusting the dough. Whisk the baking powder and salt into the remaining flour.

MAKE THE DOUGH

Food Processor Method

1. In a food processor, process the sugar and orange zest until the zest is very fine.

Continues

2. With the motor running, add the egg mixture and process until completely blended. Scrape down the sides of the bowl.

3. With the motor running, gradually add the oil, processing until blended.

4. Add the sliced almonds and process until finely chopped.

5. Add the flour mixture and process just until it is almost completely incorporated and some of the mixture is still clinging to the sides of the bowl, about 7 seconds.

Stand Mixer Method

1. Finely chop the orange zest.

2. Grind the sliced almonds in batches with a little of the flour mixture in a spice mill, or use a rotary nut grinder.

3. Whisk the orange zest and ground almonds into the (remaining) flour mixture.

4. In the bowl of a stand mixer fitted with the flat beater, beat the sugar and egg mixture on medium speed for 2 to 3 minutes, until lighter in color and very thick.

5. Gradually beat in the oil.

6. On low speed, gradually beat in the flour mixture.

Both Methods

7. Lightly dust a counter with a little of the reserved flour. Scrape the dough on top and knead it, adding as little additional flour as possible, to form a soft, tacky (slightly sticky) dough.

SHAPE THE CYLINDERS

8. Divide the dough in half (about 400 grams each). Form each piece of dough into a 2½ inch wide by about 7½ inch long cylinder.

9. If using the whole almonds, line them up lengthwise down the cylinders of dough (to make slicing the baked mandelbrot easier) and press them firmly into the dough. Pinch the dough together to enclose them.

10. Set the cylinders pinched side down on the counter and roll lightly, maintaining the diameter of 2½ inches.

11. Place the cylinders 2 inches apart on a cookie sheet.

BAKE THE CYLINDERS

12. Set the cookie sheet on the upper oven rack and bake for 20 minutes. Rotate the pan halfway around. Continue baking for 10 to 20 minutes, or until the mandelbrot is lightly browned and very firm. There will likely be some cracks along the sides. Reduce the oven temperature to 325°F / 160°C.

COOL THE CYLINDERS

13. Set the cookie sheet on a wire rack. Wet a full-size paper towel or two half-size ones and squeeze out the excess water. Lay on top of the cylinders, then cover with a piece of aluminum foil. This will keep the top crusts soft, to facilitate slicing. Cool until warm to the touch.

CINNAMON SUGAR TOPPING

sugar	50 grams	¼ cup
ground cinnamon	·	¼ teaspoon

14. In a small bowl, stir together the sugar and cinnamon.

CUT THE CYLINDERS

15. Slide the cylinders onto a cutting mat or board; remove and discard the paper towel(s).

16. Using a serrated knife, slice each cylinder on an angle into 15 mandelbrot, about ½ inch wide. Arrange them cut side down on the two cookie sheets. They can be very close together, without touching.

17. Sprinkle the cinnamon sugar evenly over the tops of the mandelbrot. Then smooth it over the entire surface of each cookie.

BAKE THE MANDELBROT

18. Bake for 8 to 10 minutes, or until pale golden.

19. With a thin pancake turner, flip the mandelbrot over. Remove the end pieces. Sugar the tops of the remaining slices and bake for another 8 to 10 minutes, until pale golden; rotate the cookies sheets from top to bottom and front to back halfway through the baking period.

COOL THE MANDELBROT

20. Set the cookie sheets on wire racks and let the mandelbrot cool completely.

STORE Airtight: room temperature, 3 months; frozen, 6 months.

Baking Gems

♥ Unbleached all-purpose flour has a higher amount of gluten-forming proteins than bleached flour, which helps to strengthen the dough and hold in the whole almonds. Avoid adding too much flour when shaping the dough. It needs to be a bit sticky to prevent cracks from forming during baking.

♥ Wash the orange with dishwashing liquid, rinse, and dry before zesting.

♥ When cutting the baked cylinders, hold them near the portion being sliced and press gently on top.

♥ If the mandelbrot become very hard on storage, either dip them in tea or coffee or set a damp paper towel in a small foil cup or glass custard cup in the storage container for a few days to soften them.

Clockwise from top left: Candied Pineapple Biscotti (page 164), Mandelbrot (page 166), Palm Beach Pecan Biscotti (page 170), and Deeply Chocolate Biscotti (page 172).

PALM BEACH PECAN BISCOTTI

Makes: Twenty-eight 4 by 1½ inch cookies

Maida Heatter once wrote, "Happiness is baking cookies. Happiness is giving them away. And serving them, and eating them, talking about them, reading and writing about them, thinking about them, and sharing them with you." Maida was one of my earliest baking inspirations; this recipe is adapted from *Maida Heatter's Brand-New Book of Great Cookies*. The generous amount of pecans in this recipe forms an elegant and tasty mosaic in the incredibly crisp, thin biscotti slices. I prefer a bit less sugar in my sweets, so I reduced the sugar by 12 percent from Maida's original, using just ⅔ cup. But if you want to make them just like she did, use the higher amount of sugar given below.

Oven Temperature: 350°F / 175°C; 325°C / 160°C for the second bake

Baking Time: 45 to 55 minutes for the loaf, then 15 to 20 minutes for the slices

Plan Ahead: The cooled baked loaf needs to be frozen for a minimum of 3 hours to slice thinly; it can be frozen for several months.

Special Equipment: One 8½ by 4½ by 2¾ inch (6 cup) loaf pan, buttered and coated with about 8 grams / 2 tablespoons of fine dry bread crumbs; A 17¼ by 12¼ half sheet pan, no preparation needed

DOUGH *Makes: 508 grams*

unsalted butter	57 grams	4 tablespoons (½ stick)
2 large eggs	100 grams	⅓ cup plus 1 tablespoon (94 ml)
pure vanilla extract	·	½ teaspoon (2.5 ml)
unbleached all-purpose flour	105 grams	¾ cup (lightly spooned into the cup and leveled off) plus 1½ tablespoons
baking powder, preferably an aluminum-free variety	·	¼ teaspoon
fine sea salt	·	⅛ teaspoon
sugar	133 to 150 grams	⅔ to ¾ cup
pecan halves	150 grams	1½ cups

PREHEAT THE OVEN

Twenty minutes or longer before baking, set an oven rack in the lower third of the oven. Set the oven at 350°F / 175°C.

MISE EN PLACE

Thirty minutes to 1 hour ahead, cut the butter into tablespoon-size pieces. Set on the counter to soften.

Thirty minutes ahead, into a 1 cup / 237 ml glass measure with a spout, weigh or measure the eggs. Whisk in the vanilla extract. Cover tightly with plastic wrap and set on the counter.

In a medium bowl, whisk together the flour, baking powder, and salt.

MAKE THE DOUGH

1. In the bowl of a stand mixer fitted with the flat beater, beat the butter and sugar on low speed until well blended, about 30 seconds.

2. Gradually beat in the egg mixture. It will be very soupy.

3. Add the flour mixture and beat just until incorporated, about 15 seconds. Scrape down the sides of the bowl as needed.

4. Remove the bowl from the mixer stand and use a silicone spatula to stir in the pecans.

5. Scrape the dough into the prepared pan. It will be less than half full.

6. Smooth the top of the dough with the silicone spatula. Using a small offset spatula, make a long trench down the length of the pan, about ½ inch deep, to inhibit as much doming as possible.

BAKE THE LOAF

7. Bake for 30 minutes. Rotate the pan halfway around. Continue baking for 15 to 25 minutes, or until a wooden skewer inserted into the center of the loaf comes out clean.

COOL THE LOAF

8. Set the pan on a wire rack. Wet a full-size paper towel or two half-size ones and squeeze out the excess water. Lay on top of the loaf and cover the pan tightly with a piece of aluminum foil. (This will keep the top crust soft, to facilitate slicing.) Cool until warm to the touch.

UNMOLD THE LOAF

9. Set a small rack on top of the pan and invert the loaf onto it. Set a piece of plastic wrap large enough to wrap the loaf on a quarter sheet pan or small baking sheet. Reinvert the loaf onto it and remove the foil and paper towel(s).

10. Wrap the loaf with the plastic wrap and set it in the freezer for a minimum of 3 hours, so that it is firm enough to cut.

PREHEAT THE OVEN

Twenty minutes or longer before baking the slices, set an oven rack at the middle level. Set the oven at 325°F / 160°C.

SLICE THE LOAF

11. Using a serrated or very sharp knife, carefully cut the loaf into ¼ inch slices. If the loaf is too firm, allow it to sit for a few minutes to soften. As you cut each slice, set cut side down on the half sheet pan; the slices should be touching each other.

BAKE THE BISCOTTI

12. Bake for 10 minutes. Rotate the pan halfway around. Continue baking for 5 to 10 minutes (a little longer if your slices are thicker), checking carefully to prevent overbrowning. The biscotti should be pale golden and browner at the edges and feel dry and firm to the touch. They will continue to dry on cooling. If some of the slices are thinner than others, remove them as they are ready.

COOL THE BISCOTTI

13. With a thin pancake turner, remove the biscotti to a layer of paper towels, to absorb any excess butter or moisture, and cool completely.

STORE Airtight: room temperature, 1 month or longer.

Baking Gem

♥ The butter beats most easily at 70°F / 21°C; if it is colder, beat it on medium speed until it is creamy before adding the sugar in Step 1.

VARIATIONS

Maida offers two delicious additions, either of which can be stirred into the dough along with the pecans.

Crystallized Ginger: 110 grams / ½ cup, cut into small pieces.

Pistachio and Lemon Zest: 50 grams / ⅓ cup unsalted pistachios and 12 grams / 2 tablespoons loosely packed finely grated lemon zest (from about 3 large lemons). Wash the lemons with dishwashing liquid, rinse, and dry before zesting.

DEEPLY CHOCOLATE BISCOTTI

Makes: Twenty-four 4¼ by 1¼ inch cookies

Lisa Yockelson, my dear friend and author of *Chocolate Chocolate*, is the creator of the most uniquely delicious chocolate biscotti I've ever tasted. They are marvelously crunchy, and they are delicious eaten on their own or dunked into coffee or milk.

Oven Temperature: 350°F / 175°C; then 275°F / 135°C for the second bake

Baking Time: 35 to 40 minutes for the loaves, then about 20 minutes for the slices

Special Equipment: One 17 by 14 inch cookie sheet, lined with parchment and the parchment held in place with 4 pieces of masking tape; if desired, draw two 10 inch long by 2½ inch wide rectangles about 4 inches apart on the parchment to serve as guides, then flip it over

DOUGH *Makes: 1,100 grams*

unsalted butter	113 grams	8 tablespoons (1 stick)
2 large eggs	100 grams	⅓ cup plus 1 tablespoon (94 ml)
1 medium egg yolk	13 grams	2½ teaspoons (12.5 ml)
pure vanilla extract	·	2½ teaspoons (12.5 ml)
strong coffee, freshly brewed	20 grams	4 teaspoons (20 ml)
fine-quality unsweetened or 99% cacao chocolate	20 grams (0.7 ounce)	·
bleached all-purpose flour	290 grams	2⅓ cups (lightly spooned into the cup and leveled off) plus 1 tablespoon
unsweetened alkalized cocoa powder	56 grams	¾ cup (sifted before measuring)
cornstarch	6 grams	2 teaspoons
baking powder, preferably an aluminum-free variety	4.5 grams	1 teaspoon
fine sea salt	4 grams	¾ teaspoon
sugar, preferably superfine	200 grams	1 cup

dark chocolate chips, 52% to 63% cacao (see Baking Gem)	283 grams (10 ounces)	1⅔ cups
granulated sugar, for topping the loaves	37 grams	3 tablespoons

PREHEAT THE OVEN

Twenty minutes or longer before baking, set an oven rack at the middle level. Set the oven at 350°F / 175°C.

MISE EN PLACE

Thirty minutes to 1 hour ahead, cut the butter into tablespoon-size pieces. Set on the counter to soften.

Thirty minutes ahead, into a 1 cup / 237 ml glass measure with a spout, weigh or measure the eggs and egg yolk. Whisk in the vanilla extract. Cover tightly with plastic wrap and set on the counter.

Into a small bowl, weigh or measure the hot coffee. Cover with plastic wrap and cool to room temperature.

Melt the Chocolate: Twenty to 30 minutes before baking, chop the unsweetened chocolate into coarse pieces. In a small microwavable bowl, heat the chocolate, stirring every 15 seconds with a silicone spatula, until almost completely melted (or heat the chocolate in the top of a double boiler set over hot, not simmering, water—do not let the bottom of the container touch the water—stirring often, until almost completely melted).

Remove the chocolate from the heat source and stir until fully melted. Let it cool until it is no longer warm to the touch but still fluid (80° to 85°F / 27° to 29°C).

In a medium bowl, whisk together the flour, cocoa powder, cornstarch, baking powder, and salt. Sift the flour mixture onto a sheet of parchment.

MAKE THE DOUGH

1. In the bowl of a stand mixer fitted with the flat beater, beat the butter on medium speed until smooth and creamy, about 2 minutes.

2. Gradually add the sugar in three parts, beating for 45 seconds after each addition. Scrape down the sides of the bowl.

3. With the mixer on medium-low speed, gradually add the egg mixture, beating just until incorporated. Scrape down the sides of the bowl. The mixture will not be smooth.

4. Add the coffee and melted chocolate and beat until well mixed. Scrape down the sides of the bowl.

5. Add half the sifted flour mixture and mix on low speed just until the flour is absorbed. Add the remaining flour mixture along with the chocolate chips and mix just until the flour is absorbed.

SHAPE THE DOUGH

6. Divide the dough in half (550 grams each). Scrape the dough into 2 rough strips on the prepared cookie sheet.

7. Lightly wet your fingers and shape each strip into a rectangular loaf 10 inches long by 2½ inches wide (following the lines drawn on the parchment, if using); the loaves will be about 1 inch high. Remove the tape used to secure the parchment.

8. Heavily sprinkle the top of each rectangle with half of the granulated sugar.

BAKE THE BISCOTTI LOAVES

9. Bake the biscotti loaves for 20 minutes. Rotate the cookie sheet halfway around. Continue baking for 15 to 20 minutes, or until the loaves are set and baked through and a wooden skewer inserted into the center comes out clean.

COOL THE BISCOTTI LOAVES

10. Set the cookie sheet on a wire rack and let the biscotti cool for 10 minutes. Reduce the oven temperature to 275°F / 135°C.

CUT THE BISCOTTI

11. Slip an offset spatula underneath the baked loaves to loosen them from the parchment. Carefully transfer one rectangle to a cutting board.

12. Using a serrated knife, slice the loaf on an angle into cookies slightly under 1 inch thick. Return them, cut side down, to the cookie sheet.

13. Repeat with the second loaf.

BAKE THE BISCOTTI

14. Bake the cookies for 20 minutes, or until they are firm and dry, turning them over once or twice. The cut surfaces of the cookies should look dry on both sides. (Avoid overbaking so as not to compromise the flavor.)

COOL THE BISCOTTI

15. Let the cookies sit on the cookie sheet for 5 minutes. Then carefully use tongs to transfer the biscotti to a wire rack. Cool completely.

STORE Airtight: room temperature, 3 weeks; frozen, 3 months.
*Biscotti keep well but have the fullest flavor within 3 days of baking.

CHAPTER 4

ROLLED
AND CUT

TIPS FOR ROLLING DOUGH FOR CUTOUT COOKIES

Rolled and cutout cookies are most easy to make in a cool room. If the room is warm and the dough starts to soften, slipping the dough onto a cookie sheet, covering it with plastic wrap, and refrigerating it until firm is a great help. The scraps from some doughs, such as that for chocolate sablés, don't need rechilling, because as a little extra flour gets added during rolling the first batch, they tend to be less sticky. In general, I try to avoid adding much extra flour when rolling.

Some moister, sticky doughs are easiest to roll between sheets of plastic wrap. This also helps to keep the top of the dough from cracking. I like to flatten the dough into a disc, wrap it, and refrigerate it to give the moisture a chance to distribute and the dough to become firm enough to roll to the proper thickness. If you are rolling a large piece of dough, you can overlap multiple sheets of plastic wrap to make it large enough or simply roll a smaller amount of dough at a time.

MY BASIC METHOD FOR TWO BATCHES OF ROLLED COOKIES IS AS FOLLOWS:

1. Divide the dough into two equal parts, shape each into a disc, and wrap them in plastic wrap. Refrigerate if necessary.

2. Roll out the first piece of dough and cut out the shapes. Set them on the first cookie sheet.

3. Wrap and refrigerate the scraps.

4. Roll the second disc and cut as many shapes as needed to fill the first cookie sheet. Set any extra cut cookies on the second sheet.

5. Add the scraps from the second batch to the ones in the refrigerator to make a third batch. Wrap and refrigerate.

6. Continue rolling, cutting, and refrigerating until all the scraps are used.

Note: Some cookies keep their shape best when refrigerated before baking.

ALFAJORES

Makes: Ten 2¾ inch round sandwich cookies

These Latin-American sandwich cookies are made with a very special dough that has an airy, crumbly, exquisite texture when baked. The dough is delicate, soft, and silky and a pleasure to shape. Though it is traditionally made with cornstarch, using cassava starch (tapioca flour) makes the cookies even lighter. The cookies can be filled with jam, but my favorite fillings are dulce de leche, especially my homemade version (page 394), and lemon curd (page 403).

Oven Temperature: 300°F / 150°C	**Baking Time:** 18 to 22 minutes (for each of two batches)

Special Equipment: Two 17 by 14 inch cookie sheets, no preparation needed or lined with parchment; A 2¼ inch to 2⅜ inch round cookie cutter

DOUGH *Makes: 486 grams*

unsalted butter	85 grams	6 tablespoons (¾ stick)
2 (to 3) large egg yolks (see page xxvi)	37 grams	2 tablespoons plus 1 teaspoon (35 ml)
1 large egg white	30 grams	2 tablespoons (30 ml)
pure vanilla extract	·	1 teaspoon (5 ml)
lemon zest, finely grated	2 grams	1 teaspoon (loosely packed)
cassava starch (tapioca flour)	150 grams	1¼ cups (sifted, then lightly spooned into the cup and leveled off)
all-purpose flour, preferably bleached	70 grams	½ cup (lightly spooned into the cup and leveled off) plus 1 tablespoon

baking powder, preferably an aluminum-free variety	5.6 grams	1¼ teaspoons
fine sea salt	·	⅛ teaspoon
sugar, preferably superfine (see Baking Gems)	100 grams	½ cup
dulce de leche, homemade (page 394) or store-bought, or cajeta (page 395), for filling	200 grams	½ cup plus 2 tablespoons
unsweetened shredded coconut, for coating the filling (optional)	4 grams	2 teaspoons

Continues

MISE EN PLACE

For the Food Processor Method: Thirty minutes ahead or longer, cut the butter into ½ inch cubes. Wrap and refrigerate.

For the Stand Mixer Method: Thirty minutes to 1 hour ahead, cut the butter into tablespoon-size pieces. Set on the counter to soften.

Into a 1 cup / 237 ml glass measure with a spout, weigh or measure the egg yolks and egg white. Whisk in the vanilla extract. Cover tightly with plastic wrap and set on the counter.

With dishwashing liquid, wash, rinse, and dry the lemon. Zest it into a small bowl.

In a medium bowl, whisk together the cassava, flour, baking powder, and salt.

MAKE THE DOUGH

Food Processor Method

1. In a food processor, process the sugar for several minutes, until very fine.

2. Add the cold butter cubes and pulse until all the sugar coats the butter.

3. Add the cassava mixture and lemon zest and pulse until the mixture resembles coarse meal.

4. Add the egg mixture and pulse several times to begin to incorporate it. Scrape down the sides of the bowl.

5. Process for 30 seconds, or until the mixture begins to form a cohesive dough.

Stand Mixer Method

1. In the bowl of a stand mixer fitted with the flat beater, beat the butter, sugar, and lemon zest on medium speed for about 5 minutes, or until the mixture lightens in color.

2. Gradually add the egg mixture, beating until it is incorporated.

3. Add the cassava mixture and beat on low speed just until fully incorporated and a soft, cohesive dough forms.

Both Methods

6. Scrape the dough onto a piece of plastic wrap and use the plastic wrap to knead it together until smooth.

ROLL AND CUT THE DOUGH

7. Divide the dough in half (about 243 grams each). Wrap each piece loosely in plastic wrap and press to flatten into a 7 inch disc, about ¾ inch thick.

For the food processor method: You can shape the dough now, or you can wrap it in two layers of plastic wrap and refrigerate for up to 2 days.

For the stand mixer method: Refrigerate for 1 to 2 hours, up to 2 days.

PREHEAT THE OVEN

Twenty minutes or longer before baking, set an oven rack at the middle level. Set the oven at 300°F / 150°C.

8. Work with one disc of dough at a time; keep the other one refrigerated. Between two sheets of plastic wrap, gently roll the first piece of dough into a ¼ inch thick oval.

9. Cut out the cookies and transfer them to a cookie sheet, spacing them a minimum of 1 inch apart. Continue with the second dough disc, until you have 10 cookies on the cookie sheet. Place any extra cookies on the second sheet. Cover the second sheet with plastic wrap until you are ready to add more cookies.

10. Cover the first sheet with plastic wrap and refrigerate for a minimum of 15 minutes before baking.

11. Use plastic wrap to knead together all the dough scraps and shape them into a disc. Cover with the plastic wrap and refrigerate until firm enough to roll and cut.

12. Continue rolling and cutting the remaining dough until you have used all the dough.

Continues

BAKE THE COOKIES

13. Bake the first cookie sheet for 10 minutes. Rotate the pan halfway around. Continue baking for 8 to 12 minutes, or just until the surfaces of the cookies are pale gold and set. When pressed lightly, there should not be any give.

COOL THE COOKIES

14. Set the cookie sheet on a wire rack and let the cookies cool completely. Use a thin pancake turner to transfer half of the cookies, bottom side up, to the counter if ready to fill them, or transfer all the cookies to a storage container.

15. Bake and cool the second batch.

SANDWICH THE ALFAJORES

16. Use a small spoon to spread about 1 tablespoon (20 grams) of dulce de leche or cajeta onto each of the bottoms of 10 cookies.

17. Set the remaining 10 cookies, bottom side down, on top to create sandwiches. Press gently so that the dulce de leche oozes a little past the edges.

OPTIONAL: COAT THE EDGES WITH COCONUT

18. If desired, arrange the coconut in a small bowl in a short mounded strip. Roll the alfajores down the strip to attach the coconut to the filling.

STORE Filled, airtight: room temperature, 2 days; frozen, 2 months.
Unfilled, airtight: room temperature, 1 week; frozen, 2 months.

Baking Gems

♥ Alfajores are often described as soft, but a more apt description is "dissolving." For the best texture, they need to be baked until crisp inside and out but not browned. That is why I prefer bleached flour, which is slower to brown, for these.

♥ My preference is to use a food processor to make the dough. The cookies will have the best texture when made with superfine sugar; if you are using a food processor, granulated sugar can be easily processed to superfine consistency. In addition, the dough doesn't need to be chilled before shaping, because the butter stays colder.

♥ My personal preference is without the coconut but dusted lightly with powdered sugar before serving.

COCONUT CRISPS

Makes: Twenty-two 2¼ inch round cookies

Flaked unsweetened coconut gives this cookie an exceptionally crisp texture as well as a lingering coconut flavor.

Oven Temperature: 375°F / 190°C	**Baking Time:** 10 to 14 minutes (for each of two batches)	**Special Equipment:** Two 17 by 14 inch cookie sheets, no preparation needed or lined with parchment; A 2¼ inch scalloped or plain round cookie cutter

DOUGH *Makes: 360 grams*

unsalted butter, cold	113 grams	8 tablespoons (1 stick)
1 large egg	50 grams	3 tablespoons plus ½ teaspoon (47 ml)
bleached all-purpose flour	150 grams	1¼ cups (lightly spooned into the cup and leveled off)
sugar	50 grams	¼ cup
flaked unsweetened coconut	30 grams	¼ cup plus 2 tablespoons
fine sea salt	·	⅛ teaspoon

MISE EN PLACE

Thirty minutes ahead or longer, cut the butter into ½ inch cubes. Wrap and refrigerate.

Into a custard cup or small bowl, weigh or measure the egg. Whisk lightly and set on the counter.

MAKE THE DOUGH

1. In a food processor, process the flour, sugar, coconut, and salt until the coconut is finely ground.

2. Add the cold butter cubes and pulse until the butter pieces are no larger than small peas.

3. Add the egg and pulse just until incorporated, about 8 times. The dough will be in crumbly pieces.

4. Empty the dough into a plastic bag and press it from the outside of the bag just until it holds together. Remove the dough from the plastic bag and place it on a very large piece of plastic wrap. Using the plastic wrap, knead the dough a few times, just until it becomes one smooth piece. There should be no visible pieces of butter. If there are, use the heel of your hand to press them in a forward motion to smear them into the dough.

CHILL THE DOUGH

5. Divide the dough into two pieces, about two-thirds / 250 grams and one-third / 110 grams. Wrap each piece loosely with plastic wrap and press to flatten into a ½ inch thick disc.

6. Rewrap them tightly and refrigerate for 30 minutes, or until firm enough to roll.

The dough can be refrigerated for up to 3 days or frozen for up to 6 months.

PREHEAT THE OVEN

Thirty minutes or longer before baking, set an oven rack at the middle level. Set the oven at 375°F / 190°C.

Continues

ROLL AND CUT THE DOUGH

7. Roll out the larger dough disc between sheets of plastic wrap to a thickness of ¼ inch, lightly flouring both sides of the dough as needed to prevent sticking. (If the dough has been chilled for more than 30 minutes, let it sit for about 5 to 10 minutes, until it is malleable enough to roll.) If the dough softens, slide it onto a cookie sheet and refrigerate for about 15 minutes, or until firm enough to make the cutouts. From time to time as you roll, flip the dough with the plastic wrap, and lift off and smooth out the plastic wrap as necessary to make sure it does not wrinkle into the dough.

8. Cut out eleven or twelve 2¼ inch cookies. Remove the scraps and add them to the other dough disc. Use the plastic wrap to lift and gently remove the shapes and place them about ½ inch apart on a prepared cookie sheet; if necessary, refrigerate them until firm enough to lift.

BAKE THE COOKIES

9. Bake the cookies for 5 minutes. Rotate the cookie sheet halfway around. Continue baking for 5 to 9 minutes, or until the cookies are pale gold and brown around the edges.

COOL THE COOKIES

10. Set the cookie sheet on a wire rack and use a thin pancake turner to transfer the cookies to another wire rack. Cool completely.

11. Repeat with the second batch, kneading the dough scraps into the disc before rolling and cutting the dough.

STORE Airtight: room temperature, 3 weeks; frozen, 3 months.

LES PIQUE-NIQUES

Makes: Eighteen 2¾ inch round sandwich cookies

This is my adaptation of one of the Bernachon family's favorite cookies, which the legendary chocolatiers created for their book *La Passion du Chocolat*. They told me it is called "picnic" cookie dough because the cookies hold up so well for packing in a picnic basket. They are indeed firm, but exceptionally crisp and deeply chocolaty, and they soften very slightly when filled with the creamy ganache. The dough is exceptionally easy to roll and shape.

Oven Temperature:	Baking Time:	Plan Ahead: Several hours before	Special Equipment: Two or
350°F / 175°C	10 to 12 minutes (for each of three batches)	you are ready to fill the cookies, make the half recipe of Dark Chocolate Ganache, which is 119 grams / ¼ cup plus 3 tablespoons.	three 17 by 14 inch cookie sheets, lined with parchment; A 2¾ inch round cookie cutter

DOUGH *Makes: 720 grams*

unsalted butter	134 grams	9½ tablespoons (1 stick plus 1½ tablespoons)
1 large egg	50 grams	3 tablespoons plus ½ teaspoon (47.5 ml)
milk	30 grams	2 tablespoons (30 ml)
pure vanilla extract	·	½ teaspoon (2.5 ml)
bleached all-purpose flour	250 grams	2 cups (lightly spooned into the cup and leveled off) plus 1 tablespoon
unsweetened alkalized cocoa powder	50 grams	⅔ cup (sifted before measuring)
fine sea salt	·	¹⁄₁₆ teaspoon (a pinch)
unblanched sliced almonds	50 grams	½ cup
sugar	175 grams	¾ cup

MISE EN PLACE

Thirty minutes ahead or longer, cut the butter into ½ inch cubes. Wrap in plastic wrap and refrigerate.

Into a small bowl, weigh or measure the egg. Whisk in the milk and vanilla extract. Cover tightly with plastic wrap and set on the counter.

MAKE THE DOUGH

1. In a medium bowl, whisk together the flour, cocoa, and salt. Pass it through a fine mesh strainer onto a piece of parchment.

2. In a food processor, process the almonds until finely chopped. Add the sugar and process for about 1 minute, until the sugar is finely ground.

3. Add the cold butter cubes and pulse until the butter pieces are the size of peas. Add the flour mixture and pulse until the butter pieces are no larger than small peas. Add the egg mixture and pulse just until incorporated, about 8 times. The dough will be in very crumbly pieces.

Continues

4. Empty the dough into a plastic bag and press it from the outside of the bag just until it holds together. Remove the dough from the plastic bag and place it on a very large sheet of plastic wrap. Using the plastic wrap, knead the dough a few times, just until it becomes one smooth piece.

5. Divide the dough into three pieces. Work with one piece at a time; wrap the other two pieces in plastic wrap. If it is warm in the room and the dough softens, refrigerate it briefly until firm.

PREHEAT THE OVEN

Twenty minutes or longer before baking, set an oven rack at the middle level. Set the oven at 350°F / 175°C.

ROLL AND CUT THE DOUGH

6. Roll the dough between sheets of plastic wrap to a thickness of ⅛ inch.

7. Cut out the cookies and place them no closer than ½ inch apart on a prepared cookie sheet. Gather up the scraps of dough, cover, and set aside.

8. Roll and cut out the second piece of dough to finish filling the first cookie sheet and start filling the second sheet (12 cookies per sheet). Add the scraps of dough to the first bunch of scraps.

9. Roll and cut out the third piece of dough to finish filling the second cookie sheet and start filling the third sheet. (If you only have two cookie sheets, place the last batch on a sheet of parchment.)

10. Combine all the scraps and reroll and cut them as many times as needed until you have used all the dough and filled the third cookie sheet.

BAKE THE COOKIES

11. Set the first cookie sheet in the oven and bake for 5 minutes. Rotate the cookie sheet halfway around. Continue baking for 5 to 7 minutes, or until the tops of the cookies are set and firm but still feel a little soft when pressed with a fingertip. The cookies will continue to harden when cooling.

COOL THE COOKIES

12. Set the cookie sheet on a wire rack and let the cookies cool completely. Use a thin pancake turner to transfer half of the cookies, bottom side up, to the counter if ready to fill them; or transfer all the cookies to a storage container.

13. Repeat with the remaining two batches. (If you don't have a third cookie sheet, after baking the first two batches, slip one of the cooled cookie sheets under the parchment to bake the third batch.)

DARK CHOCOLATE GANACHE

½ recipe Dark Chocolate Ganache (page 279)	119 grams	¼ cup plus 3 tablespoons

SANDWICH THE COOKIES

14. Use a small offset spatula to spread about 2 teaspoons (10 grams) of ganache onto the bottoms of half the cookies.

15. Set the remaining cookies bottom side down on top to create sandwiches.

STORE Filled, airtight: room temperature, 1 day; refrigerated, 5 days, frozen, 3 months. Unfilled, airtight: room temperature, 5 days; refrigerated, 1 week; frozen, 3 months.

BUTTERED RUM COOKIES

Makes: Sixteen 2 inch round sandwich cookies

One of the most touching Christmas cookie stories I know comes from my friend Jeanne Bauer, whose mother was a great cookie baker. Every year, when making Christmas cookies, her mother would save some of the dough for Jeanne's annual visit so that they could bake together. Jeanne said that somehow, when hands are busy, one finds it easier to confide intimate things.

This Bauer recipe is one of my favorites. I love it so much I even created a second cookie without rum, Raspberry Almond Cookies (see the Variation), using the same buttery, tender cookie dough as the base.

| **Oven Temperature:** 325°F / 160°C for the almonds; 375°F / 190°C for the cookies | **Baking Time:** 7 minutes for the almonds; 8 to 10 minutes for the cookies (for each of two batches) | **Plan Ahead:** Fill the cookies the day of serving so that they remain crisp. | **Special Equipment:** Two 17 by 14 inch cookie sheets, nonstick or lined with parchment; A 2¼ inch scalloped round cookie cutter; A ¾ inch plain round cookie cutter or ¾ inch plain pastry tube |

DOUGH *Makes: 275 grams*

sliced unblanched almonds	15 grams	2½ tablespoons
unsalted butter	113 grams	8 tablespoons (1 stick)
powdered sugar	29 grams	¼ cup (lightly spooned into the cup and leveled off)
fine sea salt	·	⅛ teaspoon
pure almond extract	·	¼ teaspoon (1.25 ml)
light rum	14 grams	1 tablespoon (15 ml)
bleached all-purpose flour	113 grams	1 cup (lightly spooned into the cup and leveled off) minus 1 tablespoon

PREHEAT THE OVEN

Twenty minutes or longer before baking, set an oven rack at the middle level. Set the oven at 325°F / 160°C.

MISE EN PLACE

Toast the Almonds: Spread the almonds evenly on a baking sheet and bake for about 7 minutes, or until pale gold. Set the baking sheet on a wire rack and cool completely.

Thirty minutes to 1 hour ahead, cut the butter into tablespoon-size pieces and set on the counter to soften.

MAKE THE DOUGH

Food Processor Method

1. In a food processor, process the almonds with the powdered sugar and salt until powder fine.

2. With the motor running, add the butter one piece at a time and process until smooth and creamy. Scrape down the sides as needed.

3. Pulse in the almond extract and rum.

4. Pulse in the flour just until the dough starts to hold together in clumps, scraping down the

Continues

sides of the bowl as needed. Scrape the dough into a bowl.

Stand Mixer Method

1. Finely grind the almonds in a spice mill with a little of the powdered sugar, or use a rotary nut grinder.

2. In a medium bowl, whisk together the flour, ground nuts, and salt.

3. In the bowl of a stand mixer fitted with the flat beater, beat the butter and (remaining) sugar on medium speed for 2 to 3 minutes, until lighter in color and fluffy.

4. On low speed, gradually beat in the almond extract and rum.

5. Gradually beat in the flour mixture just until incorporated, scraping down the sides of the bowl as needed.

Both Methods

6. Cover the bowl tightly with plastic wrap and refrigerate for a minimum of 2 hours, up to 2 days.

PREHEAT THE OVEN

Thirty minutes or longer before baking, set an oven rack at the middle level. Set the oven at 375°F / 190°C.

ROLL AND CUT THE DOUGH

This fragile dough softens quickly, so work with only a small amount at a time, keeping the rest refrigerated.

7. Lightly knead a piece of the dough until it is malleable but still well chilled.

8. Set the dough on a lightly floured (see Baking Gems) dough mat or sheet of plastic wrap. Lightly flour the dough and roll it ⅛ inch thick. From time to time, move the dough to make sure it is not sticking.

9. Cut out the cookies and use a small metal spatula to transfer them to a cookie sheet, 1 inch apart. Dip the cookie cutter in flour every few cuts to prevent sticking.

10. Use plastic wrap to knead together the scraps and shape them into a disc. Cover with the plastic wrap and refrigerate.

11. Continue with the remaining dough until you have 16 cookies on the first cookie sheet. Place any extra cookies on the second sheet and cover with plastic wrap.

12. Use the ¾ inch plain cookie cutter or pastry tube to cut out windows in half the cookies. Add the dough scraps to the remaining refrigerated dough.

BAKE THE COOKIES

13. Bake for 5 minutes. Rotate the cookie sheet halfway around. Continue baking for 3 to 5 minutes, or until the cookies are lightly browned.

COOL THE COOKIES

14. Set the cookie sheet on a wire rack and use a thin pancake turner to transfer the cookies to another rack. Cool completely.

15. Roll and cut out the rest of the refrigerated dough until all the dough has been used, then bake the second batch.

BUTTERED RUM CREAM FILLING

unsalted butter	21 grams	1½ tablespoons
powdered sugar	57 grams	½ cup (lightly spooned into the cup and leveled off)
light rum	·	½ teaspoon (2.5 ml)
heavy cream	·	1 teaspoon (5 ml)

MAKE THE FILLING

1. Thirty minutes ahead, set the butter on the counter to soften.

2. In a small bowl, using a handheld mixer, or in the bowl of a stand mixer fitted with the flat beater, beat the butter and sugar on low speed for 2 to 3 minutes, until smooth and creamy.

3. Beat in the rum and cream until incorporated.

SANDWICH THE COOKIES

16. Set the cookies without cutouts bottom side up on the counter. Use a small offset spatula or butter knife to spread each one with a rounded ½ teaspoon of cream filling.

17. Set the cookies with the cutouts bottom side down on top of the filling. Very gently press the two cookies together to create sandwiches.

STORE Filled, uncovered: room temperature, 1 day (do not freeze, because the filling would cause the cookies to soften on thawing). Unfilled, airtight: room temperature, 2 months; frozen, 6 months.

Baking Gems

♥ Powdered sugar makes the cookies' texture extra tender.

♥ Wondra flour works wonderfully to prevent sticking when rolling. Don't be afraid to add extra flour, as the cookies will still be very tender.

♥ Wilton makes a seven-piece Linzer cookie cutter set designed to make windows for sandwich cookies. It includes a 2 inch cutter and six different center shapes, which can be inserted into the large cutter to make perfectly centered cutouts. As that cutter is ¼ inch smaller than the one listed here, you will get a few extra cookies.

♥ If the dough softens after cutting the cookies, cover and refrigerate before lifting them off the surface so that they keep their shape.

Raspberry Almond Cookies

Use ½ teaspoon / 2.5 ml pure almond extract and replace the rum with ½ teaspoon / 2.5 ml pure vanilla extract. Instead of the Buttered Rum Cream Filling, sandwich the cookies with a thin layer of raspberry jam, preferably seedless. You will need 78 grams / ¼ cup jam. Filled with jam, the cookies will keep at room temperature, tightly covered, for up to 3 weeks.

LEMON JAMMIES

Makes: Eighteen 2¼ inch round sandwich cookies

This cookie is very similar to the Buttered Rum Cookies (page 185) and Rose's Crescents (page 111), but it uses extra flour in place of the nuts. It also has almost double the sugar, which makes it tender in texture and serves to balance the lemon zest and tart lemon curd or raspberry filling. You could even make these using a combination of the two fillings.

Oven Temperature: 350°F / 175°C	**Baking Time:** 10 to 12 minutes (for each of two batches)	**Plan Ahead:** Fill the cookies the day of serving so that they remain crisp.	**Special Equipment:** Two 17 by 14 inch cookie sheets, nonstick or lined with parchment; A 2¼ inch round scalloped cookie cutter; A ¾ inch plain round cookie cutter or ¾ inch pastry tube

DOUGH *Makes: 336 grams*

unsalted butter	92 grams	6½ tablespoons (¾ stick plus ½ tablespoon)
½ large egg, lightly beaten before measuring	25 grams	1½ tablespoons (22.5 ml)
pure vanilla extract	·	½ teaspoon (2.5 ml)
lemon zest, finely grated (from 1 to 2 lemons)	6 grams	1 tablespoon (loosely packed)
sugar	66 grams	⅓ cup
fine sea salt	·	⅛ teaspoon
bleached all-purpose flour	160 grams	1⅓ cups (lightly spooned into the cup and leveled off)
lemon curd (page 403) or raspberry jam, for the filling	67 grams	¼ cup

MISE EN PLACE

Thirty minutes to 1 hour ahead, cut the butter into tablespoon-size pieces and set it on the counter to soften.

Thirty minutes ahead, into a 1 cup / 237 ml glass measure with a spout, weigh or measure the egg. Whisk in the vanilla extract. Cover tightly with plastic wrap and set on the counter.

With dishwashing liquid, wash, rinse, and dry the lemons before zesting them.

MAKE THE DOUGH
Food Processor Method

1. In a food processor, process the sugar, salt, and lemon zest until the sugar is very fine.

2. With the motor running, add the butter one piece at a time and process until smooth and creamy. Scrape down the sides as needed.

3. With the motor running, add the egg mixture and process until incorporated, scraping down the sides as needed.

4. Pulse in the flour just until incorporated. The dough should hold together if pinched.

Stand Mixer Method

1. Grind the sugar, salt, and lemon zest in a spice mill until the sugar is finely ground. (Alternatively, use superfine sugar and chop the lemon zest very fine.)

2. In the bowl of a stand mixer fitted with the flat beater, beat the butter and sugar–lemon zest

Continues

mixture on medium speed for 2 to 3 minutes, until lighter in color and fluffy.

3. On low speed, gradually beat in the egg mixture until incorporated.

4. Gradually beat in the flour just until it is incorporated and the dough starts to come away from the sides of the bowl.

Both Methods

5. Scrape the dough onto a large piece of plastic wrap and use the plastic wrap to press the dough together, kneading it lightly until smooth.

6. Divide the dough in half (about 168 grams each). Wrap each piece loosely in plastic wrap and press to flatten it into a 5 inch disc. Refrigerate for a minimum of 2 hours, up to 2 days.

PREHEAT THE OVEN

Twenty minutes or longer before baking, set an oven rack at the middle level. Set the oven at 350°F / 175°C.

ROLL AND CUT THE DOUGH

7. Work with one disc of dough at a time, leaving the other one refrigerated. Set it on a lightly floured (see Baking Gems) dough mat or sheet of plastic wrap. Lightly flour the top of the dough and set a second sheet of plastic wrap on top. If the dough has become too firm to roll without cracking, allow it to sit at room temperature for a few minutes.

Roll the dough ⅛ inch thick. From time to time, move the dough to make sure it is not sticking.

8. Cut out the cookies and use a small metal spatula to transfer them to a cookie sheet, ½ inch apart. Dip the cookie cutter in flour every few cuts to prevent sticking. Then roll out the remaining dough disc and cut out cookies until you have 18 cookies on the first cookie sheet. Place any extra cookies on the second sheet and cover with plastic wrap.

9. Use the ¾ inch cookie cutter or pastry tube to cut out round windows in half the cookies.

10. Use plastic wrap to knead together all the dough scraps and shape them into a disc. Cover with the plastic wrap and refrigerate until firm enough to roll and cut.

BAKE THE COOKIES

11. Bake the first batch for 5 minutes. Rotate the cookie sheet halfway around. Continue baking for 5 to 7 minutes, or until the cookies are lightly browned.

COOL THE COOKIES

12. Set the cookie sheet on a wire rack and use a thin pancake turner to transfer the cookies to another rack. Cool completely.

13. Roll and cut the remaining refrigerated dough until all the dough has been used, then bake the second batch.

SANDWICH THE COOKIES

14. Set the cookies without the cutouts bottom side up on the counter. Use a small offset spatula or butter knife to spread each one with a rounded ½ teaspoon of lemon curd or raspberry jam.

15. Set the cookies with the cutouts bottom side down on top of the filling. Very gently press the two cookies together to create sandwiches.

STORE Filled, airtight: room temperature, 3 weeks (do not freeze, because the filling would cause the cookies to soften on thawing).
Unfilled, airtight: room temperature, 2 months; frozen, 6 months.

Baking Gems

🖤 Wondra flour works wonderfully to prevent sticking when rolling. Don't be afraid to add extra flour, as the cookies will still be very tender.

🖤 If the dough softens after cutting the cookies, cover and refrigerate before lifting them off the surface so that they keep their shape.

THE ISCHLER

Makes: Forty 2½ inch round sandwich cookies

This exquisite, melt-in-the-mouth Austrian cookie has a special history. It was created in 1849 at the Zauner bakery in the town of Bad Ischl, the summer residence of the emperor Franz Joseph. These cookies were said to be his favorites. I feel a special connection to this cookie because I made my first strudel dough at bakery Zauner, and my great grandfather Adolf Lansman fought in Franz Joseph's army. But, most of all, I adore the fragile texture and glorious combination of buttery almond cookie with apricot and chocolate fillings.

Oven Temperature: 350°F / 175°C	**Baking Time:** 6 to 10 minutes (for each of four batches)	**Special Equipment:** Two 17 by 14 inch cookie sheets, nonstick or lined with parchment; A 2¼ inch scalloped or plain round or heart-shaped cookie cutter

DOUGH *Makes: 780 grams*

unsalted butter	227 grams	16 tablespoons (2 sticks)
about ½ large egg, lightly beaten before measuring	21 grams	4 teaspoons (20 ml)
pure vanilla extract	·	1 teaspoon (5 ml)
bleached all-purpose flour	220 grams	1¾ cups (lightly spooned into the cup and leveled off) plus 1 tablespoon
fine sea salt	·	¼ teaspoon
sliced almonds, preferably unblanched (see Baking Gems)	200 grams	1 cup
powdered sugar	133 grams	1 cup (lightly spooned into the cup and leveled off) plus 3 tablespoons

MISE EN PLACE

For the Food Processor Method: Thirty minutes ahead or longer, cut the butter into ½ inch cubes. Wrap and refrigerate.

For the Stand Mixer Method: Thirty minutes to 1 hour ahead, cut the butter into tablespoon-size pieces. Set on the counter to soften.

Thirty minutes ahead, into a 1 cup / 237 ml glass measure with a spout, weigh or measure the egg. Whisk in the vanilla extract. Cover tightly with plastic wrap and set on the counter.

In a medium bowl, whisk together the flour and salt.

MAKE THE DOUGH
Food Processor Method

1. Process the almonds and sugar until the almonds are very fine. Add the butter and process until smooth and creamy.

2. Add the egg mixture and process until incorporated, scraping the sides of the bowl as needed.

3. Add the flour mixture and pulse just until incorporated. The mixture will be in moist and crumbly particles but should hold together if pinched.

Stand Mixer Method

1. Grind the almonds in batches in a spice mill with a little of the sugar, or use a rotary nut grinder.

2. In the bowl of a stand mixer fitted with the flat beater, beat the butter, almonds, and (remaining)

Continues

sugar on low speed until the sugar is incorporated. Raise the speed to medium and beat for 2 to 3 minutes, until lighter in color and fluffy.

3. Add the egg mixture and beat until blended.

4. On low speed, gradually add the flour mixture, mixing until it is incorporated and the dough just begins to come away from the sides of the bowl.

Both Methods

CHILL THE DOUGH

5. Scrape the mixture into a plastic bag and, using your knuckles and heels of your hands, press it together. Transfer it to a large sheet of plastic wrap and use the wrap to press down on the dough, kneading it until it is smooth.

6. Divide the dough into quarters (about 195 grams each). Wrap each piece loosely with plastic wrap and press to flatten it into a 6 inch disc, about ¾ inch thick. Refrigerate for a minimum of 2 hours, up to 2 days placed in a gallon-size reclosable freezer bag, to firm the dough and give it a chance to absorb the moisture evenly.

PREHEAT THE OVEN

Twenty minutes or longer before baking, set an oven rack in the middle of the oven. Set the oven at 350°F / 175°C.

ROLL AND CUT THE DOUGH

7. Set one of the discs on a lightly floured counter. Lightly flour the top of the dough and set a sheet of plastic wrap on top. Let the dough sit for about 10 minutes, or until malleable enough to roll without cracking.

8. Roll the dough ⅛ inch thick, moving it from time to time and adding more flour if needed to keep it from sticking. If it becomes very sticky, return it to the refrigerator briefly to firm.

9. Cut out the cookies and place them a minimum of ½ inch apart on a cookie sheet. Cover loosely with plastic wrap while you roll and cut more

cookies. Set aside any scraps, covered with plastic wrap; add the scraps from the next 3 batches as you roll them, then knead all the scraps together and roll them.

10. Continue with the remaining dough discs and scraps until you have 20 cookies on each cookie sheet.

If you only have two cookie sheets, refrigerate the remaining dough until after you have baked the first two sheets. Be sure to cool the cookie sheets completely before setting the next batch of cookie cutouts on top.

BAKE THE COOKIES

11. Bake for 4 minutes. Rotate the cookie sheet halfway around. Continue baking for 2 to 6 minutes, or just until the cookies begin to brown at the edges.

COOL THE COOKIES

12. Set the cookie sheet on a wire rack and let the cookies cool for about 1 minute. Use a thin pancake turner to transfer the cookies to another wire rack. Cool completely.

13. Repeat with the remaining batches.

DARK CHOCOLATE GANACHE FILLING

Makes: 275 grams / 1½ cups

| dark chocolate, 60% to 62% cacao | 227 grams (8 ounces) | . |
| heavy cream | 58 grams | ¼ cup (59 ml) |

MAKE THE GANACHE FILLING

1. Chop the chocolate into coarse pieces. In a medium microwavable bowl, heat the chocolate, stirring every 15 seconds with a silicone spatula, until almost completely melted (or heat the chocolate in the top of a double boiler set over hot, not simmering, water—do not let the bottom of the container touch the water—stirring often, until almost completely melted).

Remove the chocolate from the heat source and, with a silicone spatula, stir until fully melted.

2. Pour the cream on top of the chocolate and stir until smooth. The ganache should drop thickly from the spatula. Set it aside in a warm place.

If the ganache thickens before you use all of it, it can be restored to a spreadable consistency in the microwave with 3-second bursts (or in a double boiler set over hot or simmering water).

The ganache keeps in an airtight container for 3 days at cool room temperature, 2 weeks refrigerated, or 6 months frozen.

APRICOT LEKVAR FILLING

Lekvar made from dried apricots is the most delicious and concentrated. The yield will vary depending on how much you push through the strainer, which is a labor of love. The Apricot Jam Glaze (see the Variation on page 194) makes a good alternative.

Makes: about 420 grams / about 1⅓ cups / 325 ml

dried apricots	227 grams (8 ounces)	1⅓ cups (firmly packed)
water	237 grams	1 cup (237 ml)
lemon zest, finely grated	2 grams	1 teaspoon (loosely packed)
sugar	225 grams	½ cup plus 2 tablespoons

Have ready a medium-fine-mesh strainer suspended over a medium bowl.

MAKE THE APRICOT LEKVAR FILLING

1. In a medium saucepan with a tight-fitting lid, combine the dried apricots with the water and let sit for 2 hours to soften.

2. Bring the water to a boil, cover the pan, and simmer over the lowest-possible heat for 20 to 30 minutes, until the apricots are very soft when pierced with a skewer. If all the water evaporates, add a little extra.

3. With dishwashing liquid, wash, rinse, and dry the lemon before zesting it.

4. In a food processor or blender, process the apricots and any remaining liquid, the sugar, and lemon zest until uniform in consistency, scraping down the sides of the bowl as needed.

5. Working in batches, use the back of a large spoon to press the mixture through the strainer, leaving the fibrous residue behind. (This is a slow process.) Scrape the mixture from the bottom of the strainer into the bowl.

6. Scrape the apricot mixture back into the saucepan and simmer, stirring constantly to prevent scorching, for 10 to 15 minutes, or until deep orange in color and very thick. A tablespoon of the mixture when lifted will take about 3 seconds to fall from the spoon.

7. Transfer the lekvar to a bowl and let it cool completely. You will need only about 200 grams / ⅔ cup / 158 ml.

Making a smaller amount of lekvar risks scorching. The extra lekvar keeps in an airtight container for 9 months refrigerated or frozen.

SANDWICH THE COOKIES

14. Set half of the cookies bottom side up on the counter. Using a small offset spatula or butter knife, spread a very thin layer of the apricot filling (about ¾ teaspoon) over each cookie.

15. Spread the bottoms of the remaining cookies with a slightly thicker layer of the ganache (about ½ tablespoon / 6 grams).

16. Set the chocolate-coated cookies chocolate side down on the apricot-coated cookies. Let them sit for a minimum of 30 minutes for the ganache to set completely.

STORE Filled, airtight: room temperature, 3 days; frozen, 6 months.
Unfilled, airtight: room temperature, 2 weeks; frozen, 6 months.

Continues

Baking Gems

♥ Unblanched almonds give a true almond flavor to the cookie. If you prefer to use blanched almonds, it is a good idea to toast them lightly to bring out more flavor. Be sure to use sliced almonds, as they are much easier than slivered or whole almonds to grind to a fine consistency.

♥ Placing plastic wrap on top of the dough when rolling helps greatly to make this dough smooth with no cracks.

♥ If you prefer a thicker cookie, it's fine to roll the dough ¼ inch thick. You will end up with half the number of sandwich cookies.

VARIATION

APRICOT JAM GLAZE

Makes: about 253 grams / ⅔ cup / 158 ml

apricot preserves	412 grams	1⅓ cups

MAKE THE APRICOT JAM GLAZE

Have ready a strainer suspended over a 2 cup / 473 ml microwavable measure with a spout.

In a microwavable container (or in a small saucepan, over low heat) bring the preserves to a boil.

Immediately pour the mixture into the strainer, scraping up all the thickened mixture that has settled on the bottom of the pan. Press the mixture through the strainer and scrape any clinging to the underside into the bowl. You should have about ¾ cup plus 2 tablespoons / 207 ml strained apricot preserves.

Reduce the apricot preserves to about 253 grams / ⅔ cup / 158 ml; they should be very thick but still fluid. If using a microwave, stir every 20 seconds. If using a saucepan, simmer, stirring constantly.

The apricot glaze is applied piping hot so that it is still spreadable in a very thin layer, but when cooled, it become deliciously intense and sticky. Set the glaze in a pan surrounded by hot water to keep it fluid, or return it to the microwave if it becomes too thick to spread. If necessary, stir in a little water. Spread the glaze on the cookies while it is hot.

The apricot glaze keeps in an airtight container for 3 days at cool room temperature, and 6 months refrigerated or frozen.

DREI AUGEN

Makes: Twenty-six 1⅝ inch round sandwich cookies

The first time I met author and baking expert Flo Braker was at the second conference of the International Association of Culinary Professionals, in New York City. Flo was planning a special demonstration of her famous miniatures. She began her talk with laughter, when most people would have been crying. She told us that all her prep for the demo was locked in the hotel refrigerator, and no one there had the key, so she would not be able to show us anything—but luckily the samples she brought were not under refrigeration and would be passed out for all of us to share. The Drei Augen miniature I managed to snag was memorably perfect. *Drei augen* is German for three eyes, referring to the three little holes in the delicate almond-and-cinnamon shortbread cookies.

Oven Temperature: 325°F / 160°C	Baking Time: 13 to 15 minutes (for each of two batches)	Special Equipment: Two 17 by 14 inch cookie sheets, lined with parchment; A 1½ inch round cookie cutter; A ⅜ inch round decorating tube

DOUGH *Makes: 272 grams*

unsalted butter	100 grams	7 tablespoons (¾ stick plus 1 tablespoon)
sliced unblanched almonds	28 grams	¼ cup plus ½ tablespoon
bleached all-purpose flour	110 grams	¾ cup (lightly spooned into the cup and leveled off) plus 2 tablespoons
ground cinnamon	·	⅓ teaspoon
sugar, preferably superfine	43 grams	3½ tablespoons

MISE EN PLACE

Thirty minutes to 1 hour ahead, cut the butter into tablespoon-size pieces. Set on the counter to soften.

MAKE THE DOUGH

1. In a small food processor, process the almonds until fine.

2. Add the flour and cinnamon and continue processing until the nuts are very fine. Check by putting a little of the mixture in your palm and, using the thumb and index finger of your other hand, rub the mixture to see the texture of the nuts.

(Alternatively, grind the nuts with a little of the flour in a spice mill, or grind them in a rotary nut grinder, until very fine. Transfer to a bowl and whisk together with the [remaining] flour and the cinnamon.)

3. In the bowl of a stand mixer fitted with the flat beater, beat the butter and sugar on medium speed for 2 to 3 minutes, until lighter in color and slightly fluffy.

4. On low speed, gradually beat in the flour mixture just until incorporated, scraping down the sides of the bowl as needed.

5. Scrape the dough onto a sheet of plastic wrap and use the plastic wrap to knead it lightly just until it holds together smoothly.

ROLL AND CUT THE DOUGH

6. Roll the dough between two sheets of plastic wrap into an 11 inch by ⅛ inch thick disc. Slip it onto a baking sheet and refrigerate for at least 2 hours, up to 24 hours before cutting.

Continues

Drei Augen and Scarlet
Raspberry Linzer
Hearts, page 198

7. Remove the top sheet of plastic wrap from the dough and replace it loosely on top. Use the bottom piece of plastic wrap to flip over the dough, then remove the bottom piece.

8. Cut out as many cookies as you can, placing them no less than ½ inch apart on a cookie sheet. Cover with plastic wrap and refrigerate. (If at any point the dough softens too much to cut perfect discs, cover and refrigerate until firm.)

9. Gather up the dough scraps and use the plastic wrap to knead them together. Reroll the dough, cover with plastic wrap, and refrigerate for at least 30 minutes, until firm enough to cut.

10. Cut out more cookies and, after filling the first cookie sheet with 26 little discs of dough, return it to the refrigerator, and set the remaining discs on the second sheet. Continue rerolling the scraps until you have a total of 52 discs. Refrigerate the second cookie sheet for at least 30 minutes for the dough to firm up.

11. Use the decorating tube to cut out 3 circles in each disc on the second cookie sheet; these will be the cookies' tops. A wooden skewer works well to remove all the dough from the holes.

PREHEAT THE OVEN
Twenty minutes or longer before baking, set an oven rack at the middle level. Set the oven at 325°F / 160°C.

BAKE THE COOKIES
12. Bake one sheet for 7 minutes. Rotate the cookie sheet halfway around. Continue baking for 6 to 8 minutes, until the cookies are pale gold and firm to the touch.

COOL THE COOKIES
13. Set the cookie sheet on a wire rack and use a thin pancake turner to transfer the cookies to another wire rack. Cool completely.

14. Repeat with the second batch.

FILLING AND TOPPING

red currant jelly	113 grams	⅓ cup
powdered sugar	6 grams	1 tablespoon

MAKE THE FILLING
1. Into a 1 cup / 237 ml microwavable measure with a spout (or a small saucepan), weigh or measure the jelly.

2. Bring the jelly to a boil in the microwave (or in the saucepan, over low heat stirring contantly), then continue cooking, for a few seconds in the microwave or about 2 minutes on the cooktop, stirring constantly to thicken it slightly.

3. Remove from the heat source, cover with plastic wrap, and allow the jelly to cool for a few minutes, until no longer hot. Stir until smooth before using it to fill the cookies.

SANDWICH THE COOKIES
15. Set the cookies without the holes bottom side up on a baking sheet or tray. Spoon a level ½ teaspoon / 3 grams of jelly onto the center of each one.

16. Lay a sheet of parchment on the counter and another wire rack on top. Place the cookies with the holes on the rack, top side up. Spoon the powdered sugar into a small fine-mesh strainer and dust the cookies with the sugar.

17. Set the cookie tops onto the jelly-coated bottoms and press down gently. The jelly should come almost to the edges and be visible.

STORE Filled, airtight: room temperature, 1 week; frozen, 2 months.
Unfilled, airtight: room temperature, 2 weeks; frozen, 2 months.

Baking Gem
♥ Store the filled cookies in a single layer in a parchment-lined airtight container.

SCARLET RASPBERRY LINZER HEARTS

Makes: Fifty 1¾ inch high by 2 inch heart-shaped sandwich cookies

I treasure my copy of *The Silver Palate*, and this special inscription from my longtime friend Sheila Lukins: "With great love, dear Rose. Do have a great amount of pleasure with our book."

These Linzer hearts, adapted from Sheila's recipe, are the most tender of all cookies, because the dough contains a combination of cornstarch and flour, powdered sugar rather than granulated, and a high amount of nuts and butter. The dough is so soft that it requires many trips back and forth to the refrigerator to firm up for shaping, but that is so worth it. The recipe makes a large amount, but it is fine to make just half or to freeze some of the dough to bake at a later time.

| **Oven Temperature:** 325°F / 160°C | **Baking Time:** 10 to 15 minutes (for each of four batches) | **Plan Ahead:** The cookie dough requires frequent chilling during shaping, so the entire process will take several hours. | **Special Equipment:** Two 17 by 14 inch cookie sheets, no preparation needed or lined with parchment; A 1¾ inch high by 2 inch wide heart-shaped cookie cutter, preferably scalloped; A ¾ inch high by ¾ inch wide heart-shaped cookie cutter, preferably scalloped |

DOUGH *Makes: 1,050 grams*

unsalted butter	170 grams	12 tablespoons (1½ sticks)
1 large egg	50 grams	3 tablespoons plus ½ teaspoon (47.5 ml)
walnut halves	200 grams	2 cups
unbleached all-purpose flour	270 grams	2¼ cups (lightly spooned into the cup and leveled off)
cornstarch	120 grams	1 cup (lightly spooned into the cup and leveled off)
powdered sugar	115 grams	1 cup (lightly spooned into the cup and leveled off)

MISE EN PLACE

Thirty minutes to 1 hour ahead, cut the butter into tablespoon-size pieces. Set on the counter to soften.

Into a 1 cup / 237 ml glass measure with a spout, weigh or measure the egg. Whisk it lightly. Cover tightly with plastic wrap and set on the counter.

MAKE THE DOUGH

1. In a food processor, process the walnuts with 60 grams / ¾ cup of the flour until finely ground. (Alternatively, grind the nuts with a little of the flour in a spice mill, or use a rotary nut grinder.)

2. In a medium bowl, whisk together the remaining 210 grams / 1½ cups flour and the cornstarch.

3. In the bowl of a stand mixer fitted with the flat beater, beat the butter and sugar on medium speed until lighter in color and fluffy, about 2 minutes.

4. Gradually add the egg, beating until incorporated. Scrape down the sides of the bowl.

5. Add the walnut mixture and beat on low speed just until evenly incorporated, about 10 seconds.

6. Remove the flat beater. Sift the flour mixture onto the mixture in the bowl and then use the flat beater to stir it in. Reattach the beater and, on low speed, beat until well blended, about 10 seconds.

7. Divide the dough among three pieces of plastic wrap (about 350 grams each). Set a second sheet of plastic wrap on top of each one and gently roll or shape the dough into a roughly 6 inch disc. Slip the discs onto a baking sheet and chill for at least 2 hours, up to 24 hours, until firm enough to roll.

ROLL AND CUT THE DOUGH

Work with one disc of dough at a time, leaving the rest refrigerated. If the dough has become too firm to roll without cracking, allow it to sit at room temperature for a few minutes.

8. Remove the top sheet of plastic wrap and flour the top of the dough. Replace the plastic wrap and use the bottom piece of plastic wrap to flip over the dough. Remove the other piece of plastic wrap, flour the dough, and replace the plastic wrap. Roll the dough ¼ inch thick. From time to time, lift off the plastic wrap on both sides; if the dough starts to stick, it's fine to add more flour, but if it is very sticky, return it to the refrigerator to firm.

9. Use the plastic wrap to slip the dough onto a cookie sheet. Remove the top sheet of plastic wrap and cut out cookie hearts with the larger cutter. Cover with a large sheet of plastic wrap and refrigerate until firm enough to remove the scraps from around the cookies. Set the scraps on another piece of the plastic wrap. Use the plastic wrap to knead them together and shape them into a disc. Refrigerate until firm enough to reroll.

10. Use the plastic wrap to lift and gently remove 25 of the hearts and place them about 1 inch apart, alternating in direction, on one of the cookie sheets. When the dough starts to soften too much, return it briefly to the refrigerator along with the cookies on the cookie sheet, covered with plastic wrap.

11. Continue with the second cookie sheet until it is filled with 25 cookies. Using the smaller cutter, cut heart-shaped windows in the cookies. Knead the scraps into one of the remaining discs. You can bake the cookies right away or refrigerate, covered with plastic wrap, for up to 2 days. If you only have two cookie sheets, refrigerate the remaining dough until after you have baked the first two sheets. Be sure to cool the cookie sheets completely before setting the next batch of cut-out cookies on it.

12. Continue rolling and cutting the rest of the dough, cutting heart-shaped windows into half of the cookies. (You can also set the wrapped dough discs in reclosable freezer bags and freeze them for up to 2 months to bake at a later date. Defrost overnight, refrigerated.)

PREHEAT THE OVEN

Twenty minutes or longer before baking, set an oven rack at the middle level. Set the oven at 325°F / 160°C.

BAKE THE COOKIES

13. Bake the first batch for 7 minutes. Rotate the cookie sheet halfway around. Continue baking for 3 to 8 minutes, until the cookies are lightly browned and slightly darker toward the edges.

COOL THE COOKIES

14. Set the cookie sheet on a wire rack and allow the cookies to cool until just warm or room temperature. Use a thin pancake turner to transfer the cookies to a another wire rack. Cool completely.

15. Repeat with the remaining batches.

Continues

RASPBERRY FILLING AND POWDERED SUGAR TOPPING

raspberry preserves	156 grams	½ cup
powdered sugar	14 grams	2 tablespoons

SANDWICH THE COOKIES

16. Set the cookies without the cutouts bottom side up on the counter. Use a small offset spatula or butter knife to spread each one with a thin layer of the jam.

17. Set a wire rack over a sheet of parchment and set the cookies with the cutouts on the rack, bottom side down. Spoon the powdered sugar into a fine-mesh strainer and dust the cookies with the powdered sugar.

18. Set the cookie tops gently on top of the jam-coated bottoms.

STORE Filled or unfilled, airtight: room temperature, 2 weeks; frozen, 2 months.

Baking Gems

♥ This dough is very low in flour, so don't be concerned if you need to add a little extra when rolling. The cookies will still be incredibly tender. A combination of chilling and flouring works well.

♥ You can make sandwich cookies without cutting out windows in the tops. If not cutting out windows, you will end up with 2 fewer cookies.

♥ There is no need to chill the cutout cookies before baking. I've tried it both ways, and they look identical. This soft dough holds its shape perfectly.

GIANT JAM BIRTHDAY COOKIE

Makes: One 12 inch round cookie (serves 12)

There are actually those who prefer cookies to cake, so why not a birthday cookie! This cookie requires two main things: precision and enough freezer space for chilling the shaped dough.

Oven Temperature:	Baking Time:	Special Equipment:
350°F / 175°C	30 to 35 minutes	One 13 to 14 inch round pizza pan or a baking sheet, lined with parchment; A cookie sheet or a 13 inch or larger cardboard round; An expandable flan ring or 12 inch diameter round cardboard template; A small decorative cookie cutter; Two cookie sheets, lightly coated with nonstick cooking spray

DOUGH *Makes: 810 grams*

unsalted butter	227 grams	16 tablespoons (2 sticks)
2 large eggs	100 grams	⅓ cup plus 1 tablespoon (94 ml)
bleached all-purpose flour	400 grams	3⅓ cups (lightly spooned into the cup and leveled off) minus 1 teaspoon
fine sea salt	·	¼ teaspoon
turbinado sugar, preferably Sugar in the Raw (or superfine sugar if mixing by hand)	100 grams	½ cup
jam of your choice, for the filling	357 grams	1 cup plus 2 tablespoons

MISE EN PLACE

Thirty minutes ahead or longer, cut the butter into ½ inch cubes. Wrap in plastic wrap and refrigerate.

Into a 1 cup / 237 ml glass measure with a spout, weigh or measure the egg. Whisk lightly, cover tightly with plastic wrap, and refrigerate.

MAKE THE DOUGH
Food Processor Method

1. In a medium bowl, whisk together the flour and salt.

2. In a food processor, process the turbinado sugar until fine.

3. Add the cold butter cubes and pulse until the sugar disappears.

4. Add the flour mixture and pulse until the pieces of butter are no larger than small peas.

5. Add the egg and pulse just until it is incorporated and the dough is in crumbly pieces.

6. Empty the dough into a plastic bag and press it from the outside of the bag just until it holds together. Remove the dough from the bag and set it on a very large sheet of plastic wrap. Use the plastic wrap to knead the dough a few times, just until it holds together in one smooth piece. If there are visible pieces of butter, use the heel of your hand in a forward motion to smear them into the dough.

Hand Method

1. In a medium bowl, whisk together the flour, superfine sugar, and salt.

Continues

2. With a pastry cutter or two knives, cut in the cold butter until the mixture resembles coarse meal.

3. Use a blending fork or silicone spatula to stir in the egg until the dough comes together and can be formed into a large ball.

4. Set the dough on a large piece of plastic wrap and use it to knead the dough just until smooth.

Both Methods

7. Divide the dough in half (about 405 grams each). Wrap each piece loosely with plastic wrap and press to flatten into a 6 inch disc. Refrigerate for 30 minutes, or until firm enough to roll.

The dough can be refrigerated for up to 3 days or frozen for up to 6 months.

ROLL AND CUT THE DOUGH

8. Remove one piece of dough from the refrigerator and set it on a lightly floured large sheet of plastic wrap. Lightly flour the dough and set another piece of plastic wrap on top. If the dough has been chilled for more than 30 minutes, let it sit until it is malleable enough to roll, about 5 to 10 minutes.

9. Roll the dough between the two pieces of plastic wrap until it is a round a little larger than 12 inches in diameter and ⅛ inch thick.

10. Remove the upper piece of plastic wrap. Use the lower piece to lift the dough onto the cookie sheet or cardboard round. Lay the prepared pizza pan on top and invert the dough onto it. Remove the plastic wrap and, using the expandable flan ring or cardboard template, cut a 12 inch disc of dough: If using the flan ring, press it down like a large cookie cutter to cut the dough. If not using a flan ring, use a pizza wheel or small knife to cut out the dough, but take care not to cut through the parchment. Cover the dough with the plastic wrap and refrigerate for at least 30 minutes, or freeze for 5 to 10 minutes, until firm.

11. Repeat with the second dough disc, but leave it on the cookie sheet, trim it to 12 inches, and freeze for at least 10 minutes. Use a long sharp

knife to score 12 wedges, being careful not to cut all the way through the dough (see Baking Gem).

12. Use a small decorative cookie cutter to cut a shape from every other wedge, this time going all the way through the dough, but don't remove the cutout. Cover the dough with plastic wrap and freeze for 10 minutes, or until the decorative cutouts can be lifted out.

13. Remove the dough from the freezer. Carefully use the decorative cookie cutter to recut each shape along the same cut marks. Lift out each cutout with the aid of a small metal spatula. Place the cutouts on a plastic wrap–lined cookie sheet, cover them with plastic wrap, and keep them chilled. Use a wooden skewer, if necessary, to go around the cutout holes so that they are cleanly and precisely cut.

14. Place the dough disc with the cutout openings in the freezer for at least 15 minutes, or until frozen solid and rigid.

Any leftover dough scraps can be rerolled and formed into small cookies.

PREPARE THE JAM FILLING

15. In a 2 cup / 473 ml microwavable measure with a spout, lightly coated with nonstick cooking spray, heat the jam, stirring every 15 seconds, until it is reduced to 317 grams / 1 cup. Or cook the jam over medium-low heat in a medium saucepan, preferably with a nonstick lining, stirring often, until reduced to 317 grams / 1 cup. (Jams vary in consistency, so use your judgment as to the ideal consistency.) Cover tightly and let it come to room temperature. The glaze should be thick but spreadable. If necessary, stir in a little water.

COMPOSE THE COOKIE

16. Remove the plastic wrap from the dough disc on the pizza pan and spread the jam glaze evenly over it to within ½ inch from the edges. Lightly brush a little water onto this ½ inch border.

Continues

17. Remove the second dough disc from the freezer. Set one of the prepared cookie sheets on top of it and invert it. Peel off the plastic wrap and reinvert the dough onto the second prepared cookie sheet. Quickly, before it softens, slide the chilled, rigid dough on top of the glazed dough so that the edges meet. Brush each cutout piece of dough with a little water and place them on the dough wedges without the cutouts.

18. Use a fork to press the edges of the dough together, making a radiating design in the pastry. Use a wooden skewer to make many little holes in the dough, avoiding the cutouts.

19. Cover with plastic wrap and refrigerate for at least 15 minutes, up to 24 hours, before baking.

PREHEAT THE OVEN

Twenty minutes or longer before baking, set an oven rack at the middle level. Set the oven at 350°F / 175°C.

BAKE THE COOKIE

20. Bake the cookie for 15 minutes. Rotate the pan halfway around. Continue baking for 15 to 20 minutes, or until the cookie is pale golden and lightly browned at the edges. The glaze visible through the cutouts will be bubbling.

COOL AND SERVE THE COOKIE

21. Set the pan on a wire rack and let cool for at least 30 minutes, or until room temperature, before serving.

22. Slip a large pancake turner under the cookie to dislodge it and then slide it onto a large flat plate or cutting board. Cut through the score lines to the bottom of the cookie to separate the wedges.

STORE Airtight: room temperature, 10 days; refrigerated, 3 weeks; frozen, 6 months.

Baking Gem

♥ For scoring the dough into 12 pieces, a 30-60-90-degree drafting / arts triangle is very helpful. First score the dough into quarters, then use the triangle to score each quarter into 3 equal wedges.

THE DUTCH PECAN SANDIES

Makes: Thirty-one 2 inch round cookies

These exquisitely fragile cookies are a perfect balance of sugar, spice, and salt that makes you unable to stop at just one. Master baker Kierin Baldwin created this treasure of recipe when she was pastry chef at The Dutch in SoHo, New York City.

Oven Temperature:	Baking Time: 20 to	Special Equipment: Two 17 by 14 inch cookie sheets,
325°F / 160°C	22 minutes (for each of two batches)	lined with parchment or nonstick; A cookie sheet or thin cutting board; A 2 inch round cookie cutter

DOUGH *Makes: 640 grams*

unsalted butter	227 grams	16 tablespoons (2 sticks)
pecan halves	150 grams	1½ cups
unbleached all-purpose flour, preferably gold medal or heckers	207 grams	1⅔ cups (lightly spooned into the cup and leveled off) plus 2 teaspoons
whole wheat flour	22 grams	2½ tablespoons
ground cinnamon	·	½ plus ⅛ teaspoon
granulated sugar	37 grams	3 tablespoons
turbinado sugar, preferably Sugar in the Raw	30 grams	2½ tablespoons
light Muscovado (or dark brown sugar)	37 grams	2 tablespoons plus 2 teaspoons (firmly packed)
vanilla powder (or pure vanilla extract)	·	⅛ plus 1/16 teaspoon (or ½ tablespoon/ 7.5 ml)
fine sea salt	3.7 grams	½ plus ⅛ teaspoon

MISE EN PLACE

Clarify and Brown the Butter: Have ready a fine-mesh or cheesecloth-lined strainer suspended over a 2 cup / 473 ml glass measure with a spout.

In a medium heavy saucepan, melt the butter over very low heat, stirring often with a light-colored silicone spatula. Raise the heat to low and boil, stirring constantly, until the milk solids on the spatula become little brown specks. An instant-read thermometer should read 285° to 290F° / 140° to 143°C. Immediately pour the butter through the strainer into the glass measure, scraping the solids into the strainer. Refrigerate or freeze the milk solids for future use, or discard them.

Weigh or measure 161 grams / ¾ cup plus 1 tablespoon / 192 ml of the browned butter. Let it cool until solid, or refrigerate it for 1 to 1½ hours, until set but still soft. (If it becomes too hard, let it soften until malleable.)

In a food processor, pulse the pecans, all-purpose flour, whole wheat flour, and cinnamon until the pecans are coarsely chopped. (Alternatively, in a medium bowl, combine the flours and cinnamon. Coarsely chop the pecans in a spice mill in batches and add them to the flour and cinnamon.)

PREHEAT THE OVEN

Twenty minutes or longer before baking, set an oven rack at the middle level. Set the oven at 325°F / 160°C.

Continues

MAKE THE DOUGH

1. In the bowl of a stand mixer fitted with the flat beater, beat the sugars, vanilla powder or extract, and salt on low speed until combined.

2. Add the browned butter and beat, starting on low speed and gradually raising the speed to medium, then continue beating on medium speed for 1 minute. The mixture will become the consistency of buttercream.

3. Add the flour mixture and beat on low speed for 10 to 15 seconds, or until the dough is well blended and comes away from the sides of the bowl.

4. Scrape the mixture onto a large sheet of plastic wrap. Use the wrap to knead the dough lightly just until smooth.

ROLL AND CUT THE DOUGH

5. Lightly flour a sheet of plastic wrap and set the dough on top. Lightly flour the top of the dough.

6. Roll the dough into a ⅜ inch thick oval. Slide the plastic wrap with the dough onto a cookie sheet.

7. Cut out as many cookies as possible, but do not remove them from the rest of the dough yet.

8. Cover the dough with plastic wrap and refrigerate for 10 minutes, or until rigid.

CINNAMON SUGAR TOPPING

granulated sugar	19 grams	1½ tablespoons
ground cinnamon	.	¾ teaspoon
turbinado sugar, preferably Sugar in the Raw	9 grams	2 teaspoons

MAKE THE TOPPING

9. In a large custard cup or small bowl with a flat bottom, whisk the granulated sugar and cinnamon until uniform in consistency.

10. Place the turbinado sugar in a small custard cup.

COAT THE DOUGH DISCS

11. Use a small offset spatula or your fingers to peel away the dough surrounding the cut cookies and set the dough scraps on another sheet of plastic wrap. Knead them together until smooth and cover with the plastic wrap.

12. Use the offset spatula to lift each dough disc, coat both sides of it in the cinnamon sugar mixture, and transfer to a prepared cookie sheet; place up to 16 discs on the cookie sheet, spacing them at least 1 inch apart. Occasionally stir the sugar and cinnamon.

13. Sprinkle the dough discs lightly with half of the turbinado sugar.

BAKE THE COOKIES

14. Bake for 10 minutes. Rotate the cookie sheet halfway around. Continue baking for 10 to 12 minutes, or until the cookies turn golden brown and are firm when pressed lightly with a fingertip.

COOL THE COOKIES

15. Set the cookie sheet on a wire rack. Let the cookies cool completely and allow them to stand for about 2 hours, or until firm enough to transfer. If moved too soon, they will crumble.

16. Repeat with the dough scraps for the second batch of cookies. For the very last piece of dough, set it in the cookie cutter and press it down with the handle of a wooden spoon to form an even disc. Use your fingers to push it out of the cookie cutter onto the sheet.

STORE Airtight: room temperature, 3 weeks; frozen, 3 months.

WALNUT SABLÉ MAPLE LEAVES OR HEARTS

Makes: Twenty-eight 2¾ inch wide maple leaf cookies or Thirty-two heart-shaped cookies

Sablé is the French word for sandy. The French tradition is to add the smallest amount of flour possible, to make the most buttery of cookies. This results in a wondrously fragile cookie but also a very soft dough that can be a little tricky to work with. It is not a problem, however, if you make sure to chill the dough at different stages as needed. Adding powdered sugar and ground walnuts contributes tenderness, but the cookies are also lovely without nuts (see the Variation).

Oven Temperature: 350°F / 175°C	**Baking Time:** 5 minutes for the walnuts; 10 to 12 minutes for the cookies (for each of two batches)	**Special Equipment:** Two 17 by 14 inch cookie sheets, lined with parchment; A 2¾ inch maple leaf or heart cookie cutter (measured at its widest point)

DOUGH *Makes: 360 grams*

unsalted butter	113 grams	8 tablespoons (1 stick)
walnut halves	12 grams	2 tablespoons
1 (to 2) large egg yolk (see page xxvi)	19 grams	1 tablespoon plus ½ teaspoon (17.5 ml)
pure vanilla extract	·	1 teaspoon (5 ml)
granulated sugar	50 grams	¼ cup
powdered sugar	25 grams	¼ cup (lightly spooned into the cup) minus 2 teaspoons
bleached all-purpose flour	140 grams	1 cup (lightly spooned into the cup and leveled off) plus 2 tablespoons
fine sea salt	·	⅛ teaspoon

PREHEAT THE OVEN

Twenty minutes or longer before baking, set an oven rack at the middle level. Set the oven at 350°F / 175°C.

MISE EN PLACE

Thirty minutes to 1 hour ahead, cut the butter into tablespoon-size pieces. Set on the counter to soften.

Toast the Walnuts: Spread the walnuts evenly on a baking sheet and bake for 5 minutes. Turn the walnuts onto a clean dish towel and roll and rub them around to loosen the skins. Discard any loose skins and cool the nuts completely.

Into a 1 cup / 237 ml glass measure with a spout, weigh or measure the egg yolk. Whisk in the vanilla extract. Cover tightly with plastic wrap and set on the counter.

MAKE THE DOUGH

1. In the bowl of a 5 cup food processor (see Baking Gems), process the walnuts and sugars until fine.

2. In a small bowl, whisk together the flour and salt.

3. With the motor running, add the butter to the processor one piece at a time, processing until smooth and creamy. Scrape down the sides of the bowl as needed.

Continues

4. Add the egg yolk mixture and pulse until incorporated, scraping down the sides of the bowl as needed.

5. Add the flour mixture in two parts and pulse until incorporated. Scrape down the sides of the bowl and continue to pulse until all the flour is incorporated and the dough is in crumbly pieces.

6. Spoon the dough into a plastic bag and press from the outside of the bag just until it holds together. Transfer the dough to a double layer of plastic wrap and use the plastic wrap and the heel of your hand to knead the dough until it is in one smooth piece.

7. Divide the dough in half (about 180 grams each). Flatten each piece into a 5 inch disc. Wrap each piece in plastic wrap and refrigerate for 30 minutes to 1 hour, or until firm enough to roll.

The dough can be refrigerated for up to 3 days; it will then need to be softened at room temperature for 30 minutes to an hour and kneaded lightly until malleable enough to roll.

ROLL AND CUT THE DOUGH

8. Roll out one piece of the dough between sheets of plastic wrap to a thickness of ⅛ inch. Flour both sides of the dough as needed to prevent sticking. If the dough softens, slide it onto a cookie sheet and refrigerate for about 15 minutes, or until firm enough to make the cutouts. The dough may crack slightly in places, especially if it is too cold, but when you reknead the scraps, it will be smooth and not require much, if any, extra flour.

9. Cut out the dough and remove the scraps to reroll. Use the plastic wrap to lift and gently remove the shapes and place them about ½ inch apart on a prepared cookie sheet (if necessary, refrigerate until firm enough to lift off the cookie cutouts; see Baking Gems).

10. Knead together the scraps and shape them into a disc. You can reroll them right away or chill them,

wrapped in plastic wrap, if too soft. Continue with the remaining scraps until you have 18 cookies on the cookie sheet.

BAKE THE COOKIES

11. Bake the cookies for 5 minutes. Rotate the cookie sheet halfway around. Continue baking for 5 to 7 minutes, or until the cookies puff slightly and feel firm to the touch. They should just be beginning to brown at the edges and deepen slightly in color.

COOL THE COOKIES

12. Set the cookie sheet on a wire rack and let the cookies cool completely. Use a thin pancake turner to transfer the cookies to a storage container.

13. Repeat with the second batch.

STORE Airtight: room temperature, 3 weeks; frozen, 3 months.

Baking Gems

♥ If you do not have a 5 cup food processor, see the Chocolate Sablé recipe (page 210) for an alternative method, and use a spice mill to grind the nuts with the sugars.

♥ If the cut dough is slightly soft, it works very well to lift up the plastic wrap and carefully peel off the cutouts of dough to maintain their shape.

VARIATIONS
Nutless Sablés

To make sablés without nuts, omit the walnuts and add an additional 2 tablespoons flour, using a total of 155 grams / 1¼ cups plus ½ tablespoon.

CHOCOLATE SABLÉS

Makes: Twenty-six 2½ by ¼ inch thick round cookies or Fifty-two 2½ by ⅛ inch thick round cookies

This is the ultimate chocolate cookie: sandy (as the French name implies), crisp, and dissolving. I enjoy the flavor that comes from using part brown sugar, and I prefer to make the dough in a smaller 5 cup food processor so that all the sugar gets ground as fine as possible, which makes the crumb tighter and crisper. However, I give the mixer method below as well if you don't have this size food processor. The thinner version has a smooth surface, while the thicker version has attractive cracks. The thinner one is ideal for sandwiching with caramel or ganache (see the Variation; the spiciness of Wicked Good Ganache, page 397, is divine with these), but the cookie really doesn't need anything more. It is pure chocolate perfection as it is.

Oven Temperature: 350°F / 175°C	**Baking Time:** 12 to 14 minutes for the ¼ inch cookies, 8 to 10 minutes for the ⅛ inch cookies (for each of two batches of the thicker cookies or four batches of the thinner cookies)

Special Equipment: Two 17 by 14 inch cookie sheets, lined with parchment; A 2 inch round cookie cutter

DOUGH *Makes: 473 grams*

unsalted butter	113 grams	8 tablespoons (1 stick)
dark chocolate, 60% to 62% cacao	71 grams (2.5 ounces)	·
1 (to 2) large egg yolk (see page xxvi)	19 grams	1 tablespoon plus ½ teaspoon (17.5 ml)
pure vanilla extract	·	1 teaspoon (5 ml)
bleached all-purpose flour	140 grams	1 cup (sifted into the cup and leveled off) plus 2 tablespoons
unsweetened alkalized cocoa powder (see Baking Gems)	28 grams	¼ cup plus 2 tablespoons (sifted before measuring)
baking soda	2.7 grams	½ teaspoon
fine sea salt	·	⅛ teaspoon
light brown sugar, preferably Muscovado	54 grams	½ cup (firmly packed)
granulated sugar	50 grams	½ cup

MISE EN PLACE

Thirty minutes to 1 hour ahead, cut the butter into tablespoon-size pieces. Set on the counter to soften.

Thirty minutes or longer ahead, chop the chocolate into coarse pieces and refrigerate.

Thirty minutes ahead, into a 1 cup / 237 ml glass measure with a spout, weigh or measure the egg yolk. Whisk in the vanilla extract. Cover tightly with plastic wrap and set on the counter.

For the Food Processor Method: In a 5 cup food processor, process the chocolate into fine but not powder-fine particles. Transfer the chocolate to a medium bowl (don't worry if a little chocolate remains in the processor bowl; it will get mixed in during Step 4.

For the Stand Mixer Method: Finely chop the chocolate with a chef's knife. Place the chocolate in a small bowl.

Continues

For Both Methods: Refrigerate the ground or chopped chocolate to keep it from clumping together.

In a medium bowl, whisk together the flour, cocoa, baking soda, and salt. Sift the mixture onto a piece of parchment.

MAKE THE DOUGH

Food Processor Method

1. In the food processor, process the sugars until fine.

2. With the motor running, add the butter one piece at a time, processing until smooth and creamy. Scrape down the sides of the bowl as needed.

3. Add the egg yolk mixture and pulse until incorporated, scraping down the sides of the bowl as needed.

4. Add the flour mixture in two parts and pulse until it is incorporated and the dough is in coarse particles. Scrape down the sides of the bowl and add the ground chocolate. Pulse until the dough turns dark brown and is in crumbly pieces.

5. Spoon the mixture into a plastic bag and press from the outside of the bag just until it holds together. Transfer the dough to a double layer of plastic wrap and use the plastic wrap and the heel of your hand to knead it together until it is a smooth piece of dough.

Stand Mixer Method

1. Grind the sugars in a spice mill in batches.

2. In the bowl of a stand mixer fitted with the flat beater, beat the butter and sugars together on medium speed for 2 to 3 minutes, or until lighter in color and fluffy.

3. Gradually add the egg yolk mixture, beating until incorporated. Scrape down the sides of the bowl.

4. On low speed, beat in the flour mixture in two parts, then beat in the chopped chocolate, scraping down the sides of the bowl as needed.

Both Methods

6. Divide the dough in half (about 236 grams each). Flatten each piece into a 6 inch disc, wrap in plastic wrap, and refrigerate for 30 minutes to an hour, or until firm enough to roll.

The dough can be refrigerated for up to 3 days; it will need to be softened at room temperature for 30 minutes to an hour and kneaded lightly until malleable enough to roll.

PREHEAT THE OVEN

Twenty minutes or longer before baking, set an oven rack at the middle level. Set the oven at 350°F / 175°C.

ROLL AND CUT THE DOUGH

7. Roll out half the dough at a time, between sheets of plastic wrap, to a thickness of ¼ inch if making thicker cookies, or ⅛ inch if making thinner cookies. If the dough softens, slide it onto a cookie sheet and refrigerate it for about 15 minutes, or until firm enough to make the cutouts.

8. Cut out the dough and remove the scraps to reroll. (If necessary, refrigerate the dough until firm enough to lift off the cookie cutouts.) Place the cutouts no closer than 1 inch apart on a prepared cookie sheet.

9. Knead together the scraps and shape them into a disc. You can reroll them right away if the dough is not too soft, or chill them, wrapped in plastic wrap, until firm again. Continue rolling and cutting the remaining dough until you have 13 cookies on each cookie sheet.

BAKE THE COOKIES

10. Bake the first sheet of thicker cookies for 7 minutes. Rotate the cookie sheet halfway around. Continue baking for 5 to 7 minutes, or until the cookies puff slightly and then deflate, and they feel firm to the touch but still a little soft in the centers. Or, for ⅛ inch cookies, bake for 4 minutes, rotate, and continue baking for 4 to 6 minutes.

COOL THE COOKIES

11. Set the cookie sheet on a wire rack and use a thin pancake turner to transfer the cookies to another wire rack. Cool completely.

12. Repeat with the second batch (or remaining batches).

STORE Airtight: room temperature, 2 weeks; frozen, 3 months.

Baking Gems

♥ I love using Cacao Barry Extra Brute cocoa for these cookies. It adds a deep, mellow chocolate flavor.

♥ When rolling out half the dough ¼ inch thick, or one quarter the dough ⅛ inch thick, it will be a 9 by 6 inch oval. The dough can even be rolled ¹⁄₁₆ inch thick, which makes a very delicate sandwich cookie.

♥ If the cut dough is slightly soft, it works very well to lift up the plastic wrap and carefully peel off the discs of dough to maintain their round shape.

VARIATION

To fill the sablés with ganache, you will need 87 grams / ⅓ cup for the thicker cookies or 174 grams / ⅔ cup for the thinner ones. To fill with caramel, you will need 100 grams / ⅓ cup for the thicker cookies or 200 grams / ⅔ cup for the thinner ones.

For each sandwich cookie, use a rounded teaspoon / 6 grams each of ganache (page 397) or 7 grams each of caramel (page 329). The ganache is easy to pipe or spread, but the caramel must be soft enough but not too soft. Use two small spoons to drop the caramel onto the flat bottoms of half the cookies. It is best to make one sandwich at a time so that the caramel stays fluid; if necessary, reheat the caramel with 3-second bursts in the microwave, or set the container of caramel in a pan of very hot water. Set a second cookie, flat bottom side down, on top of each to create a sandwich. Press down very gently so that the caramel comes almost to the edges.

Filled with ganache, the cookies will keep airtight for 3 days at room temperature, 3 months frozen.

Filled with caramel, the cookies will keep 1 month at room temperature, 2 months frozen.

CHOCOLATE WAFERS

Makes: Twenty-six 2 inch square wafers

These crisp and deeply chocolatey cookies can be used to make the best Bourbon Balls (page 260) and crumb piecrusts, but they are also delicious eaten on their own.

Oven Temperature: 350°F / 175°C	**Baking Time:** 16 to 20 minutes (for each of two batches)

Plan Ahead: Make the dough a minimum of 4 hours before rolling it (the dough can be refrigerated overnight).

Special Equipment: Two 17 by 14 inch cookie sheets, lined with parchment

DOUGH *Makes: 370 grams*

unsalted butter	42 grams	3 tablespoons
1½ large egg whites, lightly beaten before measuring	45 grams	3 tablespoons (45 ml)
pure vanilla extract	·	¾ teaspoon (3.75 ml)
bleached all-purpose flour	86 grams	⅔ cup (lightly spooned into the cup and leveled off) plus 2 teaspoons
unsweetened alkalized cocoa powder	42 grams	½ cup plus 1 tablespoon (sifted before measuring)
fine sea salt	·	⅛ teaspoon
light brown sugar, preferably Muscovado	81 grams	¼ cup plus 2 tablespoons (firmly packed)
granulated sugar	75 grams	¼ cup plus 2 tablespoons

MISE EN PLACE

Thirty minutes to 1 hour ahead, cut the butter into tablespoon-size pieces. Set on the counter to soften.

Into a 1 cup / 237 ml glass measure with a spout, weigh or measure the egg whites. Whisk in the vanilla extract. Cover tightly with plastic wrap and set on the counter.

In a medium bowl, whisk together the flour, cocoa, and salt.

MAKE THE DOUGH

1. In the bowl of a stand mixer fitted with the flat beater, beat the sugars and butter on medium speed until well mixed and lighter in color, about 5 minutes, scraping the sides of the bowl as needed.

2. Gradually add the egg white mixture, beating until smoothly incorporated. Scrape down the sides of the bowl.

3. Add the flour mixture and mix on low speed until incorporated.

4. Scrape the dough onto a large piece of plastic wrap, overlap the ends to cover the dough, leaving enough room to shape it, and press it into a rectangle. Divide the dough in half (about 185 grams each). Wrap each piece of dough in plastic wrap and set them on a small baking sheet.

5. Refrigerate the dough until it is firm, a minimum of 4 hours, up to overnight. The dough should be firm enough to roll but still malleable.

PREHEAT THE OVEN

Twenty minutes or longer before baking, set an oven rack at the middle level. Set the oven at 350°F / 175°C.

ROLL AND CUT THE DOUGH

6. Set one piece of dough on a lightly floured sheet of plastic wrap. Lightly flour the dough and cover it with a second sheet of plastic wrap. Roll the dough into a ¼ inch thick rectangle, 10 by 6 inches, using a bench scraper butted up against the sides to keep them even. To make cutting easier, slide the shaped dough onto a cookie sheet and set it in the freezer for about 5 minutes or the refrigerator for about 20 minutes.

7. With a pizza wheel or chef's knife, cut the dough into roughly 2 inch squares. Any irregular shapes can be baked alongside the squares.

8. Use a thin pancake turner to place the dough squares a minimum of 1 inch apart on a cookie sheet. With a fork, pierce each one several times to prevent excess puffing.

BAKE THE WAFERS

9. Bake the wafers for 8 minutes. Rotate the cookie sheet halfway around. Continue baking for 8 to 12 minutes, or until the wafers are firm and slightly puffed but still a little soft.

10. While the first batch is baking, roll and cut the wafers for the second batch.

COOL THE WAFERS

11. Set the cookie sheet on a wire rack and let the wafers cool completely. Use a thin pancake turner to transfer the cookies to a storage container.

12. Bake and cool the second batch.

STORE Airtight: room temperature, 1 week; refrigerated, 2 weeks; frozen, 3 months.

TURKISH GINGER LIME COOKIES

Makes: Fourteen 2¼ inch round cookies

This book would not be complete without this unusual cookie from blogger Cenk Sönmezsoy, author of the stunning book *The Artful Baker*. The texture is super-crisp, and the flavor is buttery and aromatic, with a perfect balance of lime and ginger. Try not to eat them all at once. The flavors become even more pronounced starting the day after baking.

Oven Temperature: 325°F / 160°C

Baking Time: 15 to 20 minutes

Special Equipment: One 17 by 14 inch cookie sheet, lined with parchment; A 2 inch round cookie cutter

DOUGH *Makes: 250 grams*

unsalted butter	50 grams	3½ tablespoons
lime zest, finely grated (see Baking Gem) from 2 limes	4 grams	2 teaspoons (loosely packed)
all-purpose flour, preferably unbleached	105 grams	¾ cup (lightly spooned into the cup and leveled off) plus 1½ tablespoons
baking powder, preferably an aluminum-free variety	3.4 grams	¾ teaspoon
fine sea salt	·	⅛ teaspoon
fresh ginger, a 2 inch piece, peeled and grated	9 grams	½ tablespoon (grated)
1 (to 2) large egg yolk (see page xxvi)	19 grams	1 tablespoon plus ½ teaspoon (17.5 ml)
granulated sugar	25 grams	2 tablespoons
powdered sugar	40 grams	¼ cup (lightly spooned into the cup and leveled off) plus 2 tablespoons

MISE EN PLACE

Thirty minutes to 1 hour ahead, cut the butter into tablespoon-size pieces. Set on the counter to soften.

With dishwashing liquid, wash, rinse, and dry the limes (page xxix).

In a medium bowl, whisk together the flour, baking powder, and salt.

Use a fine Microplane grater to grate the ginger into a small bowl. It will measure about ½ tablespoon. Cover with plastic wrap and set on the counter.

Shortly before mixing, into a 1 cup / 237 ml glass measure with a spout, weigh or measure the egg yolk.

MAKE THE DOUGH

1. Use a fine Microplane grater to grate the lime zest into the bowl of a stand mixer.

2. Add the granulated sugar and, with your fingers, rub it into the lime zest.

3. Add the butter and powdered sugar to the bowl. Attach the flat beater and beat on low speed until the sugar is incorporated. Raise the speed to

Continues

medium and beat for 2 to 3 minutes, until lighter in color and fluffy.

4. Add the grated ginger and egg yolk and beat until incorporated. Scrape down the sides of the bowl.

5. Add the flour mixture and beat on low speed just until it is incorporated and large clumps form, scraping down the sides of the bowl as needed.

6. Remove the bowl from the stand and use your hand to press the dough together into a large ball.

ROLL AND CUT THE DOUGH

7. Set the dough on a piece of plastic wrap and top it with a second piece of plastic wrap. Press down to flatten it and then roll it ¼ inch thick.

8. Slip the dough onto a cookie sheet and refrigerate it for 1 to 2 hours, or until firm enough to cut out the cookies.

9. Lift off the top piece of plastic wrap, cut out the cookies, and transfer them to the cookie sheet, a minimum of 1 inch apart. Use plastic wrap to knead together the dough scraps and shape them into a disc. Cover with the plastic wrap and refrigerate until firm enough to roll and cut.

10. Continue with the refrigerated dough until you have used all the dough. Refrigerate the cookie sheet, lightly covered, for 20 to 30 minutes, up to 1 hour.

PREHEAT THE OVEN

Twenty minutes or longer before baking, set an oven rack at the middle level. Set the oven at 325°F / 160°C.

BAKE THE COOKIES

11. Bake for 10 minutes. Rotate the cookie sheet halfway around. Continue baking for 5 to 10 minutes, or until the cookies are golden around the edges.

COOL THE COOKIES

12. Set the cookie sheet on a wire rack and use a thin pancake turner to transfer the cookies to another wire rack. Cool completely.

STORE Airtight: room temperature, many days. (Cenk says longer than he knows!)

Baking Gem

🤍 Cenk has a great tip about citrus zest: He zests it right into the mixer bowl so as not to lose any of the precious aromatic oils. This is easy to do if you can set the bowl on a scale, tare out the weight, and zest away. But if you are measuring the zest by volume instead of weighing it, rest assured that 2 limes will be just right, so not to worry.

MORAVIAN SPICE CRISPS

Makes: Twenty-eight 2½ by ¹⁄₁₆ inch thick cookies

Shirley Corriher is one of my oldest and most treasured friends in the food community. We have shared many culinary adventures here and abroad and have enjoyed endless discussions about the science of cooking and, especially, baking. As a research biochemist, Shirley has had a profound influence on my baking life.

The recipe for this traditional paper-thin German cookie was given to Shirley by her son's mother-in-law—a family recipe that has been passed down over more than 200 years. The recipe is especially meaningful to me because I now live full time in Hope, New Jersey, which was settled by the Moravians of Bohemia over 250 years ago.

Oven Temperature: 325°F / 160°C	**Baking Time:** 7 to 10 minutes (for each of two batches)	**Plan Ahead:** It is best to make the dough a minimum of 8 hours ahead, up to 3 days before rolling it.	**Special Equipment:** Two 17 by 14 inch cookie sheets, nonstick or lightly coated with nonstick cooking spray; A 2⅝ inch scalloped round cookie cutter; Optional: ¹⁄₁₆ inch Fast Tracks (for rolling the dough; see page xxi)

DOUGH   *Makes: 241 grams*

solid white vegetable shortening, preferably Spectrum	25 grams	2 tablespoons
all-purpose flour	98 grams	¾ cup (lightly spooned into the cup and leveled off) plus 1 tablespoon
baking soda	3.4 grams	½ plus ⅛ teaspoon
ground ginger	·	½ teaspoon
ground cinnamon	·	¼ plus ⅛ teaspoon
ground cloves	·	¼ teaspoon
light brown sugar, preferably Muscovado	36 grams	2 tablespoons plus 2 teaspoons (firmly packed)
light molasses, preferably Grandma's brand	80 grams	¼ cup (59 ml)
all-purpose flour, for kneading	15 to 23 grams	2 to 3 tablespoons

MISE EN PLACE

Thirty minutes ahead, weigh or measure the shortening. Set on the counter to soften.

MAKE THE DOUGH

1. In a small bowl, whisk together the flour, baking soda, ginger, cinnamon, and cloves until well mixed.

2. In the bowl of a stand mixer fitted with the flat beater, beat the shortening and brown sugar on medium speed for 1 to 2 minutes, until smooth and creamy, scraping down the sides of the bowl as needed.

3. Gradually beat in the molasses until evenly incorporated.

4. On low speed, gradually beat in the flour mixture, mixing just until the flour is incorporated, scraping down the sides of the bowl as needed. The dough should be slightly sticky.

Continues

5. Scrape the dough onto a sheet of plastic wrap. Flatten it into an oval, wrap it tightly, and let it sit at room temperature for a minimum of 8 hours, up to 3 days. If storing it for longer than 8 hours, set it in a cool place or refrigerate and then bring to room temperature before rolling.

PREHEAT THE OVEN

Twenty minutes or longer before baking, set an oven rack at the middle level. Set the oven at 325°F / 160°C.

ROLL AND CUT THE DOUGH

6. Set the dough on a sheet of floured plastic wrap and flour the top of the dough. Roll it into a rough rectangle about 15 by 10 inches by 1/16 inch thick. If you slip your fingers under the plastic wrap and lift the dough, you should be able to see the faint impression of your fingers.

7. Remove the top piece of plastic wrap and dust the surface of the dough with more flour. Spread the flour evenly with your fingertips. Then cut out as many cookies as possible. The dough will be flexible, But if it is too soft to handle, slip it onto a cookie sheet, cover it with plastic wrap, and refrigerate until firm. It works well to lift each cookie, using the plastic wrap, to gently separate it from the dough. Then flip it top side down onto the cookie sheet. Place the cookies no closer than 1/4 inch apart, with 14 cookies on each sheet.

BAKE THE COOKIES

8. Bake the first batch for 5 minutes. Rotate the cookie sheet halfway around. Continue baking for 2 to 5 minutes, until the cookies are golden brown and firm to the touch. Watch carefully after the first 7 minutes of baking; if they get too dark brown, they will be bitter.

COOL THE COOKIES

9. Set the cookie sheet on a wire rack and let the cookies cool for about 30 seconds, until firm enough to lift from the sheet. Use a thin pancake turner to transfer the cookies to another wire rack. Cool completely.

10. Repeat with the second batch.

STORE Airtight: room temperature, 3 months.

Baking Gems

💜 If you prefer a spicier flavor, use up to ¾ teaspoon each of the ginger, cinnamon, and cloves.

💜 The traditional way of rolling the dough is to use a floured pastry cloth and a rolling pin with a floured sleeve. The dough picks up the amount of flour from the cloth as needed to prevent sticking. I now use plastic wrap, which is easier and stocked in most kitchens.

PFEFFERNÜSSE

Makes: Sixteen dozen 1 inch round cookies

Pfeffer is the German word for pepper (and *nüsse* means nut), but in medieval days, it referred to spices in general. Many pfeffernüsse recipes evolved using different mixtures of spices, but all include pepper. The original recipes did not use butter or nuts, resulting in a famously long shelf life. This recipe, which I got many years ago in Switzerland, includes almonds, which soften the texture slightly. Because almonds have a low oil content, they are far less prone to rancidity than other nuts; these cookies keep well for up to six months. The flavor and aroma of ground cloves, with their soothing quality, temper the sting of the pepper (and remind me of my mother's dental office, where oil of clove was used to alleviate discomfort). What is most unusual about this recipe is that the pfeffernüsse are shaped into flat discs rather than into mounds, which makes the firm cookies much easier to eat.

Oven Temperature: 350°F / 175°C	**Baking Time:** 14 to 16 minutes (for each of three batches)	**Plan Ahead:** Bake the cookies a minimum of 2 weeks ahead (or up to 6 months).	**Special Equipment:** Two 17 by 14 inch cookie sheets, lined with parchment or nonstick; A 1 inch round cookie cutter

DOUGH *Makes: 910 grams*

3 large eggs	150 grams	½ cup plus 1½ tablespoons (140 ml)
bleached all-purpose flour	435 grams	3½ cups (lightly spooned into the cup and leveled off) plus 4 teaspoons
baking powder, preferably an aluminum-free variety	·	¼ teaspoon
fine sea salt	·	¼ teaspoon
white or black pepper	2.7 grams	1 teaspoon
ground cinnamon	4.4 grams	2 teaspoons
ground cloves	1.3 grams	½ teaspoon
candied lemon peel, preferably homemade (page 398); see Baking Gems	74 grams	½ cup (chopped into ¼ inch pieces)
sliced unblanched almonds	50 grams	½ cup
sugar	200 grams	1 cup

MISE EN PLACE

Thirty minutes ahead, into a 1 cup / 237 ml glass measure with a spout, weigh or measure the eggs. Whisk lightly, cover tightly with plastic wrap, and set on the counter.

In a large bowl, whisk together the flour, baking powder, salt, pepper, cinnamon, and cloves.

PREHEAT THE OVEN

Twenty minutes or longer before baking, set an oven rack at the middle level. Set the oven at 350°F / 175°C.

MAKE THE DOUGH

Food Processor Method

1. In a food processor, process the candied lemon peel, almonds, and sugar until very fine.

2. With the motor running, add the eggs, processing until blended.

3. Add the flour mixture and pulse just until incorporated. The dough will be crumbly.

Continues

4. Scrape the dough back into the bowl and press it together to form a ball.

Stand Mixer Method

1. Grind the nuts in batches in a spice mill with a little of the sugar, or use a rotary nut grinder.

2. Grind the candied lemon peel in a spice mill with a little of the sugar until very fine, or finely chop it with a chef's knife lightly coated with nonstick cooking spray.

3. In the bowl of a stand mixer fitted with the flat beater, beat the eggs and (remaining) sugar on medium speed for 2 to 3 minutes, until lighter in color and fluffy.

4. Add the lemon peel and almonds and beat on low speed until blended.

5. Gradually beat in the flour mixture until smoothly incorporated, scraping down the sides of the bowl as needed.

Both Methods

6. Divide the dough in half (about 455 grams each). Knead each piece on the countertop until smooth and then flatten into a 6 by ¾ inch thick disc.

7. Wrap each disc of dough in plastic wrap and refrigerate until firm enough to roll, 30 minutes up to 1 hour. The dough is dry but will hold together well when rolled.

ROLL AND CUT THE DOUGH

8. Roll one piece of the dough between sheets of plastic wrap into a 10 inch oval, ¼ inch thick.

9. Cut out as many cookies as possible and place them a minimum of ½ inch apart on a cookie sheet, 64 to a sheet.

10. Knead together the scraps. Wrap with plastic wrap and set aside.

BAKE THE COOKIES

11. Bake for 7 minutes. Rotate the cookie sheet halfway around. Continue baking for 7 to 9 minutes, or until the cookies are lightly browned.

COOL THE COOKIES

12. Set the cookie sheet on a wire rack and use a thin pancake turner to transfer the cookies to another wire rack. Cool completely.

13. Repeat with the second batch. Knead the scraps from the second batch into the first batch of scraps, flatten into a disc, and cover with plastic wrap until ready to roll, cut, and bake the remaining dough.

POWDERED SUGAR TOPPING

powdered sugar	115 grams	1 cup (lightly spooned into the cup and leveled off)
apple slices as needed	.	.

14. Place the powdered sugar in a gallon-size reclosable freezer bag. Add a few cookies at a time and shake to coat well. Then transfer to an airtight storage container.

15. Make a small cup with a piece of aluminum foil and set an apple slice in it. Store the cookies in the airtight container with the apple slice for at least 2 weeks before eating; replace the apple slice every week, or as needed.

STORE Airtight: room temperature, 6 months.

Baking Gems

♥ White pepper, which is traditionally used in this cookie, is slightly milder than black pepper.

♥ If using commercial candied lemon peel rather than homemade, it is a good idea to boost the flavor of the dough by adding 12 grams / 2 tablespoons loosely packed freshly grated lemon zest from 3 to 4 lemons that have been washed with dishwashing soap, rinsed, and dried.

♥ Be sure to wait at least 2 weeks, until the cookies soften and the spices bloom and ripen, before tasting them. And be sure to age them with the apple slice, or they will be rock hard! At first, you should replace the apple slice every week, or as needed. After a few weeks, the cookies will be less hard and will soften after a few seconds in your mouth.

QUICK PUFF PASTRY

Makes: 567 grams / 1¼ pounds

Puff pastry is called a laminated dough because it is made by rolling layers of butter between layers of dough through a series of folds. When the dough bakes, the moisture in the butter turns to steam and causes the layers of dough to separate and rise, resulting in wondrously crisp and flaky pastry.

It was Julia Child who came up with this faster, easier method for making puff pastry, which takes a shortcut by mixing together a rough dough before folding. The pastry is a little bit less flaky than the classic version, but it is also more tender and keeps its shape better, which makes it ideal for cookies. This is my first choice for making Palmiers (page 227). Puff pastry freezes well, so make the full amount even if you are only planning to use part of it. To make traditional puff pastry, see the Variation to Classic Chocolate Puff Pastry, page 229.

DOUGH

unsalted butter, preferably high-fat (see Baking Gems)	255 grams	18 tablespoons (2¼ sticks)
unbleached all-purpose flour	185 grams	1½ cups (lightly spooned into the cup and leveled off) plus ½ tablespoon
bleached cake flour	35 grams	¼ cup (lightly spooned into the cup and leveled off) plus 1 tablespoon
fine sea salt	4 grams (or 6 grams for savory pastry)	¾ teaspoon (or 1 teaspoon)
ice water, or more as needed	79 grams	⅓ cup (79 ml)

MISE EN PLACE

Thirty minutes ahead or longer, cut the butter into ½ inch cubes. Wrap and refrigerate.

MAKE THE DOUGH

Mixer Method

1. In the bowl of a stand mixer fitted with the flat beater, beat together the all-purpose flour, cake flour, and salt on low speed for about 1 minute to mix well.

2. Add the butter and mix just until it forms lumps about the size of lima beans.

3. Pour the ice water evenly over the top and mix only until the dough roughly masses together. The butter pieces should remain about the same size. If the dough does not come together, add more ice water by the teaspoon.

Hand Method

1. In a large bowl, whisk together the all-purpose flour, cake flour, and salt until well mixed.

2. Add the butter and, with a fork, toss to coat it with the flour. Press the butter cubes between your fingers to form 1 inch flakes.

3. Pour the ice water evenly over the top. Use a large silicone spatula to mix in the water to form a rough dough. If there are still dry flour particles, add more ice water by the teaspoon.

Both Methods

4. Scrape the dough onto a lightly floured surface. Quickly pat the dough into a rectangle about 10 inches long by 8 inches wide.

5. Lightly flour the top of the dough. Using a bench scraper or ruler as a guide, fold the dough in thirds by flipping the bottom one third of the way up and then flipping the top down over it so that the top edge reaches the bottom edge.

6. Clean the work surface and reflour it lightly. Position the dough so that the closed edge faces to the left.

7. Lightly flour the top of the dough. With a rolling pin, roll the dough into a 10 inch by 8 inch rectangle again.

8. Fold the dough in thirds again, clean and reflour the work surface, and place the dough on it again so that the closed edge faces to the left.

9. Repeat these steps two more times so that you have made four "turns" (folding the dough into thirds four times). Each time you roll and fold the dough, it will become smoother and you will see the sheets of butter spreading through the layers of dough. Lightly press your fingertips into the dough to make four shallow indentations—this is the traditional way to keep track of the number of turns.

10. Wrap the dough tightly in plastic wrap and refrigerate for a minimum of 40 minutes, up to 1 day. Then make two more turns for a total of six turns.

STORE Airtight: refrigerated, 2 days; frozen, 1 year.

Baking Gems

♥ High-fat butter stays more malleable and will be easier to roll even when cold.

♥ Work quickly so that the butter remains cold. If at any point the dough starts to soften and stick, transfer it to a cookie sheet, cover it with plastic wrap, and refrigerate it just until firm, but no longer than 30 minutes. Any longer, and the butter may get so hard that it will not soften evenly at room temperature. After the first four turns, the butter layer will have become thin enough so that it will not be a problem to chill it longer.

QUICK-PUFF PALMIERS

Makes: Sixteen 3½ inch wide palmiers

Quick puff pastry works wonderfully for making palmiers. These are slightly more tender than those made with classic puff pastry (page 233) but just as crisp and flaky.

Oven Temperature: 425°F / 220°C	**Baking Time:** 14 to 15 minutes (for each of two batches)	**Plan Ahead:** The dough needs to be refrigerated for a minimum of 8 up to 12 hours before cutting the cookies.	**Special Equipment:** Two 17¼ by 12¼ half sheet pans, lined with parchment

DOUGH

Quick Puff Pastry (page 224)	567 grams/ 1¼ pounds	.
sugar, preferably superfine	150 grams	¾ cup, *divided*

PREHEAT THE OVEN
Forty-five minutes or longer before baking, set an oven rack at the middle level. Set the oven at 425°F / 220°C.

ROLL AND CUT THE DOUGH
1. Remove the dough from the refrigerator. If necessary, allow it to sit for a few minutes to soften slightly.

2. Sprinkle about 50 grams / ¼ cup of the sugar on the counter. Set the dough on top and sprinkle another 50 grams / ¼ cup of the sugar on top of it.

3. Roll the dough into a rectangle 7 inches long by 12 inches wide by ¼ inch thick. Try to incorporate as much of the sugar as possible. Use a bench scraper to lift any of the sugar remaining on the counter onto the dough and to butt the sides of the dough to help keep them straight and even. Then use a sharp knife to trim the edges of the dough so that they are straight and even.

4. With the back of a knife, mark the center (lengthwise) of the dough. Fold over each side of the dough so the edges almost meet in the center (about a ¼ inch gap). Then fold one half over onto the other half. The folded dough will resemble a book.

5. Wrap the dough in plastic wrap and refrigerate for a minimum of 8 hours, up to 12 hours. This will allow some of the sugar to become syrupy, making it possible to add more sugar to the cut slices of dough. It will also help to keep the folds from separating during baking.

CUT THE COOKIES
6. Put the remaining 50 grams / ¼ cup sugar in a shallow bowl. Use a sharp knife to slice the dough into ⅜ inch thick pieces (they will resemble hearts). Dip both sides and the edges of each one into the sugar and place them in alternating directions on the prepared sheet pans, spacing them evenly. I like to do two rows of 3 to 4 (6 to 8 per sheet). Cover one sheet of palmiers with plastic wrap and refrigerate while you bake the other sheet.

BAKE THE PALMIERS
7. Bake the palmiers for 8 minutes, or until the edges start to become golden brown. Remove

Continues

the pan from the oven and flip each palmier over. Rotate the pan halfway around and return to the oven. Continue baking for 6 to 7 minutes, or until both sides and the edges are caramelized and crisp. (An instant-read thermometer inserted into the center of a palmier should read 212°F / 100°C.)

COOL THE PALMIERS

8. Set the sheet pan on a wire rack and use a thin pancake turner to transfer the palmiers to another wire rack. Cool completely.

9. Repeat with the remaining batch.

STORE Airtight: room temperature, 5 days.

Baking Gems

♥ You can shape the palmiers ahead of time: Set them all on a parchment-lined cookie sheet and freeze just until frozen solid, then transfer to an airtight container or reclosable freezer bags and freeze for up to 3 months. Bake them straight from the freezer, increasing the baking time by 3 to 5 minutes; if they are browning too quickly, reduce the oven temperature to 400°F / 200°C.

♥ It is best to use half sheet pans rather than cookie sheets to catch any butter that leaks out of the puff pastry.

CLASSIC CHOCOLATE PUFF PASTRY

Makes: 1,511 grams / 3.3 pounds

This is the traditional way of making puff pastry, made even more indulgent with the addition of cocoa powder. The steps may look complex, but making it is actually a lot easier than writing about how to do it! Just follow the instructions. The finished dough is a dream to work with. To make classic puff pastry, when you start to incorporate the block of butter into the dough, it is critical that both the butter and the dough be at the same temperature. If the butter is colder than the dough, it will break through the dough, destroying some of the layering. I find 60°F / 15°C up to 70°F / 21°C the ideal temperature range for rolling.

Plan Ahead: The actual hands-on time needed to roll and fold the dough is minimal, but be prepared to be around the kitchen over several short periods of time for the better part of an afternoon.

Special Equipment: I recommend a 6 quart or larger stand mixer to avoid taxing the motor when making the dough; A 5 quart mixer will work if you finish the dough by hand (see Step 6)

BUTTER BLOCK

unsalted butter	567 grams (1¼ pounds)	5 sticks, *divided*
bread flour, preferably King Arthur	29 grams	3½ tablespoons
unsweetened alkalized cocoa powder	42 grams	½ cup plus 1 tablespoon (sifted before measuring)

MISE EN PLACE

One hour ahead or longer, cut each stick of the butter for the butter block (454 grams / 4 sticks) into 6 to 8 pieces, and the butter for the dough (113 grams / 1 stick) into 4 pieces. Set them on the counter to soften.

In a medium bowl, whisk together the bread flour and cocoa for the butter block.

MAKE THE BUTTER BLOCK

1. Cut an 18 by 13 inch piece of parchment paper and place it on your counter with one of the shorter sides facing you. (It helps to draw a 9 by 6 inch rectangle, about 1 inch from the edge of the parchment, with the 9 inch lines facing you, to use as a guide for shaping the butter. Flip the parchment over so that the writing is facing down.) Tape down the parchment to make it easier to spread the butter.

2. Add the butter to the flour mixture and use a wooden spoon or spatula to mix the butter and flour until evenly combined. Scoop the butter mixture onto the lower third of the parchment paper (onto the drawn rectangle). Use an offset spatula to spread the soft butter mixture into the rectangle 9 inches by 6 inches and ½ inch thick. Use the side of the spatula to help keep the edges squared off as you work.

3. Fold the upper part of the parchment down onto the butter block. With your hands on the outside of the parchment, square off the

Continues

edges. Leave the parchment folded over the butter block and refrigerate it while you make the dough.

DOUGH

bread flour, preferably King Arthur	367 grams	2¾ cups (lightly spooned into the cup and leveled off)
unbleached all-purpose flour	200 grams	1⅔ cups (lightly spooned into the cup and leveled off)
unsweetened alkalized cocoa powder	28 grams	¼ cup plus 2 tablespoons (sifted before measuring)
fine sea salt	6 grams	1 teaspoon
softened unsalted butter, reserved from above	113 grams	8 tablespoons (1 stick)
cold water	287 grams	1 cup plus 3½ tablespoons (287 ml)

MAKE THE DOUGH

4. In the bowl of a stand mixer, whisk together the bread flour, all-purpose flour, cocoa, and salt.

5. Attach the dough hook and add the butter to the bowl. On low speed, mix until it is fully incorporated and the mixture looks a little crumbly.

6. Add the cold water and mix the dough for 4 minutes. Increase the speed to high and mix for 1 to 2 minutes more, until the dough is smooth. (If using a 5 quart mixer, mix on medium speed for 1 minute and then remove the bowl from the stand and knead the dough with your hands to avoid taxing the motor.)

7. Empty the dough onto a large piece of plastic wrap and form it into a rough rectangle. Wrap the dough tightly in the plastic wrap and refrigerate for 30 to 40 minutes. This lets the dough rest and also allows it to come to a similar temperature and texture as the butter block.

MAKE THE DOUGH PACKAGE

8. When the dough and the butter are both chilled but still flexible (60° to 70°F / 15° to 21°C), on a lightly floured surface, roll out the dough into a 13 by 10 inch rectangle, ⅓ inch thick, with one of the 10 inch sides facing you.

9. Pull the top part of the paper up off the butter block. Then use the paper to help you invert the butter block onto the bottom half of the dough, with one of the 9 inch sides facing you so that there is a ½ to ¾ inch margin of dough around the sides and bottom of the block.

10. Fold the top of the dough over the butter block so that the edges of the dough meet. Press the edges of the dough firmly together all around to seal. Then fold the excess dough at the base and edges under itself. The block of dough should be about 10 by 6 inches. If it is still firm but pliable, it is ready to roll. If it has softened, wrap it with plastic wrap, set it on a parchment-lined baking sheet, and refrigerate it for up to 30 minutes before rolling and making the folds.

ROLL THE DOUGH BEFORE EACH FOLD

11. After the dough has been refrigerated for 30 minutes, on a lightly floured counter, roll it into a 19 by 13 inch, ½ inch thick rectangle, with a 19 inch side facing you.

FOLD THE DOUGH FOUR TIMES

12. Make the folds in the following order, brushing off excess flour from the surface of the dough when folding and before wrapping, and refrigerating the dough after each fold for 30 minutes. Then reroll the dough to its original dimensions and fold again:

1. four-fold

2. three-fold

3. four-fold

4. three-fold

Continues

HOW TO MAKE THE FOLDS

There are two kinds of folds: a *four-fold* and a *three-fold*.

FOR THE FOUR-FOLD: Position the dough so one of the longer sides is facing you. Roll the dough to a 19 by 13 inch rectangle. Fold the left side over toward the center, about three quarters of the way over the dough. Fold the right side over the dough to meet the left edge. It will look like an open book with an off-center spine. Then fold the larger side over the shorter side. You will now have 4 layers of dough.

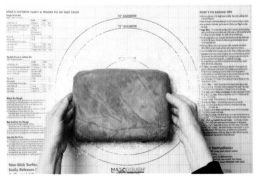

For either fold, position the dough with a longer side facing you.

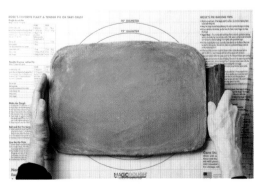

Roll the dough into a rectangle.

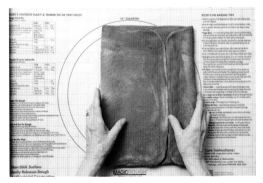

For a four-fold: Fold the left side over, then fold the right side over to meet the left edge.

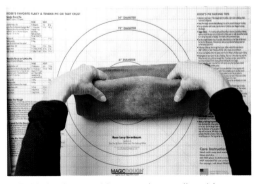

Fold the larger side over the smaller side.

FOR THE THREE-FOLD (BUSINESS-LETTER FOLD): Position the dough so one of the longer sides is facing you. Roll the dough to a 19 by 13 inch rectangle. Fold the left side of the dough one third of the way over the dough. Fold the right side over so that it rests on the piece of dough you just folded over. You will now have 3 layers of dough).

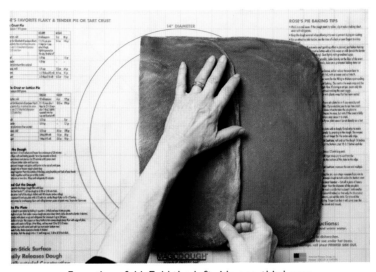

For a three-fold: Fold the left side one-third over.

Fold the right side over to resemble a business letter.

You will have 3 layers of dough.

CHILL THE DOUGH

13. After the final fold, the dough will be about 13 by 6 inches. Wrap the dough and refrigerate for about 30 minutes to relax it before shaping.

*You can store the wrapped dough refrigerated for up to 3 days or frozen for up to 3 months. (Defrost overnight in the refrigerator before rolling and shaping.)

Baking Gems

♥ Each time you roll the dough, be sure to square off the edges, straightening them by butting up against them with a bench scraper. This helps to ensure that when you fold the dough, the edges will match and your layers will be in the best shape.

♥ It is important to roll the dough and do the folds after refrigerating for 30 minutes, no longer. If the dough gets too cold, it will not soften evenly and will not roll out well. Once the final fold is completed, though, the layers of butter are so thin the dough can be rolled as soon as you take it out of the refrigerator, or after a few minutes, but it's still a good idea to let it rest for 30 minutes in the refrigerator before rolling.

♥ Marble is the ideal surface for rolling puff pastry because it retains the chill.

Classic Puff Pastry

For the Butter Block: Omit the cocoa powder. Use 71 grams / ½ cup (lightly spooned into the cup and leveled off) plus 2 teaspoons bread flour.

For the Dough: Omit the cocoa powder. Use 395 grams / 3 cups (lightly spooned into the cup and leveled off) plus 1 tablespoon bread flour and the 200 grams / 1⅔ cups (lightly spooned into the cup and leveled off) all-purpose flour.

CHOCOLATE PALMIERS

Makes: Thirty to Thirty-two 3¾ inch wide palmiers

When I was writing the foreword to Erin Jeanne McDowell's first book, *The Fearless Baker*, this stunning cookie caught my eye and I couldn't resist rising to the challenge of making chocolate puff pastry. Erin's instructions were so spot on it was a thrill to make the dough, and the cookies came out absolutely perfectly. They are crisp, flaky, and deeply chocolatey. This is one amazing cookie from one amazing baker, friend, and colleague.

Oven Temperature: 400°F / 200°C

Baking Time: 18 to 22 minutes (for each of four batches)

Special Equipment: Two 17 by 14 inch cookie sheets, lined with parchment

DOUGH AND SUGAR

Classic Chocolate Puff Pastry (page 229)	1,511 grams/ 3.3 pounds	.
sugar, preferably superfine	200 grams	1 cup, *divided*

PREHEAT THE OVEN

Forty-five minutes or longer before baking, set an oven rack at the middle level. Set the oven at 400°F / 200°C.

ROLL AND CUT THE DOUGH

1. Cut the dough in half into two rectangles (about 6½ by 6 inches / 755 grams each). Wrap and refrigerate one piece while you roll the other for the first two batches. If necessary, allow the dough to sit for a few minutes to soften slightly. (Weigh or measure 100 grams / ½ cup of the sugar.)

2. On a lightly floured counter, roll the dough into a rectangle 15 by 10 inches by ½ inch thick, with a 15 inch side facing you. Use a bench scraper butted up against the sides of the dough to help keep it straight and even.

3. When you get close to these dimensions, sprinkle 37 grams / 3 tablespoons of the sugar on the counter and set the dough on top. Sprinkle another 37 grams / 3 tablespoons of the sugar onto the surface of the dough and finish rolling it out. Use a sharp knife to trim the edges of the dough edges so that they are straight and even.

4. With the back of a knife, mark the center (lengthwise) of the dough. Fold over the sides of the dough so the edges almost meet in the center (a gap of no more than ½ inch). Then fold one half over onto the other half. The folded dough will resemble a book. If it has softened, wrap it with plastic wrap, set it on a parchment-lined baking sheet, and refrigerate for about 15 minutes until firm enough to cut.

5. Use a sharp knife to slice the dough into ½ inch thick pieces (they will resemble hearts). Put the remaining 26 grams / 2 tablespoons sugar in a shallow bowl and add any sugar remaining on the counter. Dip both sides and the edges of each palmier into the sugar and then arrange them evenly spaced in alternating directions on the prepared cookie sheets. Cover the second sheet with plastic wrap and refrigerate while you bake

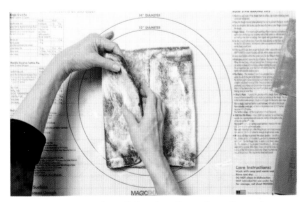

Fold over the sides of the dough so the edges almost meet in the center.

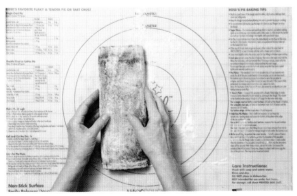

Fold one half over the other half.

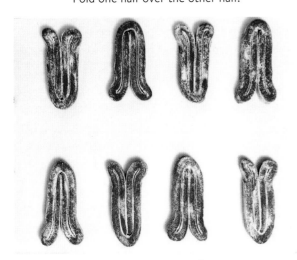

Cut the dough into slices.

the first sheet. (The unbaked palmiers can be refrigerated, tightly covered, for up to 3 days.)

BAKE THE PALMIERS

6. Bake the palmiers for 10 to 12 minutes, until firm enough to lift. Remove the pan from the oven and flip each palmier over. Rotate the pan halfway around and continue baking for 8 to 10 minutes, or until both sides and the edges are caramelized and crisp. (An instant-read thermometer inserted into a palmier should read 212°F / 100°C.)

COOL THE PALMIERS

7. Set the cookie sheet on a wire rack and use a thin pancake turner to transfer the palmiers to another wire rack. Cool completely.

8. Repeat baking and cooling with the second sheet.

9. Repeat with the second half of the dough and sugar, or freeze the dough to shape and bake at a later time.

STORE Airtight: room temperature, 5 days.

Baking Gems

💜 The trimmed end pieces, if too thick, can be covered by a piece of plastic wrap and rolled to ½ inch thickness, dipped in sugar, and baked.

💜 You can shape and sugar the palmiers ahead of time: Set them all on a parchment-lined cookie sheet and freeze just until frozen solid. Transfer the frozen palmiers to an airtight container or reclosable freezer bags and freeze for up to 3 months. Bake them without thawing; increase the baking time by 3 to 5 minutes. If the palmiers are getting too dark around the edges, reduce the oven temperature to 375°F / 190°F.

💜 If using "classic" puff pastry, it is best to use half sheet pans rather than cookie sheets to catch any butter that leaks out of the puff pastry.

ROSEBUDS

Makes: Eighteen to Twenty 2 inch oval cookies

I created this recipe as an attractive and delicious way to use my collection of piecrust dough scraps from the freezer. But I ended up liking the crisp, buttery cookies so much, I sometimes make the dough just so I can make these.

Oven Temperature: 425°F / 220°C

Baking Time: 8 to 13 minutes (for each of two batches)

Special Equipment: Two 17 by 14 inch cookie sheets, no preparation needed or lined with parchment

Makes: 256 grams

any pie dough scraps (or Cream Cheese–Butter Dough for Rugelach page 130); see Baking Gems	227 grams (8 ounces)	.
superfine sugar (see Baking Gems)	30 grams	2 tablespoons plus 1 teaspoon
ground cinnamon	.	¼ teaspoon
turbinado sugar, preferably Sugar in the Raw, for coating	12.5 grams	about 1 tablespoon

PREPARE THE DOUGH SCRAPS

If using the Cream Cheese–Butter Dough, skip to step 4.

1. If using dough scraps, cut them into similar lengths and lay them on a sheet of plastic wrap, overlapping them slightly. Sprinkle the dough lightly with flour and cover with a second sheet of plastic wrap.

2. Roll lightly to press the dough into one large piece. Then lift away the plastic wrap and use the bottom sheet to help fold the dough in thirds, like a business letter.

3. Wrap the dough well and refrigerate it for a minimum of 20 minutes.

MAKE THE SUGAR MIXTURE

4. In a small bowl, stir together the superfine sugar and cinnamon until evenly mixed.

ROLL THE DOUGH

5. Divide the dough in half (about 113 grams each). One at a time, set each piece between sheets of plastic wrap and roll into a 12 by 6 inch rectangle, ⅛ inch thick. Discard the top sheet of plastic wrap and sprinkle the dough evenly with the sugar mixture.

6. Use the bottom sheet of plastic wrap to lift up each rectangle of dough from a long side and tightly roll up into a cylinder, about 1 inch in diameter.

7. Wrap each cylinder in the bottom sheet of plastic wrap and refrigerate for at least 1 hour, up to 8 hours.

PREHEAT THE OVEN

Twenty minutes or longer before baking, set an oven rack at the middle level. Set the oven at 425°F / 220°C.

8. Unwrap one cylinder of dough. With a sharp knife, cut the cylinder on a diagonal into 1 inch thick slices. Any gaps will seal on rolling.

9. Roll out each slice into a 2 inch long by 1½ inch wide oval to resemble a rosebud. If necessary, use your fingers to perfect the shape. For a glimmer of sparkle, lightly sprinkle the tops with the turbinado sugar.

10. Place the slices a minimum of 1 inch apart on a cookie sheet.

BAKE THE COOKIES

11. Bake for 6 to 9 minutes, or until the cookies are browned on the first side. Flip each cookie over, rotate the cookie sheet, and continue baking for 2 to 4 minutes, or until the other side browns.

COOL THE COOKIES

12. Set the cookie sheet on a wire rack and use a thin pancake turner to transfer the cookies to another wire rack. Cool completely.

13. Repeat with the second batch.

STORE Airtight: room temperature, 3 weeks; frozen, 6 months.

Baking Gems

♥ The Cream Cheese–Butter Dough makes 312 grams, so if you want to use the entire amount of dough, multiply the sugars by 1.3 (39 grams / 3 tablespoons superfine sugar and 16 grams / 4 teaspoons turbinado sugar) and add a small extra pinch of cinnamon. Roll each piece into a 12 by 7¼ inch rectangle.

♥ If you are using a mild-tasting cinnamon or you prefer a stronger cinnamon flavor, increase the cinnamon to ½ teaspoon.

♥ Refrigerating the dough before cutting it firms the dough enough to cut it evenly. It also causes the sugar to dissolve slightly, helping the layers of dough adhere to each other.

BONE À FIDOS

Makes: about Fifty-five 3½ inch long bone-shaped cookies or about Forty 2½ inch round cookies

When I was writing *Rose's Christmas Cookies* many years ago, my brother, Michael, who owned several stores in the San Francisco Bay Area called Pet Food Express, insisted that I include a cookie for dogs, saying his customers loved their dogs so much that they had expressed a desire to make them treats. The original recipe was given to me by a family friend, Barbara Vanderbilt. My brother now owns more than sixty stores, so he must know what dogs and their owners value!

Oven Temperature: 300°F / 150°C	Baking Time: 45 to 60 minutes (for each of two batches)	Special Equipment: Two 17 by 14 inch cookie sheets, lined with parchment; A 3 to 3½ inch bone-shaped cookie cutter or a 2½ inch round cookie cutter

DOUGH *Makes: About 1,060 grams*

all-purpose flour, preferably unbleached	250 grams	2 cups (lightly spooned into the cup and leveled off) plus 1 tablespoon
whole wheat flour	156 grams	1 cup (lightly spooned into the cup and leveled off) plus 3 tablespoons
rye flour	73 grams	½ cup (lightly spooned into the cup and leveled off) plus 1 tablespoon
cracked wheat or bulgur	120 grams	about 1 cup (lightly spooned into the cup and leveled off)
nonfat dry milk	20 grams	¼ cup
kelp powder	4 grams	2 teaspoons
instant yeast	3.2 grams	1 teaspoon
beef or chicken broth	340 to 454 grams	1½ to 2 cups (355 to 473 ml)

PREHEAT THE OVEN

Twenty minutes or longer before baking, set two oven racks in the upper and lower thirds of the oven. Set the oven at 300°F / 150°C.

MAKE THE DOUGH

1. In a medium bowl, whisk together the all-purpose flour, whole wheat flour, rye flour, cracked wheat, dry milk, kelp powder, and yeast.

2. Add about 340 grams / 1½ cups / 355 ml of the broth. Use your hands to mix until the dough becomes smooth and supple. If needed, add more broth.

ROLL AND CUT THE COOKIES

3. Set the dough on a lightly floured counter and knead it lightly.

4. Without letting it rest, roll the dough into an 18 inch by 13 inch rectangle ¼ inch thick.

5. Cut out as many cookies as possible and place them on the prepared cookie sheets, a minimum of ½ inch apart (18 or 19 to a sheet).

6. Knead together the dough scraps, and set the dough on the counter at room temperature.

OPTIONAL SHINY GLAZE

½ large egg, lightly beaten before measuring	25 grams	1½ tablespoons (22.5 ml)
milk	15 grams	1 tablespoon (15 ml)

7. In a small bowl, whisk together the egg and milk. Brush it onto the cookies. Cover and set aside for the third batch.

BAKE THE COOKIES

8. Bake for 30 minutes. Rotate the cookie sheets halfway around and reverse them top to bottom. Continue baking for 15 to 30 minutes, or until the cookies are golden brown and firm.

COOL THE COOKIES

9. Set the cookie sheets on wire racks and use a thin pancake turner to transfer the cookies to other wire racks. Cool completely.

10. Repeat with the remaining batch.

STORE Airtight: room temperature, 6 months.

Baking Gem

♥ Cracked wheat and bulgur vary in volume depending on brand and fineness of grind, so the volume for those will be approximate, and the amount of broth will require more or less liquid.

CHAPTER 5

HOLIDAY COOKIES

HOLIDAY COOKIE CUTOUTS

Makes: Twenty-four 3 inch cutout cookies

I designed this dough to make cookies strong enough to decorate, hang from a tree, or ship as gifts, and also to be thin, crisp, tender, and flavorful.

Oven Temperature: 350°F / 175°C	**Baking Time:** 8 to 12 minutes (for each of two batches)

Special Equipment: Two 17 by 14 inch cookie sheets, no preparation needed or lined with parchment; Your favorite cookie cutters

DOUGH *Makes: 340 grams*

unsalted butter	85 grams	6 tablespoons (¾ stick)
½ large egg, lightly beaten before measuring	25 grams	1½ tablespoons (22.5 ml)
pure vanilla extract	·	½ teaspoon (2.5 ml)
bleached all-purpose flour	160 grams	1⅓ cups (lightly spooned into the cup and leveled off)
fine sea salt	·	⅛ teaspoon
lemon zest, finely grated	3 grams	½ tablespoon (loosely packed)
sugar	75 grams	¼ cup plus 2 tablespoons

MISE EN PLACE

For the Food Processor Method: Thirty minutes ahead or longer, cut the butter into ½ inch cubes. Wrap and refrigerate.

For the Mixer Method: Thirty minutes to 1 hour ahead, cut the butter into tablespoon-size pieces. Set on the counter to soften.

Thirty minutes ahead, into a 1 cup / 237 ml glass measure with a spout, weigh or measure the egg.

Whisk in the vanilla extract. Cover tightly with plastic wrap and set on the counter.

In a small bowl, whisk together the flour and salt.

With dishwashing liquid, wash, rinse, and dry the lemon before zesting it. Set the zest in a small bowl.

MAKE THE DOUGH

Food Processor Method

1. In a food processor, process the sugar with the lemon zest until very fine.

2. Add the butter and pulse until all the sugar disappears. Scrape down the sides of the bowl as needed.

3. With the motor running, add the egg mixture and process until uniform. Scrape down the sides of the bowl as needed.

4. Add the flour mixture and pulse just until the dough begins to clump together. Pinch a little of the dough, and if it doesn't hold together, pulse in a few drops of water.

Stand Mixer Method

1. Chop the lemon zest into very fine pieces.

2. In the bowl of a stand mixer fitted with the flat beater, beat the butter, sugar, and lemon zest on

Continues

low speed until the sugar is incorporated. Raise the speed to medium and beat for 2 to 3 minutes, until lighter in color and fluffy.

3. Gradually add the egg mixture, beating until blended.

4. On low speed, gradually add the flour mixture, mixing until incorporated. Add just a few drops of water and continue beating until the dough just begins to come away from the sides of the bowl.

Both Methods

5. Scrape the dough onto a sheet of plastic wrap. Use it to knead the dough together. Wrap the dough in the plastic and flatten it into a thick disc.

6. Refrigerate the dough for at least 2 hours, up to 2 days. If it's been refrigerated for longer than 3 hours, allow the dough to sit at room temperature to soften enough for rolling.

PREHEAT THE OVEN

Twenty minutes or longer before baking, set an oven rack at the middle level. Set the oven at 350°F / 175°C.

ROLL AND CUT THE DOUGH

7. Have ready a small bowl of flour for dipping the cookie cutters.

8. Set the dough on a lightly floured dough mat or sheet of plastic wrap. Lightly flour the dough and cover it with plastic wrap. Roll the dough ⅛ inch thick.

9. Before cutting out the first cookie, run a small piece of dough along the edges of the cookie cutter so that the flour will adhere. Then dip the cutter in flour every few cuts to prevent sticking.

10. Cut out 12 cookies and use a small metal spatula to transfer them to a cookie sheet, no closer than 1 inch apart.

11. To paint the cookies with edible tempera color before baking, see opposite. Royal Icing decorations (page opposite) can be added after baking and cooling (see Gingerbread Folks, page 247). If you are planning to hang the cookies, make a small hole in each one with the blunt end of a wooden skewer.

12. Gather up the scraps and press together to reroll. Wrap and refrigerate.

BAKE THE COOKIES

13. Bake for 5 minutes. If you have made holes in the cookies and they have become too small, set the cookie sheet on a wire rack and enlarge the holes with the skewer. Rotate the cookie sheet halfway around. Continue baking for 3 to 7 minutes, or until the cookies are pale gold and the edges have deepened slightly in color.

COOL THE COOKIES

14. Set the cookie sheet on a wire rack and use a thin pancake turner to lift the cookies onto another wire rack to cool completely.

15. Repeat with the second batch.

STORE Airtight: room temperature, 3 months.

Baking Gems

♥ Rolling the dough with plastic wrap on top prevents cracking.

♥ If the dough softens, refrigerate the cutout cookies before lifting them off the rolling surface. If using a dough mat, set it on a cookie sheet.

TEMPERA FOOD COLORING

This method of painting on canvas dates back to ancient Egypt. It works brilliantly for unbaked cookies, as the color magically deepens and brightens on baking.

You will need about 2 large egg yolks (37 grams / 2 tablespoons plus 1 teaspoon / 35 ml) for five colors. Put about 1 teaspoon / 5 ml yolk into each of five eggshells set in egg cups or five small bowls. Mix in the colors according to the chart below.

LIQUID FOOD COLOR

Red: ½ teaspoon (2.5 ml)

Green: ¼ teaspoon (1.25 ml)

Yellow: ½ teaspoon (2.5 ml)

Blue: ¼ teaspoon (1.25 ml)

Black: Green: 1½ teaspoons (7.5 ml)

Red: 1½ teaspoons (7.5 ml)

Blue: 5 drops

Use a small clean paintbrush to paint the cookies before baking.

ROYAL ICING

Royal icing is both decorative and useful as an edible "glue" to attach other decorative elements such as dragées, edible glitter, or colored sparkling sugar. Royal icing is easy to make, but it can also be purchased at candy supply stores.

ROYAL ICING

Makes: 530 grams / 2¼ cups

powdered sugar, or more as needed	460 grams	4 cups (lightly spooned into the cup and leveled off)
3 large egg whites	90 grams	¼ cup plus 2 tablespoons (89 ml)

MISE EN PLACE

Into the bowl of a stand mixer, weigh or measure the powdered sugar.

Into a 1 cup / 237 ml glass measure with a spout, weigh or measure the egg whites.

MAKE THE ROYAL ICING

1. Pour the egg whites into the sugar.

2. Attach the whisk beater and beat on low speed until the sugar is moistened.

3. Gradually raise the speed to high and beat until the icing is very glossy and stiff peaks form that curve slightly when the beater is raised slowly, about 6 minutes. If necessary, scrape down the sides of the bowl. If the icing is too thin, beat in more powdered sugar.

4. Use a silicone spatula to scrape the mixture into a small bowl. Keep the bowl covered with a damp towel until ready to use.

STORE Airtight in a glass container (plastic is petrol-based and can break down the icing): room temperature, 3 days. Rebeat lightly before using.

Baking Gems

♥ It is best to avoid making royal icing on humid days.

♥ The mixer bowl, glass measure, whisk, spatula, small bowl, pastry bag, and decorating tips must be entirely free of fat, which includes oil or egg yolk.

♥ When piping decorations, be sure to keep the pastry tip covered with a damp cloth when not in use so that the icing doesn't harden in the tube.

♥ Adding ½ teaspoon / 2.5 ml glycerine, which is available in candy and cake decorating supply stores, will keep the royal icing soft longer.

Continues

VARIATIONS

If you want to add food color to royal icing, use only a type that is free of fat, such as liquid or powdered food color.

For a light chocolate royal icing, add 7 grams / 1½ tablespoons of unsweetened cocoa powder to the powdered sugar.

If you would like to paint the royal icing onto cookies, thin it with water a few drops at a time, until, when some of it is lifted with a spoon, it disappears completely into the surface. Use a fine artist's brush (reserved for this purpose) to brush it evenly onto the cookies. Then immediately sprinkle with sparkling sugar or edible glitter and attach any other decorative elements. Work quickly, as royal icing dries and hardens very fast.

GINGERBREAD FOLKS

Makes: Eighteen 5 by 3 inch cookies

Not only is this amazing dough easy to work with, it freezes perfectly for as long as a year, and the baked cookies also have a long shelf life. It is delicious baked into cookies, which are also lovely to hang on Christmas trees, but with a minor change of ingredients (see the Variation), it is sturdy enough to use for building gingerbread houses.

Oven Temperature: 350°F / 175°C

Baking Time: 10 to 12 minutes (for each of two batches)

Special Equipment: Two 17 by 14 inch cookie sheets, nonstick or lightly coated with nonstick cooking spray; Gingerbread men and women cookie cutters, 5 inches high by about 3 inches wide; A disposable pastry bag and small round decorating tube for the Royal Icing

DOUGH *Makes: 490 grams*

unsalted butter	85 grams	6 tablespoons (¾ stick)
½ large egg, lightly beaten before measuring	25 grams	1½ tablespoons (22.5 ml)
light molasses, preferably Grandma's brand	80 grams	¼ cup (59 ml)
bleached all-purpose flour	212 grams	1¾ cups (lightly spooned into the cup and leveled off)
baking soda	2.7 grams	½ teaspoon
fine sea salt	·	⅛ teaspoon
ground ginger	1.8 grams	1 teaspoon
ground cinnamon	·	½ teaspoon
grated nutmeg	·	¼ teaspoon
ground cloves	·	⅛ teaspoon
dark brown sugar, preferably Muscovado	91 grams	⅓ cup plus 1 tablespoon (firmly packed)
Royal Icing (page 245), for decoration	530 grams	2¼ cups
décor: raisins, currants, and/or candies	·	·

MISE EN PLACE

Thirty minutes to 1 hour ahead, cut the butter into tablespoon-size pieces. Set on the counter to soften.

Thirty minutes ahead, into a 1 cup / 237 ml glass measure with a spout, weigh or measure the egg. Whisk lightly, cover tightly with plastic wrap, and set on the counter.

Into a 1 cup / 237 ml glass measure with a spout, lightly coated with nonstick cooking spray, weigh or measure the molasses. Cover and set on the counter.

In a medium bowl, whisk together the flour, baking soda, salt, and spices.

MAKE THE DOUGH

1. In the bowl of a stand mixer fitted with the flat beater, beat the butter and brown sugar on medium speed for 2 to 3 minutes, until lighter in color and fluffy.

2. Gradually add the egg and molasses, beating until blended. Scrape down the sides of the bowl.

3. On low speed, gradually beat in the flour mixture just until incorporated, scraping down the sides of the bowl as needed.

Continues

4. Scrape the dough onto a sheet of plastic wrap and use the wrap to press the dough together and form a ½ inch thick disc. Wrap it in the plastic wrap and refrigerate for a minimum of 2 hours, up to overnight.

PREHEAT THE OVEN

Twenty minutes or longer before baking, set an oven rack at the middle level. Set the oven at 350°F / 175°C.

ROLL AND CUT THE DOUGH

5. Set the dough on a well-floured dough mat or sheet of plastic wrap. Lightly flour the dough and cover it with plastic wrap. Roll the dough ⅛ inch thick.

6. Use the gingerbread cutters to cut out the shapes. Dip the cutters in flour every few cuts to prevent sticking. Gently brush off any flour on top of the dough. Gather up and press together the scraps to reroll. Wrap and refrigerate until firm. Roll the scraps the same day because if stored overnight, the cookies will darken on baking.

7. With a small offset metal spatula or pancake turner, lift the cut dough onto the cookie sheets, placing the cutouts about 1 inch apart. If planning to hang the cookies, use the blunt end of a wooden skewer to make a hole at the top of each cookie.

BAKE THE COOKIES

8. Bake the first sheet of cookies for 5 minutes. If you made holes in the cookies and they have become too small, set the cookie sheet on a wire rack and enlarge the holes with the wooden skewer. Rotate the cookie sheet halfway around. Continue baking for 5 to 7 minutes, or until the cookies are barely soft to the touch.

COOL THE COOKIES

9. Set the cookie sheet on a wire rack and use a thin pancake turner to transfer the cookies to another wire rack. Cool completely.

10. Repeat with the second batch.

DECORATE THE COOKIES

11. Use the royal icing to attach decorative elements such as pieces of raisins, currants, cinnamon red hots, or other candy to the cookies The royal icing also can be piped onto the cookies for attractive details. If necessary, use a lightly moistened brush to correct any imperfections.

STORE Airtight: room temperature, 3 months; frozen, 6 months.

Baking Gems

♥ If the dough softens after cutting, cover and refrigerate before lifting the cut dough off the surface to maintain the cookies' shape.

♥ If you like thicker, softer cookies, roll the dough ¼ inch thick and bake just until, when gently pressed with a fingertip, the cookies are set but still slightly soft.

VARIATION

Sturdy Gingerbread for Houses

(makes 820 grams)

Make a double batch of the dough, with the following modifications:

Omit the egg

Use only 113 grams / 8 tablespoons / 1 stick butter

Use only 120 grams / ½ cup plus 2 teaspoons (firmly packed) dark brown Muscovado sugar or dark brown sugar.

Work with one piece of dough at a time, about the size of an orange. Keep the rest of the dough tightly covered to prevent drying.

CHRISTMAS WREATHS

Makes: Eighteen 2 inch round cookies

I discovered this old-time recipe more than forty-five years ago, when I was working in the test kitchen of *Ladies' Home Journal*. They are an adorable holiday decoration—fun, magical, and easy for children to help make—and also delicious to eat. The cornflakes have a lovely crunchy texture and toasty flavor and the melted marshmallows, butter, and vanilla give the cookies a sticky texture and sweet mellow flavor.

No-Bake | **Special Equipment:** One 17 by 14 inch cookie sheet, lined with parchment and lightly coated with nonstick cooking spray; Two small spoons, lightly coated with nonstick cooking spray

INGREDIENTS *Makes: 485 grams*

unsalted butter	113 grams	8 tablespoons (1 stick)
30 large marshmallows	208 grams	3 cups
green liquid food coloring	.	1¾ teaspoons (8.75 ml)
pure vanilla extract	.	1 teaspoon (5 ml)
cornflakes	140 grams	4 cups
cinnamon red hots (candies)	30 grams	2 tablespoons

MISE EN PLACE

Thirty minutes ahead, cut the butter into tablespoon-size pieces. Set on the counter to soften.

MAKE THE CORNFLAKE MIXTURE

1. Coat a medium saucepan with nonstick cooking spray.

2. Add the butter and melt over low heat.

3. Add the marshmallows and cook, stirring constantly, until melted and smooth, about 6 minutes.

4. Remove the pan from the heat and whisk in the food coloring and vanilla extract until evenly blended.

5. Add the cornflakes. Stir them in gently until well coated.

6. Set the pan in a larger saucepan or a skillet filled with 1 inch of hot tap water to keep the mixture soft enough to shape. Replace the hot water as needed.

SHAPE THE WREATHS

7. Work quickly to keep the mixture from hardening. Use the two small spoons or your lightly oiled fingers to drop small mounds (about 2 heaping tablespoons) of the mixture onto the prepared cookie sheet. Use your fingers to form the mounds into wreaths (with open centers).

8. Immediately, while the wreaths are still sticky, attach 5 red hots to each one. (Alternatively, they can be attached later using a tiny dab of Royal Icing, page 245.)

9. Let the wreaths dry for several hours until they are firm and hold their shape. Eat them, set them on the mantelpiece for decoration, or use nylon string or fine gold ribbon to hang them on the Christmas tree.

STORE Airtight: room temperature, 1 month (for eating); several weeks as decorations.

Baking Gem

♥ You can melt the mixture in a microwave, but you will need to use a very large bowl because the marshmallows initially swell considerably on heating.

SPRITZ COOKIES

Makes: Twenty-six to Twenty-eight 2 inch round cookies

These rank as many people's favorite Christmas cookies because of their subtle almond flavor and crisp but melting texture. The cassava or cornstarch in the dough makes it easier to pipe or press it using a cookie press. If desired, you can shape the cookies by hand (see Baking Gems).

| **Oven Temperature:** 325°F / 160°C for the almonds; 375°F / 190°C for the cookies | **Baking Time:** 7 minutes for the almonds; 10 to 12 minutes for the cookies (for each of two batches) | **Special Equipment:** Two 17 by 14 inch cookie sheets, no preparation needed (see Baking Gems); A large pastry bag fitted with a ½ inch star pastry tube or a cookie press |

DOUGH *Makes: 375 grams*

unsalted butter	113 grams	8 tablespoon (1 stick)
blanched sliced almonds	22 grams	¼ cup minus ½ tablespoon
bleached all-purpose flour	128 grams	1 cup (lightly spooned into the cup and leveled off) plus 2 teaspoons
cassava (ground tapioca) or cornstarch (see Baking Gems)	15 grams	1 tablespoon plus 2 teaspoons
fine sea salt	·	a tiny pinch
½ large egg, lightly beaten before measuring	25 grams	1½ tablespoons (22.5 ml)
pure vanilla extract	·	½ teaspoon (2.5 ml)
pure almond extract	·	½ teaspoon (2.5 ml)
sugar	75 grams	¼ cup plus 2 tablespoons
glacéed cherries, sugar sprinkles, or dragées, for decorating (optional)	·	·

PREHEAT THE OVEN

Twenty minutes at longer before baking, set an oven rack at the middle level. Set the oven at 325°F / 160°C.

MISE EN PLACE

Thirty minutes to 1 hour ahead, cut the butter into tablespoon-size pieces. Set on the counter to soften.

Toast the Almonds: Spread the almonds evenly on a baking sheet and bake for about 7 minutes, or until pale gold. Stir once or twice to ensure even toasting and avoid overbrowning. Set the baking sheet on a wire rack and cool completely. Raise the oven temperature to 375°F / 190°C.

In a medium bowl, whisk together the flour, cassava, and salt.

Into a 1 cup / 237 ml glass measure with a spout, weigh or measure the egg. Whisk in the vanilla and almond extracts. Cover tightly with plastic wrap and set on the counter.

MAKE THE DOUGH
Food Processor Method

1. In a food processor, process the almonds and sugar until finely ground.

2. With the motor running, add the butter one piece at a time, processing until smoothly incorporated. Scrape down the sides of the bowl as needed.

3. Add the egg mixture and process until incorporated. Scrape down the sides of the bowl.

4. Add the flour mixture and pulse just until blended.

Stand Mixer Method

1. Grind the almonds in a spice mill with a little of the sugar, or use a rotary nut grinder. Whisk into the flour mixture.

2. In the bowl of a stand mixer fitted with the flat beater, beat the butter and (remaining) sugar on medium speed for 2 to 3 minutes, or until lighter in color and fluffy.

3. Gradually add the egg mixture, beating until incorporated. Scrape down the sides of the bowl.

4. On low speed, gradually beat in the flour mixture just until incorporated, scraping down the sides of the bowl as needed.

SHAPE THE COOKIES

5. The dough is easiest to shape when it is between 70° and 75°F / 21° and 24°C. If necessary, cover and refrigerate it briefly. If it is too cold, it will be hard to pipe. Scoop the dough into the prepared pastry bag (or spoon some of the dough into the cookie press and cover the remaining dough).

6. Pipe 14 stars about 1¾ inches in diameter (13 to 14 grams) onto a cookie sheet, spacing them no less than 1 inch apart. For the best shape, hold the bag in a vertical position (straight up and down) with the toothed edge of the tube just slightly above the cookie sheet. Squeeze the bag firmly, without moving it, until the shape is as wide as desired, just at the point when the lines in the dough are on the verge of curving. Stop squeezing the tube and push the tube down slightly, then lift it straight up and away. (If using a cookie press, lift it straight up and away with a sharp movement to make the most precise shape.) If the dough starts to soften, chill it briefly.

7. Decorate with the optional glacéed cherries set in the centers of the cookies, or with sugar sprinkles or dragées.

BAKE THE COOKIES

8. Bake for 5 minutes. Rotate the cookie sheet halfway around. Continue baking for 5 to 7 minutes, or until the cookies are pale golden.

9. While the first batch of cookies is baking, shape the dough for the second batch.

COOL THE COOKIES

10. Set the cookie sheet on a wire rack and use a thin pancake turner to lift the cookies onto another wire rack. Cool completely.

11. Bake and cool the second batch.

STORE Airtight: room temperature, 1 month; refrigerated or frozen, 3 months.

Baking Gems

♥ Cassava results in a finer, more dissolving texture than cornstarch.

♥ If you have never used a pastry bag before, don't be afraid. It's just as easy to use as a cookie press. But if desired, you can shape the cookies by hand: Roll scant tablespoons of the dough (13 to 14 grams) into 1 inch balls and then flatten them with a decorative press or with your fingers to about 1¾ inches in diameter.

♥ If not using a cookie press, if desired, you can line the cookie sheets with parchment for easy cleanup. But if using a cookie press, when lifting it off the surface, parchment would lift with it and distort the shape of the cookies.

♥ If using a stand mixer and using a rotary nut grinder to grind the nuts, it is best to use superfine sugar, which will give the cookies a finer texture.

SWISS LEBKUCHEN

Makes: Twenty-eight 2 inch round cookies

Lebkuchen is a type of gingerbread. It is one of the world's oldest cookies, dating back to the honey and spice cakes of Mesopotamia in around 2,000 BCE, when the dough was made as long as a year ahead to encourage fermentation for flavor and leavening. Lebkuchen comes in myriad varieties and is a traditional Christmas cookie in Germany and Switzerland. My favorite is adapted from Eichenberger Bakery in Bern, Switzerland. Their original version had no flour, but I include just a little to slightly temper the stickiness of the dough. The result is a sticky-chewy texture and nutty-candied flavor.

Oven Temperature: 350°F / 175°C for the nuts; 400°F / 200°C for the cookies	**Baking Time:** 7 minutes for the nuts; 6 to 8 minutes for the cookies (for each of two batches)	**Plan Ahead:** Bake the cookies a minimum of 2 weeks ahead for the fullest flavor (but if you can't resist tasting, they are also delicious soon after baking).	**Special Equipment:** Two 17 by 14 inch cookie sheets, nonstick or lined with parchment

DOUGH *Makes: 365 grams*

1 large egg white	30 grams	2 tablespoons (30 ml)
unblanched whole hazelnuts	70 grams	½ cup
unblanched whole almonds	50 grams	⅓ cup
lemon zest, finely grated	2 grams	1 teaspoon (loosely packed)
bleached all-purpose flour	22 grams	2 tablespoons plus 1 teaspoon
ground cinnamon	·	¼ teaspoon
sugar	150 grams	¾ cup
mixed candied fruit	20 grams	2½ tablespoons (cut into small pieces)
honey	21 grams	1 tablespoon (15 ml)
28 whole almonds, unblanched or blanched, for topping	36 grams	¼ cup

PREHEAT THE OVEN

Twenty minutes or longer before baking, set an oven rack at the middle level. Set the oven at 350°F / 175°C.

MISE EN PLACE

Thirty minutes ahead, into a 1 cup / 237 ml glass measure with a spout, weigh or measure the egg white. Cover tightly with plastic wrap and set on the counter.

Toast the Nuts: Spread the hazelnuts and almonds evenly on a half sheet pan and bake for 7 minutes, until aromatic. Shake the pan once or twice to ensure even toasting. Set the pan on a wire rack and cool completely.

Raise the oven temperature to 400°F / 200°C.

With dishwashing liquid, wash, rinse, and dry the lemon before zesting it.

MAKE THE DOUGH

Food Processor Method

1. In a small bowl, whisk together the flour and cinnamon.

Continues

2. In a food processor, process the sugar, toasted hazelnuts and almonds, candied fruit, and lemon zest until finely chopped.

3. Add the honey, egg white, and flour mixture and process until blended, scraping down the sides of the bowl as needed.

4. Scrape the dough into a bowl.

Stand Mixer Method

1. Grind the nuts in batches in a spice mill with a little of the sugar, or use a rotary nut grinder.

2. With a chef's knife lightly coated with nonstick cooking spray, chop the candied fruit into fine pieces.

3. In the bowl of a stand mixer fitted with the flat beater, mix the flour, cinnamon, and (remaining) sugar on low speed until well mixed.

4. Add the ground hazelnuts and almonds, candied fruit, lemon zest, honey, and egg white and beat until blended. Scrape down the sides of the bowl, reaching to the bottom.

SHAPE THE DOUGH

5. Scoop out 14 pieces of dough (2 level teaspoons / 13 grams each). Roll each piece of dough between the palms of your hands into a 1 inch ball and place them a minimum of 1½ inches apart on a prepared cookie sheet. Cover the remaining dough with plastic wrap.

6. Lightly coat the flat bottom of a glass tumbler with nonstick cooking spray and use it to flatten the dough into 1½ inch discs, ¼ inch thick.

7. Gently press a whole almond into the center of each cookie.

OPTIONAL SHINY GLAZE

gum Arabic (see Baking Gem)	14.6 grams	1½ tablespoons
water	45 grams	3 tablespoons (45 ml)

8. In a small microwavable bowl or small saucepan, combine the gum Arabic and water and, stirring often, bring the mixture to a boil. Remove from the heat source. The glaze will stay liquid at room temperature, but cover it with plastic wrap to prevent evaporation. While the glaze is hot or at room temperature, brush onto the cookies before baking.

BAKE THE COOKIES

9. Bake for 3 minutes. Rotate the cookie sheet halfway around. Continue baking for 3 to 5 minutes, or until the cookies are golden brown. They should be slightly soft when pressed, as they will harden during cooling.

COOL THE COOKIES

10. **For very crunchy cookies,** set the cookie sheet on a wire rack and let the cookies cool completely. Then use a thin pancake turner to transfer the cookies to a storage container.

For softer, chewy cookies, set the cookie sheet on a wire rack and let the cookies cool for 5 minutes, or until firm enough to lift from the sheet. To remove the cookies, it works best to lift the parchment and peel each cookie off with your other hand. Transfer the cookies to another wire rack. Cool completely.

11. Repeat with the second batch.

STORE Airtight: room temperature, 2 months.

Baking Gem

♥ Gum Arabic produces a clear and flawlessly shiny glaze; an egg glaze would be absorbed by this dough. Gum Arabic is available in candy-making supply stores.

PIZZELLE

Makes: Eighteen to Twenty-eight 4 to 4½ inch rounds

These crisp cookies are a cherished Christmas tradition in Italian families. My dear friend Mariella Esposito, whose family owns Fante's in the Italian Market in Philadelphia, told me that anise is the usual flavoring for pizzelle (see Baking Gems), but because her dad disliked it, they used almond extract instead. I also like the floral flavor of vanilla extract here.

Cooking Time: About 1½ minutes per batch, depending on the pizzelle maker and setting

Special Equipment: A pizzelle maker, preferably electric (see Baking Gems)

VANILLA BATTER *Makes: 740 grams*

unsalted butter	113 grams	8 tablespoons (1 stick)
4 large eggs	200 grams	¾ cup plus 2 teaspoons (187 ml)
pure vanilla or almond extract	.	2 teaspoons (10 ml)
sugar	200 grams	1 cup
all-purpose flour, preferably bleached	228 grams	1¾ cups (lightly spooned into the cup and leveled off) plus 2 tablespoons
baking powder, preferably an aluminum-free variety	4.5 grams	1 teaspoon
fine sea salt	4.5 grams	¾ teaspoon

CHOCOLATE BATTER *Makes: 790 grams*

unsalted butter	113 grams	8 tablespoons (1 stick)
4 large eggs	200 grams	¾ cup plus 2 teaspoons (187 ml)
pure vanilla or almond extract	.	2 teaspoons (10 ml)
sugar	268 grams	1⅓ cups
all-purpose flour, preferably bleached	152 grams	1¼ cups (lightly spooned into the cup and leveled off)
unsweetened alkalized cocoa powder	56 grams	¾ cup (sifted before measuring)
baking powder, preferably an aluminum-free variety	4.5 grams	1 teaspoon
fine sea salt	4.5 grams	¾ teaspoon

Continues

MISE EN PLACE FOR BOTH BATTERS

In a 1 cup / 237 ml microwavable measure with a spout (or in a small saucepan over low heat stirring often) melt the butter. Allow it to cool until no longer hot.

Into a medium bowl, weigh or measure the eggs. Whisk in the vanilla extract. Cover tightly with plastic wrap and set on the counter.

MAKE THE VANILLA BATTER

1. Add the sugar to the egg mixture and whisk for about a minute, until light and foamy. Whisk in the melted butter.

2. In a medium bowl, whisk together the flour, baking powder, and salt.

3. Scrape the flour mixture into the egg mixture and use the whisk to stir it in. When all the flour mixture is moistened, whisk for 15 seconds, or until smooth.

MAKE THE CHOCOLATE BATTER

1. Add the sugar to the egg mixture and whisk for about a minute, until light and foamy. Whisk in the melted butter.

2. In a medium bowl, whisk together the flour, cocoa, baking powder, and salt.

3. Scrape the flour mixture into the egg mixture and use the whisk to stir it in. When all the flour mixture is moistened, whisk for 15 seconds, or until smooth.

MAKE THE PIZZELLE

4. Follow the instructions for your pizzelle maker, dropping portions of batter onto the center of the preheated pizzelle maker. I like to use a rounded tablespoon / 15 ml / 23 grams for each pizzella. The average cooking time is 1 to 1½ minutes, depending on the setting. I set the Cuisinart pizzelle maker at the highest setting. The chocolate batter takes about 10 seconds less than the vanilla batter.

COOL THE PIZZELLE

5. Use a thin pancake turner to lift each pizzella onto a wire rack to cool. If desired, any cookie extending past the outer rim of the design can be trimmed with scissors.

STORE Airtight: room temperature, 1 week; frozen, 2 months.
If the pizzelle soften slightly in humid weather, they can be recrisped in a 325°F / 160°C oven for a few minutes.

Baking Gems

🖤 For an anise flavor, replace 1 teaspoon / 5 ml of the vanilla or almond extract with 1 teaspoon / 5 ml anise extract.

🖤 Traditionally, pizzelle did not contain baking powder, but old-fashioned pizzelle makers produced thinner and crisper pizzelle. To achieve this style, I include baking powder; the lid of the pizzelle maker doesn't allow the batter to rise during cooking, but instead causes it to spread out, resulting in thinner, crisper cookies.

🖤 My favorite pizzelle maker is produced by Cuisinart and makes two 4 inch pizzelle at a time. I use a rounded tablespoon of batter for each pizzella, weighing 23 grams.

🖤 For the most picture-perfect, evenly browned pizzelle, I rotate them after the first minute of cooking.

BOURBON BALLS

Makes: Twenty-two 1¼ inch balls

These no-bake cookies are the number-one most requested of all my holiday recipes. Traditional for that time of year, they are very appreciated all year round. They richly deserve homemade chocolate wafers (as do you!).

No-Bake	**Plan Ahead:** Make these a minimum of 1 day ahead, up to 6 weeks.

DOUGH *Makes: 450 grams*

unsalted butter, cold	28 grams	2 tablespoons
chocolate wafers, preferably homemade (page 214)	192 grams (6.7 ounces)	.
pecan halves	75 grams	¾ cup
powdered sugar	72 grams	½ cup (lightly spooned into the cup and leveled off) plus 2½ tablespoons
unsweetened alkalized cocoa powder	25 grams	⅓ cup (sifted before measuring)
corn syrup	41 grams	2 tablespoons (30 ml)
bourbon, preferably Woodford Reserve or Maker's Mark (see Baking Gems)	22 to 37 grams	1½ to 2½ tablespoons (22.5 to 37.5 ml)
granulated sugar, for coating the balls	75 grams	¼ cup plus 2 tablespoons

MISE EN PLACE

Thirty minutes to 1 hour ahead, cut the butter into 4 pieces. Set on the counter to soften.

For the Food Processor Method: In several batches, pulverize the wafers into fine crumbs. Empty them into a large bowl.

For the Hand Method: Smash the wafers into crumbs by placing them in a reclosable freezer bag and rolling with a rolling pin.

MAKE THE DOUGH

Food Processor Method

1. Process the pecans with the powdered sugar and cocoa until finely ground.

2. Add the butter and corn syrup. Process until combined.

3. Scrape the mixture into the wafer crumbs and, with your fingers or a wooden spoon, mix until evenly incorporated.

Hand Method

1. Finely grind the pecans in batches in a spice mill with a little of the powdered sugar, or use a rotary nut grinder.

2. In a medium bowl, whisk together the (remaining) powdered sugar, cocoa, and wafer crumbs.

3. Add the butter, pecans, and corn syrup. With a wooden spoon, stir until the mixture is uniform in consistency.

Continues

4. Add 1½ tablespoons / 22.5 ml of the bourbon to the cookie crumb mixture. With a wooden spoon, stir until the mixture is uniform in consistency and begins to clean the sides of the bowl. Add up to 1 more tablespoon / 15 ml bourbon a teaspoon / 5 ml at a time if the mixture is too dry to hold together.

5. Let the mixture sit, covered, for 30 minutes to absorb the bourbon evenly. Add more bourbon if needed.

ROLL THE BOURBON BALLS AND COAT WITH SUGAR

6. Scoop out level tablespoons (20 grams each) of the mixture and press and roll between the palms of your hands to shape into 1¼ inch balls.

7. Place the granulated sugar in a small bowl. Add one ball at a time and roll it around in the sugar.

The coating is most attractive when the balls are dipped three times. Redip after the sugar starts to disappear.

8. Place the balls in a paper towel– or crumpled parchment–lined airtight container.

STORE Airtight: room temperature, 6 weeks.

Baking Gems

♥ A mixture of 30 grams / 2 tablespoons / 30 ml water and ½ tablespoon / 7.5 ml pure vanilla extract can be substituted for the bourbon.

♥ I prefer granulated sugar for coating the balls. Superfine sugar will give them a whiter appearance.

KOULOURAKIA

Makes: Fifty-two 4 by 1 inch cookies

These airy, crispy, and toasty Greek Easter cookies are from our beloved senior managing editor at HarperCollins, Marina Padakis, who coordinated the production of this book. They were passed down to her by her grandmother, and improved by her mom, Connie. The dough is a dream to work with and can be formed into a variety of shapes, making this an ideal project to do with young children. After all, isn't it more fun for them to shape cookie dough they can eat, rather than modeling clay?

Oven Temperature: 375°F / 190°C

Baking Time: 18 to 22 minutes (for each of three batches)

Special Equipment: Two or three 17 by 14 inch cookie sheets, no preparation needed or lined with parchment

DOUGH *Makes: 1,182 grams*

unsalted butter	227 grams	16 tablespoons (2 sticks)
3 large eggs (see Baking Gems)	150 grams	½ cup plus 1½ tablespoons (140 ml)
orange zest, freshly grated	6 grams	1 tablespoon (loosely packed)
sugar	200 grams	1 cup
orange juice, freshly squeezed	15 grams	1 tablespoon (15 ml)
brandy, preferably Metaxa (see Baking Gems)	15 grams	1 tablespoon (15 ml)
pure vanilla extract	·	½ teaspoon (2.5 ml)
unbleached all-purpose flour, preferably King Arthur	576 grams	4¾ cups (lightly spooned into the cup and leveled off)
baking powder, preferably an aluminum-free variety	13.5 grams	1 tablespoon

MISE EN PLACE

Thirty minutes to 1 hour ahead, cut the butter into tablespoon-size pieces. Set on the counter to soften.

Into a medium bowl, weigh or measure the eggs.

With dishwashing liquid, wash, rinse, and dry the orange before zesting it.

MAKE THE DOUGH

1. In a medium bowl, with a handheld mixer or whisk, beat the eggs for about 1 minute, or until foamy.

2. In the bowl of a stand mixer fitted with the flat beater, beat the butter on medium speed for about 30 seconds, or until very smooth and creamy.

3. Gradually add the sugar and then beat for 3 minutes, until light and fluffy.

4. Gradually add the eggs, beating until incorporated.

5. Add the orange zest, orange juice, brandy, and vanilla extract and mix on low speed for a few seconds, until incorporated.

6. In a medium bowl, whisk together the flour and baking powder.

7. On low speed, gradually add the flour mixture and mix just until a soft dough forms. The dough can be shaped right away or refrigerated for about 1 hour and then allowed to come to room temperature before shaping.

Continues

PREHEAT THE OVEN

Thirty minutes or longer before baking, set an oven rack at the middle level. Set the oven at 375°F / 190°C.

SESAME SEED TOPPING

½ large egg, lightly beaten before measuring	25 grams	1½ tablespoons (22.5 ml)
hulled sesame seeds (see Baking Gems)	88 grams	½ cup plus 2 tablespoons
water	.	¼ teaspoon (1.25 ml)

MAKE THE SESAME SEED TOPPING

8. Into a small bowl, weigh or measure the egg. Whisk lightly and strain it into a 1 cup / 237 ml glass measure with a spout, pushing it through with the back of a spoon or allowing it to sit for a few minutes until it flows through the strainer. Cover tightly with plastic wrap and set on the counter.

9. Place the sesame seeds in a shallow dish.

SHAPE THE DOUGH

Shape the dough one piece at a time, keeping the rest of the dough covered in the bowl to prevent drying.

10. Scoop out 1 lightly rounded tablespoon (about 22 grams) of dough and roll it in the palms of your hands to form a 1¼ inch ball. Roll the ball into an 8 inch rope. It will be about ⅓ inch wide.

11. Twist the rope into one of the shapes shown (opposite). Don't worry about any imperfections, because they will puff away during baking!

TOP THE COOKIES

12. Brush the top of the cookie with the strained egg, then dip it in the sesame seeds, coated side down. Place each cookie on a cookie sheet, spacing them no closer than 1 inch apart, in 3 rows of 6 cookies each.

13. Repeat with the remaining two batches of cookies. (If you don't have a third cookie sheet, set the cookies on parchment and, after the first is baked and the cookie sheet is cool, slide the parchment onto the cookie sheet.)

14. After all the cookies are topped with sesame seeds, stir the ¼ teaspoon water into the remaining egg. Brush it on top of the cookies to give them a shine when baked.

BAKE THE COOKIES

15. Bake the first sheet of cookies for 10 minutes. Rotate the cookie sheet halfway around. Continue baking for 8 to 12 minutes, or until the cookies are golden brown.

COOL THE COOKIES

16. Set the cookie sheet on a wire rack and use a thin pancake turner to transfer the cookies to another wire rack. Cool completely.

17. Bake and cool the remaining batches.

STORE Airtight: room temperature, 1 month or longer; frozen, 3 months.

Baking Gems

♥ Because egg yolks vary in size, for the best texture and to make sure you get the full amount of yolk, separate the eggs for the dough and then add more yolk if needed. The amount of yolk should be 56 grams / 3½ tablespoons / 52 ml, and the whites should be 90 grams / ¼ cup plus 2 tablespoons / 89 ml. Then combine the yolks and whites.

♥ The brandy can be replaced with an equal weight or volume of orange juice for a total of 30 grams / 2 tablespoons / 30 ml juice.

HAMANTASCHEN

Makes: Twenty-four 2½ inch cookies

Hamantaschen are the cookies traditionally made for the Jewish holiday Purim. They are named for the ancient villain Haman, who wore a tricornered hat—hence their shape. They are easy to shape but less easy to bake, because if the dough is tender, the lovely shape tends to collapse. Bakers often compensate for this by making a sturdier dough, which is then less delicious. I am delighted to offer this simple solution: Make reusable aluminum foil "pans" to provide support for picture-perfect little pastries.

Apricot and prune fillings (see the Variation) are also delicious, but I always reach for the poppy seed hamantaschen. I love the slightly crunchy poppy seed filling with the crisp, tender, buttery dough. I find a smaller cookie most appealing and easiest to eat, and no one is going to stop you from eating two or even three!

Oven Temperature: 350°F / 175°C	Baking Time: 15 to 20 minutes	Special Equipment: One 17 by 14 inch cookie sheet lined with parchment; a 3 inch scalloped or plain round cookie cutter; twenty-four 4 inch discs cut from heavy-duty aluminum foil

SWEET COOKIE DOUGH (PÂTE SUCRÉE)

Makes: 420 grams

unsalted butter, cold	113 grams	8 tablespoons (1 stick)
1 (to 2) large egg yolk (see page xxvi)	19 grams	1 tablespoon plus ½ teaspoon (17.5 ml)
heavy cream	43 grams	3 tablespoons (45 ml)
all-purpose flour, preferably unbleached	200 grams	1⅔ cups (lightly spooned into the cup and leveled off)
fine sea salt	·	⅛ teaspoon
turbinado sugar, preferably Sugar in the Raw, or granulated sugar	50 grams	¼ cup

MISE EN PLACE

Thirty minutes ahead or longer, cut the butter into ½ inch cubes. Wrap in plastic wrap and refrigerate.

Into a 1 cup / 237 ml glass measure with a spout, weigh or measure the yolk and cream and whisk them lightly. Cover tightly with plastic wrap and refrigerate.

In a medium bowl, whisk together the flour and salt.

MAKE THE DOUGH

1. In a food processor, process the sugar until fine. Add the cold butter cubes and pulse until the sugar disappears. Add the flour mixture and pulse until the butter pieces are no larger than small peas. Add the egg mixture and pulse just until incorporated, about 8 times. The dough will be in crumbly pieces.

2. Empty the dough into a plastic bag and press it from the outside of the bag just until it holds together. Remove the dough from the plastic bag and place it on a very large sheet of plastic wrap. Using the plastic wrap, knead the dough just a few times, until it becomes one smooth piece. There should be no visible pieces of butter.

Continues

CHILL THE DOUGH

3. Divide the dough in half (about 210 grams each). Wrap each piece loosely in plastic wrap and press to flatten it into a 4 inch disc. Refrigerate for a minimum of 30 minutes, or until firm enough to roll.

The dough can be refrigerated for up to 3 days or frozen, well wrapped, for up to 6 months.

POPPY SEED FILLING

Makes: 290 grams / 1 cup

poppy seeds (see Baking Gems)	113 grams	⅔ cup plus 2 tablespoons
milk	81 grams	⅓ cup (79 ml)
sugar	50 grams	¼ cup
honey	28 grams	1 tablespoon plus 1 teaspoon (20 ml)
lemon zest, finely grated (see Baking Gems)	4 grams	2 teaspoons (loosely packed)
Apricot Lekvar (page 193) or apricot preserves (see Baking Gems)	38 grams	2 tablespoons (30 ml), *divided*

MAKE THE FILLING

1. In a spice mill or blender, grind the poppy seeds. (There will be about ¾ cup.)

2. In a small saucepan, heat the milk over low heat until hot. Add the poppy seeds and stir for a few seconds, until the milk is absorbed.

3. Remove the pan from the heat and stir in the sugar, honey, lemon zest, and 1 tablespoon / 15 ml / 19 grams of the apricot lekvar until incorporated. Cool the filling to room temperature.

4. Place the remaining apricot lekvar in a small bowl, and cover tightly with plastic wrap, and reserve for glazing the hamantaschen.

EGG GLAZE

1 (to 2) large egg yolk (see page xxvi)	19 grams	1 tablespoon plus ½ teaspoon (17.5 ml)
milk	5 grams	1 teaspoon (5 ml)

5. In a small bowl, whisk together the egg yolk and milk. Strain the mixture into another small bowl, pushing it through with the back of a spoon or allowing it to sit for a few minutes so it flows through the strainer. Cover tightly with plastic wrap and set on the counter.

ROLL THE DOUGH AND CUT OUT THE COOKIES

4. Remove a disc of dough from the refrigerator. If the dough has been chilled for more than 30 minutes, allow it to sit for about 5 to 10 minutes, until it is malleable enough to roll.

5. Lightly dust a large piece of plastic wrap with flour. Set the dough on top and lightly flour the top. Cover with another piece of plastic wrap and roll the dough into a ⅛ inch thick oval.

6. Remove the top piece of plastic wrap and cut out the cookies. Place each one on a foil disc and set on the countertop. Gather up the scraps and knead them together lightly. Shape into a flat patty, wrap in plastic wrap, and refrigerate until firm enough to reroll.

7. Repeat with the remaining disc of dough. Gather up the scraps and add them to the scraps from the first batch. Once all the hamantaschen from the first two batches have been shaped, the dough scraps can be used to make more.

FILL AND SHAPE THE HAMANTASCHEN

8. One at a time, brush the outer ½ inch of each dough round with a thin coating of egg glaze. (Alternatively, water will also work almost as well to seal the dough.) Place 2 teaspoons / 12 grams poppy seed filling mounded in the center of the round. Firmly pinch the dough together at three equally spaced places to form the three-corner-hat effect. Press the foil up against the sides of the dough to conform to the shape, then fold in the excess foil at each corner to secure it. Bend back the top edges of the foil slightly so they don't rise above the dough.

9. Place the hamantaschen about 1½ inches apart on the prepared cookie sheet. Refrigerate, covered with plastic wrap, for at least 30 minutes, up to overnight, or until firm.

PREHEAT THE OVEN

Twenty minutes or longer before baking, set an oven rack at the middle. Set the oven at 350°F / 175°C.

BAKE THE HAMANTASCHEN

10. Bake for 8 minutes. Rotate the cookie sheet halfway around. Continue baking for 7 to 12 minutes, or until the hamantaschen are lightly browned.

COOL AND GLAZE THE HAMANTASCHEN

11. Set the cookie sheet on a wire rack. Use the edges of the foil "pans" to lift the hamantaschen to another wire rack to cool completely.

12. When the cookies are cool, brush the poppy seed filling with the remaining 1 tablespoon of apricot lekvar (or sieved apricot preserves; see Baking Gems). If necessary, stir in a little apricot brandy or hot water to make it more liquid. Remove the hamantaschen from the foil "pans."

STORE Lightly covered: room temperature, 5 days. Airtight: frozen, 3 months.

VARIATION

Replace the poppy seed filling with an equal volume (about 300 grams / 1 cup) of Apricot Lekvar (page 193) or Prune Lekvar (page 404).

Baking Gems

♥ I find that whole poppy seeds have a slightly bitter quality when used in this quantity. As I like the crunch, I only heat the ground poppy seeds for a short time. To make a smoother poppy seed paste, I use fewer poppy seeds and cook them longer, which also causes them to increase in volume. In a poppy seed grinder or blender, grind only 84 grams / ½ cup plus 1 tablespoon poppy seeds. (There will be about ¾ cup.) Place the ground poppy seeds in a small saucepan. Add 89 grams / ¼ cup plus 2 tablespoons / 89 ml hot water and cook over low heat, stirring often, for 3 to 6 minutes. The poppy seeds will gradually absorb the water, swelling and becoming more paste-like. Add water by the tablespoon as needed to keep the mixture from scorching. When the poppy seed paste has the consistency of peanut butter, remove it from the heat. Cool completely. There will be a little under ¾ cup of paste. The paste can be stored in an airtight container in the freezer for several months. If using this paste as a filling in place of the poppy seeds cooked in milk, continue with step 3 of make the filling.

♥ Poppy seeds have a high oil content and are therefore prone to rancidity, especially if purchased ground rather than whole. When poppy seeds start to become rancid, they taste very bitter. Store whole or ground poppy seeds in the freezer. If you are purchasing ground poppy seeds and don't have a scale, measure out ¾ cup.

♥ The best way to grind poppy seeds is in a specially designed poppy seed grinder. A blender will work but not quite as well, a food processor will not work at all.

♥ If using apricot preserves instead of lekvar for the filling and glaze, place 78 grams / about ¼ cup apricot preserves in a microwavable container and bring them to a boil. (Alternatively, place in a small saucepan and bring to a boil over medium-low heat, stirring constantly.) Using the back of a spoon, push the preserves through a strainer into a small bowl; discard the small amount of pulp.

CHAPTER 6

BAR AND CAKE COOKIES

FUDGY PUDGY BROWNIES

Makes: Sixteen 2 inch square by 1 inch high brownies

Is this not what most people in their heart of hearts want a brownie to be: dense, moist, and fudgy? These brownies are great with or without nuts, but they stand up especially well to the slight crunch and assertive flavor of walnuts. The unsweetened chocolate and white chocolate add cocoa butter to the brownies, which contributes to the chewy texture and melt-in-the-mouth flavor.

Oven Temperature: 350°F / 175°C	**Baking Time:** 5 minutes for the walnuts; 30 to 40 minutes for the brownies

Special Equipment: One 8 inch square by 2 inch high baking pan, wrapped with a cake strip (see Baking Gem), lined with two crisscrossed 16 by 8 inch strips of heavy-duty aluminum foil, extending a few inches past the edges of the pan, then lightly coated with baking spray with flour

BATTER

unsalted butter	170 grams	12 tablespoons (1½ sticks)
3 large eggs	150 grams	½ cup plus 1½ tablespoons (140 ml)
pure vanilla extract	·	½ teaspoon (2.5 ml)
walnut halves	100 grams	1 cup
fine-quality unsweetened or 99% cacao chocolate	142 grams (5 ounces)	·
white chocolate containing cocoa butter	85 grams (3 ounces)	·
unsweetened alkalized cocoa powder	16 grams	3½ tablespoons (sifted before measuring)
sugar	267 grams	1⅓ cups
all-purpose flour, bleached or unbleached	91 grams	¾ cup (lightly spooned into the cup and leveled off)
fine sea salt	·	1/16 teaspoon (a pinch)

PREHEAT THE OVEN

Twenty minutes or longer before baking, set an oven rack at the middle level. Set the oven at 350°F / 175°C.

MISE EN PLACE

Thirty minutes ahead, cut the butter into tablespoon-size pieces. Set on the counter to soften.

Into a 1 cup / 237 ml glass measure with a spout, weigh or measure the eggs. Whisk in the vanilla extract. Cover tightly with plastic wrap and set on the counter.

Toast and Chop the Walnuts: Spread the walnuts evenly on a baking sheet and bake for about 5 minutes. Stir once or twice to ensure even toasting and prevent overbrowning. Turn the walnuts onto a dish towel and roll and rub them around to loosen the skins. Discard any loose skins and cool completely, then chop into coarse pieces.

Chop both chocolates into small pieces.

Continues

MAKE THE BATTER

1. In a large heatproof bowl set over hot, not simmering, water (do not let the bottom of the container touch the water), heat the chocolates and butter, stirring often, until completely melted. Remove the bowl from the heat source.

2. Whisk the cocoa into the melted chocolate mixture and then mix in the sugar until incorporated.

3. Whisk in the egg mixture, mixing until the mixture becomes thick and glossy.

4. Stir in the flour and salt just until the flour is moistened.

5. Add the walnuts and stir, reaching to the bottom of the bowl, until evenly incorporated.

6. Scrape the batter into the prepared pan and smooth the surface, mounding the batter slightly in the center, which tends to dip on baking.

BAKE THE BROWNIE

7. Bake for 20 minutes. Rotate the pan halfway around. Continue baking for 10 to 20 minutes, or until a toothpick inserted 1 inch from the edge of the pan comes out almost clean. (An instant-read thermometer inserted in the center should read about 190°F / 88°C.)

COOL AND UNMOLD THE BROWNIE

8. Let the brownie cool in the pan on a wire rack for 10 minutes.

9. Run a small metal spatula between the pan and the foil in case batter has leaked through and stuck to the sides. Invert the brownie onto a wire rack lined with plastic wrap and lift off the pan. Carefully peel off the foil and reinvert the brownie onto another rack. Cool completely.

CUT THE BROWNIE

10. Transfer the brownie to a cutting mat or board. Use a long serrated knife to cut it into 2 inch squares.

STORE Airtight: room temperature, 1 week; refrigerated, 1 month; frozen, 3 months.

Baking Gem

♥ Cake strips are designed to slow down the baking at the sides of the pan, which bake and set faster than the middle. This not only keeps the edges of the brownies or cake from drying, it also helps to promote more even baking and keeps the surface more level. My Rose's Heavenly Cake Strips are made from silicone, because silicone is a poor conductor of heat. You can also make your own cake strip from a long strip of aluminum foil wrapped around wet paper towels and secured with a paper clip or clamp.

COCOA BROWNIES

Makes: Sixteen 2 inch square by 1 inch high brownies

These were the first brownies I ever created, more than thirty years ago. They have a crisp top but stay moist even on standing. The chocolate component is 100 percent cocoa powder, which means they have very little cocoa butter. At room temperature, they are soft; I prefer them chilled, which makes them more fudgy.

Oven Temperature: 325°F / 160°C	**Baking Time:** 5 minutes for the pecans; 30 to 40 minutes for the brownies	**Plan Ahead:** Chill the brownies for a minimum of 6 hours before serving.	**Special Equipment:** One 8 inch square by 2 inch high baking pan, wrapped with a cake strip (see page 274), lined with two crisscrossed 16 by 8 inch strips of heavy-duty aluminum foil, extending a few inches past the edges of the pan, then lightly coated with baking spray with flour

BATTER

unsalted butter	200 grams	14 tablespoons (1¾ sticks)
3 large eggs	150 grams	½ cup plus 1½ tablespoons (140 ml)
pure vanilla extract	.	2 teaspoons (10 ml)
pecan halves	100 grams	1 cup
unsweetened alkalized cocoa powder	50 grams	⅔ cup (sifted before measuring)
sugar	238 grams	1 cup plus 3 tablespoons
all-purpose flour, bleached or unbleached	70 grams	½ cup (lightly spooned into the cup and leveled off) plus 1 tablespoon
fine sea salt	.	¹⁄₁₆ teaspoon (a pinch)

PREHEAT THE OVEN

Twenty minutes or longer before baking, set an oven rack at the middle level. Set the oven at 325°F / 160°C.

MISE EN PLACE

Thirty minutes ahead, cut the butter into tablespoon-size pieces. Set on the counter to soften.

Into a 1 cup / 237 ml glass measure with a spout, weigh or measure the eggs. Whisk in the vanilla extract. Cover tightly with plastic wrap and set on the counter.

Toast and Chop the Pecans: Spread the pecans evenly on a baking sheet and bake for 5 minutes, or just until they start to smell fragrant but are not beginning to brown. Stir once or twice to ensure even baking. Let the pecans cool completely, then chop them medium fine.

MAKE THE BATTER

1. In a medium microwavable bowl, or in a saucepan over medium-low heat, melt the butter, stirring often. Remove from the heat source.

2. Whisk the cocoa into the melted butter and then mix in the sugar until incorporated.

3. Add the egg mixture and whisk until the mixture becomes thick and glossy.

Continues

4. Stir in the flour, salt, and nuts just until the flour is moistened.

5. Scrape the batter into the prepared pan and smooth the surface, mounding the batter slightly in the center, which tends to dip on baking.

BAKE THE BROWNIE

6. Bake for 20 minutes. Rotate the pan halfway around. Continue baking for 10 to 20 minutes, until a toothpick inserted in the center comes out with a few moist crumbs clinging to it, or until the batter has set up to 1 inch from the edges and a toothpick inserted 1 inch from an edge comes out clean. (An instant-read thermometer inserted in the center should read 190° to 195°F / 88° to 90°C.)

COOL AND UNMOLD THE BROWNIE

7. Let the brownie cool in the pan on a wire rack for 10 minutes.

8. Run a small metal spatula between the pan and the aluminum foil in case any batter has leaked through and stuck to the sides. Invert the brownie onto another wire rack lined with plastic wrap and lift off the pan. Carefully peel off the aluminum foil and reinvert the brownie onto a wire rack. It will be very soft at this point. Cool completely.

REFRIGERATE AND CUT THE BROWNIE

9. Transfer the brownie to a cutting mat or board. Cover tightly and refrigerate for a minimum of 6 hours before serving.

10. Use a long serrated knife to cut the brownie into 2 inch squares. Serve chilled.

STORE Airtight: room temperature, 1 week; refrigerated, 1 month; frozen, 3 months.

VARIATIONS

Malt powder will add roundness and intensity of chocolate flavor to the brownies. If desired, add 17 grams / 2 tablespoons (or double, for a more pronounced taste) in Step 2 together with the sugar.

Dress Brownies

For a special occasion, make a double recipe of Ganache Pools (see Brownie Doughnuts, page 280) and spread it on top of the brownie before chilling. Cover the pan with plastic wrap, being careful not to allow the plastic wrap to touch the ganache until it is set. To cut the brownie, run the knife under hot water and wipe dry between cuts.

BARCELONA BROWNIES

Makes: Fourteen 3 by 1 inch by 1⅛ inch high brownies

I call these Barcelona Brownies because I created them years ago for a series of talks and demonstrations at culinary schools in Barcelona. I love making brownies in individual silicone molds because they give them a lovely shape and produce a fine crust on all sides of every brownie, which keeps them moist and fresh. You can also bake a larger version in an 8 inch square by 2 inch high baking pan; use the ingredient quantities given for the batter in Woody's Luxury Brownies (page 283).

Oven Temperature: 325°F / 160°C

Baking Time: 12 to 15 minutes

Special Equipment: Financier mold(s), preferably silicone, 3 by 1 by 1¼ inches high (¼ cup / 59 ml capacity), coated with baking spray with flour; A disposable pastry bag with a small semicircle cut from the tip

BATTER *Makes: 650 grams*

2 large eggs	·	¼ cup plus 2 tablespoons (89 ml)
pure vanilla extract	·	1½ teaspoons (7.5 ml)
full-fat cream cheese	56 grams	scant ¼ cup
unsalted butter	130 grams	9 tablespoons (1 stick plus 1 tablespoon)
pecan halves	75 grams	¾ cup
dark chocolate, 60% to 62% cacao	57 grams (2 ounces)	·
unsweetened alkalized cocoa powder	33 grams	¼ cup plus 3 tablespoons (sifted before measuring)
sugar	156 grams	¾ cup plus 1½ tablespoons
all-purpose flour, bleached or unbleached	50 grams	¼ cup (lightly spooned into the cup and leveled off) plus 2½ tablespoons
fine sea salt	·	⅟₁₆ teaspoon (a pinch)

PREHEAT THE OVEN
Twenty minutes or longer before baking, set an oven rack at the middle level. Set the oven at 325°F / 160°C.

MISE EN PLACE
Thirty minutes ahead, into a 1 cup / 237 ml glass measure with a spout, weigh or measure the eggs. Whisk in the vanilla extract. Cover tightly with plastic wrap and set on the counter.

About 30 minutes ahead, cut the cream cheese into a few pieces and set on the counter to soften.

Cut the butter into tablespoon-size pieces and set on the counter to soften.

Chop the pecans medium-fine.

Melt the Chocolate and Butter: Chop the chocolate into coarse pieces. In the top of a double boiler over hot, not simmering, water (do not let the bottom of the container touch the water), melt the butter and chocolate, stirring often. Remove the pan from the heat source.

Continues

MAKE THE BATTER

Stand Mixer Method

1. Scrape the melted chocolate mixture into the bowl of a stand mixer.

2. Attach the flat beater, add the cocoa and sugar, and beat on medium speed until incorporated.

3. Gradually beat in the egg mixture. The mixture will become thick and glossy.

4. Beat in the cream cheese until it is almost completely incorporated and only a few small bits remain.

5. Add the flour and salt and beat on low speed just until incorporated, scraping down the sides of the bowl as needed.

6. Add the pecans and beat for a few seconds, just until evenly incorporated.

Hand Method

1. Scrape the melted chocolate mixture into a large bowl.

2. Whisk in the cocoa and then the sugar until incorporated.

3. Add the egg mixture and whisk until the mixture becomes thick and glossy.

4. With a blending fork or wooden spoon, stir in the cream cheese until it is almost completely incorporated and only a few small bits remain.

5. Add the flour and salt and stir only until the flour is fully moistened.

6. Stir in the pecans.

Both Methods

7. Scrape half the batter into the prepared pastry bag.

FILL THE MOLDS

8. Pipe or spoon the batter into the cavities of the financier mold(s), filling them about three-quarters full (45 grams each). With a small offset spatula, smooth the tops. Refill the pastry bag as needed until you have used all the batter.

BAKE THE BROWNIES

9. If using silicone mold(s), set them on a wire rack and then on a half sheet pan(s) or cookie sheet(s). Bake the brownies for 12 to 15 minutes, or until the batter has set. The batter will puff and rise a little above the top of the cavities and then sink slightly on cooling; if pressed lightly with a fingertip, the brownies will spring back. (An instant-read thermometer inserted into the center of a brownie should read about 194°F / 90°C.)

COOL AND UNMOLD THE BROWNIES

10. **If using silicone mold(s),** set them on a wire rack and cool completely. To unmold, push out each brownie by pressing your finger against the bottom of the mold.

If using metal mold(s), set on a wire rack and let the brownies cool for 10 minutes. To unmold, run a small metal spatula between the sides of the molds and the brownies, pressing firmly against the molds. Invert the brownies onto a wire rack and reinvert them onto another wire rack. Cool completely.

STORE Airtight, layered between sheets of parchment: room temperature, 1 week; refrigerated, 1 month; frozen, 3 months.

Baking Gem

♥ If you like chewy brownies, try these frozen or chilled. For a softer, creamier texture, eat them at room temperature.

VARIATION

Dark Chocolate Ganache Infusion Brownies

It's an extra wow to encounter the chocolate creaminess of ganache against the chewy, moist, cakey texture of the brownies when biting into them. The ganache needs to be added as soon as the brownies come out of the oven.

Special Equipment: A disposable pastry bag fitted with a ¼ inch round decorating tube, or a small spoon; A chopstick or ¼ inch thick wooden dowel

Makes: 127 grams / ½ cup

dark chocolate, 60% to 62% cacao	56 grams (2 ounces)	.
heavy cream	77 grams	⅓ cup (79 ml)

MAKE THE CHOCOLATE GANACHE INFUSION

1. Chop the chocolate into coarse pieces. In a food processor, pulse the chocolate until finely chopped. (Alternatively, use a chef's knife to chop the chocolate.) Empty it into a small bowl.

2. In a 1 cup / 237 ml or larger microwavable measure with a spout (or in a small saucepan over medium heat, stirring often), scald the cream (heat it to the boiling point; small bubbles will form around the periphery).

3. Pour the hot cream over the chocolate. Cover the bowl and let sit for 1 minute to melt the chocolate.

4. Using a silicone spatula, gently stir together the chocolate and cream until smooth.

5. Let the mixture cool and thicken to a soft pipeable consistency (about 72°F / 22°C), about 30 minutes. If longer, cover it tightly to prevent evaporation. (To speed cooling, you can set it in the refrigerator, stirring gently every 10 minutes. If it becomes too firm, reheat it in the microwave with 3-second bursts, or in the top of a double boiler.)

6. Oil the blunt end of the chopstick (or dowel) and insert it into each brownie in three evenly spaced intervals, going all the way to the bottom. Twist it gently as you insert and withdraw it.

7. Pipe or spoon ganache into each opening until slightly rounded above the surface of each one.

8. The ganache will sink slightly as it cools, so more can be added. If desired, you can set the brownies under a hot lamp to make the ganache plugs perfectly smooth.

BROWNIE DOUGHNUTS

Makes: Twenty-four mini brownie doughnuts

These mini doughnut-shaped brownies are moist, fudgy, and elevated to extra deliciousness by a puddle of ganache in their centers.

Oven Temperature: 325°F / 160°C	Baking Time: 8 to 10 minutes	Special Equipment: Two (or one) mini doughnut pans, preferably silicone, with 12 cavities each, coated with baking spray with flour; Two disposable pastry bags (one for the batter and one for the ganache pools) with a small semicircle cut from the tip of each one

BROWNIE BATTER

Make a half recipe of the Barcelona Brownie batter (see page 277), but use only 67 grams / ⅓ cup sugar. This will make 316 grams of batter.

FILL THE MOLDS

If you only have one pan, scrape half the batter into the prepared pastry bag and refrigerate the rest of the batter until ready to fill the second pan.

1. Scrape the batter into a prepared pastry bag. Pipe the batter into the doughnut pan cavities, filling them about three-quarters full (about 13 grams each). With a small offset spatula, smooth the tops.

BAKE THE BROWNIE DOUGHNUTS

If using silicone pans, set them on a wire rack and then on a half sheet pan or cookie sheet.

2. Bake for 8 to 10 minutes, or until the batter has set. The batter will puff slightly and sink slightly on cooling. If pressed lightly with a fingertip, the brownie doughnuts will spring back. (An instant-read thermometer should read about 194°F / 90°C.)

COOL AND UNMOLD THE BROWNIE DOUGHNUTS

3. If using metal pans, set the pan on a wire rack and cool for 5 minutes. If using a silicone pan, cool completely on the rack. Unmold the doughnuts onto a sheet pan lined with a nonstick silicone baking mat or aluminum foil.

If you only have one doughnut pan, wash, dry, and coat it and repeat with the remaining batter.

GANACHE POOLS

Make the ganache shortly before filling the doughnuts. If necessary, reheat it in the microwave with 3-second bursts, or in the top of a double boiler, until it softens enough to pipe it. It needs to be warm and liquid enough to flatten into pools in the centers of the doughnuts.

Makes: about 160 grams / ⅔ cup

dark chocolate, 60% to 62% cacao	74 grams (2.6 ounces)	.
heavy cream	86 grams	¼ cup plus 2 tablespoons (89 ml)

Continues

MAKE THE GANACHE

1. Chop the chocolate into coarse pieces. In a small food processor, process the chocolate until very fine. (Alternatively, use a spice mill or rotary nut grinder to grind the chocolate.) Empty it into a small bowl.

2. In a 1 cup / 237 ml microwavable measure with a spout (or in a small saucepan over medium heat, stirring often) scald the cream (heat it to the boiling point; small bubbles will form around the periphery).

3. Pour the hot cream on top of the chocolate. Cover with plastic wrap and let sit for 1 minute to melt the chocolate.

4. Stir the ganache until smooth, then pour it into the second prepared pastry bag.

FILL THE BROWNIE DOUGHNUTS

5. Pipe the ganache into the centers of the brownies. Allow it to set for 1 hour, or until firm. Slide an offset spatula under each brownie to transfer it to a serving plate or storage container.

STORE Airtight, layered between sheets of parchment: room temperature, 1 week; refrigerated, 1 month; frozen, 3 months. If you like chewy brownies, try the brownie doughnuts frozen or chilled. For a softer, creamier texture, eat them at room temperature.

WOODY'S LUXURY BROWNIES

Makes: Sixteen 2 inch square by 1½ inch high brownies

Woody always looked forward to his mother's traditional bourbon brownies at Christmastime; they were covered with white icing and topped with melted dark chocolate. He adapted her recipe components using favorites of mine: Barcelona Brownies, White Chocolate Buttercream, and Dark Chocolate Ganache Glaze. Admittedly labor-intensive, this brownie is so gorgeous, elegant, and luscious it is well worth the effort for special occasions.

Oven Temperature: 325°F / 160°C

Baking Time: 5 minutes for the pecans; 25 to 35 minutes for the brownies

Plan Ahead: A minimum of 4 hours ahead, make the buttercream and glaze.

Special Equipment: One 8 inch square by 2 inch high baking pan, wrapped with a cake strip (see page 274), lined with two crisscrossed 16 by 8 inch strips of heavy-duty aluminum foil, extending a few inches past the edges, then lightly coated with baking spray with flour

BATTER

3 large eggs	150 grams	½ cup plus 1½ tablespoons (140 ml)
pure vanilla extract	·	2 teaspoons (10 ml)
full-fat cream cheese	85 grams	⅓ cup
unsalted butter	200 grams	14 tablespoons (1¾ sticks)
pecan halves	113 grams	1 cup plus 2 tablespoons
dark chocolate, 60% to 62% cacao	85 grams (3 ounces)	·
unsweetened alkalized cocoa powder	50 grams	⅔ cup (sifted before measuring)
sugar	200 grams	1 cup
all-purpose flour, bleached or unbleached	75 grams	½ cup (lightly spooned into the cup) plus 1½ tablespoons
fine sea salt	·	1/16 teaspoon (a pinch)

PREHEAT THE OVEN

Twenty minutes or longer before baking, set an oven rack at the middle level. Set the oven at 325°F / 160°C.

MISE EN PLACE

Thirty minutes ahead, into a 1 cup / 237 ml glass measure with a spout, weigh or measure the eggs. Whisk in the vanilla extract. Cover tightly with plastic wrap and set on the counter.

Thirty minutes ahead, cut the cream cheese into a few pieces and set on the counter to soften.

Thirty minutes ahead, cut the butter into tablespoon-size pieces and set on the counter.

Toast the Pecans: Break the pecans into medium pieces. Spread them evenly on a baking sheet and bake for 5 minutes, or just until they start to smell fragrant but are not beginning to brown. Stir once or twice to ensure even baking. Set the baking sheet on a wire rack and cool completely.

Continues

Melt the Chocolate and Butter: Chop the chocolate into coarse pieces. In a large heatproof bowl set over hot, not simmering, water (do not let the bottom of the container touch the water), heat the chocolate and butter, stirring often, until completely melted. Remove the bowl from the heat source.

MAKE THE BATTER

Stand Mixer Method

1. Scrape the melted chocolate mixture into the bowl of a stand mixer.

2. Attach the flat beater, add the cocoa and sugar, and beat on medium speed until incorporated.

3. Gradually beat in the egg mixture. The mixture will become thick and glossy.

4. Beat in the cream cheese until it is almost completely incorporated and only small bits remain.

5. Add the flour and salt and beat on low speed just until incorporated, scraping down the sides of the bowl as needed.

6. Add the pecans and beat for a few seconds, just until evenly incorporated.

Hand Method

1. Whisk the cocoa and then the sugar into the bowl of melted chocolate until incorporated.

2. Add the egg mixture and whisk until the mixture becomes thick and glossy.

3. With a blending fork or wooden spoon, stir in the cream cheese until it is almost completely incorporated and only small bits remain.

4. Stir in the flour and salt just until the flour is moistened.

5. Add the pecans and stir, reaching to the bottom of the bowl, until evenly incorporated.

Both Methods

7. Scrape the batter into the prepared pan. With an offset spatula, smooth the surface, mounding it slightly in the center, which tends to dip on baking.

BAKE THE BROWNIE

8. Bake for 15 minutes. Rotate the pan halfway around. Continue baking for 10 to 20 minutes, or until the batter has set up to 1 inch from the edges and a toothpick inserted 1 inch from an edge comes out clean. (An instant-read thermometer inserted in the center should read 190° to 195°F / 88° to 90°C.)

COOL AND UNMOLD THE BROWNIE

9. Let the brownie cool in the pan on a wire rack for 10 minutes. Run a small metal spatula between the pan and the foil in case any batter has leaked through and stuck to the sides.

10. Grasp two of the opposite overhanging edges of foil and lift out the brownie onto another wire rack. Let the brownie cool completely.

11. For the best appearance of the finished brownies, use a long serrated knife to level the top of the brownie.

12. Wash the pan and use the foil to return the brownie to the pan. Cover the pan tightly with plastic wrap.

The unfrosted brownies can be stored airtight at room temperature for 1 week, refrigerated for 1 month, or frozen for 3 months.

Continues

WHITE CHOCOLATE BUTTERCREAM
Makes: about 370 grams / 2 cups

WHITE CHOCOLATE CUSTARD BASE
Makes: about 306 grams / 1¼ cups

unsalted butter	78 grams	5½ tablespoons (½ stick plus 1½ tablespoons)
2 large eggs	100 grams	⅓ cup plus 1 tablespoon (94 ml)
white chocolate containing cocoa butter, preferably Valrhona	150 grams (5.3 ounces)	·

MAKE THE WHITE CHOCOLATE CUSTARD BASE

1. Thirty minutes to 1 hour ahead, cut the butter into tablespoon-size pieces. Set on the counter to soften.

2. Thirty minutes ahead, into a 1 cup / 237 ml glass measure with a spout, weigh or measure the eggs. Whisk lightly. Cover tightly with plastic wrap and set on the counter.

3. Have ready a fine-mesh strainer suspended over a medium bowl.

4. Chop the white chocolate into coarse pieces. In the top of a double boiler over hot, not simmering, water (do not let the bottom of the container touch the water), melt the white chocolate and butter, stirring often with a silicone spatula, until smooth and creamy.

5. Whisk the eggs into the melted chocolate until incorporated. Continue stirring with the spatula, being sure to scrape the mixture from the bottom of the container so that it does not risk overcooking, until an instant-read thermometer reads 160°F / 71°C. The mixture will have thickened slightly.

6. Pour the mixture at once into the strainer. Press it through the strainer and scrape any mixture clinging to the underside into the bowl.

7. Cover the custard base tightly and refrigerate for about 1 hour, stirring every 15 minutes, until cool to the touch. (An instant-read thermometer should read 65° to 70°F / 18° to 21°C.) To speed cooling, you can place the bowl in an ice water bath, stirring often.

COMPLETED WHITE CHOCOLATE BUTTERCREAM

unsalted butter	71 grams	5 tablespoons (½ stick plus 1 tablespoon)
White Chocolate Custard Base	306 grams	1¼ cups
pure vanilla extract	·	1 teaspoon (5 ml)

COMPLETE THE BUTTERCREAM

8. Thirty minutes to 1 hour ahead, cut the butter into tablespoon-size pieces. Set on the counter to soften.

9. In the bowl of a stand mixer fitted with the whisk beater, beat the butter on medium-low speed until creamy, about 30 seconds.

10. Gradually beat the white chocolate custard base into the butter, scraping the sides of the bowl as needed. Raise the speed to medium-high and beat for 2 minutes. The color will lighten and stiff peaks will form when the beater is raised.

11. Cover and set aside for 1½ to 2 hours, or until the mixture is slightly thickened and spongy. It should be no warmer than 70°F / 21°C. If necessary, place the bowl in an ice water bath for a few minutes, stirring constantly, to finish cooling it.

12. Beat the mixture on medium-high speed until smooth, light, and creamy, about 30 seconds.

13. Add the vanilla extract and beat just until incorporated.

Refrigerate or freeze 95 grams / about ½ cup of the buttercream for another use.

FROST THE BROWNIE

14. Scrape the remaining white chocolate buttercream onto the brownie and, using a small offset spatula, spread it evenly.

15. Refrigerate the frosted brownie for a minimum of 1 hour to firm the buttercream before applying the ganache glaze.

DARK CHOCOLATE GANACHE GLAZE

Makes: 238 grams / ¾ cup plus 2 tablespoons

dark chocolate, 60% to 62% cacao	130 grams (4.6 ounces)	.
heavy cream	116 grams	½ cup (118 ml)
bourbon, preferably Woodford Reserve or Maker's Mark (or pure vanilla extract)	.	1 tablespoon (15 ml) (or 1 teaspoon / 5 ml)

MAKE THE CHOCOLATE GANACHE GLAZE

Have ready a fine-mesh strainer suspended over a 2 cup / 473 ml glass measure with a spout.

1. Chop the chocolate into coarse pieces. In a food processor, process the chocolate until very fine. Transfer it to a small heatproof glass bowl.

2. In a 1 cup / 237 ml or larger microwavable measure with a spout (or in a small saucepan over medium heat, stirring often) scald the cream (heat it to the boiling point; small bubbles will form around the periphery).

3. Pour the hot cream over the chocolate. Cover the bowl and let stand for 5 minutes to melt the chocolate.

4. Using a silicone spatula, gently stir together the chocolate and cream until smooth.

5. Stir in the bourbon until smooth. Press the mixture through the strainer and scrape any mixture clinging to the underside into the bowl.

6. Let the glaze cool to warm room temperature; it should still be fluid but not warm to the touch (75° to 82°F / 24° to 28°C). This only takes about 10 minutes, so set it in a warm spot to keep it pourable. If it becomes too firm, reheat it in the microwave with 3-second bursts, or in the top of a double boiler.

GLAZE THE BROWNIE

7. Starting at the center, with the measuring cup's spout just above the buttercream, slowly pour the ganache glaze over the brownie, moving the cup as needed to cover all the buttercream. With a small offset spatula, smooth the glaze evenly.

8. Refrigerate for a minimum of 1 hour to set the glaze before cutting into squares.

CUT THE BROWNIES

9. Run a small metal spatula between the foil and the glazed brownie. Lift out the brownie by grasping two of the opposite overhanging edges of foil and set it on a cutting mat or board.

If desired, for perfectly squared-off corners, use a serrated knife to trim the sides of the brownie.

10. Use a thin-bladed knife, run under hot water and wiped dry between cuts, to cut the brownie into 2 inch squares. To retain the pristine whiteness of the buttercream, cut straight down and then pull the knife straight out.

STORE Airtight, in a single layer: room temperature, 1 day; refrigerated, 1 week; frozen, 3 months.

VARIATION

Chocolate-Cherry Almond Brownies

Tart brandied cherries and dark chocolate, with a hint of almond extract, are a felicitous combination. These are light in texture yet moist and fudgy as they melt in your mouth. The cherries contribute a mellow and delightful quality, and

Continues

the almond extract enhances the cherry flavor and blends well with the chocolate. These are also delicious even without the added buttercream and ganache toppings.

CHERRIES

dried sour cherries	114 grams	1 cup
hot water	79 grams	⅓ cup (79 ml)

With scissors, cut each cherry in half.

In a small bowl, place the dried cherries and hot water. Cover with plastic wrap and let the cherries soak for about 30 minutes, until they are softened and plump, stirring once after the first 15 minutes.

Empty the cherries into a strainer set over a small bowl. Press the cherries gently to release any excess liquid. Set them on paper towels and roll them up to keep them moist but not too wet.

Replace the pecans with the soaked cherries, and replace 1 teaspoon / 5 ml of the vanilla extract with 1 teaspoon / 5 ml pure almond extract.

MINI GÂTEAUX BRETON

Makes: Thirty-eight 1⅝ inch round cookies

The dough-like batter for this classic French cake from Brittany, when baked in miniature tart pans, makes the most buttery cookies I know. They contain even more butter than sablés! They will keep for as long as a week at room temperature, making them perfect for holiday gift giving. You can also use mini muffin pans, which are double the size, to make larger cookies (see the Variation).

Oven Temperature: 325°F / 160°C	**Baking Time:** 7 minutes for the almonds; 14 to 16 minutes for the cookies

Special Equipment: 38 mini tartlet or brioche pans, 1 inch at the bottom and 1¾ inches at the top (1 tablespoon capacity), uncoated, set on a 17¼ by 12¼ half sheet pan (if you do not have enough brioche pans, bake in batches); A long thin sewing needle for unmolding

DOUGH *Makes: 380 grams*

lightly salted high-fat butter (or high-quality regular unsalted butter); see Baking Gems	128 grams (or 142 grams)	9 tablespoons (1 stick plus 1 tablespoon) (or 10 tablespoons / 1¼ sticks)
2 (to 3) large egg yolks (see page xxvi)	37 grams	2 tablespoons plus 1 teaspoon (35 ml)
pure vanilla extract	·	¾ teaspoon (3.75 ml)
blanched sliced almonds	25 grams	¼ cup
superfine sugar (see Baking Gems)	75 grams	¼ cup plus 2 tablespoons, *divided*
fine sea salt	·	¹⁄₁₆ teaspoon
kirsch, dark rum, or water	·	½ tablespoon (7.5 ml)
bleached all-purpose flour	125 grams	1 cup (lightly spooned into the cup and leveled off) plus ½ tablespoon

PREHEAT THE OVEN

Twenty minutes or longer before baking, set an oven rack at the middle level of the oven. Set the oven at 325°F / 160°C.

MISE EN PLACE

Thirty minutes to 1 hour ahead, cut the butter into tablespoon-size pieces. Set on the counter to soften.

Thirty minutes ahead, into a 1 cup / 237 ml glass measure with a spout, weigh or measure the egg yolks. Whisk in the vanilla extract. Cover tightly with plastic wrap and set on the counter.

Toast the Almonds: Spread the almonds evenly on a baking sheet and bake for about 7 minutes, or until pale gold. Stir once or twice to ensure even toasting and prevent overbrowning. Set the baking sheet on a wire rack and cool completely.

In a food processor, process the almonds with 25 grams / 2 tablespoons of the sugar and the salt until fairly fine but not powder fine. (Alternatively, grind the almonds with the sugar and salt in a spice mill, or use a rotary nut grinder to grind the nuts.)

Continues

MAKE THE DOUGH

1. In the bowl of a stand mixer fitted with the flat beater, beat together the butter and (remaining) sugar on medium speed for 1 to 2 minutes, until smooth and creamy. Scrape down the sides of the bowl.

2. On low speed, gradually beat in the egg yolk mixture until incorporated. Scrape down the sides of the bowl.

3. Add the almond mixture, the salt if you did not grind it with the nuts, and the liquor and mix until the almond mixture is moistened, then beat for about 20 seconds, until evenly incorporated.

4. Add the flour in four parts, turning off the mixer between additions and beating on the lowest speed for about 15 seconds after each one. Detach the beater and, with a silicone spatula, finish mixing in any flour that may remain, reaching to the bottom of the bowl.

5. Scrape the dough onto a piece of plastic wrap. Wrap tightly and refrigerate for 30 minutes, or until firm enough to scoop.

FILL THE TARTLET PANS

6. One piece at a time, scoop out a rounded teaspoon of dough (10 grams), roll it between the palms of your hands into a 1 inch ball, and set it into a tartlet pan. Press the dough ball into the pan. The dough will come almost to the top of the pan. (If the dough is sticky, refrigerate the dough until firmer.) Use your pinky to press the dough into the fluted edges of the pan.

7. Arrange the tartlet pans at least ½ inch apart on the sheet pan.

BAKE THE GÂTEAUX

8. Bake for 8 minutes. Rotate the sheet pan halfway around. Continue baking for 6 to 8 minutes, or until the gâteaux are deep golden brown. (An instant-read thermometer inserted in the center should read about 205°F / 96°C.)

COOL AND UNMOLD THE GÂTEAUX

9. Set the sheet pan on a wire rack to cool for 10 minutes. Slip the needle between the edge of the pan and each gâteau to loosen and pop it out, then place onto another wire rack. Cool completely.

STORE Airtight: room temperature, 5 days; refrigerated, 10 days; frozen, 3 months.

Baking Gems

♥ High-fat butter that is lightly salted, such as Vermont brand, is far less salty than regular butter labeled "lightly salted." If using good-quality unsalted regular butter, increase the salt to ⅛ teaspoon.

♥ Butter with 80 percent fat (most everyday brands) contains about 1 tablespoon more water than butter with 86 percent fat, which will result in a slightly moister crumb. If this is your preference, but you want to use the higher-fat butter, you can add 1 tablespoon of water to the dough when adding the ground almonds.

♥ To impart an especially lovely flavor to this cookie, substitute golden sugar for the superfine sugar.

VARIATION

The recipe can be baked in two mini muffin pans to make 19 gâteaux. Increase the baking time to 20 to 25 minutes.

BABY CHEESECAKES

Makes: Twenty-four 1¼ inch mini cheesecakes

This could well be my favorite way to eat cheesecake. The two-bite size offers a perfect balance of textures and a perfect excuse to have more than one. The creamy texture and tangy flavor of the filling marry wonderfully with the cranberry topping here, but you could also use lemon curd (see Baking Gems).

Oven Temperature: 350°F / 175°C	Baking Time: 10 minutes	Special Equipment: Two 12 cup mini muffin pans (1½ inches at the base), lightly coated with nonstick cooking spray and set a minimum of 1 inch apart on a cookie sheet; A disposable pastry bag with a ½ inch semicircle cut from the tip, or a demitasse spoon

CRUMB CRUST *Makes: 160 grams*

unsalted butter	57 grams	4 tablespoons (½ stick)
graham cracker crumbs (8 to 8½ double crackers, 5 by 2¼ inch)	110 grams	1 cup (lightly packed after crushing)

1. In a 1 cup / 237 ml microwavable measure with a spout (or in a small saucepan over medium-low heat, stirring often) melt the butter.

Food Processor Method

2. Break the crackers into the food processor and process into fine crumbs. Add the melted butter and pulse a few times, just until incorporated.

Hand Method

2. Place the crackers in a reclosable freezer bag and use a rolling pin to crush them into fine crumbs. Pour the crumbs into a medium bowl. With a fork, stir in the melted butter, tossing lightly to incorporate.

Both Methods

3. Spoon 2 gently rounded measuring teaspoons (6.5 grams) of the crumb mixture into each cup of the prepared pans and press it in as evenly as possible. It works best to start by pressing the crumbs against the sides with a demitasse spoon

and then using your index finger to press them evenly over the bottom.

4. Set the pans in the refrigerator so that the crust will firm up while you make the filling.

FILLING
Makes: 380 grams

full-fat cream cheese	227 grams	¾ cup plus 2 tablespoons
1 large egg	50 grams	3 tablespoons plus ½ teaspoon (47.5 ml)
sugar	67 grams	⅓ cup
lemon juice, freshly squeezed and strained	10 grams	2 teaspoons (10 ml)
pure vanilla extract	·	½ teaspoon (2.5 ml)
full-fat sour cream	30 grams	2 tablespoons

PREHEAT THE OVEN
Twenty minutes or longer before baking, set an oven rack at the middle level. Set the oven at 350°F / 175°C.

Continues

MISE EN PLACE

Thirty minutes ahead, cut the cream cheese into roughly 1 inch cubes. Cover with plastic wrap and set on the counter to soften.

Thirty minutes ahead, into a 1 cup / 237 ml glass measure with a spout, weigh or measure the egg. Whisk lightly, cover tightly with plastic, and set on the counter.

MAKE THE FILLING

1. In the bowl of a stand mixer fitted with the whisk beater, beat the cream cheese and sugar on low speed until the mixture begins to come together. Raise the speed to medium and beat for 1 minute, or until very smooth. Scrape down the sides of the bowl.

2. Gradually beat in the egg and continue beating until smooth.

3. On low speed, add the lemon juice and vanilla extract and beat until incorporated.

4. Add the sour cream and beat just until incorporated.

FILL THE CRUMB CRUSTS

5. Fill the prepared pastry bag and pipe the filling, or use a demitasse spoon to fill each crust to the top (14 to 15 grams each).

BAKE THE CHEESECAKES

6. Bake for 5 minutes. Rotate the cookie sheet halfway around. Continue baking for 5 minutes. The filling will puff up but deflate a little on cooling.

COOL AND CHILL THE CHEESECAKES

7. Set the pans on a wire rack and let the cheesecakes cool completely, then refrigerate for a minimum of 3 hours, up to overnight. It is best to invert a pan over them to prevent them from absorbing other odors in the fridge.

CRANBERRY TOPPING

water	59 grams	¼ cup (59 ml)
superfine sugar	75 grams	¼ cup plus 2 tablespoons
cranberries (fresh or frozen)	100 grams	1 cup
cornstarch	6 grams	2 teaspoons

MAKE THE CRANBERRY TOPPING

1. In a small saucepan, with a silicone spatula, stir together the water, sugar, cranberries, and cornstarch, then bring the mixture to a boil over medium heat, stirring constantly.

2. Reduce the heat to low and simmer, without stirring, for 1 minute, swirling the pan often. Allow the mixture to cool to room temperature.

TOP THE CHEESECAKES

3. Use a small spoon to place 3 or 4 cranberries, with their syrup, on each cheesecake.

UNMOLD THE CHEESECAKES

8. Fill the sink or a roasting pan with a few inches of hot tap water. Carefully dip each pan into the water for about 30 seconds; do not allow the water to reach the tops of the pans. Slip a small metal spatula between the crust and the pans to pop out the cakes.

STORE Airtight: refrigerated, 1 week.

Baking Gems

♥ Setting the mini muffin pans on a cookie sheet prevents the bottoms of the crust from overbrowning.

♥ If you'd prefer to use lemon curd instead of cranberries for the topping, halve the recipe on page 403. For the smoothest surface, add the lemon curd while it is still hot or warm: Apply 1 teaspoon / 6 grams lemon curd to the top of each cheesecake.

BANANA CUSTARD CUDDLE COOKIES

Makes: Eighteen 3 by 1 inch high round cookies

Every year, pastry chef Miro Uskokovic hosts a "Sweets & Sips" networking event at Gramercy Tavern for pastry professionals. The chefs who participate bring all manner of wonderful creations. One year, Jansen Chan, director of pastry operations at the International Culinary Center in NYC, contributed this very special recipe. What's unique about this cookie is that the raw dough is coated in cake crumbs (which I always have plenty of) or graham cracker crumbs. The crumb exterior is crunchy, soft, and creamy, all rolled into one. These are like a cross between a cookie and a cake. They are very moist and are best made a minimum of one day ahead of serving.

Oven Temperature:	Baking Time:	Plan Ahead:	Special Equipment:
350°F / 175°C	15 to 20 minutes (for each of two batches)	Set the bananas in a warm place for several days until they become very ripe and develop black spots or become totally black. The riper they are, the sweeter they will be.	Two 17 by 14 inch cookie sheets, lined with parchment; Nine or eighteen 3 by ¾ inch high pastry rings (see Baking Gems), lightly coated with nonstick cooking spray and arranged evenly spaced nine to a pan (alternatively, use muffin pans, the bottoms lined with parchment and lightly coated with nonstick cooking spray)

DOUGH *Makes: 1,160 grams*

2 large ripe bananas	227 grams	1 cup (mashed)	fine sea salt	3 grams	½ teaspoon
unsalted butter	170 grams	12 tablespoons (1½ sticks)	apple cider vinegar	·	1½ teaspoons (7.5 ml)
1 large egg	·	3 tablespoons plus ½ teaspoon (47.5 ml)	sugar	170 grams	¾ cup plus 1½ tablespoons
all-purpose flour, preferably bleached	283 grams	2⅓ cups (lightly spooned into the cup and leveled off)	light molasses, preferably Grandma's brand	10 grams	1½ teaspoons (7.5 ml)
baking powder, preferably an aluminum-free variety	2.2 grams	½ teaspoon	milk chocolate chips (or chopped milk chocolate pieces)	127 grams (4.5 ounces)	¾ cup
baking soda	2.7 grams	½ teaspoon			

Continues

MISE EN PLACE

Peel the ripened bananas and mash them in a medium bowl.

Thirty minutes to 1 hour ahead, cut the butter into tablespoon-size pieces. Set on the counter to soften.

Thirty minutes ahead, into a 1 cup / 237 ml glass measure with a spout, weigh or measure the egg. Cover tightly with plastic wrap and set on the counter.

In a medium bowl, whisk together the flour, baking powder, baking soda, and salt.

MAKE THE DOUGH

1. To the medium bowl with the mashed bananas, add the apple cider vinegar and egg and whisk them together to combine.

2. In the bowl of a stand mixer fitted with the flat beater, beat the butter, sugar, and molasses on medium speed for 2 to 3 minutes, until light and fluffy.

3. On low speed, add the flour mixture alternating with the banana mixture in three parts, beating for a few seconds after each addition until incorporated. Scrape down the sides of the bowl as needed.

4. On the lowest speed, mix in the chocolate chips.

5. Cover the bowl tightly with plastic wrap and refrigerate for 1 hour to slightly firm up the very sticky dough before shaping. (It needs to be somewhat sticky to attach the crumbs.) While the dough is chilling, make the custard filling and crumb topping.

PREHEAT THE OVEN

Twenty minutes or longer before baking, set an oven rack at the middle level. Set the oven at 350°F / 175°C.

CUSTARD FILLING

Makes: 135 grams / about ¾ cup / 177 ml

full-fat sour cream	100 grams	¼ cup plus 2½ tablespoons
sugar	25 grams	2 tablespoons
1 small egg yolk	9.5 grams	½ tablespoon (7.5 ml)
vanilla paste or pure vanilla extract	·	¼ teaspoon (1.25 ml)
fine sea salt	·	1⁄16 teaspoon

MAKE THE CUSTARD FILLING

1. In a small bowl, whisk together the sour cream and sugar. Add the egg yolk, vanilla, and salt. Whisk until smooth. Cover tightly with plastic wrap and set aside.

GRAHAM CRACKER TOPPING

1 package graham crackers (11 double crackers, 5 by 2¼ inch)	151 grams	1⅓ cups (lightly packed after crushing)
powdered sugar, for dusting	18 grams	3 tablespoons

MAKE THE TOPPING

1. Break the crackers into a gallon-size reclosable freezer bag. Use a rolling pin to break the crackers into coarse crumbs.

2. Empty the crumbs onto a quarter sheet pan or pie plate.

SHAPE AND FILL THE DOUGH

6. Use a large spoon and a small silicone spatula to drop mounds of dough (about 64 grams / 2 teaspoons each) onto the graham crackers, and then sprinkle some of the crumbs on top. Use your fingers to shape the mounds of dough into patties, using the crumbs to keep the dough from sticking to your fingers.

7. After shaping each patty, press it into a prepared ring or muffin cup until it reaches the edges.

8. Now you need to create a 2 inch wide by ¼ inch deep opening in the center of each cookie. Start by using the back of a tablespoon to make the depression and then sprinkle the depression with more crumbs so that the dough doesn't stick to your fingers while you deepen it to the proper size.

9. With a small spoon, fill each depression with about 2 teaspoons (10 ml) of the custard filling.

10. Use your fingers to sprinkle additional crumbs on top of each cookie, leaving most of the cream center exposed.

BAKE THE COOKIES

11. Bake the first batch for 10 minutes. Rotate the pan halfway around. Continue baking for 5 to 10 minutes, or until the cookies begin to puff and brown. (An instant-read thermometer inserted into the center should read about 212°F / 100°C.)

COOL THE COOKIES

12. Set the cookie sheet on a wire rack and let the cookies cool completely (about an hour) before lifting them from the parchment (the rings can be removed as soon as they are cool enough to handle and prepared for the second batch if necessary) or from the muffin pans.

13. Repeat with the second batch.

14. Dust the cookies lightly with powdered sugar.

STORE Airtight: room temperature, 3 days; refrigerated, 1 week; frozen, 3 months.

Baking Gems

♥ Disposable pastry rings can be made easily from heavy-duty aluminum foil, or reusable rings can be cut from aluminum flashing (available at most hardware and home improvements stores).

For each aluminum foil ring: Cut a 12 by 3 inch strip of foil. Mark the foil along its length at ⅝ inch. Fold the foil along the markings. Continue folding the foil two more times to form a 12 by ¾ inch strip with 4 layers of foil.

For each aluminum flashing ring: Mark, and then use metal shears or sharp utility scissors to cut a 12 by ¾ inch strip.

For either type of rings: Wrap each ring around a 3 inch diameter can. Use two small paper clips to secure the overlapping ends to form a 3¼ inch wide ring. Remove the ring from the can and adjust it if necessary so it is as round as possible.

FINANCIERS

These little cakes are soft and springy, with a fine crisp crust. They consist of flour, almond flour, sugar, browned butter (called *beurre noisette* in French because it is the color of a hazelnut), and egg white. Their only liquid comes from the egg white, but they contain plenty of fat from the almonds and browned butter, so they are very moist. Whenever anyone asks me what to do with their extra egg whites, financiers are the first thing that comes to mind.

The financier was created in France over 100 years ago by a baker whose bakery was close to the financial center of Paris. Traditionally, they were baked in the shape of bars and so became known in English as "ingots." They are now available in a wide variety of shapes, but the basic ingredients have remained the same.

Financiers have the best texture within a few hours of baking, but they will still be moist and delicious even after 5 days of refrigeration.

I like to use silicone financier molds because they result in the moistest texture. For even baking, they need to be set on a rack and then on a sheet pan, which makes it easy to transfer them in and out of the oven.

My three favorite financiers are the golden, peanut butter, and chocolate varieties.

TIPS FOR THE BEST RESULTS

Whisk or stir the browned butter constantly as it cooks and darkens to distribute the flavor of the browning solids through the butter.

For a more mellow flavor, add the browned butter to the batter while it is hot so that it partially cooks the flour.

The skins from unblanched almonds will contribute more flavor and absorb some of the oils from the nuts, which results in a better texture. If an extra-crunchy texture is desired, use whole almonds for one quarter of the total almonds and pulse them in the food processor with the flour.

If freezing the baked financiers, defrost them in the refrigerator and recrisp them briefly in a preheated oven 350°F / 175°C.

GOLDEN BUTTER FINANCIERS

Makes: Sixteen 3 by 1 by 1¼ inch high financiers

This is a butter cake-cookie in its purest form. The key to their unique buttery flavor is to use part clarified browned butter and part melted whole butter, a secret I learned from pastry chef Drew Shotts of Garrison Confections. The milk solids in the whole butter add an extra mellow dimension. The pastry or Wondra flour gives these financiers their delicate and special texture.

Oven Temperature:
325°F / 160°C for the almonds; 375°F / 190°C for the financiers

Baking Time: about 7 minutes for the almonds; 18 to 20 minutes for the financiers

Special Equipment: Financier mold(s), preferably silicone, 3 by 1 by 1¼ inches high (¼ cup/59 ml capacity), coated with baking spray with flour; A fine strainer, or a coarser strainer lined with cheesecloth; Optional: A pastry bag fitted with a ⅜ to ½ inch round pastry tube

BATTER *Makes: 480 grams*

sliced almonds, preferably unblanched	67 grams	⅔ cup
4 large egg whites	120 grams	½ cup (118 ml)
pure vanilla extract	·	¼ teaspoon (1.25 ml)
unsalted butter, for clarifying	85 grams	6 tablespoons (¾ stick)
unsalted butter, for melting	71 grams	5 tablespoons (½ stick plus 1 tablespoon)
sugar, preferably superfine	150 grams	¾ cup
pastry flour or wondra	50 grams	¼ cup (lightly spooned into the cup and leveled off) plus 3 tablespoons
baking powder, preferably an aluminum-free variety	3.4 grams	¾ teaspoon

PREHEAT THE OVEN

Twenty minutes or longer before baking, set an oven rack at the middle level. Set the oven at 325°F / 160°C.

MISE EN PLACE

Toast the Almonds: Spread the almonds evenly on a baking sheet and bake for about 7 minutes, or until pale golden. Stir once or twice to ensure even browning. Set the baking sheet on a wire rack and cool completely.

Raise the oven temperature to 375°F / 190°C.

Thirty minutes to 1 hour ahead, into a 1 cup / 237 ml glass measure with a spout, weigh or measure the egg whites. Whisk in the vanilla extract. Cover tightly with plastic wrap and set on the counter.

Clarify and Brown Part of the Butter: Have ready by the cooktop a fine-mesh strainer suspended over a 2 cup / 473 ml glass measure with a spout, and a 1 cup / 237 ml glass measure with a spout.

Continues

In a medium heavy saucepan, melt the 85 grams / 6 tablespoons butter over very low heat, stirring often with a light-colored silicone spatula. Raise the heat to low and boil, stirring constantly, until the milk solids on the spatula become little golden brown specks. (An instant-read thermometer should read between 278° and 284°F / 137° and 140°C.) Immediately pour the butter through the strainer into the glass measure.

Into the 1 cup / 237 ml glass measure, weigh or measure 50 grams / about ¼ cup / 59 ml of the clarified browned butter. Set it in a warm place so it stays hot. (Store the browned solids and extra browned butter for future use; see Baking Gem.)

MELT THE REMAINING BUTTER

In a small heavy saucepan, melt the 71 grams / 5 tablespoons butter over low heat. Pour it into the glass measure with the clarified browned butter. Return it to a warm place to stay hot, or reheat it when ready to add it to the batter.

MAKE THE BATTER

1. In a food processor, process the toasted almonds with the sugar until powder fine, scraping down the sides of the bowl as needed. (Alternatively, grind the almonds in batches in a spice mill with a little of the sugar, and then whisk them together with the remaining sugar, or use a rotary nut grinder and then whisk them together with the sugar.)

2. In the bowl of a stand mixer fitted with the flat beater, mix the almond mixture, flour, and baking powder on low speed for 30 seconds.

3. Add the egg white mixture and beat on medium speed for 30 seconds, or until evenly mixed.

4. On medium-low speed, very slowly drizzle in the hot butter mixture. It should take about 5 minutes to add all of it; the batter will emulsify to a smooth golden cream.

FILL THE MOLDS

5. Fill the prepared pastry bag with the mixture and use it to fill each cavity about half full (30 grams); or use a spoon to fill the cavities.

BAKE THE FINANCIERS

If using silicone financiers mold(s), set them on a rack and then on a half sheet pan(s) or cookie sheet(s).

6. Bake for 10 minutes. Rotate the sheet pan(s) or metal molds halfway around. Continue baking for 8 to 10 minutes, or until the financiers are golden brown and spring back when pressed lightly in the centers.

UNMOLD AND COOL THE FINANCIERS

7. **If using silicone mold(s),** set them on a wire rack and cool completely. To unmold, push out each financier with your finger pressed against the bottom of the mold.

If using metal mold(s), set on a wire rack and let the financiers cool for 5 minutes. Run a small metal spatula between the sides of the mold(s) and the financiers, pressing firmly against the molds. Invert them onto the wire rack and then reinvert them onto another wire rack. Cool completely.

STORE Airtight: room temperature, 3 days; refrigerated, 5 days; frozen, 3 months.

To reheat frozen financiers, defrost in the refrigerator and then recrisp in a preheated 350°F / 175°C oven for about 3 minutes.

Baking Gem

♥ The browned butter solids make a great addition to bread dough or a baked potato. Any leftover clarified butter can be used for sautéing.

PEANUT BUTTER FINANCIERS

Makes: Sixteen 3 by 1 by 1¼ inch high financiers

Christophe Toury comes from Chartres, France, and he started his career as a pastry chef and chocolatier at the Ritz in Paris. Although Europeans seem to prefer praline paste (which is fine to substitute for the peanut butter here), Chris created this peanut butter financier for his appreciative American clientele.

Oven Temperature:
325°F / 160°C for the almonds; 375°F / 190°C for the financiers

Baking Time: about 7 minutes for the almonds; 18 to 20 minutes for the financiers

Special Equipment: Financier mold(s), preferably silicone, 3 by 1 by 1¼ inches high (¼ cup/59 ml capacity) coated with baking spray with flour; A fine strainer, or a coarser strainer lined with cheesecloth; Optional: A pastry bag fitted with a ⅜ to ½ inch round pastry tube

BATTER *Makes: 540 grams*

sliced almonds, preferably unblanched	75 grams	¾ cup
4 large egg whites	120 grams	½ cup (118 ml)
unsalted butter	170 grams	12 tablespoons (1½ sticks)
powdered sugar	150 grams	1⅔ cups (sifted, then lightly spooned into the cup and leveled off) minus 1 teaspoon
bleached all-purpose flour	57 grams	½ cup (lightly spooned into the cup and leveled off) minus 1 teaspoon
smooth peanut butter	50 grams	3 tablespoons

PREHEAT THE OVEN

Twenty minutes or longer before baking, set an oven rack at the middle level. Set the oven at 325°F / 160°C.

MISE EN PLACE

Toast the Almonds: Spread the almonds evenly on a baking sheet and bake for about 7 minutes, or until pale golden. Stir once or twice to ensure even browning. Set the baking sheet on a wire rack and cool completely.

Raise the oven temperature to 375°F / 190°C.

Thirty minutes to 1 hour ahead, into a 1 cup / 237 ml glass measure with a spout, weigh or measure the egg whites. Cover tightly with plastic wrap and set on the counter.

Clarify and Brown the Butter: Have ready by the cooktop a fine-mesh strainer suspended over a 2 cup / 473 ml glass measure with a spout, and a 1 cup / 237 ml glass measure with a spout.

In a medium heavy saucepan, melt the butter over very low heat, stirring often with a light-colored silicone spatula. Raise the heat to low and boil, stirring constantly, until the milk solids on the spatula become little brown specks. (An instant-read thermometer should read between 278° and 284°F / 137° and 140°C.) Immediately pour the butter through the strainer into the glass measure.

Continues

Into the 1 cup / 237 ml glass measure, weigh or measure 105 grams / about ½ cup / 118 ml of the clarified browned butter. Set it in a warm place so it stays hot, or reheat it when ready to add it to the batter. (Store the browned solids and extra browned butter for another use; see Baking Gem.)

MAKE THE BATTER

1. In a food processor, process the toasted almonds with the powdered sugar until powder fine, scraping down the sides of the bowl as needed. Add the flour and process until evenly incorporated. (Alternatively, grind the almonds in a spice mill with a little of the powdered sugar, and then whisk them together with the remaining sugar, or use a rotary nut grinder, and whisk them together with the powdered sugar.)

2. In the bowl of a stand mixer fitted with the whisk beater, beat the egg whites on medium-low speed just until foamy.

3. Add the almond mixture and beat on low speed until incorporated, scraping down the sides of the bowl as needed.

4. On medium-low speed, very slowly drizzle in the hot clarified browned butter. It should take about 5 minutes to add all of it; the batter will emulsify to a smooth golden cream.

5. Add the peanut butter and mix for a few seconds, just until evenly incorporated.

FILL THE MOLDS

6. Fill the prepared pastry bag with the mixture and use it to fill each cavity about two-thirds full (33 grams); or use a spoon to fill the cavities.

BAKE THE FINANCIERS

If using silicone financiers mold(s), set them on a rack and then on a half sheet pan(s) or cookie sheet(s).

7. Bake for 10 minutes. Rotate the sheet pan(s) or metal molds halfway around. Continue baking for 8 to 10 minutes, or until the financiers spring back when pressed lightly in the centers.

UNMOLD AND COOL THE FINANCIERS

8. **If using silicone mold(s),** set them on a wire rack and cool completely. To unmold, push out each financier with your finger pressed against the bottom of the mold.

If using metal mold(s), set on a wire rack and let the financiers cool for 5 minutes. Run a small metal spatula between the sides of the mold(s) and the financiers, pressing firmly against the molds. Invert them onto the wire rack and then reinvert them onto another wire rack. Cool completely.

STORE Airtight: room temperature, 3 days; refrigerated, 5 days; frozen, 3 months. To reheat frozen financiers, thaw in the refrigerator and recrisp in a preheated 350°F / 175°C oven for about 3 minutes.

Baking Gem

♥ The browned butter solids make a great addition to bread dough or a baked potato.

CHOCOLATE FINANCIERS

Makes: Fifteen 3 by 1 by 1¼ inch high financiers

My love affair with financiers started over twenty years ago at the Monkey Bar in New York City. I so loved pastry chef Jean-François Bonnet's velvety, intensely chocolate financiers that I subsequently wrote a story on the financier for *Food Arts* magazine.

Oven Temperature: 325°F / 160°C for the almonds; 375°F / 190°C for the financiers

Baking Time: about 7 minutes for the almonds; 18 to 20 minutes for the financiers

Special Equipment: Financier mold(s), preferably silicone, 3 by 1 by 1¼ inches high (¼ cup / 59 ml capacity) coated with baking spray with flour; A fine strainer, or a coarser strainer lined with cheesecloth; Optional: A pastry bag fitted with a ⅜ to ½ inch round pastry tube

BATTER *Makes: 450 grams*

sliced almonds, preferably unblanched	50 grams	½ cup
4 large egg whites	120 grams	½ cup (118 ml)
unsalted butter	200 grams	14 tablespoons (1¾ sticks)
bleached all-purpose flour	35 grams	¼ cup (lightly spooned into the cup and leveled off) plus ½ tablespoon
cornstarch	4.5 grams	1½ teaspoons
unsweetened alkalized cocoa powder	10 grams	2 tablespoons (sifted before measuring)
superfine sugar	125 grams	½ cup plus 2 tablespoons

PREHEAT THE OVEN

Twenty minutes or longer before baking, set an oven rack at the middle level. Set the oven at 325°F / 160°C.

MISE EN PLACE

Toast the Almonds: Spread the almonds evenly on a baking sheet and bake for about 7 minutes, or until pale golden. Stir once or twice to ensure even browning. Set the baking sheet on a wire rack and cool completely.

Raise the oven temperature to 375°F / 190°C.

Thirty minutes to 1 hour ahead, into a 1 cup / 237 ml glass measure with a spout, weigh or measure the egg whites. Cover tightly with plastic wrap and set on the counter.

Clarify and Brown the Butter: Have ready by the cooktop a fine-mesh strainer suspended over a 2 cup / 473 ml glass measure with a spout, and a 1 cup / 237 ml glass measure with a spout.

In a medium heavy saucepan, melt the butter over very low heat, stirring often with a light-colored silicone spatula. Raise the heat to low and boil, stirring constantly, until the milk solids on the spatula become little brown specks. (An instant-read thermometer should read between 285° and 290°F / 140° and 143°C.) Immediately pour the butter through the strainer into the glass measure.

Into the 1 cup / 237 ml glass measure, weigh or measure 125 grams / about 10 tablespoons / 150 ml of the clarified browned butter. Set it in a warm place so it stays hot, or reheat it when ready to add it to the batter. (Store the browned solids and extra browned butter for another use; see Baking Gems.)

MAKE THE BATTER

1. In a food processor, process the toasted almonds with the flour and cornstarch until powder fine, scraping down the sides of the bowl as needed. Add the cocoa and process until evenly incorporated. (Alternatively, grind the almonds in a spice mill with a little of the flour, or use rotary nut grinder to grind the nuts, then whisk the ground nuts together with the [remaining] flour, cornstarch, and cocoa.)

2. In the bowl of a stand mixer fitted with the flat beater, stir together the egg whites and sugar until the sugar is completely moistened.

3. Add the almond mixture and beat on low speed until incorporated, scraping down the sides of the bowl as needed.

4. On medium-low speed, very slowly drizzle in the hot clarified browned butter. It should take about 5 minutes to add all of it; the batter will emulsify to a smooth brown chocolatey cream.

FILL THE MOLDS

5. Fill the prepared pastry bag with the batter and use it to fill each cavity about half full (30 grams); or use a spoon to fill the cavities.

BAKE THE FINANCIERS

If using silicone financiers mold(s), set on a rack and then on a half sheet pan(s) or cookie sheet(s).

6. Bake for 10 minutes. Rotate the sheet pan(s) or metal molds halfway around. Continue baking for 8 to 10 minutes, or until the financiers spring back when pressed lightly in the centers.

UNMOLD AND COOL THE FINANCIERS

7. **If using silicone mold(s),** set them on a wire rack and cool completely. To unmold, push out each financier with your finger pressed against the bottom of the mold.

If using metal mold(s), set on a wire rack and let the financiers cool for 5 minutes. Run a small metal spatula between the sides of the mold(s) and the financiers, pressing firmly against the molds. Invert them onto the wire rack and then reinvert them onto another wire rack. Cool completely.

STORE Airtight: room temperature, 3 days; refrigerated, 5 days; frozen, 3 months. To reheat frozen financiers, defrost in the refrigerator and recrisp in a preheated 350°F / 175°C oven for about 3 minutes.

Baking Gems

💜 Jean-François Bonnet likes to bring his beurre noisette to a darker color for chocolate financiers because chocolate can both support and benefit from the more intense flavor. He is the only pastry chef I know who takes the temperature of his browned butter!

💜 The browned butter solids make a great addition to bread dough or a baked potato.

💜 Since this recipe has no leavening, it's fine to let the filled molds sit at room temperature for a few hours before baking. Or refrigerate overnight, covered with plastic wrap, and let them come to room temperature (about 1 hour) to soften before baking. This will produce financiers that are lighter in texture.

LEMON MADELEINES

Makes: One hundred twelve mini madeleines or Twenty-eight large madeleines (or 108 mini or 26 large if not adding the poppy seeds)

My madeleine of choice is based on my signature cake from *The Cake Bible*, Lemon Poppy Seed Pound Cake. While other madeleines quickly become unappealingly dry, these stay moist and delicious for 3 days at room temperature and can also be frozen. I love the little pop of the poppy seeds, but the madeleines are wonderfully buttery and lemony without them too!

Oven Temperature: 350°F / 175°C	**Baking Time:** 10 to 12 minutes for mini madeleines; 14 to 15 minutes for large madeleines

Special Equipment: Mini madeleine molds (1½ teaspoon capacity) or large madeleine molds (2 tablespoon capacity), preferably silicone (see Baking Gems), lightly coated with baking spray with flour and, if silicone, set on wire racks and then on cookie sheets; A disposable pastry bag fitted with a ⅜ or ½ inch round pastry tube; A pastry brush; Two 17 by 14 inch cookie sheets lined with plastic wrap and then lightly coated with nonstick cooking spray

BATTER *Makes: 455 grams (474 with the poppy seeds)*

unsalted butter	120 grams	8½ tablespoons plus 2 teaspoons
2 large eggs	100 grams	⅓ cup plus 1 tablespoon (94 ml)
pure vanilla extract	·	1 teaspoon (5 ml)
lemon zest, finely grated (from 2 lemons)	4 grams	2 teaspoons (loosely packed)
milk	30 grams	2 tablespoons (30 ml)
bleached cake flour	100 grams	1 cup (sifted into the cup and leveled off)
sugar, preferably superfine	100 grams	½ cup
baking powder, preferably an aluminum-free variety	2.2 grams	½ teaspoon
fine sea salt	·	¼ teaspoon
poppy seeds, black or white (optional)	19 grams	2 tablespoons

PREHEAT THE OVEN

Twenty minutes or longer before baking, set oven racks in the upper and lower thirds of the oven. Set the oven at 350°F / 175°C.

MISE EN PLACE

Thirty minutes to 1 hour ahead, cut the butter into tablespoon-size pieces. Set on the counter to soften.

Thirty minutes ahead, into a 1 cup / 237 ml glass measure with a spout, weigh or measure the eggs. Whisk in the vanilla extract. Cover tightly with plastic wrap and set on the counter.

Wash the lemons with dishwashing liquid, rinse, and dry before zesting. Finely grate the lemon zest. Freeze any extra for future use.

Reserve the lemons for the lemon syrup.

MAKE THE BATTER

1. Add the milk to the egg mixture and whisk it in.

2. In the bowl of a stand mixer fitted with the flat beater, mix the flour, sugar, baking powder, salt,

Continues

Lemon Madeleines
and Chocolate
Sweetheart
Madeleines,
page 309

lemon zest, and optional poppy seeds on low speed for 30 seconds.

3. Add the butter and half the egg mixture and mix until the dry ingredients are moistened. Raise the speed to medium and beat for 1 minute. Scrape down the sides of the bowl.

4. With the mixer off between additions, add the remaining egg mixture in two parts. Beat after each addition, starting on medium-low speed and gradually raising the speed to medium, then beating on medium speed for 30 seconds, to incorporate the ingredients and strengthen the structure. Scrape down the sides of the bowl.

PIPE THE BATTER INTO THE MOLDS

5. Fill the prepared pastry bag about three-quarters full with the batter. Pipe the batter into the molds, filling them about three-quarters full (4 grams for each mini mold cavity, 16 grams for each large cavity). There is no need to smooth the batter. Refill the bag as needed.

BAKE THE MADELEINES

6. Bake mini madeleines for 10 to 12 minutes, large ones for 14 to 15 minutes, or until a wooden toothpick inserted near the centers comes out completely clean and the madeleines spring back when pressed lightly in the centers. While they are baking, make the lemon syrup.

LEMON SYRUP

Makes: 95 grams / about ⅓ cup / 79 ml

sugar	50 grams	¼ cup
lemon juice, freshly squeezed and strained (2 large lemons from above)	47 grams	3 tablespoons (45 ml)

MAKE THE LEMON SYRUP

7. In a 1 cup / 237 ml glass measure with a spout, stir together the sugar and lemon juice. Heat in the microwave just until the sugar is dissolved. (Or use a small saucepan over medium heat.)

BRUSH THE MADELEINES WITH SYRUP, UNMOLD, AND COOL

8. As soon as the madeleines come out of the oven, place the pans on a rack, poke the madeleines all over with a wire cake tester, and brush with about one third of the syrup.

9. **If using silicone molds,** use your fingers to push the madeleines up and out of the mold from underneath and invert onto the prepared cookie sheets.

If using metal molds, use a toothpick or pin to carefully dislodge them from the molds and then invert them onto the prepared cookie sheets.

10. Brush the madeleines with the remaining syrup and allow them to cool completely. (The syrup distributes most evenly when allowed to sit for about 2 hours.)

STORE Airtight in a single layer: room temperature, 3 days; refrigerated, 5 days; frozen, 3 months.

Baking Gems

♥ Use superfine sugar for the finest texture.

♥ After coating the molds with the baking spray with flour, use a pastry brush to brush out any excess spray to prevent air bubbles from forming in the fluted tops of the madeleines.

♥ If you do not have enough molds to bake all the madeleines soon after making the batter, chill the extra batter in the refrigerator until ready to use.

♥ Be sure to use a wooden toothpick to test for doneness. The madeleines will spring back when pressed lightly in the center even before they are done.

CHOCOLATE SWEETHEART MADELEINES

Makes: One hundred mini madeleines or Twenty-five large madeleines

These are the moistest and most delicious chocolate madeleines I've ever tasted. My big breakthrough came about when I turned to my favorite chocolate cake from *The Cake Bible*, The Chocolate Domingo, after the advent of silicone molds, which result in a fine crust and maintain moisture better than metal molds. Brushing the madeleines with a ganache glaze seals in their moisture and adds extra chocolate flavor.

Oven Temperature: 350°F / 175°C

Baking Time: 10 to 12 minutes for mini madeleines, 14 to 15 minutes for large madeleines

Special Equipment: Mini madeleine molds (1½ teaspoon capacity) or large madeleine molds (2 tablespoon capacity), preferably silicone (see Baking Gems), lightly coated with baking spray with flour and, if silicone, set on wire racks and then on cookie sheets; A disposable pastry bag fitted with a ⅜ or ½ inch round pastry tube; An artist's brush; Two 17 by 14 inch cookie sheets lined with plastic wrap, and then lightly coated with nonstick cooking spray

GANACHE GLAZE *Makes: 123 grams / ½ cup*

dark chocolate, 60% to 62% cacao	42 grams (1.5 ounces)	·
heavy cream	87 grams	¼ cup plus 2 tablespoons (89 ml)

MAKE THE GANACHE GLAZE

1. Chop the chocolate into coarse pieces. In a small food processor, process the chocolate until very fine. (If you don't have a small processor, see Baking Gems.)

2. In a 1 cup / 237 ml microwavable measure with a spout (or in a small saucepan over medium heat, stirring often) scald the cream (heat it to the boiling point; small bubbles will form around the periphery).

3. With the motor running, pour the cream through the feed tube in a steady stream. Process for a few seconds, until smooth. Scrape the ganache into a glass bowl, cover it with plastic wrap, and set it in a warm place.

BATTER *Makes: 400 grams*

unsalted butter	100 grams	7 tablespoons (¾ stick plus 1 tablespoon)
1 large egg	50 grams	3 tablespoons plus ½ teaspoon (47.5 ml)
pure vanilla extract	·	¾ teaspoon (3.75 ml)
unsweetened alkalized cocoa powder	22 grams	¼ cup plus 2 teaspoons (sifted before measuring)
full-fat sour cream	81 grams	⅓ cup
bleached cake flour	78 grams	¾ cup (sifted into the cup and leveled off) plus ½ tablespoon
superfine sugar	100 grams	½ cup
baking powder	·	⅜ teaspoon
baking soda	·	⅛ teaspoon
fine sea salt	·	¼ teaspoon

Continues

PREHEAT THE OVEN

Twenty minutes or longer before baking, set oven racks in the upper and lower thirds of the oven. Set the oven at 350°F / 175°C.

MISE EN PLACE

Thirty minutes to 1 hour ahead, cut the butter into tablespoon-size pieces and set on the counter to soften.

Thirty minutes ahead, into a 1 cup / 237 ml glass measure with a spout, weigh or measure the egg. Whisk in the vanilla extract. Cover tightly with plastic wrap and set on the counter.

MAKE THE BATTER

1. In a medium bowl, whisk the cocoa, sour cream, and egg mixture, just until the consistency of slightly lumpy muffin batter.

2. In the bowl of a stand mixer fitted with the flat beater, mix the flour, sugar, baking powder, baking soda, and salt on low speed for 30 seconds.

3. Add the butter and half the cocoa mixture and mix on low speed until the dry ingredients are moistened. Raise the speed to medium and beat for 1½ minutes. Scrape down the sides of the bowl.

4. With the mixer off between additions, add the remaining cocoa mixture in two parts. Beat after each addition, starting on medium-low speed and gradually raising the speed to medium, then beating on medium speed for 30 seconds, to incorporate the ingredients and strengthen the structure. Scrape down the sides of the bowl.

PIPE THE BATTER INTO THE MOLDS

5. Fill the prepared pastry bag about three-quarters full with the batter. Pipe the batter into the molds, filling them about half full (4 grams for each mini mold cavity, 16 grams for each large cavity). Refill the bag as needed.

BAKE THE MADELEINES

6. Bake mini madeleines for 10 to 12 minutes, large ones for 14 to 15 minutes, or until a wire cake tester inserted near the centers comes out clean and the madeleines spring back when pressed lightly in the centers.

COOL AND UNMOLD THE MADELEINES

7. Set the pans on wire racks and let the madeleines cool in the molds for 5 minutes.

If using silicone molds, use your fingers to push the madeleines up and out of the mold from underneath and invert onto the prepared cookie sheets.

If using metal molds, use a toothpick or pin to carefully dislodge them from the molds. Invert the madeleines onto the prepared cookie sheets.

GLAZE THE MADELEINES

8. If necessary, reheat the ganache glaze with 3-second bursts in the microwave, or reheat in a hot water bath. With the artist's brush, coat the tops of the madeleines with the glaze, brushing it lengthwise along the grooves. As the glaze sets, it will darken and some of it will be absorbed. Brush a second lighter coat of glaze over each madeleine to make it even and shiny.

STORE Airtight: room temperature, 3 days; refrigerated, 5 days; frozen, 3 months.

Baking Gems

♥ After coating the molds with the baking spray with flour, use a pastry brush to brush out any excess spray to prevent air bubbles from forming in the fluted tops of the madeleines.

♥ If you do not have enough molds to bake all the madeleines soon after making the batter, chill the extra batter in the refrigerator until ready to use.

♥ If you don't have a small food processor, chop the chocolate with a large chef's knife and put it in a heatproof bowl. Pour the hot cream over the chocolate and stir until melted and smooth.

WHOOPIE COOKIES

Makes: Twelve 2½ inch sandwich cookies

The whoopie pie is said to have originated in Pennsylvania Dutch country. Although it is called "pie," it is actually a richly moist and chocolatey cake. Whoopie pies are traditionally about 3½ inches in size, but they can also be made in a lovely cookie-size version, as in this recipe. Milk Chocolate Mousse Ganache (page 401) is the ideal filling.

Oven Temperature:	Baking Time:	Special Equipment: Two 17 by 14 inch cookie sheets, lined with
400°F / 200°C	8 to 10 minutes	parchment or coated with nonstick cooking spray or solid vegetable shortening; Optional: A 1½ inch diameter cookie scoop

BATTER *Makes: 512 grams*

unsalted butter	28 grams	2 tablespoons
1 large egg	50 grams	3 tablespoons plus ½ teaspoon (47.5 ml)
dark chocolate, 60% to 62% cacao	42 grams (1.5 ounces)	.
bleached all-purpose flour	125 grams	1 cup (lightly spooned into the cup and leveled off) plus ½ tablespoon
unsweetened alkalized cocoa powder	19 grams	¼ cup (sifted before measuring)
baking powder, preferably an aluminum-free variety	2.2 grams	½ teaspoon
baking soda	2.7 grams	½ teaspoon
fine sea salt	3 grams	½ teaspoon
low-fat buttermilk	121 grams	½ cup (118 ml)
canola or safflower oil	27 grams	2 tablespoons (30 ml)
dark brown sugar, preferably Muscovado	121 grams	½ cup plus 2 teaspoons (firmly packed)

PREHEAT THE OVEN

Forty-five minutes or longer before baking, set an oven rack at the middle level. Set the oven at 400°F / 200°C.

MISE EN PLACE

Thirty minutes to 1 hour ahead, cut the butter into tablespoon-size pieces. Set on the counter to soften.

Thirty minutes ahead, into a 1 cup / 237 ml glass measure with a spout, weigh or measure the egg. Cover tightly with plastic wrap and set on the counter.

Melt the Chocolate: About 30 minutes ahead, chop the chocolate into coarse pieces. In a small microwavable bowl, heat the chocolate, stirring every 15 seconds with a silicone spatula, until almost completely melted (or heat the chocolate in the top of a double boiler set over hot, not simmering, water—do not let the bottom of the container touch the water—stirring often, until almost completely melted).

Remove the chocolate from the heat source and stir until fully melted. Let cool until it is no longer warm to the touch but is still fluid.

Continues

In a medium bowl, whisk together the flour, cocoa, baking powder, baking soda, and salt. Sift the mixture to remove any lumps from the cocoa and baking soda.

Into a 2 cup / 473 ml glass measure with a spout, weigh or measure the buttermilk.

MAKE THE BATTER

1. In the bowl of a stand mixer fitted with the flat beater, beat the butter, oil, brown sugar, and egg on medium speed for about 5 minutes, until smooth and paler in color. Scrape down the sides of the bowl as needed.

2. Add the cooled melted chocolate and beat on low speed until incorporated.

3. Add one third of the dry ingredients, along with one third of the buttermilk, and beat on low speed just until incorporated. Scrape down the sides of the bowl. Repeat with another third of the ingredients and then the final third. Raise the speed to medium and beat for about 15 seconds, until smooth.

SCOOP THE BATTER

4. Measure the batter into a 1½ inch cookie scoop and level it off for each cookie, or use two spoons, to drop and shape 12 rounded mounds (21 grams each) of batter, evenly spaced, onto a prepared cookie sheet. They should be about 1½ inches wide by ¾ inch high.

BAKE THE WHOOPIES

5. Bake for 6 minutes. Rotate the pan halfway around. Continue baking for 2 to 4 minutes, or just until the cookies spring back when pressed lightly with a fingertip.

6. While the first batch is baking, scoop the remaining batter onto the second cookie sheet. Bake as soon as the first batch is removed from the oven.

COOL THE WHOOPIES

7. Set the cookie sheets on wire racks and let the cookies cool for 5 to 10 minutes, until firm enough to lift from the sheets. Use a thin pancake turner to transfer the cookies to another wire rack. Cool completely.

WHOOPIE FILLING

You will need about 220 grams / 1⅓ cups Milk Chocolate Mousse Ganache (page 401), or other filling of your choice.

SANDWICH THE WHOOPIES

8. Set 12 of the cookies flat side up on a baking sheet. Place a mound of filling (about 1½ gently rounded tablespoons) on top of each one. Set a second cookie flat side down on top. Press down lightly until the filling reaches the edges.

STORE Filled, airtight: cool room temperature, 1 day; refrigerated, 1 week; frozen, 3 months. Unfilled, airtight: room temperature, 3 days; refrigerated, 1 week; frozen, 3 months.

Baking Gem

♥ As the batter is scooped, it will gradually become a little denser, so the weight of each scoop of batter will be a gram or two heavier.

LEMON CRANBERRY SQUARES

Makes: Sixteen 2 inch squares

Inspired by my sweet cousin Ariel Butterfass, who brings a version of these cookies every Thanksgiving, I added a bright, tart layer of cranberries to my favorite lemon butter squares, and now it's hard to imagine making them any other way. For classic lemon squares, see the Variations.

Oven Temperature: 325°F / 160°C for the shortbread base; 300°F / 150°C for the topping	Baking Time: 30 to 40 minutes for the shortbread; 10 minutes for the topping	Special Equipment: One 8 by 2 inch square baking pan, lined with a 16 by 8 inch strip of heavy-duty aluminum foil, extending a few inches past the two opposite edges of the pan

DOUGH

dough for Scottish Shortbread Cookies (page 56); see step 1, below	355 grams	1 recipe
lemon zest, finely grated	3 grams	½ tablespoon (loosely packed)

PREHEAT THE OVEN

Twenty minutes or longer before baking, set an oven rack at the middle level. Set the oven at 325°F / 160°C.

MISE EN PLACE

With dishwashing liquid, wash, rinse, and dry the lemon before zesting it. Set the zest into a medium bowl.

MAKE THE DOUGH

1. After processing the sugars for the dough, add the lemon zest and process for about 30 seconds, or until evenly mixed. Proceed with the recipe through step 5.

PRESS THE DOUGH INTO THE PAN

2. Pinch off about 36 grams / 2 tablespoons of the dough and set aside. Use your fingers to press the rest of the dough evenly into the prepared pan. If the dough feels sticky, set a piece of plastic wrap on top before pressing it into the pan. (I like to roll it first between two sheets of plastic wrap to a rough approximately 7 inch square.) Divide the reserved dough into 4 pieces and shape into balls. Flatten the dough balls and press them into the corners of the pan. Use a fork to prick the dough lightly all over.

BAKE THE SHORTBREAD BASE

3. Bake for 20 minutes. Rotate the pan halfway around. Continue baking for 10 to 20 minutes, until the surface of the dough is pale golden. The edges may begin to brown lightly. Transfer the baking pan to a wire rack.

4. Reduce the oven temperature to 300°F / 150°F.

CRANBERRIES FOR THE FILLING

dried cranberries	100 grams	1 cup
water	118 grams	½ cup (118 ml)

5. With small scissors, cut the cranberries into quarters, or coarsely chop them.

6. In a small skillet or saucepan, heat the water until simmering.

Continues

7. Stir in the cranberries, remove the pan from the heat, cover it, and allow the cranberries to sit for a minimum of 30 minutes to soften.

8. Bring the cranberry mixture to a simmer over medium-low heat and simmer, stirring constantly, for a few minutes, until all the water has evaporated. Remove the cranberries to a pan or plate and allow them to cool until no longer hot.

9. Spoon the cranberries onto the baked shortbread base. Use an offset spatula to spread them as evenly as possible.

LEMON CURD

Lemon Curd (page 403 for Cranberry Squares), still hot	355 grams	1⅓ cups
powdered sugar, for dusting	12 grams	2 tablespoons

10. Pour the hot lemon curd evenly on top of the cranberries to coat them completely. Then use a small offset spatula to smooth the lemon curd as evenly as possible.

BAKE THE LEMON CRANBERRY SQUARES

11. Bake for 10 minutes to set the lemon curd.

COOL THE SQUARES

12. Set the pan on a wire rack and cool completely, Then refrigerate for 30 minutes to ensure that the lemon curd is firm enough to cut.

UNMOLD AND CUT THE SQUARES

13. Run a small metal spatula between the sides of the pan and the pastry on the two sides without the aluminum foil. Lift out the shortbread by grasping the two ends of the foil and set it on a counter. Slide the pastry off the foil onto a cutting mat or board. Use a long sharp knife to cut 16 squares.

14. Shortly before serving, spoon the powdered sugar into a small fine-mesh strainer and dust the cookies with the sugar.

STORE Airtight: room temperature, 3 days; refrigerated, 3 weeks.

Baking Gem

♥ Briefly baking the lemon curd enables the egg yolks to re-bond and makes it possible to cut the curd cleanly.

VARIATIONS

Lemon Butter Squares

Omit the cranberries and use the main Lemon Curd recipe (page 403).

Orange Butter Squares

The most intense orange flavor resides in the peel of an orange, rather than the juice. In a eureka moment one day, I decided to make lemon curd with a substantial amount of grated orange zest. This gives the curd a true orange flavor with the vibrancy of lemon. Alternatively, when Seville oranges are in season, simply replace the lemon juice with an equal weight or volume of freshly squeezed and strained Seville orange juice and use the zest from navel or blood oranges. (Seville orange peel is bitter and is generally best used for making marmalade.)

For the Dough: Substitute 18 grams / 3 tablespoons finely grated orange zest for the lemon zest.

For the Curd: Use the main Lemon Curd recipe; substitute 12 grams / 2 tablespoons loosely packed finely grated orange zest for the lemon zest.

Lime Butter Squares

Omit the cranberries. Use the main Lemon Curd recipe, but replace the lemon juice and zest with equal amounts of lime juice and zest. For a pale green color, add a few drops of green liquid food coloring.

DAVID'S DREAMIER BARS

Makes: Forty-eight 1½ inch square bars

These bar cookies are among the favorites in my book *Rose's Christmas Cookies*. This updated version is creamier because it is made in a smaller, deeper pan. It is enhanced by an optional Caramel Lace Topping.

Oven Temperature:	Baking Time:	Special Equipment:
350°F / 175°C	30 to 40 minutes	One 13 by 9 by 2 inch high baking pan, lined with a 21 by 9 inch strip of heavy-duty aluminum foil, extending a few inches past the short edges of the pan, and lightly coated with nonstick cooking spray

DOUGH *Makes: 1,760 grams*

dark chocolate, 60% to 62% cacao	170 grams (6 ounces)	.
milk chocolate	170 grams (6 ounces)	.
white chocolate containing cocoa butter	170 grams (6 ounces)	.
pecan halves	368 grams	3⅔ cups, *divided*
unsalted butter	170 grams	12 tablespoons (1½ sticks)
cinnamon graham cracker crumbs (see Baking Gems)	220 grams	2 cups (lightly packed)
sweetened flaked coconut (see Baking Gems)	113 grams	1⅓ cups
sweetened condensed milk	400 grams	1¼ cups (296 ml)

PREHEAT THE OVEN

Twenty minutes or longer before baking, set an oven rack in the middle level. Set the oven at 350°F / 175°C.

MISE EN PLACE

Cut all three chocolates into ½ inch pieces and combine them in a medium bowl.

Reserve 48 of the most attractive whole pecans. Coarsely break or chop the remaining pecans.

MAKE THE BARS

1. Melt the butter in the prepared baking pan in the hot oven for 5 to 10 minutes.

2. Spread the butter evenly over the bottom and sides of the pan by tilting the pan or using a pastry brush.

3. Sprinkle the cracker crumbs over the butter, stirring with a silicone spatula to moisten them. With your fingers, press the crumbs firmly and evenly over the bottom and about ¼ inch up the sides of the pan.

4. Strew the coconut evenly over the crumbs.

5. Scatter the broken pecans evenly over the coconut.

6. Scatter the chocolate pieces in an even layer over the pecans.

7. Slowly and evenly pour the condensed milk on top.

8. Arrange the reserved pecan halves, top side up, over the bars in 6 long rows of 8 each.

Continues

BAKE THE BARS

9. Bake for 10 minutes. Remove the pan from the oven and, using an offset spatula, press the nuts down so they adhere to the chocolate.

10. Return the pan to the oven and continue baking for 10 minutes. Rotate the pan halfway around and continue baking for 10 to 20 minutes, or just until the condensed milk bubbles up between the nuts in the center of the pan and is pale golden. Do not overbake, or the nuts and crust will be bitter.

COOL AND UNMOLD THE BARS

11. Set the pan on a wire rack and cool completely.

12. Run a small metal spatula between the pan and the bar on the two sides without the foil, pressing it firmly against the pan. Place a piece of plastic wrap on top of the cookie and then a small folded towel. (The towel should come up to the rim of the pan; this will prevent the cookie from splitting when you invert it.) Invert the cookie onto a large baking sheet and peel off the aluminum foil. Reinvert onto a cutting mat or board.

13. Lace with the caramel topping (at right) if desired.

CUT THE BARS

14. Use a long sharp knife to cut the bar lengthwise into 6 strips (each 1½ inches wide), cutting between the rows of pecans, and then crosswise into 8 strips (each 1½ inches wide).

STORE Airtight: room temperature, 5 days; frozen, 2 months. Once frozen solid, the bars can be stacked and placed in freezer bags.

Baking Gems

♥ To make your own crumbs, you will need 15 to 16 double graham crackers. You can break them into a food processor and process to crumbs, or set them in a gallon-size reclosable freezer bag and crush them with a rolling pin.

♥ Packaged sweetened flaked coconut is moister and gives a better texture to these cookies than fresh coconut.

OPTIONAL CARAMEL LACE TOPPING
Makes: 150 grams / ½ cup / 118 ml

heavy cream	43 grams	3 tablespoons (45 ml)
sugar	100 grams	½ cup
corn syrup	10 grams	½ tablespoon (7.5 ml)
cream of tartar	·	¼ teaspoon
water	30 grams	2 tablespoons (30 ml)
unsalted butter, softened	14 grams	1 tablespoon
pure vanilla extract	·	1 teaspoon (5 ml)

MAKE THE CARAMEL LACE TOPPING

Have ready a 1 cup / 237 ml glass measure lightly coated with nonstick cooking spray.

1. Into a 1 cup / 237 ml microwavable measure with a spout (or in a small saucepan over medium-low heat stirring often) weigh or measure the cream. Heat until hot, and then cover.

2. In a medium heavy saucepan, preferably nonstick (if the pan is not nonstick, lightly coat the sides with nonstick cooking spray), with a silicone spatula, stir together the sugar, corn syrup, cream of tartar, and water until all the sugar is moistened. Heat, stirring constantly, until the sugar has dissolved and the syrup is bubbling.

3. Continue boiling, without stirring, until the syrup caramelizes to deep amber. (An instant-read thermometer should read about 370°F / 188°C, or a few degrees lower, because its temperature will continue to rise.) Just as soon as it reaches the correct temperature, remove it from the heat and pour in the hot cream. The mixture will bubble up furiously. Use a clean silicone spatula to stir the mixture gently, scraping up the thicker part that has settled on the bottom.

4. Return the pan to very low heat and stir gently for 1 minute, or until the mixture is uniform in color and the caramel is fully dissolved.

5. Remove it from the heat and gently stir in the butter until incorporated. The mixture will be a little streaky but will become uniform once cooled and stirred.

6. Pour the caramel into the prepared glass measure and let it cool for 3 minutes. Gently stir in the vanilla extract and let the caramel cool, stirring three or four times, until no longer warm to the touch.

7. Pour the caramel diagonally back and forth over the top of the bars, first in one direction and then the other, to form a crisscross lattice design of caramel webbing.

Baking Gem

♥ The cream of tartar will prevent crystallization of the caramel if storing the cookies for more than 2 days.

CARAMELIZED MAPLE MACADAMIA SQUARES

Makes: Sixteen 2 inch squares

Crisp, crunchy, candied nuts in a tender cookie crust—this is one of my favorite bar cookies. It's the easiest caramel ever because the sugar mixture caramelizes by itself during baking. The cookies are at their best within three days of baking. Because maple and walnut are such a classic combination, I sometimes replace the macadamia nuts with walnuts.

Oven Temperature: 350°F / 175°C (325°F / 160°C if using a Pyrex pan)

Baking Time: 20 to 22 minutes for the crust; 9 to 10 minutes for the filling

Special Equipment: One 8 inch square by 2 inch high baking pan, lined with two crisscrossed 16 by 8 inch strips of heavy-duty aluminum foil, extending a few inches past the edges of the pan, and lightly coated with nonstick cooking spray; Uncooked rice or beans

DOUGH *Makes: 230 grams*

unsalted butter	57 grams	4 tablespoons (½ stick)
1 (to 2) large egg yolk (see page xxvi)	19 grams	1 tablespoon plus ½ teaspoon (17.5 ml)
pure vanilla extract	·	½ teaspoon (2.5 ml)
sugar, preferably superfine	50 grams	¼ cup
bleached all-purpose flour	105 grams	¾ cup (lightly spooned into the cup and leveled off) plus 1½ tablespoons

PREHEAT THE OVEN

Twenty minutes or longer before baking, set an oven rack at the middle level. Set the oven at 350°F / 175°C.

MISE EN PLACE

Thirty minutes to 1 hour ahead, cut the butter into tablespoon-size pieces. Set on the counter to soften.

Thirty minutes ahead, into a 1 cup / 237 ml glass measure with a spout, weigh or measure the egg yolk. Whisk in the vanilla extract. Cover tightly with plastic wrap and set on the counter.

MAKE THE DOUGH

1. In the bowl of a stand mixer fitted with the flat beater, beat the butter and sugar on medium speed for 2 to 3 minutes. until lighter in color and fluffy.

2. Gradually add the egg mixture, beating until incorporated. Scrape down the sides of the bowl.

3. On low speed, gradually add the flour, beating just until incorporated. Scrape down the sides of the bowl.

4. Scrape the dough onto a piece of plastic wrap and use the wrap to press it together into a smooth dough. Flatten it into a rough 5 inch square. Roll it out between two sheets of plastic wrap into an 8½ inch square. (It works best first to roll it to about 9 inches and then to use a ruler to square it off.)

5. Slip the dough onto a cookie sheet and refrigerate for 15 minutes, or until firm but still flexible.

LINE THE PAN

6. Peel off the top sheet of plastic wrap and invert the dough into the prepared pan. Leave the bottom sheet of plastic wrap in place and, with your fingers or a small pastry roller, press the dough evenly over the bottom of the pan and ½ inch up the sides. You can use a small metal spatula to even off any excess on the sides and then use it to press this dough into the corners to fill in any empty spaces. Remove the plastic wrap.

7. Press the tines of a fork lightly against the ½ inch dough border to form a design.

BAKE THE DOUGH

8. Crumple a 12 inch square of parchment so that it conforms to the shape of the pan. Lightly spray the bottom of it with nonstick cooking spray and set it on top of the dough. Add enough rice or beans to fill it about three-quarters full.

9. Bake for 15 minutes. Remove the parchment with the weights and continue baking for 5 to 7 minutes, or until the crust is light golden. Remove from the oven (leave the oven on).

FILLING

macadamia nuts	100 grams	¾ cup
light Muscovado (or dark brown sugar)	120 grams	½ cup plus 1 tablespoon (firmly packed)
unsalted butter	35 grams	2½ tablespoons
heavy cream	21 grams	1½ tablespoons (22.5 ml)
corn syrup	31 grams	1½ tablespoons (22.5 ml)
pure maple syrup, preferably dark amber	10 grams	1 tablespoon (15 ml)

MAKE THE FILLING

1. Use a chef's knife to chop the macadamia nuts very coarsely (I like to cut them into quarters). Spread them evenly over the baked crust.

2. In a small heavy saucepan, preferably nonstick, with a silicone spatula, stir together the brown sugar, butter, heavy cream, corn syrup, and maple syrup. Bring the mixture to a boil over medium heat, stirring constantly. Stop stirring and allow the mixture to boil for 1 minute to dissolve the sugar.

3. Pour the maple syrup mixture evenly over the nuts.

BAKE THE SQUARES

10. Bake for 5 minutes. Rotate the pan halfway around. Continue baking for another 4 to 5 minutes, until the filling bubbles up over the nuts and caramelizes to a deep amber.

COOL AND UNMOLD THE SQUARES

11. Set the pan on a wire rack and cool completely, about 1 hour.

12. Lift out the cookie by grasping the ends of the aluminum foil. Invert it onto a cookie sheet and peel off the foil. Reinvert onto a cutting mat or board.

CUT THE SQUARES

13. Use a long sharp knife to cut sixteen 2 inch squares.

STORE Airtight: room temperature, 3 days (on longer storage, the caramel will start to crystallize).

Baking Gem

♥ If you can find only salted macadamia nuts, set them in a strainer and rinse them under hot tap water. Then recrisp them on a baking sheet in the preheated oven for 5 to 10 minutes.

VARIATION

You can double the recipe and use a 13 by 9 inch pan to make 24 squares about 2¼ inches in size.

PECAN FREEZER SQUARES

Makes: Twenty-five 1½ inch squares

These squares have all the delicious merits of pecan pie and more! They are crunchy and butterscotch-gooey, but less sweet than most pecan pies because they are made with golden syrup and eaten frozen. The cookie crust does not get tough on freezing. These can be made weeks ahead and served straight out of the freezer.

Oven Temperature: 425°F / 220°C for the crust; 350°F / 175°C for the pecan filling

Baking Time: 25 to 35 minutes for the crust; 15 to 20 minutes for the pecan filling

Special Equipment: One 8 inch square by 2 inch high baking pan, lined with two crisscrossed 16 by 8 inch strips of heavy-duty aluminum foil, extending a few inches past the edges of the pan, and lightly coated with nonstick cooking spray; Uncooked rice or beans

SWEET COOKIE CRUST (PÂTE SUCRÉE)

Makes: 315 grams

unsalted butter	85 grams	6 tablespoons (¾ stick)
1 (to 2) large egg yolk (see page xxvi)	19 grams	1 tablespoon plus ½ teaspoon (17.5 ml)
heavy cream	29 grams	2 tablespoons (30 ml)
bleached all-purpose flour	150 grams	1¼ cups (lightly spooned into the cup and leveled off)
fine sea salt	·	⅛ teaspoon
turbinado or granulated sugar	37 grams	3 tablespoons

PREHEAT THE OVEN

Thirty minutes or longer before baking, set two oven racks at the middle and lowest levels of the oven. Set the oven at 425°F / 220°C.

MISE EN PLACE

Cut the butter into ½ inch cubes and refrigerate.

Into a 1 cup / 237 ml glass measure with a spout, weigh or measure the egg yolk. Whisk in the cream. Cover tightly with plastic wrap and refrigerate.

MAKE THE DOUGH
Food Processor Method

1. In a medium bowl, whisk together the flour and salt.

2. In a food processor, process the sugar until fine.

3. Add the cold butter cubes and pulse until the sugar coats the butter.

4. Add the flour mixture and pulse until the butter pieces are no larger than small peas.

5. Add the egg yolk mixture and pulse just until incorporated. The dough will be in crumbly pieces unless pinched.

6. Scrape the dough into a plastic bag and press it from the outside of the bag just until it holds together. Remove the dough from the plastic bag and place it on a very large sheet of plastic wrap. Use the plastic wrap to knead the dough a few times until it becomes one smooth piece. There should be no visible pieces of butter. (Visible

Continues

pieces of butter in the dough will melt and form holes during baking. If there are any visible pieces, use the heel of your hand in a forward motion to smear them into the dough.)

Hand Method

1. In a medium bowl, whisk together the flour, sugar, and salt.

2. With a pastry cutter or two knives, cut in the cold butter until the mixture resembles coarse meal.

3. With a wooden spoon, mix the egg yolk mixture into the flour mixture until the dough comes together and can be formed into a large ball.

4. Scrape the dough onto a piece of plastic wrap and use the wrap to press it together to form a smooth piece.

Both Methods

CHILL THE DOUGH

7. Flatten the dough into a rough 6 inch square. Roll it out between two sheets of plastic wrap into a 9 inch square. Use a bench scraper or ruler to square it off.

8. Slip the dough onto a cookie sheet and refrigerate for 10 to 15 minutes, or until firm but still flexible.

The dough also can be refrigerated, well wrapped, for up to 3 days or frozen for up to 6 months.

LINE THE PAN

9. Peel off the top sheet of plastic wrap and invert the dough into the prepared pan. Leave the bottom sheet of plastic wrap in place and, with your fingers or a small pastry roller, press the dough evenly into the bottom of the pan and 1 inch up the sides. You can use a small metal spatula to even off any excess on the sides and to press the dough into the corners to fill in any empty spaces. Remove the plastic wrap.

BAKE THE CRUST

10. Crumple a 12 inch square of parchment so that it conforms to the size of the pan. Lightly spray the bottom of it with nonstick cooking spray and set it on top of the dough. Add enough rice or beans to fill it about three-quarters full, pushing them up against the sides.

11. Set the pan on the lower oven rack. Bake for 5 minutes, then lower the heat to 375°F / 190°C and bake for 15 to 20 minutes, or until the dough is set. If not set, the dough will stick more to the parchment. Carefully ease away the parchment from the edges. Lift out the parchment with the weights and continue baking for 5 to 10 minutes more, until the crust is pale gold and set but still soft to the touch.

COOL THE CRUST

12. Remove the pan to a wire rack. If any holes have formed in the crust, see Baking Gems.

13. Lower the oven temperature to 350°F / 175°C.

Baking Gems

💜 Always keep the dough covered when allowing it to rest to prevent drying or crusting.

💜 Melted white or dark chocolate is ideal for sealing holes if they form in the baked dough because, unlike egg white, they will not stick to the foil, if the bottom of the pan is heated slightly before unmolding.

💜 The unbaked shaped crust can be refrigerated for 3 days or frozen for 3 months. The baked crust will keep at room temperature in an airtight container for 2 days.

PECAN FILLING

Makes: 370 grams / 1¼ cups / 296 ml

unsalted butter	57 grams	4 tablespoons (½ stick)
4 (to 6) large egg yolks (see page xxvi)	74 grams	¼ cup plus 2 teaspoons (69 ml)
pecan halves	170 grams	1⅔ cups

golden syrup (or corn syrup)	113 grams (109 grams)	⅓ cup (79 ml)
light brown sugar, preferably Muscovado	108 grams	½ cup (firmly packed)
heavy cream	58 grams	¼ cup (59 ml)
fine sea salt	·	a pinch
pure vanilla extract	·	1/16 teaspoon (a pinch)

MISE EN PLACE

Thirty minutes to 1 hour ahead, cut the butter into tablespoon-size pieces. Set on the counter to soften.

Shortly before cooking, into a medium heavy saucepan, preferably nonstick, weigh or measure the egg yolks.

Break or chop the pecans into coarse pieces.

MAKE THE FILLING

Have ready a strainer suspended over a medium bowl near the cooktop.

1. To the egg yolks in the saucepan, add the butter, golden syrup, sugar, cream, and salt and stir with a silicone spatula. Cook over medium-low heat, stirring constantly, without letting the mixture boil, until it is uniform in color and just beginning to thicken slightly, about 7 to 10 minutes. (An instant-read thermometer should read 160°F / 71°C.)

2. Immediately pour the mixture into the strainer, scraping up the thickened mixture that has settled on the bottom of the pan. Press it through the strainer and scrape any mixture clinging to the underside into the bowl. Then scrape the mixture into a 2 cup / 473 ml glass measure with a spout. Stir in the vanilla extract.

ASSEMBLE THE COOKIE

14. Sprinkle the pecans evenly over the baked crust.

15. With the cup's spout just above the pecans, slowly and evenly pour the filling over them. Once all the filling has been added, the pecans will float.

BAKE THE PECAN SQUARES

16. Set the pan on the middle oven rack and bake for 15 to 20 minutes, or until the filling is lightly puffed and golden. The filling will shimmy slightly when the pan is moved. An instant-read thermometer inserted near the center should read 190° to 200°F / 88° to 93°C. Check early to prevent overbaking, which would result in a dry filling.

COOL THE SQUARES

17. Set the pan on a wire rack and cool completely, about 45 minutes.

UNMOLD AND CUT THE SQUARES

18. Run a small metal spatula between the sides of the pan and the aluminum foil. Lift out the pastry by grasping the two opposite ends of the foil and set it on a counter. Run a small offset spatula underneath all four edges of the pastry. Then slip a large pancake turner under the pastry and use it to slide it off the foil onto a cutting mat or board.

19. Use a long sharp knife to cut twenty-five 1½ inch squares.

20. Wrap each pecan bar in plastic wrap and store them in a reclosable freezer bag in the freezer.

STORE Airtight: Frozen, up to 3 months. Eat frozen or allow to sit for 3 minutes to soften slightly.

Baking Gem

♥ Golden syrup and unrefined light brown sugar, such as Muscovado, make a real difference in quality of flavor.

Continues

VARIATION
Chocolate Lattice Topping

Decorate the top of the squares before slicing and allow the chocolate to set completely before wrapping and freezing.

Makes: 53 grams / 2½ tablespoons / 37.5 ml

dark chocolate, 60% to 62% cacao	28 grams (1 ounce)	.
heavy cream, or as needed	29 grams	2 tablespoons (30 grams / 30 ml)

MAKE THE CHOCOLATE LATTICE TOPPING

1. Chop the chocolate into coarse pieces. In a small microwavable bowl, heat the chocolate, stirring every 15 seconds with a silicone spatula, until almost completely melted (or heat the chocolate in the top of a double boiler set over hot, not simmering, water—do not let the bottom of the container touch the water—stirring often, until almost completely melted).

2. Remove the chocolate from the heat and stir until fully melted.

3. Pour the cream on top of the chocolate and stir until smooth. The mixture should drop thickly from the spatula. If it is too thin, allow it to cool for a few minutes. If too thick, add a little more heavy cream (or a little bourbon).

4. Pour the chocolate topping into a small disposable pastry bag, with a very small semicircle cut from the tip. Close the bag securely. Drizzle lines of chocolate diagonally back forth over the top of the pecans, first in one direction and then the other, to form a crisscross lattice design of chocolate webbing.

CHOCOLATE CARAMEL CANDY BARS

Makes: Thirty-two 2 inch by 1½ inch bars

This is a killer cookie. Take one look at it, and you will want to sink your teeth into it. And you won't be disappointed. This deserves the best-quality chocolate and brown sugar and homemade caramel. The crunchy walnuts, gooey caramel, and chocolate rest on a base of crisp, chewy brown sugar–oat cookies.

Oven Temperature: 350°F / 175°C (325°F / 160°C if using a Pyrex pan)	**Baking Time:** 10 minutes for the base; 20 to 22 minutes for the candy cookie	**Special Equipment:** One 13 by 9 by 2 inch high baking pan, lined with a 21 by 9 inch strip of heavy-duty aluminum foil, extending a few inches past the short edges of the pan, crisscrossed with a 17 by 13 inch strip of heavy-duty aluminum foil, extending a few inches past the long edges of the pan, and lightly coated with nonstick cooking spray (see Baking Gems)

TOPPING

walnut halves	100 grams	1 cup
dark chocolate, 60% to 62% cacao	170 grams (6 ounces)	·

MISE EN PLACE

Break or chop the walnuts into coarse pieces.

Chop the chocolate into ½ inch pieces.

BROWN SUGAR–OAT COOKIE BASE

Makes: 555 grams

unsalted butter	170 grams	12 tablespoons (1½ sticks)
bleached all-purpose flour	144 grams	1 cup (lightly spooned into the cup and leveled off) plus 2½ tablespoons
instant oats	83 grams	1 cup
light brown sugar, preferably Muscovado	163 grams	¾ cup (firmly packed)
baking soda	2.7 grams	½ teaspoon
fine sea salt	·	⅛ teaspoon

PREHEAT THE OVEN

Twenty minutes or longer before baking, set an oven rack at the middle level. Set the oven at 350°F / 175°C.

MAKE THE DOUGH

1. In a small saucepan, melt the butter over low heat, stirring occasionally. Set aside in a warm spot.

2. In the bowl of a stand mixer fitted with the flat beater, beat the flour, oats, brown sugar, baking soda, and salt on low speed for about 20 seconds, until evenly mixed.

3. On low speed, beat in the melted butter.

4. Scrape the dough into the prepared pan. With your fingers, spread it into an even layer.

BAKE THE COOKIE BASE

5. Bake for 5 minutes. Rotate the pan halfway around. Continue baking for 5 minutes. Set the pan on a wire rack.

6. Scatter the walnuts evenly on top of the cookie base. Then add chocolate: It works best to use your

Continues

fingers to place the pieces one at a time evenly over the base so that they don't clump together. Sprinkle on any loose pieces.

CARAMEL TOPPING

Makes: 460 grams / 1½ cups / 355 ml

heavy cream	174 grams	¾ cup (177 grams)
sugar	200 grams	1 cup
corn syrup	164 grams	½ cup (118 ml)
cream of tartar	·	⅜ teaspoon
unsalted butter	21 grams	1½ tablespoons
pure vanilla extract	·	1 teaspoon (5 ml)

Have ready a 2 cup / 473 ml glass measure with a spout, lightly coated with nonstick cooking spray, near the cooktop.

MAKE THE CARAMEL TOPPING

1. Into a 1 cup / 237 ml microwavable measure with a spout (or in a small saucepan over medium heat stirring often) weigh or measure the cream. Heat until hot, then cover.

2. In a medium heavy saucepan, preferably nonstick (if the pan is not nonstick, coat the sides lightly with nonstick cooking spray), with a silicone spatula, stir together the sugar, corn syrup, and cream of tartar until most of the sugar is moistened. Heat, stirring constantly, until the sugar is dissolved and the syrup is bubbling.

3. Then continue boiling, without stirring, until the syrup caramelizes to a deep amber. (An instant-read thermometer should read about 370°F / 188°C, or a few degrees lower, because its temperature will continue to rise.) Remove it from the heat as soon as it reaches temperature.

4. Add the butter and then slowly and carefully stir in the hot heavy cream; it will boil up furiously.

5. Return the pan to low heat and continuing boiling, stirring often and adjusting the heat

to keep it at a steady boil, until it reaches 240°F / 116°C.

6. Immediately pour the caramel into the prepared cup and allow it to cool for 10 minutes before stirring in the vanilla extract. Use it at once, or within an hour, so that it is still pourable. (If necessary, it can be reheated in the microwave with 3-seconds bursts, stirring gently, or set in a pan of simmering water.)

DRIZZLE THE CARAMEL TOPPING

7. Drizzle the caramel evenly over the nuts and chocolate. It will coat them completely and smoothly during baking.

BAKE THE CANDY COOKIE

8. Bake for 10 minutes. Rotate the pan halfway around. Continue baking for 10 to 12 minutes, or until the entire surface is bubbling.

COOL THE CANDY COOKIE

9. Set the pan on a wire rack and let the cookie cool completely, about 1 hour.

UNMOLD THE CANDY COOKIE

10. Cover an inverted quarter sheet pan or cookie sheet with plastic wrap. Place the plastic-wrapped sheet over the baking pan. Invert both pans onto the countertop. If necessary, tug the foil overhang to dislodge the cookie. Remove the pan, set a cutting board on top, and reinvert the cookie onto the cutting board. Peel back the foil from the sides of the cookie.

CUT THE CANDY COOKIE INTO BARS

11. Use a long serrated knife to cut the cookie lengthwise into 4 strips (each 2 inches wide), and then crosswise into 8 strips (each 1½ inches wide).

12. Peel away the foil from the bottom of each cookie bar and set the bars on paper towels for a minimum of 15 minutes to absorb any excess butter.

Continues

I like to eat these cookies within 6 hours of baking because the chocolate will still be soft. Once the chocolate hardens, it works well to put the bars on a cookie sheet in a preheated 300°F / 150°C oven for about 1 minute or until the chocolate softens, before serving. But they are also delicious even when the chocolate is firmer.

STORE Airtight, layered between sheets of parchment: room temperature, 3 weeks; frozen, 3 months.

Baking Gems

♥ Lining the pan with foil makes it easier to dislodge any caramel that has stuck from the sides of the pan. The oat cookie base has enough butter so that it will not stick. Alternatively, you can butter just the sides of the pan and run a small metal spatula between the sides of the pan and the caramel and oat cookie base before unmolding. If any of the base of caramel sticks, it is so malleable you'll be able to press it back into place.

♥ Instant oats are softer and more tender than the old-fashioned variety.

♥ Spray the measuring cup before weighing or measuring the corn syrup to make it easier to slide out.

♥ The cream of tartar will prevent crystallization of the caramel if the cookies are stored for more than 2 days.

LINZER SQUARES OR THUMBPRINTS

Makes: Sixteen 2 inch squares or Thirty-four 1¾ inch round cookies

Both of these shapes have their charms. I enjoy the attractive shape and crisper texture of the round thumbprint version of Linzers, but the squares offer a better balance of jam to crust. The squares also tend to stay moister a few days longer. Either way, hazelnuts and raspberry jam are a winning combination.

Oven Temperature:
350°F / 175°C
(300°F / 150°C if using a Pyrex pan for the squares)

Baking Time:
10 to 12 minutes for the hazelnuts; 30 to 35 minutes for the squares, 18 to 20 minutes for the thumbprints

Special Equipment: *For the Squares:* One 8 by 2 inch square baking pan, lined with a 16 by 8 inch strip of heavy-duty aluminum foil, extending a few inches past two opposite edges of the pan; A disposable pastry bag fitted with a coupler and a 5/16 inch round decorating tube
For the Thumbprints: One 17 by 14 inch cookie sheet, no preparation needed or lined with parchment; Optional: A 1¼ inch cookie scoop and a disposable pastry bag with a small semicircle cut from the tip

DOUGH *Makes: 415 grams (before adding the egg white)*

unblanched whole hazelnuts	71 grams	½ cup
unsalted butter	113 grams	8 tablespoons (1 stick)
lemon zest, finely grated	3 grams	½ tablespoon (loosely packed)

1 large egg, separated
  egg yolk
  egg white (reserve for the squares)
	19 grams
	30 grams
		1 tablespoon plus ½ teaspoon (17.5 ml)
		2 tablespoons (30 ml)

pure vanilla extract	·	½ teaspoon (2.5 ml)
bleached all-purpose flour	145 grams	1 cup (lightly spooned into the cup and leveled off) plus 3 tablespoons, *divided*
sugar	67 grams	⅓ cup
baking powder, preferably aluminum-free	2.2 grams	½ teaspoon
fine sea salt	·	⅛ teaspoon
ground cinnamon	·	½ teaspoon
seedless raspberry jam, for topping or filling	206 grams for squares, 156 grams for thumbprints	⅔ cup for squares, ½ cup for thumbprints
powdered sugar (optional), for dusting	12 grams	2 tablespoons

PREHEAT THE OVEN

Twenty minutes or longer before baking, set an oven rack at the middle level. Set the oven at 350°F / 175°C.

MISE EN PLACE

Toast the Hazelnuts: Spread the hazelnuts evenly on a rimmed baking sheet and toast for 10 to 12 minutes, stirring occasionally, until the skins crack and the exposed nuts are golden. Set the baking sheet on a wire rack and cool completely.

Continues

For the Food Processor Method: Thirty minutes ahead or longer, cut the butter into ½ inch cubes. Wrap and refrigerate.

For the Stand Mixer Method: Thirty minutes to 1 hour ahead, cut the butter into 1 tablespoon-size pieces. Set on the counter to soften.

With dishwashing liquid, wash, rinse, and dry the lemon before zesting it. Set the zest into a medium bowl.

MEASURE THE EGG

For the Squares: Thirty minutes ahead, into separate 1 cup / 237 ml glass measures with spouts, weigh or measure the egg yolk and the egg white.

For the Thumbprints: Thirty minutes ahead, into a 1 cup / 237 ml glass measure with a spout, weigh or measure the egg yolk.

For Both: Whisk the vanilla extract and lemon zest into the yolk. Cover the yolk and white tightly with plastic wrap and set on the counter.

In a small bowl, whisk together 121 grams / 1 cup of the flour, the sugar, baking powder, salt, and cinnamon.

Into a small bowl, weigh or measure the jam. With a spoon, stir the jam just until smooth.

MAKE THE DOUGH

Food Processor Method

1. In a food processor, process the nuts with the remaining 24 grams / 3 tablespoons flour until fine but not powder fine.

2. Add the flour mixture and process for a few seconds, until evenly mixed.

3. Pulse in the butter until the mixture is in fine crumbs.

4. Add the egg yolk mixture and pulse just until the crumbs are moistened and will hold together when pinched. Leave the dough in the processor.

Stand Mixer Method

1. Grind the hazelnuts with 24 grams / 3 tablespoons of the flour in a spice mill. (Alternatively use a rotary nut grinder to grind the nuts.)

2. In a medium bowl, whisk together the ground nuts, the remaining flour (all of the flour if using a rotary nut grinder), baking powder, cinnamon, salt, and lemon zest.

3. In the bowl of a stand mixer fitted with the flat beater, beat the butter and sugar on medium speed for 2 to 3 minutes, until lighter in color and fluffy.

4. Gradually add the egg yolk mixture, beating until incorporated.

5. On low speed, gradually beat in the flour mixture just until incorporated, scraping down the sides of the bowl as needed. Leave the dough in the mixer bowl.

FOR THE LINZER SQUARES

6. Remove 200 grams / 1 cup (firmly packed) of the dough and press it evenly over the bottom of the prepared pan.

7. Spread the jam to within ¼ inch of the edges.

8. Add the reserved egg white to the dough remaining in the food processor and pulse it in. Or, if using the mixer, gradually add the egg white, beating on low speed. Scrape into the prepared pastry bag.

9. Pipe the mixture to form a lattice on top of the raspberry jam filling: Begin by piping one line down the center, dividing the square in half. Then pipe 2 more lengthwise lines, dividing the square into quarters. Then pipe 4 more lines, one each between the existing lines, to divide the square into eighths. (There will be 7 lines.)

10. Turn the pan 90 degrees and repeat the process, adding 7 more lines.

11. Pipe a border around the edges of the square. (Any leftover dough can be baked as cookies; see Baking Gems.)

Continues

BAKE THE SQUARES

12. Bake for 20 minutes. Rotate the pan halfway around. Continue baking for 10 to 15 minutes, or until the dough is golden brown. The entire square will puff up a little and, depending on the thickness of the jam used, it may be bubbling.

COOL AND UNMOLD THE SQUARES

13. Set the pan on a wire rack and cool completely.

14. Run a small metal spatula between the pan and the pastry on the two sides without the foil. Lift out the pastry by grasping the two ends of the foil and set it on a counter. Slip a thin pancake turner between the bottom crust and the foil and slide the square off the foil onto a cutting mat or board.

CUT THE SQUARES

15. Use a long sharp knife to cut sixteen 2 inch squares: First cut the square into 4 rows. Then cut each row one at a time into 4 squares, cutting again through the middle of the piped lattice lines.

16. If desired, add a little extra jam to each opening shortly before serving.

FOR THE THUMBPRINTS

6. Empty the dough mixture into a bowl and knead it lightly to form a rough dough.

7. Portion the dough using the cookie scoop (12 grams each), or use two level teaspoons.

8. Roll each piece of dough between the palms of your hands into a 1 inch ball. Set the ball in the cupped palm of your hand and, with your index finger, or the ½ inch diameter handle of a wooden spoon, make an indentation in the middle.

9. Place the dough balls 1 inch apart on the cookie sheet.

10. Using the prepared pastry bag or a ¼ teaspoon measure, fill each indentation with jam. (It will sink down during baking.)

11. Cover the cookies with plastic wrap and refrigerate for a minimum of 30 minutes before baking.

BAKE THE THUMBPRINTS

12. Bake for 10 minutes. Rotate the cookie sheet halfway around. Continue baking for 8 to 10 minutes, or until the cookies are lightly browned.

COOL THE THUMBPRINTS

13. Set the cookie sheet on a wire rack and use a thin pancake turner to transfer the cookies to another wire rack. Cool completely.

OPTIONAL: FOR BOTH THE SQUARES AND THUMBPRINTS

On the day of serving, dust the cookies lightly with powdered sugar. Pipe or spoon a little more raspberry jam into the "windows" or the center to cover the powdered sugar and fill in the indentation. Leave uncovered until serving.

STORE Airtight: room temperature, 1 week; refrigerated, 3 weeks for the squares, 2 weeks for the thumbprints; frozen, 2 months.

Baking Gems

♥ The dark skin of the hazelnuts, which is usually removed to avoid bitterness, contributes a pleasant flavor to this recipe.

♥ When piping the dough for the squares, it helps to cut off the end of each line of dough with a small metal spatula, which you can also use to move the line into place if it is not perfectly straight.

♥ The small amount of leftover dough in the pastry bag can be squeezed out onto plastic wrap and chilled until firm. Then divide it into 3 or 4 pieces and shape into thumbprint cookies. For the best shape, roll the dough balls in a little flour when forming them.

JAMMY PLUM BARS

Makes: Twenty-four 2 inch square bars

My brilliant baker friend Erin Jeanne McDowell created this recipe for the *New York Times* in 2018, and it has since become one of my annual summer traditions. I love the sweet, tangy plum jam filling and super-crunchy streusel crust and topping. The glistening purple plum jam is easy to make and permeates the entire house with its perfume. The streusel couldn't be easier. And the bars are delicious at room temperature or chilled.

Oven Temperature:	Baking Time:	Special Equipment:
350°F / 175°C, 325°F / 160°C (if using a Pyrex pan)	50 to 60 minutes	One 13 by 9 by 2 inch high baking pan, lined with a 21 by 9 inch strip of heavy-duty aluminum foil, extending a few inches past the short edges of the pan, crisscrossed with a 17 by 13 inch strip of heavy-duty aluminum foil, extending a few inches past the long edges of the pan (see Baking Gems)

PLUM JAM FILLING

Makes: about 900 grams / 3 cups / 711 ml

ripe plums (red, black, or purple)	1 kilogram/ 2.2 pounds; 955 grams coarsely chopped	6 cups (coarsely chopped)
sugar	365 grams	1½ cups plus ⅓ cup, *divided*
cornstarch	30 grams	¼ cup (lightly spooned into the cup and leveled off)
pure vanilla extract	.	2 teaspoons (10 ml)

1. In a large (6 quart) pot, stir together the plums and 300 grams / 1½ cups of the sugar. Bring just to a boil over medium-low heat and cook at a slow boil, stirring often with a silicone spatula, until the plums release their juices and become very tender, about 15 minutes. Remove from the heat.

2. Purée the mixture directly in the pot with an immersion blender until fairly smooth, or transfer to a regular blender or a food processor to purée, then return to the pot.

3. Bring the mixture to a boil over medium-low heat and continue cooking, stirring often, until it thickens and reduces to about 2⅔ cups / 629 ml / 800 grams (see Baking Gems). It will pool thickly on the surface when dropped from the spoon. (An instant-read thermometer will read about 218°F / 103°C.)

4. In a small bowl, whisk together the remaining 65 grams / ⅓ cup sugar and the cornstarch. Whisk the mixture into the plum jam.

5. Bring the jam to a simmer over medium-low heat, stirring often. Continue simmering for 1 minute, stirring gently. Remove from the heat and stir in the vanilla extract. Cool completely.

The plum jam can be made up to 1 week ahead and refrigerated.

Continues

DOUGH *Makes: 1,325 grams*

unsalted butter	340 grams	24 tablespoons (3 sticks)
old-fashioned oats	240 grams	3 cups
all-purpose flour, preferably unbleached	320 grams	2⅔ cups (lightly spooned into the cup and leveled off)
whole wheat flour	90 grams	⅔ cup (lightly spooned into the cup and leveled off) plus ½ tablespoon
light brown sugar, preferably Muscovado	330 grams	1½ cups plus 1 teaspoon (firmly packed)
baking powder, preferably an aluminum-free variety	4.5 grams	1 teaspoon
fine sea salt	6 grams	1 teaspoon
ground cinnamon	2.2 grams	1 teaspoon

PREHEAT THE OVEN

Thirty minutes or longer before baking, set an oven rack in the lower third of the oven. Set the oven at 350°F / 175°C.

MAKE THE DOUGH

1. In a medium saucepan, melt the butter over medium-low heat, stirring often. Remove from the heat.

2. In a large bowl, using your fingers, mix the oats, flour, whole wheat flour, brown sugar, baking powder, salt, and cinnamon, pressing out any brown sugar lumps.

3. Using a large silicone spatula, stir the melted butter into the flour mixture until the butter moistens all the dry ingredients and the mixture forms streusel-like crumbs.

4. Press two thirds of the crumbs (875 grams) into an even layer over the bottom of the prepared pan.

5. Spread the cooled plum jam in an even layer over the crust.

6. Sprinkle the remaining crumb mixture evenly over the top of the plum jam.

BAKE THE PLUM BAR

7. Bake for 30 minutes. Rotate the pan halfway around. Continue baking for 20 to 30 minutes, or until the topping is golden brown. (An instant-read thermometer inserted near the center and touching the bottom crust should read about 230°F / 110°C.)

COOL AND UNMOLD THE PLUM BAR

8. Set the pan on a wire rack. Run a small metal spatula between the sides of the bar and the foil, and let the plum bars cool completely.

9. Lift out the plum bar by grasping the two long ends of the foil and set it on a counter. Run an offset spatula under all the edges of the bottom crust. Slip a cookie sheet between the bar and the foil and slide the bar onto a cutting mat or board.

CUT THE PLUM BARS

10. Use a long sharp knife, coated with nonstick cooking spray as needed, to cut the bar lengthwise into 4 strips (each 2 inches wide), and then crosswise into 6 strips (each 2 inches wide).

STORE Airtight: room temperature, 2 days; refrigerated, 5 days; frozen, 1 month.

Baking Gems

❤ The baked jam on the edges of the bar is very sticky, so it is best to release it right after baking, while it is still hot.

❤ If you are using a 4 cup / 1 liter glass measuring cup with a spout to check the weight or volume of the reduced plum jam, instead of then returning it to the pot, you can whisk the cornstarch mixture into it and heat it in the microwave, whisking or stirring every 15 seconds, until it thickens. This will take about 3 to 4 minutes.

BLONDIE'S BLONDIES

Makes: Twenty-four 2 inch square by ¾ inch high blondies

This is the recipe I almost hate to love, because I had always assumed that since blondies by nature are much sweeter than brownies, I wouldn't like them. But one day, during the photo shoot for *Rose's Ice Cream Bliss*, baker Erin Jeanne McDowell (who did the food styling on that book, as well as this one!) shared these s'mores blondies, and I was smitten. I loved the sticky, chewy texture so much I didn't mind the sweetness. Hidden beneath Erin's trademark bandana are golden blond curls, and hence the name I have given the recipe.

Oven Temperature:	Baking Time:	Special Equipment: One 13 by 9 by 2 inch high baking pan,
350°F / 175°C (325°F / 160°C if using a Pyrex pan)	38 to 42 minutes	lined with a 21 by 9 inch strip of heavy-duty aluminum foil, extending a few inches past the short edges of the pan, crisscrossed with a 17 by 13 inch strip of heavy-duty aluminum foil, extending a few inches past the long edges of the pan

DOUGH *Makes: 1,131 grams*

(without the marshmallows and extra chocolate topping)

unsalted butter	227 grams	16 tablespoons (2 sticks)
2 large eggs	100 grams	⅓ cup plus 1 tablespoon (94 ml)
pure vanilla extract	·	1 tablespoon (15 ml)
dark chocolate, 60% to 70% cacao	227 grams (8 ounces)	·
9 double graham crackers (5 by 2¼ inch)	135 grams	about 1 cup crumbs (lightly packed)
all-purpose flour, preferably unbleached	160 grams	1¼ cups (lightly spooned into the cup and leveled off) plus 1 tablespoon
baking powder, preferably an aluminum-free variety	5.6 grams	1¼ teaspoons
fine sea salt	6 grams	1 teaspoon
light Muscovado (or dark brown sugar)	224 grams	1 cup plus ½ tablespoon (firmly packed)
granulated sugar	100 grams	½ cup
mini marshmallows	150 grams	2½ cups

MISE EN PLACE

Thirty minutes to 1 hour ahead, cut the butter into tablespoon-size pieces. Set on the counter to soften.

Thirty minutes ahead, into a 1 cup / 237 ml glass measure with a spout, weigh or measure the eggs. Whisk in the vanilla extract. Cover tightly with plastic wrap and set on the counter.

Chop the chocolate into ½ inch pieces.

PREHEAT THE OVEN

Twenty minutes or longer before baking, set two oven racks in the upper and lower thirds of the oven. Set the oven at 350°F / 175°C.

MAKE THE DOUGH

1. Break the graham crackers into the bowl of a food processor and process to fine crumbs. (Alternatively, place the graham crackers in a reclosable freezer bag and use a rolling pin to crush them into fine crumbs.)

2. Empty the graham crackers into a medium bowl. Add the flour, baking powder, and salt and whisk together to combine evenly.

3. In the bowl of a stand mixer fitted with the flat beater, beat the butter and sugars on low speed until the butter starts to blend in. Increase the speed to medium and beat for 4 to 5 minutes, until much lighter in color and fluffy.

4. Gradually beat in the egg mixture until well combined, scraping the sides of the bowl as needed.

5. On low speed, gradually add the crumb mixture, beating just until incorporated.

6. Add 170 grams / 6 ounces (three quarters) of the chocolate and mix just until incorporated.

7. Scrape the mixture into the prepared pan. With a small offset spatula, spread the soft dough, with a back-and-forth motion, into an even layer. Or use damp hands to even the dough.

BAKE THE BLONDIES

8. Set the pan on the lower oven rack and bake for about 30 minutes, until the outer 1 inch of the edges of the blondies looks wrinkled and they start to come away from the sides of the pan. (An instant-read thermometer inserted near the center should read about 212°F / 100°C.)

9. Remove the pan from the oven and sprinkle the marshmallows evenly over the top.

10. Rotate the pan halfway around, and set it on the top rack of the oven, and bake for 6 to 8 minutes, until the marshmallows have softened and begun to brown lightly.

11. Remove the pan from the oven. Sprinkle the remaining chocolate evenly on top.

12. Return the pan to the top rack of the oven and bake for 2 to 3 minutes, until the chocolate is shiny and the marshmallows are lightly toasted and puffy. If some of the marshmallows puff more than others, for a more even appearance, use a toothpick or skewer to puncture and deflate them.

COOL THE BLONDIES

13. Set the pan on a wire rack and let the blondies cool for 45 minutes.

UNMOLD AND CUT THE BLONDIES

14. Run a small metal spatula between the sides of the bar and the foil. Lift out the blondie by grasping the two long ends of the foil and set it on a cutting mat or board. Let the blondie cool for 10 minutes. Peel back the foil from the sides of the bar.

15. Use a long sharp knife, coated with nonstick cooking spray as needed, to cut the blondies lengthwise into 4 strips (each 2 inches wide), and then crosswise into 6 strips (each 2 inches wide). Use a small offset spatula to lift each blondie onto a serving plate or into a storage container.

*Serve warm or at room temperature.

STORE Airtight: room temperature, 2 days.

CHAPTER 7

MERINGUES
AND CANDIES

TIPS FOR MAKING MERINGUE

People are always asking me what to do with leftover egg whites. I'm pleased to report that some of the most delightful and exquisite cookies, such as the Crown Jewel Macarons (page 357), are the perfect answer to that question. Egg whites freeze wonderfully for many months, and older egg whites produce an even better texture in meringues. It is ideal, in fact, to age egg whites in the refrigerator for 2 to 5 days before using them in meringue recipes. (See page xxvii for how to store leftover yolks.)

The meringues in my cookie collection come in many flavors, textures, and shapes. All have the characteristic crisp outer shell and some are slightly sticky and chewy on the inside.

My basic meringue uses superfine sugar, which dissolves more readily in the egg whites, producing a finer and lighter texture. You can make your own superfine sugar by processing granulated sugar in a food processor.

The acidity of cream of tartar adds stability and gives white meringues a whiter appearance. The ideal amount is ⅛ teaspoon of cream of tartar per 1 egg white (30 grams / 2 tablespoons / 30 ml).

MY BASIC MERINGUE PROPORTIONS

Egg whites: 2 large (60 grams / 1/4 cup / 59 ml)

Cream of tartar: ¼ teaspoon

Sugar: 107 to 112 grams (the larger amount if you are adding cocoa or chocolate)

Optional: ¼ teaspoon extract, such as vanilla or almond

Optional: For cocoa meringues, a few drops of red food color to enhance the appearance

Baking Gems

♥ It is best to make the amount of meringue specified in the recipe; you can double it, but no more than that, because it holds its shape best when piped soon after whipping.

♥ Avoid making meringues in humid weather: 50 percent humidity or under is best.

♥ The bowl and beater must be entirely free of any grease or oil, including egg yolk, or the whites will not whip to a stiff meringue.

♥ Meringues are best shaped with a pastry bag and tube, but you can also use two teaspoons. Piping them makes it possible to shape them in many different designs, such as twigs, little logs, rounds with peaks, rounds with indentations for fillings, and hearts. It can be helpful to draw circles or other shapes on the parchment (then flip it over) as guides for piping. Silicone baking mats also work well, but avoid nonstick cookie sheets, because the meringue tends to slide and not hold its shape when you pipe on them.

♥ To prevent cracking during baking, do not use the convection setting of your oven, and rotate the cookie sheets only after three quarters of the way through baking. Bake until still just a little sticky on the inside, as the meringues will continue to dry after removal from the oven.

SAUCEPANS AND SYRUPS

For making Italian meringue and other sticky syrups, I recommend a nonstick saucepan. But other than for the sugar syrup for Italian meringue, which must not have contact with any oil, if you don't have a nonstick saucepan, it works well to coat a regular saucepan lightly with nonstick cooking spray.

When making a sugar syrup, first gently stir together the sugar and liquid until the sugar is completely moistened. This will prevent sugar crystals from getting on the sides of the pan and subsequently causing crystallization by dropping into the sugar while it is boiling. If any sugar crystals should appear, either use a pastry brush dipped in water to wash them down or cover the pan with a lid for a few seconds, until the steam washes them down.

BASIC MERINGUES

Makes: Thirty-two meringues, or more or fewer depending on size and shape

With these three base recipes, you will be able to make any number and shapes of the white, chocolate, and spangled meringues of your dreams.

Oven Temperature: 200°F / 90°C

Baking Time: 1 hour for logs and buttons, 1 hour plus 20 minutes for taller kisses

Plan Ahead: For the best shape, at least 2 days, up to 5 days ahead, separate the eggs and store the egg whites in a covered container in the refrigerator to age.

Special Equipment: One or two 17 by 14 inch cookie sheets, lined with silicone baking mats or parchment; A disposable pastry bag fitted with a ½ inch star pastry tube for the spangled meringues, a ½ inch diameter star pastry tube for logs, or a ½ inch round pastry tube for buttons plus a ⁵⁄₁₆ inch round decorating tip for the filling

ALABASTER MERINGUE *Makes: 167 grams*

2 large egg whites	60 grams	¼ cup (59 ml)
cream of tartar	·	¼ teaspoon
superfine sugar	50 grams	¼ cup
powdered sugar	57 grams	½ cup (lightly spooned into the cup and leveled off)
vanilla or almond extract (optional)	·	¼ teaspoon (1.25 ml)

CHOCOLATE MERINGUE

Makes: 179 grams (200 grams for the Spangled Meringue)

2 large egg whites	60 grams	¼ cup (59 ml)
cream of tartar	·	¼ teaspoon
powdered sugar	57 grams	½ cup (lightly spooned into the cup and leveled off)
unsweetened alkalized cocoa powder	6 grams	1 tablespoon
superfine sugar	56 grams	¼ cup plus ½ tablespoon, *divided*
vanilla or almond extract (optional)	·	¼ teaspoon (1.25 ml)

For Spangled Meringues, replace the cocoa with 28 grams / 1 ounce fine-quality unsweetened or 99% cacao chocolate. In a food processor, process it together with the powdered sugar until the chocolate is in very fine particles. Cover and refrigerate.

MISE EN PLACE FOR ALL THREE MERINGUES

Thirty minutes to 1 hour ahead, into a 1 cup / 237 ml glass measure with a spout, weigh or measure the egg whites. Whisk in the cream of tartar. Cover tightly with plastic wrap and set on the counter.

MISE EN PLACE FOR CHOCOLATE MERINGUES

In a small bowl, whisk together the powdered sugar and cocoa.

MAKE ANY OF THE MERINGUES

1. In the bowl of a stand mixer fitted with the whisk beater, beat the egg whites and cream of tartar on medium speed until soft peaks form when the beater is raised slowly.

Continues

2. Gradually add ½ tablespoon of the superfine sugar if making chocolate or spangled meringues, then raise the speed to medium-high and continue beating until stiff peaks form when the beater is raised slowly.

3. Scrape down the sides of the bowl. Gradually add the remaining ¼ cup superfine sugar. Raise the speed to high and beat until the meringue is very stiff and glossy.

4. Detach the whisk beater and bowl from the stand and use the beater to fold in the powdered sugar (or powdered sugar–chocolate mixture) by hand until evenly incorporated. Shake the beater against the sides of the bowl as needed to release the meringue from the center of the whisk.

5. If using vanilla or almond extract, whisk it in.

SHAPE THE MERINGUES
6. Spoon about half the meringue into the prepared pastry bag. Pipe a small dot of meringue onto each corner of the cookie sheet(s) to secure the parchment and keep it in place when you pipe the meringue.

7. Pipe the shapes as described below. Refill the pastry bag as needed.

8. Let the meringues dry at room temperature for 30 minutes to 1 hour, or until set, before baking (if touched lightly with your finger, the meringue should barely stick to it).

PREHEAT THE OVEN
Twenty minutes or longer before baking, set an oven rack at the middle level, or set two racks in the upper and lower thirds of the oven if using two cookie sheets. Set the oven at 200°F / 90°C.

BAKE THE MERINGUES
9. Bake for 45 minutes (1 hour for taller meringues such as kisses). Rotate the cookie sheet(s) halfway around and, if baking on two racks, exchange their positions from top to bottom. Continue baking for about another 15 minutes (20 minutes for the

kisses). The meringues should be completely crisp but not beginning to brown or darken. (Test by breaking one of them or digging out a small amount with the tip of a small knife. The interiors should only be slightly sticky.) If necessary, continue baking for about 10 minutes more. To make meringues that are even crisper, turn off the oven and leave the meringues in the oven for an hour.

COOL THE MERINGUES
10. Set the cookie sheet(s) on a wire rack and use a thin pancake turner to transfer the meringues to another wire rack to cool completely. **For logs,** it is best to allow them to cool completely on the cookie sheet before transferring them.

11. Gently transfer the meringues to a covered storage container.

STORE Airtight: room temperature, 1 month.

Baking Gems for the Spangled Meringues

♥ Chilling the chocolate mixture for the spangled meringues will maintain a distinct brown and white contrast in the baked meringues.

♥ When storing, if the cover is not tightly closed, the meringues will stay crisp on the outside but become a little chewy on the inside.

SHAPING INSTRUCTIONS
Meringue Kisses: Use a ½ inch star pastry tube. Pipe 1¾ inch mounds about 1 inch apart. Hold the pastry bag straight up and down with the tip of the pastry tube a little above the surface of the cookie sheet as you pipe each one. Then stop squeezing and lift off to form a small peak.

Button Meringues: Pipe 1 inch mounds about 1 inch apart on the cookie sheets as above. After lifting off the pastry tube, use the edge to cut off the peak. Let the meringues stand for 10 minutes to dry slightly. Then use your index finger, dipped in powdered sugar, or a tiny spoon, to make a depression about ½ inch wide in the center of each mound. After baking and cooling the meringues, fill and / or top with the filling of your choice. For one of my favorite combinations, try the chocolate fudge topping below.

Hearts: Pipe the hearts 1 inch apart. Hold the pastry bag at a 45-degree angle, pointing slightly to the right. Squeeze a teardrop shape, gradually pulling the tube toward you to come to a point. Repeat, starting on the left side.

Little Logs: Hold the pastry bag at a slight angle away from you, with the tube several inches above the sheet. Starting at the top of the sheet, squeeze the meringue with steady pressure, allowing it to drop from the tube, and pipe a log all the way down the sheet. Leave about ½ inch between the lines of meringue. Do not try to make the lines perfectly straight, as a slight squiggle lends to their charm. After baking, let the meringues cool completely on the cookie sheet. Carefully remove them from the sheet and break into 4 inch long pieces.

CHOCOLATE FUDGE FILLING FOR MERINGUE BUTTONS

Makes: 128 grams / about ½ cup

dark chocolate, 60% to 62% cacao	85 grams (3 ounces)	.
unsalted butter	28 grams	2 tablespoons
1 (to 2) large egg yolk (see page xxvi)	19 grams	1 tablespoon plus ½ teaspoon (17.5 ml)
shelled unsalted pistachio nuts	19 grams	2 tablespoons

PREHEAT THE OVEN

Twenty minutes or longer before baking, set an oven rack at the middle level. Set the oven at 325°F / 160°C.

MAKE THE CHOCOLATE FUDGE FILLING

1. Chop the chocolate into coarse pieces. In the top of a double boiler set over hot, not simmering, water—do not let the bottom of the container touch the water—heat the chocolate and butter, stirring often with a silicone spatula, until completely melted.

2. Into a small custard cup, weigh or measure the egg yolk. Whisk into the hot chocolate mixture for about 1 minute. Then remove the top of the double boiler, wipe the bottom of it dry, and scrape the mixture into a small bowl.

3. Let the mixture cool to room temperature, stirring occasionally.

TOAST AND CHOP THE PISTACHIOS

4. Spread the pistachios on a baking sheet and bake in the preheated oven for 5 minutes to help loosen the peels. Empty them onto a towel, wrap them in the towel, and let them sit for 5 minutes to help the skins separate from the nuts. Then rub them in the towel to remove as much skin as possible. Chop the nuts medium coarse and set them in a small bowl.

FILL THE MERINGUE BUTTONS AND TOP WITH PISTACHIOS

5. Up to 3 days before serving, pipe or use a tiny spoon to fill the depressions in the meringue with the fudge filling.

6. Hold each meringue gently between your thumb and first two fingers and invert it into the nuts. The nuts will attach themselves to the fudge. Set them on a serving plate.

STORE Airtight: room temperature, 1 month.

LES MACARONS AU CHOCOLAT DE BERNACHON

Makes: Forty-eight 2½ inch round cookies

These intensely chocolate macarons are extraordinary. I love the contrast of the very crisp outer shells and soft, chewy interiors. The texture of the exterior is less smooth than the more refined Parisian macarons, and they are thinner and flatter. At Chez Bernachon in Lyon, they sell these as single cookies, but I discovered that they rise to a whole new level of deliciousness when sandwiched with a layer of creamy ganache (see Baking Gems).

Oven Temperature: 325°F / 160°C, then 425°F / 220°C	**Baking Time:** 10 to 12 minutes (for each of three batches)	**Plan Ahead:** Make the batter 8 to 10 hours ahead.	**Special Equipment:** Two or three 17 by 14 inch cookie sheets, lined with parchment (taped in place at each corner); A disposable pastry bag fitted with a ½ inch plain round pastry tube, or a teaspoon

BATTER *Makes: 790 grams*

5 large egg whites	150 grams	½ cup plus 2 tablespoons (150 ml)
sugar	400 grams	2 cups
sliced unblanched almonds	200 grams	2 cups
unsweetened alkalized cocoa powder	50 grams	⅔ cup (sifted before measuring)

MISE EN PLACE
Thirty minutes to 1 hour ahead, into a small bowl, weigh or measure the egg whites. Cover tightly with plastic wrap and set on the counter.

MAKE THE BATTER
1. In a food processor, process the sugar for 1 minute. Add the almonds and cocoa and process until the almonds are very finely ground. (Alternatively, grind the almonds with the sugar in a spice mill in batches, or in a rotary nut grinder, and then whisk together with the cocoa and if using a rotary nut grinder, also whisk in the sugar.)

2. Transfer the almond mixture to the bowl of a stand mixer fitted with the flat beater and add the egg whites. Beat on medium speed for about 15 seconds, until smooth.

3. Set a piece of plastic wrap that has been coated with nonstick cooking spray directly onto the surface of the batter to keep a skin from forming and place the bowl in a cool spot or in the refrigerator for 8 to 10 hours.

PREHEAT THE OVEN
Twenty minutes or longer before baking, set an oven rack at the middle level. Set the oven at 325°F / 160°C.

PIPE THE COOKIES
4. Scoop one third to one half the batter into the prepared pastry bag and pipe 1 inch balls of batter about ½ inch high onto the prepared cookie sheets, leaving about 2 inches between them (3 rows of 5 cookies, about 15 to 16 grams each). Use a pastry brush dipped in water to flatten the balls to about 2 inches in diameter. Refill the pastry bag as needed.

BAKE THE COOKIES

5. Remove the tape from the parchment and bake the cookies, one sheet at a time, for 5 minutes. Rotate the cookie sheet halfway around. Raise the oven temperature to 425°F / 220°C and continue baking for 5 to 7 minutes, or until the cookies are set. When pressed gently in the centers, they should still feel a little soft. The outside of the cookies will firm on cooling. Remove the cookie sheet to a wire rack. Turn the oven down to 325°F / 160°C and leave the door open for 3 to 5 minutes to lower the temperature.

COOL THE COOKIES

6. Allow the macarons to cool completely on the cookie sheet. To remove them, lift them off the parchment using your fingers. If they stick at all, first slide a small offset spatula under them.

7. Repeat with the remaining two batches. Any leftover batter can be baked on a small lined cookie sheet at the same time.

STORE Airtight: room temperature, 3 days (if kept longer, they become harder and more chewy); frozen, 3 months.

Baking Gems

♥ The batter needs to rest for at least 8 hours so that the cocoa powder can absorb the liquid and thicken the batter.

♥ It is very helpful to draw 1 inch circles, 3 inches apart from center to center, on the parchment sheets. Invert the parchment so that the marks are facing the cookie sheets, not the cookies.

♥ The two different baking temperatures are what create the special texture of these macarons. Raising the temperature by 100°F / 40°C after the first 5 minutes gives them a blast of hot air to set the outsides. (The oven will not actually reach that high a temperature, so when you turn it down after each next batch, it should get back to the proper temperature by the time the next batch is ready to bake.)

♥ The Bernachons unmolded the macarons by inverting them, still attached to the parchment, and brushing the parchment with water. Then they reinverted the parchment and removed the macarons. But with most of today's parchment, I find this step unnecessary.

♥ If sandwiching the macarons with ganache, you will need about 400 grams / 1½ cups, or 1 tablespoon for each. Make 1¾ times the recipe for Dark Chocolate Ganache Glaze for Woody's Luxury Brownies (page 283).

LES BATONS DE SUCCÈS

Makes: Thirty-four 3 inch bars

These batons of delicately crispy, nutty succès ("souk-SAY"—a meringue made with the addition of ground nuts) are topped with extra nuts and then a chocolate glaze. In France, succès is traditionally prepared as a cake, the meringue piped into large spiral rounds which are then filled with ganache once baked.

Oven Temperature: 350°F / 175°C	**Baking Time:** 10 to 12 minutes (for each of two batches)	**Special Equipment:** Two 17 by 14 inch cookie sheets, lined with parchment; A large disposable pastry bag, fitted with a ½ inch round pastry tube

BATTER *Makes: 390 grams*

5 large egg whites	150 grams	1 cup plus 2 tablespoons (150 ml)
cream of tartar	·	½ plus ⅛ teaspoons
slivered almonds, for topping	50 grams	⅓ cup plus ½ tablespoon
sliced blanched almonds	125 grams	1¼ cups
superfine sugar	125 grams	½ cup plus 2 tablespoons, *divided*
powdered sugar, for dusting	21 grams	3½ tablespoons

PREHEAT THE OVEN

Twenty minutes or longer before baking, set an oven rack at the middle level. Set the oven at 350°F / 175°C.

MISE EN PLACE

Into the bowl of a stand mixer, weigh or measure the egg whites. Add the cream of tartar and cover tightly with plastic wrap.

Chop the slivered almonds into coarse pieces. Place them into a small bowl and set aside for the topping.

MAKE THE BATTER

1. In a food processor, process the sliced almonds and 25 grams / 2 tablespoons of the superfine sugar until the almonds are finely ground. (Alternatively, grind the almonds in a spice mill in batches with a little of the sugar, or use a rotary nut grinder.)

2. Attach the whisk beater to the mixer and beat the egg white mixture until foamy. Gradually increase the speed to medium-high and beat until soft peaks form when the beater is raised slowly. Gradually beat in the remaining 100 grams / ½ cup sugar (all of the sugar if using a rotary nut grinder), then continue beating until very stiff but gently curved peaks form when the beater is raised slowly.

3. Detach the whisk and remove the bowl from the stand. Using the whisk or a large balloon whisk, quickly but gently fold in the ground almond mixture in three parts, deflating the meringue as little as possible.

4. Smear a small dot of meringue onto each corner of each cookie sheet to secure the parchment and keep it in place when you pipe the meringue.

PIPE AND TOP THE BATONS

5. Fill the prepared pastry bag with the batter and pipe 3 inch long bars onto a prepared cookie sheet (3 rows of 6 batons): Hold the bag at a slight angle away from you, with the tube several inches above the sheet. Starting at the top of the sheet, squeeze the meringue with steady pressure, allowing it to drop from the tube. Stop squeezing completely after each bar and lift the tube up and away.

6. Sprinkle the bars with half of the coarsely chopped almonds. Spoon half of the powdered sugar into a small fine-mesh strainer and dust the batons.

BAKE THE BATONS

7. Bake for 5 minutes. Rotate the cookie sheet halfway around. Continue baking for 5 to 7 minutes, or until the batons are lightly browned.

8. While the cookies are baking, repeat with the second batch (piping 16 batons). Set it in the oven after the first batch comes out.

COOL THE BATONS

9. Set the cookie sheet on a wire rack and allow the batons to cool completely.

DARK CHOCOLATE GLAZE

dark chocolate, 60% to 62% cacao	200 grams (7 ounces)	.

MAKE THE DARK CHOCOLATE GLAZE

10. Chop the chocolate into coarse pieces. In a medium microwavable bowl, heat the chocolate, stirring every 15 seconds with a silicone spatula, until almost completely melted (or heat the chocolate in the top of a double boiler set over hot, not simmering, water—do not let the bottom of the container touch the water—stirring often, until almost completely melted).

Remove the chocolate from the heat source and stir until fully melted (see Baking Gems).

GLAZE THE BATONS

11. Gently remove the batons, using the parchment to help peel them off. Shake off any loose powdered sugar, dip each batons in the chocolate glaze, rounded side down, and set flat side down on a counter or cookie sheet. Let stand until the chocolate dulls and sets.

STORE Airtight: room temperature, 5 days; refrigerated, 1 month; frozen, 3 months.

Baking Gems

♥ It is helpful to draw piping guidelines: 3 rows of parallel lines 3 inches apart on the parchment. Be sure to turn the parchment over so that the pen or pencil lines are facing the cookie sheet, not the cookies.

♥ You need to quick-temper the chocolate by removing it from the heat before it is fully melted and then stirring until completely melted and the temperature is no higher than 94°F / 34°C. This will keep the chocolate from "blooming" (forming gray streaks) and will give it a sharp snap when you bite into it.

♥ Keep the chocolate warm and in temper as you work by placing the container on a heating pad wrapped with foil and set to the lowest temperature, or by setting it over a bowl of warm water (no warmer than 120°F / 49°C). Stir often to equalize and maintain the temperature.

DATTELKONFEKT (DATE CONFECTIONS)

Makes: Thirty-two 2 inch round cookies

This treasured family recipe was given to me by Naomi Lewin, former host of WQXR radio. It is an heirloom, brought over from Germany by Naomi's Oma (grandmother). Chopped dates contribute a marvelously moist and chewy interior, and almonds add crunch. They are encased in thin, crisp meringue shells.

Oven Temperature:	Baking Time: 10 to	Special Equipment: Two 17 by 14 inch cookie sheets (lined
350°F / 175°C	15 minutes (for each of two batches)	with parchment if not using the Back-Oblaten); Optional: A disposable pastry bag with a ½ inch semicircle cut from the tip

DATE NUT MERINGUE *Makes: 500 grams*

2 large egg whites	60 grams	¼ cup (59 ml)
sliced almonds, preferably unblanched	167 grams	1⅔ cups
pitted dates (about 24)	167 grams	1⅓ cups
sugar	133 grams	⅔ cup
pure vanilla extract	·	¾ teaspoon (3.75 ml)
50 mm / 2 inch round back-oblaten (optional; see Baking Gem)	·	32 rounds

PREHEAT THE OVEN

Twenty minutes or longer before baking, set an oven rack at the middle level. Set the oven at 350°F / 175°C.

MISE EN PLACE

Thirty minutes to 1 hour ahead, into a 1 cup / 237 ml glass measure with a spout, weigh or measure the egg whites. Cover tightly with plastic wrap and set on the counter.

MAKE THE MERINGUE

1. In a food processor, process the almonds until fine but not beginning to become pasty. Empty them into a medium bowl. (Alternatively, grind the nuts in batches in a spice mill with a little of the sugar, or use a rotary nut grinder.)

2. Add the dates to the processor and pulse until chopped and beginning to clump together. (Alternatively, use a knife that has been lightly coated with nonstick cooking spray to chop the dates.)

3. Return the almonds to the food processor and process them together with the dates just until the dates are evenly dispersed and separate. (Alternatively, mix together the chopped dates and ground almonds in a bowl.)

4. In the bowl of a stand mixer fitted with the whisk beater, beat the egg whites on medium-low speed until soft peaks form when the beater is raised.

5. Raise the speed to medium-high and gradually beat in the sugar (or the remaining sugar if using a spice mill). Continue beating for 5 minutes.

The meringue will be very glossy but will not hold a peak when the beater is raised.

6. Add the vanilla extract and almond and date mixture and beat on low speed just until incorporated.

PIPE OR SPREAD THE MERINGUE

7. Scoop about half of the meringue into the prepared pastry bag, if using. If using the back-oblaten, hold one wafer in your hand and pipe a mound of the batter, about 1 inch high (15 grams), onto it. Leave ⅛ inch of the wafer's edges exposed, as the batter will expand outward. Set it on the cookie sheet. Alternatively, use a small metal spatula to spread the mixture onto the back-oblaten.

8. Smooth the top of the meringue mound with a fingertip, first dipped lightly in water. Pipe or spread 15 more meringue mounds.

(If not using the back-oblaten, pipe 2 inch wide mounds onto the prepared cookie sheets, leaving a minimum of 1 inch between them. If making some with back-oblaten and some without, bake each type on separate cookie sheets, as the back-oblaten cookies take longer to bake.)

BAKE THE COOKIES

9. Bake for 5 minutes. Rotate the cookie sheet halfway around. Continue baking for 5 to 10 minutes, or until the cookies are set and the tops are lightly browned.

COOL THE COOKIES

10. Set the cookie sheet on a wire rack and let the cookies cool completely. Use a thin pancake turner to transfer the cookies to a storage container.

11. Repeat with the second batch.

STORE Airtight: room temperature, 2 weeks; frozen, 2 months.

Baking Gem

♥ Back-oblaten are thin edible wafers made with flour that are used in Germany as the base for various confections to prevent sticking. They are available online. Rectangular sheets of back-oblaten can be cut easily into circles with scissors if you want to make traditional round cookies. Alternatively, you can cut the back-oblaten into 2 by 2 inch squares, mound the batter on them, and then square off the sides with a wet spatula.

MERINGUE MUSHROOMS

Makes: Thirty 1½ inch tall cookies

It always amazes me how meringue mushrooms look so much like the real thing, especially when lightly dusted with cocoa to appear as if they'd just been unearthed from the forest floor. What could be a more perfect adornment for a Bûche de Noël (Christmas cake resembling a log) or garnish for a dessert plate? Perhaps I am especially partial to mushrooms in any form because I come from a family, three generations back, of mycologists!

Oven Temperature: 200°F / 90°C	**Baking Time:** 65 minutes	**Plan Ahead:** At least 2 days, up to 5 days ahead, separate the eggs and store the egg whites in a covered container in the refrigerator to age.	**Special Equipment:** Two 17 by 14 inch cookie sheets, lined with parchment or aluminum foil; A large disposable pastry bag fitted with a ½ inch round pastry tube; A small disposable pastry bag fitted with a ¹⁄₁₆ inch round decorating tip

MERINGUE *Makes: 170 grams*

2 large egg whites	60 grams	¼ cup (59 ml)
cream of tartar	·	¼ teaspoon
superfine sugar	113 grams	½ cup plus 1 tablespoon, *divided*

MISE EN PLACE

Thirty minutes to 1 hour ahead, into the bowl of a stand mixer, weigh or measure the egg whites. Whisk in the cream of tartar. Cover tightly with plastic wrap and set on the counter.

MAKE THE MERINGUE

1. Attach the whisk beater to the mixer stand. Beat the egg white mixture on medium speed until foamy. Gradually raise the speed to medium-high and continue to beat until soft peaks form when the beater is raised. Beat in 1 tablespoon / 13 grams of the sugar and continue beating until stiff peaks form when the beater is raised slowly.

Gradually beat in the remaining sugar and beat until the whites are very stiff and glossy.

2. If using parchment, smear a small dot of meringue on each corner of the cookie sheet to secure the parchment and keep it in place when you pipe the meringue.

3. Fill the prepared pastry bags with meringue, spooning ¼ cup into the bag with the small tip and the rest into the bag with the large tube. Set the smaller bag aside.

4. **To pipe the mushroom caps,** hold the large pastry bag upright slightly above one of the cookie sheets. Squeeze with a steady pressure, gradually raising the tube as the meringue builds up but keeping the tip buried in the meringue, until you have a well-rounded shape about 1½ inches in diameter. Stop squeezing as you bring the tip to the surface. Use the edge of the tip in a clockwise movement to shave off any point that has formed. (Alternatively, use a moistened fingertip to press gently against the point.) Repeat to pipe a total of 30 mushroom caps.

Continues

5. **To pipe the stems,** hold the same pastry bag upright with the tube touching the second cookie sheet. Squeeze firmly, keeping the tip buried in the meringue, until you build a ¾ inch high cone that is wide enough at the base to support a mushroom cap, and then taper it to a point. Repeat to pipe 30 stems.

6. Let the meringue mushroom shapes sit for about 1 hour to dry. A fingertip gently pressed on the meringue should not stick.

PREHEAT THE OVEN
Twenty minutes or longer before baking, set two oven racks in the upper and lower thirds of the oven. Set the oven at 200°F / 90°C.

BAKE THE MERINGUE
7. Bake for 30 minutes. Rotate the cookie sheets halfway around and from top to bottom. Continue baking for 15 minutes, or until the meringue is firm enough to lift from the cookie sheets. Remove the cookie sheets. Leave the oven on.

ATTACH THE STEMS TO THE CAPS
8. To attach the stems to the caps, first use the tip of a small knife to make a small hole, about a ¼ inch deep, in the flat bottom sides of the caps. Then use the pastry bag with the smaller tip to pipe a tiny dab of meringue into each hole. Insert the pointed ends of the stems into the holes.

9. Return the meringue mushrooms, cap side down, to one of the cookie sheets. Set it in the oven for 20 minutes, or until the meringue is completely dry.

COOL THE MERINGUE MUSHROOMS
10. Set the cookie sheet on a wire rack and let the meringue mushrooms cool completely.

STORE Airtight: room temperature, low humidity, indefinitely.

CROWN JEWEL MACARONS

Makes: Twenty 2¼ inch round sandwich cookies

Confession: The only thing I ever really liked about macarons was their exquisite texture: crackly shells with moist, chewy interiors, sandwiching a creamy filling. Flavor-wise, I just found them to be too damn sweet.

But a few years ago, my baker friend Kimberlie pointed me to Thomas Keller's "bull's-eye" technique, which features a ring of buttercream around the edges of the filled macaron and a dot of curd or jam in the center, and the idea of the multiplicity of textures and balance of tart and sweet flavors intrigued me. I adapted the concept using my own favorite lemon curd and mousseline. These macarons are larger than usual in order to accommodate the buttercream and lemon curd. They are labor-intensive, but trust me, I wouldn't offer this recipe if I didn't think it was worth every second involved in making them. The results are not only amazingly delicious, they are empowering.

I like to keep the natural pale almond color of the macaron batter here rather than coloring it, so that when biting into the cookies, you get the happy surprise of the sunny yellow lemon curd centers.

There are three basic components for this recipe: macaron shells, lemon curd, and mousseline buttercream, which also uses some of the curd. Both the macaron shells and the mousseline require making an Italian meringue, in which a hot sugar syrup is added to the egg whites, for the best texture and stability.

Oven Temperature: 300°F / 150°C

Baking Time: 17 to 20 minutes (for each of three batches)

COMPONENTS

Lemon Curd (page 403): You will need about 250 grams / ¾ cup plus 2 tablespoons
Macaron Shells (see page 359)
Lemon Mousseline Buttercream (page 361): You will need about 240 grams / 1¼ cups plus 2 tablespoons

---

Plan Ahead: Make the lemon curd at least 2 days ahead; reserve the egg whites to make the macaron shells. The egg whites need to be refrigerated for at least 2 up to 5 days before making the macarons to age. The filled macarons need to cure in the refrigerator for at least 24 hours to enhance their flavor and soften their texture.

Special Equipment for the Macarons: Three 17 by 14 inch cookie sheets, lined with parchment or silicone baking mats. If using parchment: Trace fourteen 2¼ inch circles on each piece in 4 rows, 1 inch apart, and then flip the parchment over. If using silicone baking mats: Make three parchment templates and then slide them under the baking mats. You'll also need a disposable pastry bag fitted with a ½ inch round pastry tube.

For the Mousseline Buttercream: A disposable pastry bag fitted with a ⅜ inch round pastry tube

For the Lemon Curd: A disposable pastry bag fitted with a ¼ inch round decorating tip, or a small spoon

Continues

MACARON SHELL BATTER *Makes: 800 grams*

5 (to 6) egg whites (see page xxvi)	170 grams	scant ¾ cup (170 ml)
cream of tartar	·	½ teaspoon
almond flour	225 grams	2 cups (spooned into the cup and leveled off)
powdered sugar	225 grams	2 cups (lightly spooned into the cup and leveled off) minus 1 tablespoon
granulated sugar, preferably superfine	225 grams	1 cup plus 2 tablespoons
water	79 grams	⅓ cup (79 ml)

MISE EN PLACE

Thirty minutes to 1 hour ahead, into the bowl of a stand mixer, weigh or measure half the egg whites (85 grams / about ⅓ cup / 85 ml). Add the cream of tartar. Cover tightly and set on the counter.

Set a thick towel, slightly larger than the cookie sheets on the counter.

In a food processor, working in batches, process the almond flour with the powdered sugar until it is very fine. Strain through a medium strainer onto a large piece of parchment. Use a spice mill to process any coarse particles, which would otherwise form lumps in the macarons. Pour the almond flour mixture into a large bowl and whisk to blend it together evenly.

MAKE THE ITALIAN MERINGUE

Have ready a 1 cup / 237 ml glass measure with a spout near the cooktop.

1. In a small heavy saucepan, preferably with a nonstick lining and a spout, stir together the granulated sugar and water until all the sugar is moistened. Heat over medium heat, stirring constantly, until the sugar dissolves and the mixture is bubbling. Stop stirring and reduce the heat to the lowest setting. (If using an electric cooktop, remove the pan from the heat.)

2. Attach the whisk beater to the mixer stand and beat the egg whites and cream of tartar on medium-low speed until foamy. Raise the speed to high and beat until stiff peaks form when the beater is raised slowly.

3. Increase the heat under the sugar syrup and boil the syrup for a few minutes, until an instant-read thermometer reads 248° to 250°F / 121°C. Immediately pour the syrup into the glass measure to stop the cooking.

4. Beat the syrup into the egg whites in a steady stream; don't allow the syrup to fall onto the beater, or it will spin it onto the sides of the bowl. Use a silicone scraper to remove the syrup clinging to the measure and apply it to the beater.

5. Lower the speed to medium and continue beating just until the outside of the bowl feels warm, not hot, about 5 minutes.

COMPLETE THE MACARON BATTER

6. While the meringue is cooling, make a wide well in the almond mixture, leaving a layer of the mixture on the bottom of the bowl. Add the remaining egg whites and, with a silicone spatula, mix into the almond flour mixture until the mixture is a thick paste.

Now comes the most critical part in achieving the best appearance and texture of the macarons. It even has a name: *macaronage*, which refers to the technique for folding the meringue into the almond mixture to mix it evenly and break up large air bubbles.

7. To fold in the meringue, mash the mixture against the side of the bowl and fold it in so that it deflates and drops in thick ribbons from the spatula, a consistency often described as like molten lava.

Continues

PIPE THE MACARON MIXTURE

8. Use two small pieces of tape to attach two opposite corners of the parchment to the sides of the first cookie sheet so it doesn't slide while you pipe the batter. Fill the prepared pastry bag with about one third of the batter. Cover the batter remaining in the bowl with plastic wrap so that it doesn't dry out.

9. Holding the pastry bag straight up and ½ to 1 inch off the surface, pipe the mixture not quite to the edge of the circles on the template, about ½ inch high (18 grams each). Stop squeezing, give the bag a clockwise twist of your wrist, and when batter stops flowing, lift off. The little tails that form in the middle of the circles will disappear into the batter.

10. To eliminate irregular bubbles for a more even interior texture, hold the cookie sheet a few inches above the towel on the counter and rap it against the counter a few times, until no bubbles appear on the surface and the little tails disappear.

11. Let the macarons sit for 30 minutes or longer, until a skin forms and it doesn't feel tacky when you touch it lightly.

12. While the first batch is sitting, pipe the remaining batches. Remove the tape from the parchment.

PREHEAT THE OVEN

Twenty minutes or longer before baking, set an oven rack just below the middle level and set another rack at the lowest level. Set the oven at 300°F / 150°C.

BAKE THE MACARONS

13. Set the first cookie sheet in the oven and bake for 5 minutes. Open and close the oven door quickly to allow steam to escape. Continue baking for another 5 minutes. Again open and close the door quickly. Continue baking for 7 to 10 minutes, or until the edges and tops of the macarons feel firm. They should not begin to

color; if necessary, move them to a lower rack after the first 15 minutes.

COOL THE MACARONS

14. Set the cookie sheet on a wire rack and let the macarons stand until completely cool and firm enough to lift from the sheet with a thin pancake turner (about 10 minutes). The bottoms should feel set but still a little soft. Transfer the macarons to an airtight storage container.

15. Bake and cool the remaining batches.

STORE Airtight: room temperature, 3 days; refrigerated, 5 days; frozen, 2 weeks.

Baking Gems

♥ These larger-than-usual macarons rise most evenly when baked on silicone baking mats.

♥ If you want to make a half recipe of the macarons, it's best to use a small bowl and handheld mixer for the Italian meringue.

♥ The macarons will continue to bake while they cool. If they do not release well from the cookie sheet, return them to the oven for a few minutes and then allow them to cool before trying again. The goal is to have the outsides of the macarons crisp and the insides slightly soft and chewy.

♥ A shout-out to my dear friend Zach Townsend, who wrote a detailed article about macarons for *Food Arts* magazine, in which he compared in detail the differences between macarons made with French meringue and those made with Italian meringue. He explained that French macarons are lighter and chewier than those made with Italian meringue, which are more stable and have a more attractive "foot" and a cakier interior. He also noted that freezing the macarons causes them to break down a little more on thawing, which gives a moister texture.

♥ If the "feet" on the macarons are much wider than the shells, it is because the oven temperature was too high and/or the macaronage was overmixed. This can actually create a very pretty ruffled petticoat effect. While the macarons are still hot, use a small metal spatula to press the feet closer to the sides of the shells.

LEMON MOUSSELINE BUTTERCREAM

Makes: 390 grams / 2¼ cups

unsalted butter, preferably high-fat	227 grams	16 tablespoons (2 sticks)
2½ large egg whites, lightly beaten before measuring	75 grams	¼ cup plus 1 tablespoon (74 ml)
cream of tartar	·	½ teaspoon
sugar, preferably superfine	100 grams	½ cup, *divided*
water	30 grams	2 tablespoons (30 ml)
lemon curd	50 grams	about 3 tablespoons

MISE EN PLACE

Thirty minutes to 1 hour ahead, set the butter on the counter at cool room temperature. The butter needs to be 65° to 68°F / 18° to 20°C.

Thirty minutes to 1 hour ahead, into a medium bowl, weigh or measure the egg whites. Add the cream of tartar. Cover tightly with plastic wrap and set on the counter.

MAKE THE MOUSSELINE

Have ready a 1 cup / 237 ml glass measure with a spout near the cooktop.

1. In the bowl of a stand mixer fitted with the flat beater, beat the butter on medium-high speed until creamy, about 1 minute. Set it aside in a cool place (no warmer than 70°F / 21°C).

2. In a small heavy saucepan, preferably with a nonstick lining and a spout, stir together 75 grams / ¼ cup plus 2 tablespoons of the sugar and the water

until all the sugar is moistened. Heat over medium heat, stirring constantly, until the sugar dissolves and the mixture is bubbling. Stop stirring and reduce the heat to the lowest setting. (If using an electric cooktop, remove the pan from the heat.)

3. With a handheld mixer, beat the egg whites on medium-low speed until foamy. Raise the speed to high and beat until soft peaks form when the beater is raised. Gradually beat in the remaining 2 tablespoons sugar and continue beating until stiff peaks form when the beater is raised slowly.

4. Increase the heat under the sugar syrup and boil the syrup for a few minutes, until an instant-read thermometer reads 248° to 250°F / 121°C. Immediately pour the syrup into the glass measure to stop the cooking.

5. Beat the syrup into the egg whites in a steady stream; don't allow the syrup to fall on the beater, or it will spin it onto the sides of the bowl. Use a silicone scraper to remove the syrup clinging to the measure and apply it to the beater.

6. Lower the speed to medium and continue beating for up to 2 minutes. Refrigerate the meringue for 5 to 10 minutes, until it cools to 70°F / 21°C. Whisk it after the first 5 minutes to test and equalize the temperature.

7. Set the mixer bowl containing the butter in the stand and attach the whisk beater. Beat on medium-high speed for about 3 minutes, or until the butter lightens in color and is no warmer than 70°F / 21°C.

8. Scrape the meringue into the butter and beat on medium speed until smooth and creamy. Then beat for about 2 minutes longer, scraping down the sides of the bowl as necessary. At first the mixture will look slightly curdled. If it starts watering out, check the temperature. It should feel cool and be no lower than 68°F / 20°C, but no higher than 70°F / 21°C.

Continues

If too warm, set it in a bowl of ice water and stir gently to chill it down before continuing to whisk. If it is too cool, suspend the bowl over a pan of simmering water (do not let the bottom of the bowl touch the water) and heat for just a few seconds, stirring vigorously as soon as the mixture just starts to melt slightly at the edges. Then dip the bottom of the bowl in a larger bowl of ice water for a few seconds to cool it. Remove the bowl from the ice water and beat the buttercream by hand until smooth. If the mixture breaks down and will not come together, it can still be rescued; see Baking Gems.

9. Gradually beat in the lemon curd until uniformly incorporated. The mousseline can be stored for 1 day at room temperature, refrigerated for 3 days, or frozen for 2 months.

Baking Gems

♥ If the mousseline separates and will not come back together, squeeze out all the liquid that has separated and pour it into a measuring cup with a spout. Beat the remaining buttercream on high speed until it becomes smooth and creamy. Gradually beat in the liquid. It will be silky smooth but less airy.

♥ If not using the mousseline soon after making it, for the silkiest texture, whisk it lightly by hand before using. If it has been refrigerated or frozen, be sure to let it come to room temperature first.

COMPOSE THE MACARONS

If piping the lemon curd, fill the pastry bag fitted with the ¼ inch decorating tip with the curd.

16. Fill the pastry bag fitted with the ⅜ inch pastry tube with the buttercream. On the flat bottom of half of the macaron shells, pipe a ring (about 12 grams) just inside the edges.

Pipe a ring of buttercream around the edge of the macaron.

Fill the center with lemon curd.

Sandwich with the top cookie.

17. Pipe or spoon the lemon curd into the center (about 10 grams each).

18. Set the flat side of the remaining macaron shells on top of the filling and press down gently, twisting them slightly clockwise, until the buttercream filling comes just to the edges.

19. Refrigerate or freeze the macarons until firm, then wrap each one in plastic wrap. Store them in airtight containers or reclosable freezer bags. Allow them to "cure" for a minimum of 24 hours, during which time the moisture from the filling will soften the shells slightly and the flavors will meld together. Let them come to room temperature, still wrapped with plastic wrap, before serving, a minimum of 1 hour if frozen, 30 minutes if refrigerated.

Note: If you just can't bear to wait 24 hours to taste the first macaron, here's my speed curing method: Wrap a macaron in plastic wrap and freeze it for a least 2 hours. Bring it to room temperature for about 1 hour. It won't have the full flavor, but the texture will be great.

STORE Airtight: room temperature, 1 day; refrigerated, 3 days; frozen, 1 month.

Baking Gem

♥ To gild the lily with an enhanced lemon flavor, spread a thin film of Nielsen-Massey lemon paste on the flat surface of the top meringue shells before setting them on top of the filling.

SWISS SCHOGGI S

Makes: Eighteen 4 inch long cookies

In Switzerland, this chocolate Italian meringue is often referred to as *neve nero,* which means black snow in Italian. Italian meringue is more stable than other meringues, so it keeps its shape longer when you pipe it. Crisp on the outside, these are deliciously soft and chewy within. I love eating them with a little cup of unsweetened espresso, but, most of all, I love them crumbled over caramel, dulce de leche, or coffee ice cream.

Oven Temperature: 350°F / 175°C, then 200°F / 90°C	**Baking Time:** 10 minutes, then 18 to 20 minutes	**Plan Ahead:** For the best shape, at least 2 days, up to 5 days, ahead, separate the eggs and store the egg whites in a covered container in the refrigerator to age.	**Special Equipment:** Two 17 by 14 inch cookie sheets, nonstick or lined with parchment or silicone baking mats; A large disposable pastry bag fitted with a ¾ inch diameter star pastry tube

CHOCOLATE ITALIAN MERINGUE

Makes: 460 grams

4 large egg whites	120 grams	½ cup (118 ml)
cream of tartar	·	½ teaspoon
fine-quality unsweetened or 99% cacao chocolate	57 grams (2 ounces)	·
instant espresso powder	2.5 grams	2 teaspoons
boiling water	·	½ teaspoon (2.5 ml)
red liquid food coloring (optional)	·	4 drops
sugar, preferably superfine	285 grams	1¼ cups plus 3 tablespoons, *divided*
water	79 grams	⅓ cup (79 ml)

MISE EN PLACE

Thirty minutes to 1 hour ahead, into the bowl of a stand mixer, weigh or measure the egg whites. Add the cream of tartar. Cover tightly with plastic wrap and set on the counter.

Melt the Chocolate: Chop the chocolate into coarse pieces. In a medium microwavable bowl, heat the chocolate, stirring every 15 seconds with a silicone spatula, until completely melted (or melt the chocolate in the top of a double boiler set over hot, not simmering, water—do not let the bottom of the container touch the water—stirring often). Remove it from the heat source and set it aside in a warm place (100° to 120°F / 38° to 49°C).

Have ready a 1 cup / 237 ml glass measure with a spout near the cooktop.

MAKE THE MERINGUE

1. In a custard cup or small bowl, stir together the espresso powder and the boiling water. Then stir in the red food color, if using. Cover and set aside near the mixer.

2. In a small heavy saucepan, preferably with a nonstick lining and a spout, stir together 250 grams / 1¼ cups of the sugar and the water until the sugar is completely moistened. Heat over medium heat, stirring constantly, until the sugar dissolves and the syrup is bubbling. Stop stirring and turn down the heat to the lowest setting. (If

Continues

using an electric cooktop, remove the pan from the heat.)

3. Attach the whisk beater to the mixer and beat the egg whites and cream of tartar on medium-high speed until soft peaks form when the beater is raised.

4. Gradually beat in the remaining 35 grams / 3 tablespoons sugar until stiff peaks form when the beater is raised slowly.

5. Increase the heat under the saucepan and boil the syrup until an instant-read thermometer reads 248° to 250°F / 121°C. Immediately pour the syrup into the glass measure to stop the cooking.

6. With the mixer off, pour a small amount of syrup over the whites. Immediately beat at high speed for 5 seconds. Stop the mixer and add a larger amount of syrup. Beat at high speed for 5 seconds. Continue with the remaining syrup. For the last addition, use a silicone scraper to remove the syrup clinging to the measure and apply it to the beater, then beat for 1 minute.

7. Detach the whisk beater and mixer bowl from the stand. Scrape the espresso mixture into the meringue and use the whisk beater to stir it in slightly. Immediately pour in the warm melted chocolate. Continuing with the whisk beater by hand, stir and gently fold in the chocolate just until incorporated. (If overmixed, the meringue will be too soft and will not hold the attractive ridges.) With a silicone spatula, reach to the bottom of the bowl.

8. Scrape the mixture at once into the prepared pastry bag and pipe the meringue while it is still hot. Pipe a small dot of meringue on each corner of the cookie sheet to secure the parchment and keep it in place when you pipe the meringue.

SHAPE THE MERINGUES

9. Pipe large, high, tight 3½ inch long S shapes onto the cookie sheets: Let the meringue fall from the bag and avoid flattening it by having the tip of the decorating tube too low. Leave a minimum of 1½ inches between the meringues (9 to a cookie sheet).

10. Let the meringues dry at room temperature for 2 hours before baking, or until set (when a meringue is touched lightly with your finger, it doesn't stick to it).

PREHEAT THE OVEN

Twenty minutes or longer before baking, set two oven racks in the upper and lower thirds of the oven. Set the oven at 350°F/175°C.

BAKE THE MERINGUES

11. Bake for 10 minutes. Lower the heat to 200°F / 90°C and bake, without opening the oven door, for 18 minutes, or until the meringues can be removed easily from the cookie sheet using a thin pancake turner.

12. If further baking is needed, rotate the cookie sheets halfway around, exchange their positions from top to bottom, and bake for about another 2 minutes. The meringues should still be very moist inside, because they will continue to dry on cooling. The undersides can have a tiny amount of give, but they will firm up within minutes as they cool.

COOL THE MERINGUES

13. Set the cookie sheets on wire racks and use a thin pancake turner to transfer the meringues to another wire rack to cool completely.

14. Gently transfer the meringues to a covered storage container.

STORE Airtight: room temperature, 3 to 5 days.

Baking Gems

♥ The few drops of red food color produce a richer chocolate color.

♥ The sugar syrup needs to reach 248°F / 120°C, but for the ideal stability of the meringue, it should not exceed 250°F / 121°C.

DACQUOISE MERINGUE PUFFS

Makes: Thirty 1½ inch round meringue puffs

Dacquoise is a meringue with either hazelnuts or a combination of hazelnuts and almonds mixed in. These charming little puffs feature both plain meringue shells and a dacquoise filling, so they pack a variety of textures and flavors—from crisp, sweet meringue to crunchy, nutty, and slightly sticky filling.

Oven Temperature: 350°F / 175°C for the hazelnuts; 200°F / 90°C for the puffs	**Baking Time:** About 10 minutes for the hazelnuts; 1 hour for the puffs	**Plan Ahead:** At least 2 days and up to 5 days ahead, separate the eggs and store the egg whites in a covered container in the refrigerator to age.	**Special Equipment:** One 17 by 14 inch cookie sheet, nonstick or lined with parchment; A disposable pastry bag fitted with a ½ inch pastry tube (for the meringue shells); A disposable pastry bag fitted with 5/16 inch round decorating tip

HAZELNUTS

water	237 grams	1 cup (237 ml)
baking soda	22 grams	4 teaspoons
whole unblanched hazelnuts	47 grams	⅓ cup
sugar	·	1 teaspoon

PREHEAT THE OVEN
Twenty minutes or longer before baking, set an oven rack at the middle level. Set the oven at 350°F / 175°C.

REMOVE THE HAZELNUT SKINS
Have ready a colander placed in the sink, and a large bowl filled half full with cold water.

1. In a medium saucepan, bring the water to a boil. Remove it from the heat and stir in the baking soda. The water will bubble vigorously.

2. Add the hazelnuts and return the pan to the heat. Boil the nuts for 3 minutes. Test a nut by running it under cold water. The skin should slip off easily. If not, boil for a couple of minutes longer.

3. Pour the nuts into the colander and rinse them under cold running water. Place the nuts in the bowl of cold water. Use both hands to slide off the skins under water, scraping lightly in places if necessary. As each nut is peeled, set it on a clean towel to dry. Then roll and rub the nuts around to dry them.

TOAST THE HAZELNUTS
4. Spread the hazelnuts on a rimmed baking sheet and bake for about 10 minutes, or until their oils rise to the surface and they become slightly shiny and turn a deep golden brown. Shake the baking sheet two or three times to ensure even toasting. Set the sheet pan on a wire rack and cool completely.

5. Lower the oven temperature to 200°F / 90°C.

6. Using a food processor fitted with the grater or shredder disc, grate the nuts.

7. Switch to the metal blade and process the nuts with the 1 teaspoon sugar until very fine. (Alternatively, use a rotary nut grinder to grind the nuts.)

Continues

8. Scrape the hazelnut mixture into a medium bowl (add the 1 teaspoon sugar if you used a rotary nut grinder for the nuts).

MERINGUE *Makes: 160 grams*

2 large egg whites	60 grams	¼ cup (59 ml)
cream of tartar	·	¼ teaspoon
superfine sugar	100 grams	½ cup, *divided*
pure almond extract, for the dacquoise filling	·	¼ teaspoon (1.25 ml)
cornstarch	8 grams	1 tablespoon

MISE EN PLACE
Thirty minutes to 1 hour ahead, into the bowl of a stand mixer, weigh or measure the egg whites. Add the cream of tartar. Cover tightly with plastic wrap and set on the counter.

MAKE THE MERINGUES
1. Attach the whisk beater to the mixer and beat the egg whites and cream of tartar on medium speed until soft peaks form when the beater is raised slowly.

2. Gradually add ½ tablespoon of the sugar. Raise the speed to medium-high and continue beating until thick and glossy and droopy peaks form when the beater is raised slowly.

3. Scrape down the sides of the bowl. Gradually add the remaining sugar. Raise the speed to high and beat until the meringue is very stiff and glossy.

MAKE THE DACQUOISE FILLING
4. Scoop out 54 grams / ⅔ cup of the meringue and gently fold it into the nut mixture. Fold in the almond extract. Spoon the mixture into the pastry bag fitted with the ⁵⁄₁₆ inch decorating tip.

PIPE THE MERINGUE SHELLS
5. Spoon the rest of the meringue into the pastry bag fitted with the ½ inch tube.

6. Pipe a small dot of meringue on each corner of the cookie sheet to secure the parchment and keep it in place when you pipe the meringue.

7. Pipe 1 inch wide mounds of meringue (about 3 grams each) about 1 inch apart onto the cookie sheet. After lifting off the pastry tube, use the edge to cut off the peak. Let them stand for 20 minutes to dry slightly.

FILL THE MERINGUE SHELLS
In a custard cup or small bowl, place a spoonful of cornstarch.

8. Working with one row at a time, use your index finger, dipped in cornstarch, to dab a shallow depression in the center of each mound.

9. Insert the tip of the decorating tube almost to bottom of each meringue shell and pipe enough dacquoise filling into each depression to fill it to the top (about 3 grams each). The openings will enlarge to about ¾ inch as you fill them and the meringue shells will expand to about 1¼ inches in diameter.

10. After finishing each row, moisten your index finger with water and press the top of the dacquoise filling so that it is level with the meringue shell.

11. If there is any remaining dacquoise filling, pipe it into 1 inch mounds and bake it on the same cookie sheet along with the meringue puffs.

BAKE THE PUFFS
12. Bake 45 minutes. Rotate the cookie sheet halfway around. Continue baking for another 15 minutes to dry the meringue. The dacquoise centers should still be a little moist and sticky.

COOL THE PUFFS
13. Set the cookie sheet on a wire rack and let the puffs cool completely. Use a thin pancake turner to transfer the puffs to a covered storage container.

STORE Airtight: room temperature, 1 month.

MERINGUE BIRCH TWIGS

Makes: Forty 11½ inch long twigs

These delicate piped meringues, with a subtle raspberry flavoring enhancing the chocolate stripes, are lovely for garnishing desserts or to eat on their own with espresso. Set in a crystal vase or tall glass, they make a spectacular presentation.

   I was inspired to make these to decorate my dear friend Nathan Fong's wedding cake. His bridegroom, Michel Chicoine, designed the theme of the winter wedding to feature birch trees. So I surprised them by using meringue birch twigs to surround the chocolate cake layers. Nathan tragically passed away in 2020.

Oven Temperature:	Baking Time:	Plan Ahead:	Special Equipment:
225°F / 105°C	1 hour plus 20 minutes, then 1 or 2 hours in the turned-off oven	At least 2 days, up to 5 days, ahead, separate the eggs and store the egg whites in a covered container in the refrigerator to age.	Two 17 by 14 inch cookie sheets, lined with silicone baking mats or parchment; A large disposable pastry bag fitted with a ¼ inch round decorating tip; Optional: A small artist's brush; A small disposable pastry bag (for the chocolate drizzle)

MERINGUE *Makes: 190 grams*

3 large egg whites	90 grams	¼ cup plus 2 tablespoons (89 ml)
cream of tartar	.	⅜ teaspoon
superfine sugar	100 grams	½ cup
pure vanilla extract	.	¼ teaspoon (1.25 ml)
fine-quality raspberry flavoring, or another flavoring of your choice (see Baking Gems)	.	⅛ teaspoon

PREHEAT THE OVEN

Twenty minutes or longer before baking, set two oven racks in the upper and lower thirds of the oven. Set the oven at 225°F / 105°C.

MISE EN PLACE

Thirty minutes to 1 hour ahead, into the bowl of a stand mixer, weigh or measure the egg whites. Add the cream of tartar and cover tightly with plastic wrap and set on the counter.

MAKE THE MERINGUE

1. Attach the whisk beater to the mixer and beat the egg whites and cream of tartar on medium-low speed until foamy. Gradually raise the speed to medium-high and beat until soft peaks form when the beater is raised.

2. Beat in the sugar, 1 tablespoon at a time, and continue beating until stiff peaks form when the beater is raised slowly. Scrape down the sides of the bowl.

3. Add the vanilla and flavoring and beat for 30 seconds. Scrape down the sides of the bowl. Continue beating for 1 more minute. The meringue should be stiff and glossy.

PIPE THE MERINGUE TWIGS

4. Fill the prepared pastry bag with the meringue. If using parchment, pipe a small dot of meringue on each corner of each cookie sheet to secure the parchment and keep it from lifting when you pipe the twigs.

5. Pipe 11½ inch long twigs (the width of the pans) in rows about ⅜ inch apart on the sheets (20 per sheet, piped widthwise). Use a damp artist's brush or moistened fingertip to tamp down the peak that forms when you lift the tip away.

BAKE THE MERINGUE TWIGS

6. Bake for 1 hour and 20 minutes, without opening the oven door. Turn off the oven and let the meringue dry for 2 hours (1 hour if the oven has a pilot light).

COOL THE MERINGUE TWIGS

7. Set the cookie sheets on wire racks or on a heat-resistant surface. Cool completely.

DARK CHOCOLATE DRIZZLE GLAZE

dark chocolate, 60% to 70% cacao	85 grams (3 ounces)	.

DRIZZLE THE MERINGUE TWIGS WITH MELTED CHOCOLATE

8. Chop the chocolate coarsely. In a small microwavable bowl, heat the chocolate, stirring every 15 seconds with a silicone spatula, until almost completely melted (or heat the chocolate in the top of a double boiler set over hot, not simmering, water—do not let the bottom of the container touch the water—stirring often, until almost completely melted).

Remove the chocolate from the heat source and stir until fully melted (see Baking Gems).

9. Pour the chocolate into the small pastry bag. Cut a very small semicircle into the tip of the bag.

10. Drizzle the melted chocolate back and forth over the rows of meringue twigs to stripe the twigs so they resemble birch trunks. Let the chocolate set before removing the twigs from the sheets. Then carefully loosen the meringue twigs with a small offset spatula.

STORE Airtight: room temperature, low humidity, 3 months.

Baking Gems

♥ Intense and pure chef's flavorings are available from Mandy Aftel of Aftelier Perfumes.

♥ These meringues are very delicate because they use slightly less than half the amount of sugar as the sturdier basic meringues.

♥ You need to quick-temper the chocolate by removing it from the heat before it is fully melted and then stirring until it is completely melted and the temperature is no higher than 94°F / 34°C. This will keep the chocolate from "blooming" (forming gray streaks) and will give it a sharp snap when you bite into it.

♥ If you would like to use these to decorate a cake, as I did, paint the underside of each twig with melted white chocolate to prevent the meringues from softening from the moisture in the frosting. Avoid making or serving them on humid days.

PECAN PRALINE MERINGUE ICE CREAM SANDWICH COOKIES

Makes: Twenty 2½ inch round sandwich cookies

This is my top favorite cookie for sandwiching ice cream, but it is also perfectly delicious on its own. The brown sugar pecan meringues are airy, slightly chewy, crunchy, and flavorful. They pair well with dulce de leche ice cream; coffee ice cream would also be a great choice.

Oven Temperature: 350°F / 175°C	**Baking Time:** 5 minutes for the pecans; 10 to 15 minutes for the cookies (for each of two batches)

Special Equipment: Two to four 17 by 14 inch cookie sheets, lined with parchment; Two tablespoons; A 2 inch ice cream scoop or a ¼ cup measure

PECAN PRALINE MERINGUE COOKIES

Makes: 700 grams

4 large egg whites	120 grams	½ cup (118 ml)
light brown Muscovado sugar or dark brown sugar	300 grams	1¼ cups plus 2 tablespoons (firmly packed)
pecan halves	300 grams	3 cups, *divided*

PREHEAT THE OVEN

Twenty minutes or longer before baking, set two oven racks in the upper and lower thirds of the oven. Set the oven at 350°F / 175°C.

MISE EN PLACE

Thirty minutes to 1 hour ahead, into the bowl of a stand mixer, weigh or measure the egg whites. Whisk in the brown sugar. Cover tightly with plastic wrap.

Toast and Prepare the Pecans: Spread the pecans evenly on a baking sheet, set the pan on the upper rack, and bake for about 5 minutes, just until they start to smell fragrant but are not beginning to brown. Stir once or twice to ensure even toasting and prevent overbrowning. Cool completely.

Divide the pecans into two equal groups. Leave one group whole and chop the other group into medium-fine pieces.

MAKE THE PECAN PRALINE MERINGUE

1. Attach the whisk beater and beat the egg white mixture on medium speed until well mixed, about 1 minute. Scrape down the sides of the bowl. Raise the speed to medium-high and beat for about 5 minutes, or until very thick and lighter in color.

2. Remove the bowl from the mixer stand. Add all of the pecans and, using a silicone spatula, fold them into the meringue.

SHAPE THE MERINGUES

3. Use the two tablespoons to spoon 10 dollops each of the pecan meringue (about 17 grams each) onto two prepared cookie sheets a minimum of 1½ inches apart. Using a small offset spatula, shape the dollops into ½ inch high by 2¼ inch wide discs. They will spread to about 2½ inches but will not widen during baking. Stir the mixture from time to time as you work to ensure that each spoonful includes some of the nuts.

BAKE THE MERINGUES

4. Bake for 10 to 15 minutes. The meringues will crack slightly in an attractive design. Check for doneness by inserting a metal cake tester into one of the cracks: It should come out sticky and the cookie should give slightly to pressure. (An instant-read thermometer should read about 190°F / 88°C.) If longer baking is required, rotate the cookie sheets halfway around, reverse their positions from top to bottom, and continue baking for a few more minutes.

5. While the first batch of meringues is baking, shape the second batch of meringues. If you only have two cookie sheets, spoon the second batch of meringue onto two sheets of parchment and then slide them onto the cooled cookie sheets to bake.

COOL THE MERINGUES

6. Set the cookie sheets on wire racks and let the cookies cool completely on the sheets. They will firm on sitting and become easy to lift off the parchment using a thin pancake turner.

7. Bake and cool the second batch.

The cookies can be stored in an airtight container for 2 months at room temperature.

ICE CREAM FILLING

ice cream of your choice, softened (see Baking Gems)	.	about 1½ quarts

Set sheet pans or cookie sheets in the freezer to chill.

Assemble only half of the ice cream sandwiches at a time to keep the ice cream from melting.

SANDWICH THE COOKIES WITH ICE CREAM

8. Set 10 of the cookies, bottom side up, on one of the chilled sheet pans. Set a scoop of ice cream, about ¼ cup, on top of each cookie. Place a second cookie, bottom side down, on top.

9. When the ice cream is soft enough to press down easily, evenly press the top of each cookie until the ice cream comes almost to the edges. The ice cream should be about ½ inch thick.

10. Cover the sandwiches with a sheet of plastic wrap and set them in the freezer until firm. Then wrap each sandwich separately in plastic wrap and store them in an airtight container in the freezer.

11. Repeat with the remaining cookies.

STORE Airtight: frozen, 3 days.

Baking Gems

♥ Refrigerate the ice cream for 20 minutes before sandwiching the cookies to soften it slightly.

♥ You can make these as "open-faced" sandwich cookies by making a half batch of the cookies and just topping them with ice cream.

VARIATION

Fudgy Pecan Praline Meringue Ice Cream Sandwich Cookies

The addition of unsweetened chocolate creates meringues with a fudgy interior and a crisp crust. The chocolate, together with the molasses in the brown sugar, helps to temper the sweetness of the meringues.

In Step 2: Fold in 56 grams / 2 ounces / about ⅓ cup (loosely packed) grated fine-quality unsweetened or 99% cacao chocolate before folding in the pecans.

In Step 3: Each dollop should weigh about 20 grams.

PECAN PRALINE CHOCOLATE SCHEHERAZADES

Makes: Sixteen 2 inch round pralines or Thirty-two 1 inch praline balls or 1½ inch praline batons

These pralines are caramel at its finest moment! Smooth, chewy, and creamy, they are delicious even when frozen. Dipped in melted chocolate, they have all the elements of chocolate pecan turtles grown up.

This confection deserves the best ingredients: golden syrup, Muscovado sugar, crème fraîche, bourbon vanilla, fleur de sel, high-quality dark chocolate, and lightly toasted pecans. The golden syrup and crème fraîche add a lilting flavor and slight tang to balance the delicious butterscotchy sweetness.

I named this favorite confection after my favorite childhood story. Scheherazade was the beautiful and clever woman who saved her life by intriguing her murderous husband with a thousand and one unfinished stories, so delicious that he kept her alive each night in anticipation of the next. (This may well be what inspired me to become a storyteller.) These confections, like Scheherazade's stories, are so delicious one can never have enough.

Oven Temperature: 325°F / 160°C | **Baking Time:** 5 minutes for the pecans | **Special Equipment:** A medium heavy saucepan, preferably nonstick (minimum 1 quart / 1 liter)

PECAN PRALINE MIXTURE *Makes: 360 grams*

unsalted butter	21 grams	1½ tablespoons
pecan halves	50 grams	½ cup
crème fraîche (or heavy cream)	87 grams	¼ cup plus 2 tablespoons (89 ml)
golden syrup (or corn syrup)	127 grams (123 grams)	¼ cup plus 2 tablespoons (89 ml)
light brown Muscovado sugar or dark brown sugar	72 grams	⅓ cup (firmly packed)
granulated sugar	33 grams	2 tablespoons plus 2 teaspoons
fine sea salt	·	¼ teaspoon
cream of tartar (optional)	·	⅛ teaspoon
pure vanilla extract	·	½ teaspoon (2.5 ml)
fleur de sel, for topping (optional)	·	⅛ teaspoon

PREHEAT THE OVEN
Twenty minutes or longer before baking, set an oven rack at the middle level. Set the oven at 325°F / 160°C.

MISE EN PLACE
Thirty minutes ahead, cut the butter into 4 pieces. Set on the counter to soften.

Chop and Toast the Pecans: Chop the pecans into medium-small pieces and place them in a coarse strainer. Shake the strainer to remove the nut dust and discard (or reserve for another use). Spread the pecan pieces evenly on a baking sheet

Continues

and bake for 5 minutes, or just until they start to smell fragrant but are not beginning to brown. Empty the pecans into a medium glass bowl.

MAKE THE PRALINES

1. In the saucepan, stir together the crème fraîche, butter, golden syrup, sugars, salt, and optional cream of tartar until the sugar is moistened. Bring the mixture to a boil over medium heat, stirring constantly with a silicone spatula.

2. Continue boiling for 10 to 15 minutes, stirring constantly but gently, until an instant-read thermometer reads 260°F / 127°C or a few degrees lower, because the temperature will continue to rise.

3. Remove the saucepan from the heat and, as soon as the mixture reaches temperature, pour it over the pecans in the bowl. Use the silicone spatula to scrape out all the caramel and then to fold the nuts into the caramel. Let the mixture cool to 175°F / 79°C, about 6 to 12 minutes. Stir in the vanilla extract.

SHAPE THE PRALINES

4. On the counter, set a silicone baking mat or a sheet of nonstick aluminum foil, or foil lightly coated with nonstick cooking spray.

5. Use two tablespoons, fronts and backs lightly coated with nonstick cooking spray, to drop rounds of the mixture (20 grams each) onto the mat or foil. Use a small offset spatula or the back of one of the spoons to smooth and shape the pralines into 2 inch rounds. If the mixture becomes too stiff, soften it in the microwave with 5-second bursts.

6. While the pralines are still warm, sprinkle them with the fleur de sel if desired, and press it in lightly.

COOL THE PRALINES

7. Let the pralines cool completely.

DARK CHOCOLATE COATING

dark chocolate, 61% to 70% cacao	57 grams (2 ounces)	.

MAKE THE CHOCOLATE COATING

8. In a small microwavable bowl, heat the chocolate, stirring every 15 seconds with a silicone spatula, until almost completely melted (or heat the chocolate in the top of a double boiler set over hot, not simmering, water—do not let the bottom of the container touch the water—stirring often, until almost completely melted).

Remove the chocolate from the heat source and stir until fully melted (see Baking Gems).

COAT THE PRALINES

9. Tilt the bowl and dip each praline partially in the melted chocolate. Remove any excess by knocking it against the side of the bowl. Set the coated pralines back on the mat until the chocolate dulls and sets. You can also slip a cookie sheet under the mat and set in the refrigerator for 10 minutes if the room is warm.

10. Wrap each praline in a small piece of plastic wrap.

STORE Airtight: room temperature, low humidity, 1 month; refrigerated, 6 months; frozen, 9 months.

Baking Gems

♥ If you don't have a nonstick saucepan, coat your saucepan lightly with nonstick cooking spray.

♥ The cream of tartar will extend the shelf life of the caramel, preventing any fine crystallization.

♥ Keep the pralines at cool room temperature and away from direct sunlight to prevent them from softening.

♥ The recipe can be doubled using a larger pan, but it will be helpful to set the bowl of praline mixture on a tray that has been lined with foil and heated in the oven to keep the mixture malleable and to catch any spills.

♥ Compared to my favorite caramel sauce recipe (page 329), this recipe has part light brown sugar and 30 grams / 2 tablespoons / 30 ml less cream, which makes it thicker and chewier.

♥ The pralines are most attractive when partially dipped in the chocolate, but you can instead use a small offset spatula to coat the entire tops. You will need to increase the chocolate to 85 grams / 3 ounces.

♥ You need to quick-temper the chocolate by removing it from the heat before it is fully melted and then stirring until it is completely melted and the temperature is no higher than 94°F / 34°C. This will keep the chocolate from "blooming" (forming gray streaks) and will give it a sharp snap when you bite into it.

♥ Keep the chocolate warm and in temper as you work by placing the container on a heating pad wrapped with foil and set to the lowest temperature, or by setting it over a bowl of warm water (no warmer than 120°F / 49°C). Stir often to equalize and maintain the temperature.

VARIATION
Yum Balls or Batons

I created these Yum Balls—a pop-in-the-mouth-size variation—for my husband, Elliott, who wanted to avoid having sticky fingers. He gave them their name. I also like shaping them as two-bite batons, which can be dipped in chocolate.

When the praline mixture is no longer hot but still warm enough to shape, roll heaping teaspoons of the mixture between the palms of your hands to form 1 inch round balls or 1½ inch long batons (10 grams each). Let them cool to room temperature. For the batons, dip one end of each baton in the melted dark chocolate and allow it to set. Wrap each ball or baton in a small piece of plastic wrap.

LACY SUSANS

Makes: Forty-eight 2½ inch round cookies

Sue Zelickson, a much-beloved and accomplished food personality from Minneapolis, created this wonderful recipe. The cookies caramelize during baking, resulting in a butterscotch flavor, crisp texture, and—yes indeed—lacy appearance. Sue suggests, in addition to eating them as cookies, molding them while still hot and flexible to use as dessert dishes, or crumbling the cooled cookies and using them as a topping for ice cream.

Oven Temperature: 375°F / 190°C	**Baking Time:** 4 to 6 minutes (for each of four batches)	**Special Equipment:** Two 17 by 14 inch cookie sheets, nonstick or lined with parchment (do not use insulated or cushioned sheets); A disposable pastry bag or a ½ teaspoon measure

BATTER *Makes: 230 grams*

unsalted butter	85 grams	6 tablespoons (¾ stick)
½ large egg, lightly beaten before measuring	25 grams	1½ tablespoons (22.5 ml)
pure vanilla extract	·	½ teaspoon (2.5 ml)
unbleached all-purpose flour	36 grams	¼ cup (lightly spooned into the cup and leveled off) plus 2 teaspoons
baking soda	·	¼ teaspoon
fine sea salt	·	1/16 teaspoon (a pinch)
granulated sugar	25 grams	¼ cup
light brown sugar, preferably Muscovado	68 grams	¼ cup plus 1 tablespoon (firmly packed)
mini semisweet chocolate chips, 46% to 50% cacao	28 grams (1 ounce)	2 tablespoons plus 2 teaspoons

PREHEAT THE OVEN

Thirty minutes or longer before baking, set an oven rack at the middle level. Set the oven at 375°F / 190°C.

MISE EN PLACE

Thirty minutes to 1 hour ahead, cut the butter into tablespoon-size pieces. Set on the counter to soften.

Thirty minutes ahead, into a 1 cup / 237 ml glass measure with a spout, weigh or measure the egg. Whisk in the vanilla extract. Cover tightly with plastic wrap and set on the counter.

MAKE THE BATTER

1. Into the bowl of a stand mixer fitted with the flat beater, sift together the flour, baking soda, salt, and granulated sugar. Add the light brown sugar and whisk the mixture together evenly.

2. Add the butter and the egg mixture and beat on medium speed until smooth, scraping down the sides of the bowl as needed.

3. Add the chocolate chips and beat for a few seconds on low speed, until evenly incorporated.

SHAPE THE BATTER

4. Scrape the batter into the pastry bag. Cut a small semicircle from the tip.

5. Pipe twelve ½ inch mounds (about 5 grams each) onto a cookie sheet, spaced no closer than 3 inches apart. (Alternatively, use the ½ teaspoon measure and the tip of your finger to portion out the batter.)

BAKE THE COOKIES

6. Bake for 3 minutes. Rotate the cookie sheet halfway around. Continue baking for 1 to 3 minutes, or until the cookies are deep amber and bubbling. Watch carefully to prevent burning.

COOL THE COOKIES

7. Set the cookie sheet on a wire rack and let the cookies cool for 2 to 3 minutes, until firm enough to lift from the sheet. Use a thin pancake turner, starting around the edges, to transfer the cookies to paper towels to absorb any excess butter. Cool completely.

8. Repeat with the remaining three batches.

STORE Airtight, layered between sheets of parchment: room temperature, low humidity, 1 week; refrigerated, 3 months.

Baking Gem

♥ There is no need to cool the cookie sheets between batches.

BRANDY SNAPS

Makes: Twelve to Fourteen 4 to 4½ inch long cookies

I adapted this recipe from one given to me many years ago by Sanford D'Amato of Sanford's Restaurant in Milwaukee, Wisconsin. I enjoy the buttery/brandied caramel flavor and delicate chewy/crisp texture of the brandy snap shells. The mascarpone pastry cream filling, lightened with whipped cream, is delicious. The orange zest, dried currants, and cherries add a contrasting tartness.

Oven Temperature: 350°F / 175°C for the brandy snaps; 300°F / 150°C for the pistachios

Baking Time: 7 to 10 minutes for the brandy snaps; 7 minutes for the pistachios

Plan Ahead: The brandy snaps, pastry cream, and pistachio garnish can be prepared up to 3 days ahead. The snaps should not be filled more than 2 hours ahead of serving to maintain crispness.

Special Equipment: Two 17 by 14 inch cookie sheets, nonstick or lightly coated with nonstick cooking spray (do not use insulated or cushioned sheets); A ¾ inch diameter dowel or cannoli mold, lightly coated with nonstick cooking spray; A large disposable pastry bag fitted with a ⅝ inch star pastry tube; Optional: extra dowels or cannoli molds

BATTER *Makes: 285 grams (if making more cookies, see Baking Gems, page 382)*

unsalted butter	75 grams	5 tablespoons plus 1 teaspoon
golden syrup (or corn syrup)	113 grams (109 grams)	⅓ cup (79 ml)
light Muscovado (or dark brown sugar)	27 grams	2 tablespoons (firmly packed)
ground ginger	·	¾ teaspoon
fine sea salt	·	1/16 teaspoon (a pinch)
bleached all-purpose flour	72 grams	½ cup (lightly spooned into the cup and leveled off) plus 4 teaspoons
brandy	·	2 teaspoons (10 ml)

PREHEAT THE OVEN
Twenty minutes or longer before baking, set two oven racks in the upper and lower thirds of the oven. Set the oven at 350°F / 175°C.

MISE EN PLACE
Thirty minutes ahead, cut the butter into tablespoon-size pieces. Set on the counter to soften.

MAKE THE BATTER
1. In a 2 cup / 473 ml microwavable measure with a spout, lightly coated with nonstick cooking spray (or a small heavy saucepan over medium heat, stirring often), combine the butter, golden syrup, brown sugar, ginger, and salt and bring the mixture to a boil in the microwave, watching it carefully so that it does not bubble over if using a microwave.

Continues

2. Remove from the heat source and whisk in the flour and brandy. If using a saucepan, transfer the batter to a heated 2 cup / 473 ml glass measure with a spout.

3. Pour the batter onto the cookie sheets, 6 to 7 per sheet, to form 2 to 2¼ inch rounds, spacing them 3 inches apart; the batter will spread to about 4 to 4½ inches. (If the batter begins to thicken, heat it in the microwave for a few seconds or place the glass measure in a pan of hot water. A thinner batter makes lacier cookies.)

BAKE THE BRANDY SNAPS

4. Bake for 4 minutes. Rotate the cookie sheets halfway around and reverse their position from top to bottom. Continue baking for 3 to 6 minutes, or until the cookies are a deep golden brown and filled with holes.

COOL THE BRANDY SNAPS

5. Set the cookie sheets on wire racks and let the cookies cool on the sheets for about 1 minute, or until they can be lifted without wrinkling but are still flexible.

SHAPE THE BRANDY SNAPS

6. Use a pancake turner to lift the cookies one at a time from the sheets, shaping each one before removing the next so that the remaining cookies stay warm and flexible. Roll each cookie loosely around the dowel (or cannoli mold), with the smooth side against the dowel, so that the edges overlap just enough to seal. The wrapped cookie shell should be no more than 1 inch in diameter. Leave the dowel in the cookie and press down firmly on the seam for a few seconds. Then place the cookie seam side down on another wire rack to cool.

7. If the cookies become too rigid to roll, return them briefly to the oven. If a cookie begins to sag while cooling, reshape it into a cylinder. (Alternatively, if you have more than one dowel or cannoli mold, leave the dowels in the cookies until they harden enough to keep their shape.)

The cookies can be stored in an airtight container at room temperature for up to 1 week.

Baking Gems

♥ If increasing the recipe, use a proportionally larger microwavable cup or saucepan. To keep the batter fluid for subsequent batches, set the container with the remaining batter in a pan of hot water and cover the top of the container with plastic wrap.

♥ In order to maintain the cookies' shape and crisp texture, I advise you not to make brandy snaps in humid weather.

♥ The color of the baked cookies needs to be just a deep golden brown. A darker brown cookie will become too fragile for filling and serving.

MASCARPONE PASTRY CREAM FILLING
Makes: 650 grams / 2½ cups

PASTRY CREAM
Makes: 166 grams / ½ cup plus 2 tablespoons

½ large egg, lightly beaten before measuring	25 grams	1½ tablespoons (22.5 ml)
cornstarch	7 grams	2¼ teaspoons
half-and-half	121 grams	½ cup (118 ml), *divided*
sugar	25 grams	2 tablespoons
vanilla bean, split lengthwise (or vanilla extract)	.	½ inch piece (or ¼ teaspoon/ 1.25 ml)
fine sea salt	.	1/16 teaspoon (a pinch)
unsalted butter	5 grams	1 teaspoon

MAKE THE PASTRY CREAM
Have ready a fine-mesh strainer suspended over a small bowl near the cooktop.

1. In a 1 cup / 237 ml glass measure with a spout, whisk the egg. Weigh or measure it into a small bowl.

2. Add the cornstarch and whisk to combine. Gradually add 30 grams / 2 tablespoons / 30 ml of the half-and-half, whisking until the mixture is smooth and the cornstarch is dissolved.

3. In a medium saucepan, place the sugar and vanilla bean (not the extract). Use your fingers to rub the seeds into the sugar. Stir in the remaining 91 grams / 6 tablespoons / 89 ml half-and-half and the salt.

4. Bring the mixture to a full boil over medium heat, stirring constantly.

5. Whisk 2 tablespoons / 30 ml of this hot mixture into the egg mixture. Pass the egg mixture through the strainer into the small bowl and scrape any mixture clinging to the underside into the bowl.

6. Bring the half-and-half mixture back to a boil over medium heat. Remove the vanilla pod (rinse and dry it for future use). Quickly add all of the egg mixture, whisking rapidly. Continue whisking rapidly for about 20 to 30 seconds, being sure to get into the bottom edges of the pan. The mixture will become very thick.

7. Remove the mixture from the heat and whisk in the butter. (If using, whisk in the vanilla extract.) Immediately pour the mixture into a bowl and place a piece of plastic wrap, lightly coated with nonstick cooking spray, directly on top of the cream to keep a skin from forming.

8. Let it cool to room temperature, about 45 minutes, then refrigerate until cold.

MASCARPONE PASTRY CREAM FILLING

Pastry Cream	130 grams	½ cup
mascarpone, preferably imported, or whipped cream cheese	227 grams	¾ cup plus 2 tablespoons
heavy cream, cold	116 grams	½ cup (118 ml)

blanched shelled unsalted pistachio nuts, for sprinkling	56 grams	¼ cup plus 2 tablespoons
orange zest, finely grated	12 grams	2 tablespoons (loosely packed)
dried cherries	28 grams	¼ cup
dried currants	28 grams	¼ cup
bourbon, preferably Woodford Reserve or Maker's Mark	56 grams	¼ cup (59 ml)
sugar	25 grams	2 tablespoons
grand marnier liqueur	14 grams	1 tablespoon (15 ml)

PREHEAT THE OVEN

Twenty minutes or longer before toasting the nuts, set an oven rack at the middle level. Set the oven at 300°F / 150°C.

MISE EN PLACE

Twenty minutes ahead, weigh or measure the pastry cream and mascarpone into two small bowls to soften slightly.

Toast and Chop the Pistachios: Spread the pistachios on a baking sheet and bake for about 7 minutes, or until they barely begin to color, to enhance their flavor. Cool completely and chop.

Into a medium bowl, pour the heavy cream and refrigerate for at least 10 minutes. (Chill the handheld mixer's beaters alongside the bowl.)

Coarsely chop the pistachios.

With dishwashing liquid, wash, rinse, and dry the orange before zesting it.

With kitchen scissors, cut the dried cherries and currants into ¼ inch pieces.

COMPLETE THE FILLING

9. In a small saucepan, preferably nonstick, place the cherries, currants, bourbon, sugar, and orange zest and bring to a boil, stirring often with

Continues

a silicone spatula. Simmer the mixture for 3 to 4 minutes, scraping the liquid onto the fruits, until almost all the liquid has evaporated. Transfer the mixture to a small bowl and let it cool completely.

10. Starting on low speed and gradually raising the speed to medium-high as it thickens, whip the cream just until soft peaks form when the beater is raised.

11. In a medium bowl, place the mascarpone and fold in the dried fruits. Fold in the pastry cream and Grand Marnier.

12. Gently fold in the whipped cream just until evenly blended.

The completed filling can be stored, refrigerated, for up to 24 hours.

FILL THE BRANDY SNAPS

13. Up to 2 hours before serving, place the filling in the prepared pastry bag and pipe the mixture into the brandy snaps. To make a decorative star finish, as you reach the end, gradually ease the pressure as you pull the tube away. Pipe another star into the opposite end.

14. Sprinkle the ends with the chopped pistachio nuts.

STORE Loosely covered: room temperature, 2 hours. Do not refrigerate or freeze the filled rolls, because the brandy snaps will lose their crispness.

DOUBLE CHOCOLATE TOFFEE

Makes: 454 grams / 1 pound

This irresistible combination of chocolate, caramel, and almonds is a time-honored crowd pleaser. The molasses in the brown sugar gives the toffee its butterscotch flavor. The baking soda creates tiny bubbles which is the secret to the perfectly crunchy and not sticky texture.

Oven Temperature: 325°F / 160°C	**Baking Time:** 5 minutes for the almonds	**Special Equipment:** One silicone baking mat set on a 17¼ by 12¼ half sheet pan, or a nonstick or buttered cookie sheet, set near the cooktop; An instant-read thermometer

TOFFEE BATTER

unsalted butter	113 grams	8 tablespoons (1 stick)
sliced almonds, preferably blanched	175 grams	1¾ cups, *divided*
dark chocolate, 53% to 70% cacao	340 grams (12 ounces)	*divided*
light Muscovado (or dark brown sugar)	270 grams	1¼ cups (firmly packed)
corn syrup	82 grams	¼ cup (59 ml)
water	30 grams	2 tablespoons (30 ml)
pure vanilla extract	·	1 teaspoon (5 ml)
baking soda	2.7 grams	½ teaspoon

PREHEAT THE OVEN

Twenty minutes or longer before baking, set an oven rack at the middle level. Set the oven at 350°F / 175°C.

MISE EN PLACE

Thirty minutes ahead, cut the butter into tablespoon-size pieces. Set on the counter to soften.

Toast the Almonds: Spread the almonds evenly on a baking sheet and bake for about 5 minutes, or until pale gold. Stir once or twice to ensure even toasting and prevent overbrowning. Allow the almonds to cool completely.

In a food processor, process the nuts until medium-fine. Divide the almonds equally between two small bowls. Wipe out the food processor bowl.

Chop the chocolate into coarse pieces. In the food processor, finely process the chocolate. (Alternatively, finely chop it on a cutting board.)

Place half of the chocolate in a small bowl and half in either a microwavable bowl or the top of a double boiler.

MAKE THE TOFFEE

1. In a medium heavy saucepan, preferably nonstick, using a wooden spatula or spoon, stir together the brown sugar, corn syrup, butter, and water. (Do not use a silicone spatula unless it has a wooden handle.) Bring the mixture to a boil over medium heat, stirring constantly. Continue boiling, stirring gently, until an instant-read thermometer reads 285°F / 140°C.

2. The ideal temperature is 285° to 290°F / 140° to 143°C. Stir in the vanilla and baking soda, then stir well to distribute the baking soda evenly. The mixture will become lighter in color and thicker.

Continues

POUR AND COAT THE TOFFEE

3. Pour the toffee mixture evenly into roughly a 12 by 10 inch oval onto the prepared half sheet pan. If necessary, spread it with a silicone spatula so it is even.

4. Immediately scatter the chocolate from the small bowl over the hot toffee.

5. As soon as the chocolate starts to melt, use a long metal spatula, preferably offset, to spread the chocolate in an even layer over the toffee.

6. Sprinkle half of the chopped almonds on top of the melted chocolate and use a small offset spatula to move them gently into an even layer.

7. Refrigerate for about 40 minutes to 1 hour, or until the toffee is cool and the chocolate is set. The almonds should barely move when pressed gently. (An instant-read thermometer should read about 65°F / 18°C when inserted into the chocolate.)

8. Carefully lift the toffee from the silicone baking mat and flip it over. Allow to sit for 30 to 40 minutes to warm up so that the chocolate doesn't harden before adding the nuts.

MELT THE REMAINING CHOCOLATE

9. In a small microwavable bowl, heat the remaining chocolate, stirring every 15 seconds with a silicone spatula, until almost completely melted (or heat the chocolate in the top of a double boiler set over hot, not simmering, water—do not let the bottom of the container touch the water—stirring often, until almost completely melted).

Remove the chocolate from the heat source and stir until fully melted.

COAT THE SECOND SIDE OF THE TOFFEE

10. Pour the chocolate onto the toffee and use the long metal spatula to spread it evenly over the surface. If the chocolate hardens too much, wave a hair dryer over it to soften it so that the almonds will stick.

11. Immediately sprinkle the remaining chopped almonds evenly over the chocolate, using the small offset spatula to press them into the chocolate.

12. Refrigerate the toffee again for about 30 minutes, or until the chocolate has set firmly, around 62°F / 17°C.

13. Break the toffee into irregular pieces.

STORE Airtight: room temperature, 1 month. (After 1 month, the toffee will still be delicious but the sugar may start to crystallize.)

Baking Gems

🖤 An instant-read thermometer is essential for this recipe because the correct temperature is critical to achieve the ideal texture.

🖤 The higher the temperature of the finished toffee mixture, the crunchier the texture will be, but if it's too high, it will taste burnt and have a crumbly texture.

🖤 The corn syrup helps ensure a smooth texture.

VARIATION
Chocolate Butterscotch Toffee

If you prefer to coat only one side of the toffee, you will need only half the amount of chocolate (170 grams / 6 ounces).

All of the other ingredients are the same measurements.

Mise en Place will be same as above except for the following instructions:

After processing the toasted almonds, sprinkle half of them in a roughly 11 by 9 inch oval onto the prepared half sheet pan. With a small offset spatula, spread them into an even layer.

Make the Toffee.

Pour and Coat the Toffee.

Pour the toffee over the almonds. If necessary, spread it with the back of a silicone spatula to make it even.

Continue with Steps 4 through 7.

APRICOT MARZIPAN BÂTARDS

Makes: Twenty-four 2 inch round cookies

This soft, chewy, and crunchy cookie rides the cusp between cookie and candy. The flavor combination of almond and apricot, accented with a spark of salt, is soul satisfying. I call these cookies Bâtards because I discovered them at Drew Nieporent's wonderful restaurant Bâtard in New York City. Use the finest-quality marzipan you can find for the silkiest texture and best flavor (see Baking Gems).

Oven Temperature: 350°F / 175°C	**Baking Time:** 12 to 14 minutes	**Special Equipment:** One 17¼ by 12¼ half sheet pan or one 17 by 14 inch cookie sheet, lined with parchment

DOUGH *Makes: 408 grams*

fine-quality marzipan, preferably Lübeck (see Baking Gems)	250 grams	¾ cup plus 1½ tablespoons
sugar, preferably superfine	125 grams	½ cup plus 2 tablespoons
honey	25 grams	1 tablespoon plus ½ teaspoon (17.5 ml)
1 large egg white	30 grams	2 tablespoons (30 ml)
sliced blanched almonds	100 grams	1 cup

MISE EN PLACE

Thirty minutes to 1 hour ahead, into the bowl of a stand mixer, weigh or measure the marzipan, sugar, honey, and egg white. Cover.

MAKE THE DOUGH

1. Attach the flat beater and mix on low speed until all the ingredients are smoothly combined. Scrape the mixture into a small bowl, cover tightly with plastic wrap pressed against the surface, and refrigerate for at least 2 hours, up to 24 hours.

PREHEAT THE OVEN

Twenty minutes or longer before baking, set an oven rack at the middle level. Set the oven at 350°F / 175°C.

2. Arrange the sliced almonds on a sheet pan or large plate in a single layer.

Have a small bowl of water on the counter to moisten your fingers and palms lightly, which will help prevent the marzipan mixture from sticking.

SHAPE THE COOKIES

3. Weigh out or measure twenty-four 1 inch balls (17 grams) of dough.

4. One at a time, roll the balls in the almonds to coat and then press them down into the almonds to flatten to 1½ inches in diameter by ½ inch high.

5. Set the cookies 1 inch apart on the prepared pan. Cover lightly with plastic wrap and refrigerate for a minimum of 30 minutes, up to 8 hours.

BAKE THE COOKIES

6. Bake for 6 minutes. Rotate the pan halfway around. Continue baking for 6 to 8 minutes, or until the cookies are lightly browned and, when pressed in the center, have only a slight give.

COOL THE COOKIES

7. Set the sheet pan on a wire rack and let the cookies cool for about 10 minutes before brushing them with the apricot glaze.

APRICOT GLAZE

apricot preserves, strained (see Baking Gems)	62 grams	3 tablespoons
water	·	¾ teaspoon (3.75 ml)
sea salt, preferably Maldon, for sprinkling	·	¼ teaspoon

8. In a small microwavable bowl or cup, combine the strained apricot preserves and water and heat until just beginning to bubble. (Alternatively, heat them in a small saucepan over low heat.)

GLAZE THE COOKIES

9. Brush a very thin layer of apricot glaze onto each cookie. You will need only about 2 tablespoons glaze in all. Then sprinkle each cookie with just a tiny bit of the salt.

10. Use a thin pancake turner to transfer the cookies to a serving plate. Allow the cookies to cool for at least 20 minutes before serving.

STORE Airtight: room temperature or refrigerated, 1 week. (They will stay soft and chewy.)

Baking Gems

♥ Lübeck marzipan contains a higher percentage of almonds than American brands. If you can't find it, substitute an equal weight of almond paste (¾ cup plus 2 tablespoons). Do not use American marzipan, which would result in flat puddles instead of chewy cookies.

♥ My favorite brand of apricot preserves is Darbo from Austria. You will need to start with 87 grams / about 4½ tablespoons of preserves to get 62 grams / 3 tablespoons strained preserves.

BRAZILIAN QUINDIM

Makes: Twenty-four 1¾ to 2 inch round cookies

This traditional Brazilian recipe actually originated in Portugal, known for its rich egg yolk desserts. Quindim is very rich and very yellow, with a creamy blend of egg yolk, sugar, and butter and a macaroon-like bottom of coconut. I've incorporated lemon zest and coconut milk in my version, the lemon to temper the sweetness and the coconut milk for a creamier texture; it also helps keep the coconut in the middle of the cookies instead of sinking to the bottom.

Oven Temperature: 350°F / 175°C	Baking Time: 25 to 30 minutes	Special Equipment: Two nonstick mini muffin pans, 12 cavities each (1¾ to 2 inches wide at the top by ¾ inch deep), coated with nonstick cooking spray; A 17¼ by 12¼ half sheet pan

BATTER *Makes: 510 grams*

unsalted butter	75 grams	5 tablespoons plus 1 teaspoon
6 (to 9) large egg yolks (see page xxvi)	112 grams	¼ cup plus 3 tablespoons (104 ml)
lemon zest, finely grated (from about 2 lemons) and minced	8 grams	4 teaspoons (loosely packed)
sweetened grated coconut (see Baking Gems)	85 grams	1 cup
coconut milk, stirred before measuring	114 grams	½ cup (118 ml)
sugar	133 grams	⅔ cup

PREHEAT THE OVEN

Twenty minutes or longer before baking, set an oven rack at the middle level. Set the oven at 350°F / 175°C.

MISE EN PLACE

Thirty minutes to 1 hour ahead, cut the butter into tablespoon-size pieces. Set on the counter to soften.

Thirty minutes ahead, into a 1 cup / 237 ml glass measure with a spout, weigh or measure the egg yolks. Whisk lightly, cover tightly with plastic wrap, and set on the counter.

With dishwashing liquid, wash, rinse, and dry the lemons before zesting them. Use a sharp knife to mince the zest as finely as possible.

In a medium bowl, place the grated coconut. Use scissors to snip the coconut into shorter pieces. Stir in the coconut milk.

MAKE THE BATTER

1. In the bowl of a stand mixer fitted with the flat beater, beat the sugar, lemon zest, and butter on medium speed until well combined.

2. Gradually beat in the egg yolks. Raise the speed to high and beat for about 3 minutes, until pale yellow, scraping down the sides of the bowl halfway through beating.

3. Scrape in the coconut mixture and mix on low speed until evenly incorporated.

4. Transfer the batter to a 2 cup / 473 ml glass measure with a spout and fill each muffin cup to about ⅛ inch from the top (about 20 grams each).

5. Set the muffin pans on the half sheet pan and carefully add enough hot tap water to the sheet pan to come about halfway up the sides of the muffin pans.

BAKE THE QUINDIM

6. Bake for 15 minutes. Rotate the sheet pan halfway around. Continue baking for 10 to 15 minutes, or until the quindim are dark golden brown and feel set when pressed lightly on top with a fingertip.

COOL THE QUINDIM

7. Lift the muffin pans out of the water bath and set them on a wire rack to cool for 5 minutes.

UNMOLD THE QUINDIM

8. Run a small metal spatula around the sides of each quindim, pressing it away from the sides of the pan, and then lift it out and onto a serving plate. If any of the custard is left on the bottom of the pan, simply use the spatula to spread it back into place on the bottoms of the quindim. Cool completely before serving or storing.

STORE Airtight: room temperature, 1 day; refrigerated, 2 weeks; frozen, 3 months.

Baking Gems

♥ Sweetened coconut is preferable to unsweetened because it is more flavorful.

♥ Nonstick mini muffin pans make unmolding the quindim much easier.

♥ You can add a teaspoon of cream of tartar to the water in the sheet pan to prevent staining it.

VARIATION

For a chewier texture, omit the coconut milk. Fill the muffin cups only three quarters full.

CHAPTER 8

EXTRA SPECIALS

DULCE DE LECHE

Makes: 350 grams / 1 full cup / 270 ml

I like to make my own dulce de leche because I've found the flavor and texture to be superior to commercial brands. The process is very simple: Sweetened condensed milk is cooked until the sugar in it caramelizes. Dulce de leche is paler in color than caramel, and not as deeply caramelized. Because it is more mellow, it makes a less intense filling, ideal for more delicately flavored sandwich cookies. If you have a canning pot, you can make several jars at once.

Special Equipment: One deep pot; A 2 cup / 473 ml canning jar

one 14 ounce can sweetened condensed milk	396 grams	1 cup plus 3 tablespoons (281 ml)

1. Fill a canning pot or deep pot fitted with a rack with hot water and bring it to a boil.

2. Scrape the condensed milk into the canning jar. Cover with the lid and the screw cap. Set it on the rack.

3. Make sure the water covers the jar by at least 2 inches; add more water if needed. Cover the pot and simmer for about 3 hours, or until the dulce de leche reaches the desired dark tan color, checking the level of the water every 30 minutes and adding more boiling water if needed.

Note: If you can set your burner so that the water is just below a simmer, the process will take about 6½ hours, but you will end up with the silkiest, smoothest-possible dulce de leche.

4. Remove the jar to a wire rack and allow it to cool completely, then refrigerate. Bring the dulce de leche to room temperature before using it.

STORE Refrigerated, unopened, 1 month; once opened, 2 weeks.

Baking Gem

♥ Use a new canning jar to avoid the risk of the bottom of the jar fracturing off into the water bath.

CAJETA (GOAT'S MILK "CARAMEL")

Makes: 355 grams / rounded 1 cup / 245 ml

Cajeta is like dulce de leche concentrated from goat's milk. Dulce de leche (opposite) is usually made from sweetened condensed cow's milk and is thicker in texture, with a more intense flavor. Cajeta requires long cooking and frequent stirring, but I encourage you to try it at least once to experience the gentler pure caramel flavor. A thin layer is delicious in sandwich cookies such as Alfajores (page 177) and Sablés (page 209).

Special Equipment: One shallow 5 quart / 4.7 liter nonreactive pot

goat's milk, preferably fresh	964 grams	1 quart (946 ml)
granulated sugar	175 grams	¾ cup plus 2 tablespoons
baking soda (optional; see Baking Gem)	2.7 grams	½ teaspoon
heavy cream, if needed in step 5	.	.

1. Measure the goat's milk, sugar, and optional baking soda into the large pot (the mixture will bubble up if using fresh goat's milk).

2. Cook over medium heat, stirring constantly, until the sugar dissolves and the milk becomes foamy.

3. Adjust the heat to maintain a simmer. Cook, stirring frequently with a silicone spatula and scraping the sides and bottom of the pot, until the milk turns a light brown color and thickens, 40 to 60 minutes.

4. Adjust the heat if necessary to maintain a simmer, which may require taking the pot off the heat to stir down the caramelizing milk if it foams up. Continue cooking until it is reduced to a little more than one quarter of its original volume, and a "bare trail" remains open for 1 second when a spatula is scraped through the cajeta across the bottom of the pot.

5. Scrape the cajeta into a heatproof container. If the cajeta weighs less than 355 grams / is less than 1 cup in volume, whisk in enough heavy cream to reach that quantity. Cool to room temperature.

6. Cover the container tightly with plastic wrap and refrigerate it for at least 4 hours to thicken the cajeta before using.

STORE Airtight: room temperature, 4 hours; refrigerated, 2 weeks.

Baking Gem

♥ The optional baking soda lowers the required temperature for caramelization and reduces bubbling, making it easier to assess when the cajeta is done.

WICKED GOOD GANACHE

Makes: 390 grams / 1½ cups

This is the darkest, shiniest, smoothest ganache. It is enriched with unsweetened chocolate and corn syrup. The optional cayenne pepper gives it a luxuriously long finish. I love the spiciness when used as a filling for chocolate cookies, and it also blends well with the slight heat of ginger cookies.

fine-quality unsweetened or 99% cacao chocolate	24 grams (0.8 ounce)	.
dark chocolate, 60% to 62% cacao	170 grams (6 ounces)	.
heavy cream	170 grams	¾ cup minus 1 teaspoon (172 ml)
corn syrup	61 grams	3 tablespoons (45 ml)
cayenne pepper (optional)	.	½ teaspoon

MISE EN PLACE

Chop both the chocolates into coarse pieces. Transfer to a food processor.

Into a 1 cup / 237 ml microwavable measure with a spout (or a small saucepan), weigh or measure the cream.

MAKE THE GANACHE

Have ready a fine-mesh strainer suspended over a medium glass bowl near the cooktop.

1. Process the chocolate until very fine.

2. In the microwavable measure (or saucepan over medium heat, stirring often) scald the cream (heat it to the boiling point; small bubbles will form around the periphery).

3. With the motor running, pour the cream through the feed tube in a steady stream and continue processing for a few seconds, until smooth.

4. Add the corn syrup and optional cayenne pepper and pulse briefly to incorporate.

5. Press the mixture through the strainer and scrape any mixture clinging to the underside into the bowl.

6. Let the ganache sit for 1 hour. Then cover it with plastic wrap and let it sit for 3 to 4 hours, until it reaches a soft frosting consistency.

STORE Airtight: cool room temperature, 3 days; refrigerated, 10 days; frozen, 3 months. If you chill the ganache, allow it to come to room temperature before using to spread on cookies.

CANDIED ORANGE OR LEMON PEEL

Makes: about 150 grams / 1 cup chopped

Homemade candied orange and lemon peel are a world apart in flavor from commercial varieties. They have the brightest color, truest flavor, and a chewy yet crisp texture that is totally unlike any brand I have ever tasted. Chopped into small pieces, the candied peel makes a delightful addition to cookie dough. It requires an extended heating process, but the only laborious part is cutting the peel and removing the bitter pith. I learned this method of candying citrus at Bernachon chocolatier in Lyon, France.

Plan Ahead: The process of making the peels takes about 8 to 9 days but very little time as far as hands on involvement.

Special Equipment: A large wire rack, lightly coated with nonstick cooking spray and set over a 17¼ by 12¼ half sheet pan; An instant-read thermometer

2 large thick-skinned oranges or 3 to 5 lemons	about 500 grams (about 1¼ pounds)	.
water	500 grams	2 cups plus 2 tablespoons (500 ml)
sugar	375 grams	1¾ cups plus 2 tablespoons
1 vanilla bean, split lengthwise	.	.
glucose (or corn syrup)	21 grams	1 tablespoon (15 ml)

MAKE THE CANDIED PEEL

1. Wash the oranges or lemons with dishwashing detergent and rinse them well.

2. Score the peel of each orange or lemon into 6 vertical pieces and remove the ovals of peel. Use a sharp paring knife to cut and scrape off as much of the white pith as possible.

3. Add a few handfuls of ice to a large bowl and add cold water to make an ice water bath.

4. Bring a medium nonreactive saucepan of water to a boil. Add the citrus peels and boil for 5 minutes.

5. Drain the citrus peels and immediately add to the ice water bath to set their color. Then drain them again.

6. In the same saucepan, stir together the 500 grams / 2 cups plus 2 tablespoons / 500 ml water, sugar, and vanilla bean. Bring to a boil over medium heat, stirring constantly.

7. Add the citrus peels, swirling the pan but not stirring, and boil for 5 minutes. Remove from the heat, cover tightly, and allow the citrus peels to sit for 3 to 4 hours.

8. Set the saucepan over medium-low heat and cook the citrus peels, uncovered, for about 5 minutes, or until the instant-read thermometer reads 212°F / 100°C. Remove the pan from the heat, cover, and set aside overnight. (When removing the lid the next day, allow any condensation to fall back into the pan.)

9. Repeat cooking the peels for the next 7 or 8 days, each day bringing the temperature 1°F / 0.5°C higher. This usually takes 1 to 2 minutes after the syrup reaches a boil. On the day the temperature reaches 218°F / 103°C, add the glucose and swirl it in.

Continues

10. On the day the temperature reaches 220°F / 104°C, cover the pan and remove from the heat. Allow to sit for 2 or 3 hours before draining the peels.

11. Use tongs to arrange the peels in a single layer on the coated wire rack set over the sheet pan to catch any falling syrup. Set the pan in a warm area for several hours, until the peels are barely sticky. (A dehydrator set at 110° to 125°F / 43° to 52°C or an oven warmed by the pilot light will speed the process.)

12. Use sharp kitchen scissors to cut the candied peel into long strips about ¼ inch wide. Set them back on the rack and continue to dry them until no longer sticky but still flexible. This will take several hours. (For longer storage, let them stand until totally dry, which can take as long as 24 hours.)

13. Transfer the dried candied peel to a canning jar or other container with a tight-fitting lid.

On storage, a fine layer of sugar crystals will form on the outside of the peels, which adds a pleasant texture.

STORE Airtight: room temperature or refrigerated 1 month; frozen, 6 months.

Baking Gems

♥ Use a stainless steel, enamel, glass, or nonstick saucepan.

♥ The classic method of making candied peel uses an instrument called a densimeter to determine the density of the syrup; for the ideal consistency, the syrup should read 1310 Baumé (a unit of relative density). I was delighted to discover on testing with an instant-read thermometer that this correlates precisely with a reading of 220°F / 104°C! The slow 8- or 9-day process enables the peel to absorb the syrup completely into its structure.

Speed Version

Boiling the peels in several changes of water removes most of the bitterness.

2 large thick-skinned oranges or 3 to 5 lemons	about 500 grams (about 1¼ pounds)	.
fine sea salt	3 grams	½ teaspoon
orange or yellow liquid food color	.	a few drops
sugar	150 grams	¾ cup, *divided*

1. Wash, score, and peel the oranges as above, but leave some of the pith attached.

2. Cut the peels lengthwise into ½ inch strips.

3. In a medium saucepan, cover the strips of peel with cold water. Bring the water to a boil. Add the salt and continue boiling for 5 minutes.

4. Drain and rinse the peels. Add fresh cold (unsalted) water to cover again and bring to a boil. Boil for 5 minutes. Drain, rinse, and repeat the boiling process once more with fresh unsalted water, adding a few drops of liquid food color if desired. Drain well.

5. In a large skillet, place the peels in a single layer and sprinkle with 100 grams / ½ cup of the sugar. Cook over very low heat, uncovered, for 30 minutes to 1 hour, turning them over occasionally, until the peels are translucent and all of the syrup has been absorbed.

6. Dry the candied peels on a nonstick wire rack (or coat the rack lightly with nonstick cooking spray) for 1 to 1½ hours. They should be quite dry.

7. Dip the strips of peel in the remaining 50 grams / ¼ cup sugar, coating each one on both sides.

8. Allow the candied peels to dry for 1 to 2 days before storing.

STORE Airtight: refrigerated, 1 week; frozen, 2 months.

MILK CHOCOLATE MOUSSE GANACHE

Makes: 330 grams / 2 cups

This light whipped ganache is perfect for Whoopie Cookies (page 311), but it is also lovely for sandwiching other cookies. It uses double the cream of a classic ganache, so it has the flavor profile of milk chocolate and can be whipped to a much lighter consistency.

dark chocolate, 53% to 62% cacao	113 grams (4 ounces)	·
heavy cream	232 grams	1 cup (237 ml)
pure vanilla extract	·	1 teaspoon (5 ml)

MISE EN PLACE

Chop the chocolate into coarse pieces. Transfer it to a food processor.

Into a 2 cup / 473 ml microwavable measure with a spout (or a small saucepan) weigh or measure the cream.

MAKE THE GANACHE

1. Process the chocolate until very fine.

2. In the microwavable measure (or saucepan over medium heat stirring often) scald the cream (heat it to the boiling point; small bubbles will form around the periphery).

3. With the motor running, pour the cream through the feed tube in a steady stream and continue processing for a few seconds, until smooth.

4. Pour the mixture into the bowl of a stand mixer and refrigerate until cold, 40 minutes to an hour, stirring every 30 minutes. (You can speed chilling by setting the bowl in an ice water bath and stirring often.) Do not allow the mixture to get too cold, or it will be too stiff to incorporate air. The ideal temperature is 65° to 68F° / 18° to 20°C.

5. Add the vanilla extract and attach the whisk beater. Beat on low speed for about 30 seconds, or just until the mixture forms very soft, floppy peaks when the beater is raised. It will continue to thicken after a few minutes at room temperature. The safest way to prevent overbeating is to use the stand mixer until the ganache starts to thicken and then finish by hand with a whisk.

STORE Airtight: cool room temperature, 1 day; refrigerated, 1 week; frozen, 3 months.

Baking Gem

♥ If the ganache gets overbeaten and becomes grainy, you can restore it by remelting, chilling, and rebeating it.

LEMON CURD

Makes: 330 grams / 1¼ cups (355 grams / 1⅓ cups with the extra sugar option)

I love the pure, lilting flavor of lemon, and its ultimate expression is lemon curd. I like to keep my lemon curd tart because it tempers the sweetness of cookies such as Mrs. Swallows's Perfect Lemon Cookies (page 117) and Crown Jewel Macarons (page 357). If you prefer it sweeter, it's fine to add more sugar, as in the variation.

unsalted butter	57 grams	4 tablespoons (½ stick)
lemon zest, finely grated	4 grams	2 teaspoons (loosely packed)
lemon juice, freshly squeezed and strained (about 3 lemons)	95 grams	¼ cup plus 2 tablespoons (89 ml)
5 (to 8) large egg yolks (see page xxvi)	93 grams	¼ cup plus 2 tablespoons (89 ml)
sugar	150 grams	¾ cup
fine sea salt	·	1⁄16 teaspoon (a pinch)

MISE EN PLACE

Thirty minutes to 1 hour ahead, cut the butter into tablespoon-size pieces. Set on the counter to soften.

Wash the lemons with dishwashing liquid, rinse, and dry before zesting them. Set the lemon zest in a medium bowl. Suspend a fine-mesh strainer over the bowl.

Into a 1 cup / 237 ml glass measure with a spout, weigh or measure the lemon juice.

Into a small heavy saucepan, preferably nonstick, weigh or measure the egg yolks.

MAKE THE LEMON CURD

1. Add the butter and sugar to the yolks and whisk until blended.

2. Whisk in the lemon juice and salt.

3. Cook over medium-low heat, stirring constantly with a silicone spatula and scraping the sides of the pan as needed, until the mixture is thickened and resembles hollandaise sauce. It should thickly coat the spatula but still be liquid enough to pour. It will change from translucent to opaque as it cooks and begin to take on a yellow color on the back of the spatula. Do not let it boil, or it will curdle. If steam appears, remove the pan briefly from the heat, stirring constantly, to keep the mixture from boiling.

4. When the curd has thickened and will pool slightly when a little is dropped on its surface, immediately pour it into the strainer. Press it through the strainer and scrape any mixture clinging to the underside into the bowl.

5. Stir gently to mix in the lemon zest in the bowl.

6. Cover tightly with plastic wrap or pour into an airtight container. Cool completely and then refrigerate. The curd will continue to thicken during cooling and chilling.

STORE Airtight: refrigerated, 3 weeks. Longer storage dulls the fresh citrus flavor.

VARIATION

Lemon Curd for Lemon Cranberry Squares

If you are making the Lemon Cranberry Squares on page 315, add 25 grams / 2 tablespoons more sugar to balance the tartness of the cranberries.

PRUNE LEKVAR (AKA DRIED PLUM JAM)

Makes: 312 grams / 1 cup / 237 ml

This dark and delicious condiment makes a great velvety substitution for the poppy seed filling in Hamantaschen (page 266).

pitted prunes	226 grams	2 cups (tightly packed)
water	237 grams	1 cup (237 ml)
lemon zest, finely grated	.	1 teaspoon (loosely packed)
sugar	25 grams	2 tablespoons

MAKE THE PRUNE LEKVAR

1. In a medium saucepan with a tight-fitting lid, combine the prunes and water and let sit, uncovered, for 2 hours to soften. (If the prunes are cut in half, this will take only 1 hour.)

2. Bring the water to a boil, cover the pan, and simmer over the lowest-possible heat for 20 to 30 minutes, until the prunes are very soft when pierced with a skewer. If the water evaporates, add a little extra.

3. With dishwashing liquid, wash, rinse, and dry the lemon before zesting it. Set the zest into a small bowl.

4. In a food processor or blender, place the prunes and any remaining liquid, the sugar, and lemon zest and process until smooth.

5. Scrape the prune mixture back into the saucepan and simmer, stirring constantly with a silicone spatula or spoon to prevent scorching, for 10 to 15 minutes, or until the lekvar is a deep, rich brown and very thick. A tablespoon of the mixture when lifted will take about 3 seconds to fall from the spoon. Transfer the lekvar to a small bowl and let cool completely.

STORE Airtight: refrigerated or frozen, 9 months.

RASPBERRY JAM

Makes: 1,175 grams / 1 quart / 1 liter (4 half-pint jars plus ½ cup)

I created this jam for filling cookies or adding to buttercream, although, of course, it is also lovely on your morning toast! The jam is very concentrated, intensely flavorful, and less sweet than most commercial jams. It is well worth the effort.

Plan Ahead: The jam takes 2 days to thicken fully in the jars.

Special Equipment: Four ½ pint / 237 ml canning jars; A canning pot or large pot with a rack (see Baking Gems); A jar lifter or tongs

sugar	425 grams	2 cups plus 2 tablespoons
water	267 grams	1 cup plus 2 tablespoons (267 ml)
raspberries	1,361 grams (3 pounds)	3 quarts

MISE EN PLACE

Sterilize the canning jars by filling them with boiling water. Pour boiling water over the inside of the lids. Set the rack in the bottom of the canning pot and bring enough water to a boil to cover the jars by a minimum of 1 inch.

Have ready a colander suspended over a large bowl.

MAKE THE JAM

1. In a large wide pot, bring the sugar and water to a boil, stirring constantly. Boil for 1 minute.

2. Add 340 to 454 grams / 3 to 4 cups of the berries, just enough to make a single layer, and boil for 1 minute. Use a slotted skimmer to remove the berries to the colander.

3. Reduce the syrup in the pot to about 2 cups / 473 ml. Add another batch of berries and boil for 1 minute. Remove the berries to the colander and again reduce the syrup in the pot to about

2 cups / 473 ml. Repeat with the remaining batches of berries, returning the syrup that drains from the berries in the bowl to the pot and always reducing it to about 2 cups / 473 ml. Skim and discard the white foam from the surface of the boiling syrup.

4. When the last batch of berries has been added to the bowl, again boil the syrup down to 2 cups / 473 ml. It will read 210°F / 99°C on an instant-read thermometer. Remove the pot from the heat and set it aside.

5. Pass the berries through a sieve or food mill to remove most of the seeds. You should have about 2 cups / 473 ml raspberry pulp.

6. Scrape the raspberry pulp into the syrup in the pot and simmer the mixture for about 10 minutes, until reduced to 4 cups / 946 ml. Remove from the heat.

FILL THE CANNING JARS

7. Drain out the water from the sterilized canning jars and fill them with the jam, leaving ⅜ inch of headspace. (Spoon the remaining ½ cup jam into a small jar and refrigerate. It will keep for several weeks.) Return the water in the canning pot to a full boil. Screw on the caps and lower them

Continues

into the boiling water. Cover and, after the water returns to a boil, leave undisturbed for 10 minutes.

8. Set a folded kitchen towel on the counter. Remove the jars from the boiling water and set them on the towel to cool completely. Then check the seal. If you press on the center of each lid with your finger, it should not yield to pressure. If they don't seal, store in the refrigerator.

9. Allow the jam to sit for 2 days to continue to thicken before using.

STORE Airtight (unopened): in a dark cool area, as long as 2 years. The flavor remains, but the color will darken.

Baking Gems

♥ Small batches of jam offer the best flavor, so it is best to do no more than 1,361 grams / 3 pounds / 3 quarts of berries at a time. The basic formula is: 454 grams / 1 pound raspberries to 142 grams / 5 ounces sugar to 85 grams / 3 ounces / 90 ml water.

♥ Raspberries frozen without sugar will give just as excellent a flavor. Allow them to thaw overnight in a colander set over a bowl in the refrigerator. Add the juice to the sugar syrup and proceed as with fresh berries.

♥ The jars must sit on a rack in the water bath to allow the water to flow all around them. The water must be deep enough to cover the jars by a minimum of 1 inch. They must be upright to expel any air inside the jars, producing a vacuum, which seals the jars. As an alternative to boiling them, you can invert the just-filled jars onto a folded towel until cool. The air trapped in the headspace will travel upward through the hot jam and be sterilized.

♥ Be sure to use only new canning jars. Used ones can fracture at the bottom in the boiling water bath.

♥ Half-pint jars will hold only 7 fluid ounces / 207 ml because of the ⅜ inch headspace required at the top.

APPENDIX

Flourless and Eggless Recipes

Mom's Coconut Snowball Kisses, page 79

Christmas Wreaths, page 251

Pecan Praline Scheherazades, page 374

Double Chocolate Toffee, page 385

Recipes Using Only Egg Whites

1 White: 30 grams / 2 tablespoons / 30 ml

Les Biarritz, page 101

Turkish Ginger Lime Cookies, page 217

Swiss Lebkuchen, page 254

Pecan Freezer Squares, page 322

Apricot Marzipan Bâtards, page 388

1½ Whites: 45 grams / 3 tablespoons / 45 ml

Chocolate Wafers, page 214

Bourbon Balls, page 260

2 Whites: 60 grams / ¼ cup / 59 ml

Basic Meringues, page 345

Dattelkonfekt (Date Confections), page 352

Meringue Mushrooms, page 354

Dacquoise Meringue Puffs, page 367

3 Whites: 90 grams / ¼ cup plus
2 tablespoons / 89 ml

Langues de Chats (Cats' Tongues), page 94

Meringue Birch Twigs, page 370

4 Whites: 120 grams / ½ cup / 118 ml

Golden Butter Financiers, page 299

Peanut Butter Financiers, page 301

Chocolate Financiers, page 304

Swiss Schoggi S, page 364

Fudgy Pecan Praline Meringue Ice Cream
Sandwiches, page 373

5 Whites: 150 grams / ½ cup plus
2 tablespoons / 148 ml

French Tuiles, page 99

Les Macarons au Chocolat Bernachon, page 348

Les Batons de Succès, page 350

Crown Jewel Macarons, page 357

Recipes Using Only Egg Yolks

1 Yolk: 18.7 to 19 grams / 1 tablespoon plus
½ teaspoon / 17.5 ml

Lemon Poppy Seed Cookies, page 21

Kourambiethes, page 36

Pumpkin Pecan Cookies, page 46

Walnut Sablé Maple Leaves or Nutless Sablés
page 207

Chocolate Sablés, page 210

Hamantaschen, page 266

2 Yolks: 37 grams / 2 tablespoons plus
1 teaspoon / 35 ml

Mini Gâteaux Breton, page 289

5 Yolks: 93 grams / ¼ cup plus
2 tablespoons / 89 ml

Lemon Curd, page 403

6 Yolks: 112 grams / ¼ cup plus
3 tablespoons / 104 ml

Brazilian Quindim, page 390

Flourless Cookie Recipes

Eggless Recipes

INDEX